WILLIAM COWPER, Esq.,

COMPILED FROM HIS CORRESPONDENCE,

Condensed and Annotated.

WILLIAM COWPER, Esq., COMPILED FROM HIS CORRESPONDENCE

By Thomas Taylor

Condensed Version, Edited by Gary Lee Roper

PUBLISHED BY R. B. SEELEY AND W. BURNSIDE:

AND SOLD BY L. AND J. SEELEY,'

FLEET STREET, LONDON.

MDCCCXXXV.

1835

CONTENTS

Mary Unwin..19

CHAPTER I...20

His parentage—Loss of his mother—Verses to her Memory—First school—Cruelty he experienced there —First serious impressions—Entrance upon Westminster School—Character while there—Removal thence—Entrance upon an attorney's office—Want of employment there — Unfitness for his profession — Early melancholy impressions...20

CHAPTER II. Entrance at the Temple—Employment there—Depression of his mind—Religious impressions—Visit to Southampton—Sudden removal of sorrow—Death of his father—Appointment to the office of reading clerk to the House of Lords—Dread of appearing in public —Consequent abandonment of the situation—Is proposed as Clerk of the Journals—Preparation for entering upon his office—Distressing sensations on the occasion—Is compelled to relinquish it—Serious attack of depression—Visit of his brother..26

CHAPTER III. His removal to St. Alban's—Painful state of his mind there—Receives a visit from his brother—Good effects of it—His recovery—How it was effected—His subsequent happiness—Pleasing conversation with Dr. Cotton — The delightful manner in which he now passed his time—Description of his experience—His gratitude to God—Employs his brother to look out for him a new residence—Leaves St. Albans—Feelings on the occasion...43

CHAPTER IV. Removal to Huntingdon—Sensations there—Engages in public worship for the first time after his recovery—Commences a regular correspondence with some of his friends—

Pleasure he experienced in writing on religious subjects — Anxiety of his mind for the spiritual welfare of his former associates—Attributes their continuance in sin chiefly to infidelity—Absurdity of attributing events to second causes instead of to the overruling providence of God—Forms some connections—Becomes acquainted with the Unwin family—Happiness he experienced in their company..........................55

CHAPTER V. Cowper becomes an inmate with Mr. Unwin's family— Is much delighted with their society—His opinion respecting the knowledge which Christians will have of each other in heaven—Just views of Christian friendship—Strength of his religious affections— Humbling views of himself—Melancholy death of Mr. Unwin—Cowper's reflections upon it—Mr. Newton's visit to Mrs. Unwin—Cowper's determination to remain with the family—Their removal from Huntingdon to Olney. 68

CHAPTER VI. Commencement of Cowper's intimacy with Mr. Newton —Pleasure it afforded him—His charitable disposition —Means provided for its indulgence, by the munificence of the late J. Thornton, Esq.—Mr. Thornton's death—Cowper's poetic tribute to his memory— His great anxiety for the spiritual welfare of his correspondents — Consolatory remarks addressed to his cousin—Severe affliction of his brother—Cowper's great concern on his behalf—Happy change in his brother's sentiments on religious subjects —His death- Cowper's reflections on it—Deep impression it made upon his mind—Description of his brother's character—Engages with Mr. Newton to write the Olney Hymns—Cowper's severe indisposition..78

CHAPTER VII. Great severity of Cowper's mental depression—His presentiment of it—Its consequences—Remarks upon its probable cause—Absurdity of attributing it, in any degree, to religion—Mrs. Unwin's great attention to him—His aversion to the company of strangers— Symptoms of his recovery—Domesticates three leverets—Amusement they afforded him—Mr. Newton's removal from Olney—Introduction of Mr. Bull to Cowper—His translation of Madame de la Guyon's poems, at Mr. Bull's request—Commences his original productions, at the suggestion of Mrs. Unwin— Renews his correspondence with Mr. and Mrs. Newton—Describes the state of his mind. 96

CHAPTER VIII. Makes preparation for publishing his first volume— Reasons assigned for it—Beneficial effects of composition on his mind—His comparative indifference to the success of his volume—Great care, nevertheless, with which he composed it—His readiness to avail himself of the assistance and advice of his friends— The interest which Mr. Newton took in his publication — Writes the preface for the volume—Cowper's judicious reply to some objections that had been made to it — Publication of the volume—Manner in which it was received— Continuance of Cowper's depression—State of his mind respecting religion—Ardent desires to make his volume the means of usefulness to others. 121

CHAPTER IX. Commencement of Cowper's acquaintance with Lady Austen—Poetic epistle to her ladyship—Beneficial influence of her conversational powers on Cowper's mind—Occasion of his writing John Gilpin—Lines composed at Lady Austen's request—Induced by her to commence writing The Task—Principal object he had in view in composing it—Sudden and final separation from Lady Austen—Occasional severity of his depressive malady—Hopes entertained by his friends of his ultimate recovery—His own opinion of it—Pleasing proofs of the power of religion on his mind—Tenderness of his conscience—Aversion to religious deception and pretended piety—Sympathy with the sufferings of the poor—Enviable condition of such of them as are pious, compared with the rich who disregard religion...138

CHAPTER X. Publication of Cowper's second volume of poems— Manner in which it was received by the public—His feelings on the occasion—Great self-abasement—Renewal of his correspondence with Lady Hesketh— Acceptance of her proffered assistance—Her projected visit to Olney—Cowper's pleasing anticipations of its results—Her arrival—Cowper's removal from Olney to Weston—His intimacy with the Throckmortons—Happiness it afforded him. 160

CHAPTER XI. Extracts from his correspondence—Description of the deep seriousness generally pervading his mind— His remarks to justify his removal from Olney—Vindicates himself and Mrs. Unwin from unjust aspersions—Reasons for undertaking the translation of Homer—Immense pains he bestowed upon it— His readiness to avail himself of the assistance of others — Vexation he experienced from a multiplicity of critics—Just remarks upon criticism—Determination to persevere in his work — Justifies himself for undertaking it — Pleasure he took in relieving the poor—Renewal of his correspondence with General Cowper and the Rev. Dr. Bagot—Consolatory letter to the latter. 174

CHAPTER XII. Pleasure he enjoyed in his new residence—Sudden death of Mrs. Unwin's son—Cowper's distress on the occasion—Experiences a severe attack of illness—Is compelled to relinquish, for a time, his labours of translation—Mr. Rose's first visit to him—His sudden recovery—Manner of spending his time—Peculiarities of his case—Is dissuaded from resuming his translation—His determination to persevere in it—Applies to it with the utmost diligence—Great care with which he translated—His admiration of the original—Providential preservation of Mrs. Unwin—His painful depression unremoved. 193

CHAPTER XIII. Pressing invitations of his friends to write a poem on the Slave Trade—Reasons for declining it—Correspondence with Mrs. King—Particular description of his feelings—Death of Sir Ashley Cowper—Description of his character—Great severity of Cowper's depression—Is again urged to write on the Slave Trade —Again declines it—Assigns particular reasons for it—His indefatigable application to Homer—Notice he took of passing events—Mr. and Mrs. Newton's visit to Weston—The pleasure it afforded Cowper— Lady Hesketh's visit—Completion of the *Iliad*, and commencement of the *Odyssey*—His unwearied application to Homer not allowed to divert his attention from religion— Occasional composition of original poetry —Readiness to listen to any alteration that might be suggested in his productions. ...210

CHAPTER XIV. Mrs. Unwin much injured by a fall— Cowper's anxiety respecting her—Continues incessantly engaged on his Homer—His regret that it should have suspended his correspondence with his friends—Revises a small volume of poems for children—State of his mind —Receives as a present from Mrs. Bodham, a portrait of his mother—Feelings on the occasion— Interesting description of her character—Translates a series of Latin letters from a Dutch minister of the gospel— Continuance of his depression—Is attacked with a nervous fever—Completion of his translation— Death of Mrs. Newton— His reflections on the occasion—Again revises his Homer—His unalterable attachment to religion. 224

CHAPTER XV. Publication of his Homer—To whom dedicated—Benefits he had derived from it—Feels the want of employment—Mrs. Unwin's first attack of paralysis—Manner in which it affected Cowper—Remarks on Milton's labours —Reply to Mr. Newton's letter on original composition—Continuance of his depression—First letter from Mr. Hayley—Unpleasant circumstance respecting it —Mr. Hayley's first visit to Weston— Kind manner in which he was received—Mrs. Unwin's second severe paralytic attack—Cowper's feelings on the occasion —Mr. Hayley's departure—Cowper's warm attachment to him— Reflections on the recent changes he had witnessed—Promises to visit Eartham—Makes preparations for the journey—Peculiarity of his feelings on the occasion...243

CHAPTER XVI. Journey to Eartham—Incidents of it—Safe arrival— Description of the place—Employment there—Reply to a letter from Mr. Hurdis, on the death of his sister — State of Cowper's mind at Eartham—His great attention to Mrs. Unwin—Return to Weston —Interview with General Cowper — Safe arrival at their beloved retreat — Regrets the loss of his studious habit — Warmth of his affection for Mr. Hayley—Dread of January—Prepares for a second edition of Homer — Commences writing notes upon it — Labour it occasioned him—His close application—Continuance of his depression — Judicious consolatory advice he gives to his friends—Letter to Rev. J. Johnson on his taking orders—Reply to Mr. Hayley respecting a joint literary undertaking. 263

CHAPTER XVII. Mr. Hayley's second visit to Weston—Finds Cowper busily engaged—Great apprehensions respecting him—Mrs. Unwin's increasing infirmities—Cowper's feelings on account of them—Vigour of his own mind at this period—Severe attack of depression—Deplorable condition to which he was nmu reduced—Management of his affairs kindly undertaken by Lady Hesketh— Mr. Hayley's anxieties respecting him—Is invited by Mr. Greatheed to pay Cowper another visit—Complies with the invitation—Arrival at Weston—How he is received by Cowper—Inefficiency of the means employed to remove the depression—Handsome pension allowed by his Majesty—His removal from Weston to Norfolk, under the care of the Rev. J. Johnson— Death of Mrs. Unwin—How it affected Cowper. 283

CHAPTER XVIII. Cowper undertakes the revisal of his Homer—Depth of his depression—Means pursued by his kinsman to remove it—Lady Spencer's visit to the poet—His removal to Mundesley—His letter to Lady Hesketh— Returns to Dereham—Manner in which he was occasionally employed—His last original poem—His declining strength—New models a passage in his Homer —Rapid increase of his weakness—Last illness and death—Description of his person, his disposition, his piety—His attachment to the Established Church— His religious sentiments—Depth of his piety—His aversion to flattery and ostentation—The warmth of his friendship—His industry and perseverance — Manly independence—Happy manner in which he could console the afflicted—Occasional intervals of enjoyment—Rhyming letter, *etc.* 305

CHAPTER XIX. Cowper's scholastic attainments—Character as a writer —Originality of his productions—Comparison between him and other poets—The severity of his sarcasm— Review of his original poems—Table Talk—Expostulation—Hope—Charity—Conversation—Retirement—The Task—His minor poems—His prose productions—Remarks on his letters—List of his works—Extract from an anonymous critic—Lines descriptive of his poetic character—On seeing his picture—On visiting his garden and summer-house. 334

PREFACE.

Many lives of Cowper have already been published. Why, then, it may be asked, add to their number? Simply because, in the opinion of competent judges, no memoir of him has yet appeared that gives a full, fair, and unbiased view of his character.

It is remarked by Dr. Johnson, the poet's kinsman, in his preface to the two volumes of *Cowper's Private Correspondence*, that Mr. Hayley omitted the insertion of several interesting letters in his excellent *Life* of the poet, out of kindness to his readers. In doing this, however amiable-and considerate his caution must appear, the gloominess, which he has taken from the mind of Cowper, has the effect of involving his character in obscurity. People read 'The Letters' with 'The Task' in their recollection (and vice versa), and are perplexed. They look for the Cowper of each in the other, and find him not. Hence the character of Cowper is undetermined; mystery hangs over it; and the opinions formed of him are as various as the minds of the inquirers.

In alluding to these alluding to these suppressed letters, the late highly esteemed Rev. Legh Richmond once emphatically remarked, "Cowper's character will never be clearly and satisfactorily understood without them, and they should be permitted to exist for the demonstration of the case. I know the importance of it from numerous conversations I have had both in Scotland and in England, on this most interesting subject. Persons of truly religious principles, as well as those of little or no religion at all, have greatly erred in their estimate of this great and good man."

Dr. Johnson's two volumes of *Private Correspondence* have satisfactorily supplied this deficiency to all those who have the means of consulting them, and the four volumes by Mr. Hayley. The author of this memoir has attempted not only to bring the substance of these six volumes into one, but to communicate information respecting the poet which cannot be found in either of those works. He is fully aware of the peculiarities of Cowper's case, and has endeavoured to exhibit them as prominently as was compatible with his design, without giving to the memoir too much of that melancholy tinge by which the life of its subject was so painfully distinguished.

In every instance where he could well accomplish it, he has made Cowper his own biographer; convinced that it is utterly impossible to narrate any circumstance in a manner more striking, or in a style more chaste and elegant, than Cowper has employed in his inimitable letters.

To impart ease and perspicuity to the memoir, and to compress it into as small a compass as was consistent with a full development and faithful record of the most interesting particulars of Cowper's life, the author has, in a few cases, inserted in one paragraph remarks extracted from different letters, addressed more frequently, though not invariably, to the same individual. He has, however, taken care to avoid doing this where it could lead to any obscurity.

He has made a free use of all the published records of Cowper within his reach, besides availing himself of the valuable assistance and advice of the Rev. Dr. Johnson, Cowper's kinsman, to whom he hereby respectfully tenders his grateful acknowledgements for his condescension and kindness, in undertaking to examine the manuscript, and for the useful and judicious hints respecting it he was pleased to suggest.

Without concealing a single fact of real importance, the author has carefully avoided giving that degree of prominence to any painful circumstance in the poet's life, which would be likely to excite regret in the minds of any of his surviving relatives, and which, for reasons the most amiable and perfectly excusable, they might have wished had been suppressed; and he hopes it will be found that he has admitted nothing that can justly offend the most fastidious.

It is particularly the wish of the author to state, that he makes no pretensions to originality in this memoir. He wishes it to be regarded only as a compilation; and all the merit he claims for it, if indeed he has any, is for the arrangement of those materials which were already furnished for his use.

He has attempted to make the work interesting to all classes, especially to the lovers of literature and genuine piety, and to place within the reach of general readers, many of whom have neither the means nor the leisure to consult larger works, all that is really interesting respecting that singularly afflicted individual, whose productions, both poetic and prose, can never be read but with delight.

Availing himself of some remarks kindly made by some of his friends, and of the hints of the different reviewers who have noticed the work, the author has, in this edition, made a few trifling alterations of some parts of the Memoir; and besides adding an entire new chapter, of what may be called the Christian philosophy of the volume, he has inserted a number of additional extracts from the poet's correspondence, all of which he hopes will be found illustrative of his character.

For the flattering manner in which the work has been noticed by the reviewers, and received by the public, the author begs to express his grateful acknowledgments; ascribing it much less to any merit of his work, than to their unabated, and he hopes, increasing attachment to the memory and productions of Cowper.

The author,
Sept. 14, 1833.

FAMILY:

Father – Reverend John Cowper D. D. (Chaplain to King George II).

Mother – Ann Donne Cowper (a descendant of poet John Donne) died at 34 in childbed.

Anne Donne Cowper

When sent a portrait of his mother by one of his female cousins, a vivid childhood came to his mind of his mother stroking his hair.

> And thou was happier than myself, the while,
> Wouldst softly speak,
> and stroke my head, and smile.
> Could those few pleasant days again appear,
> Might one wish bring them,
> would I wish them here?

John – William's brother, a poet. Cambridge educated.

EXTENDED FAMILY:

William Cowper – Great uncle - became Lord High Chancellor in 1707. (Anne and George I)
Spenser Cowper – Grandfather - became Chief Justice of Chester in 1717, a judge in the court of Common Pleas.
Judith – Spenser's daughter – a poet.
John – Spenser's son – father of William.
Roger Donne – father of his mother, Ann.
Rev. Martin Madan – William's first cousin. Chaplin to the Lock Hospital. The oldest son of Colonel Madan, married the daughter of Judge Cowper.
Uncle Ashley – father of Cousin Theodora and Cousin Harriet.
Theodora Cowper – The cousin William fell in love with, and who anonymously sent money to help him in later years. Neither ever married. After a minor quarrel with her, Cowper wrote a friend, "All is comfortable and happy between us at present and I doubt not will continue so forever. Indeed we had neither of us any great reason to be dissatisfied and perhaps quarrel'd merely for the sake of the reconciliation – which you may be sure made ample amends!
Major or Colonel or General Cowper – cousin of William who married the sister of Martin Madan. (Mrs. Cowper)
Mrs. Cowper – (of the letters) sister of Martin Madan.
Rev. Roger Donne – William's mother's brother. Had the children Harriet, Anne, Elizabeth, and Castres.
John Donne – A very distinguished and accomplished poet, an ancestor of his mother.

Mrs. Anne Bodham, "Rose" – His cousin.

FRIENDS:

Rev. John Newton – Reverend at Olney and then St. Mary Woolnoth. Very close friend of William.

Lady Hesketh – Cousin Harriet Cowper, who married Sir Thomas Hesketh, and then widowed. She was his patron and good friend. He loved Harriet deeply but was not "in love" with her. In August 1763, he wrote to her, "So much as I love you; I wonder how the deuce it has happened I was never in love with you."

Lady Austen – the widow of a Baronet, Sir Robert Austin. Moved to Olney. She became good friends with William and Mrs. Unwin.

Lady Austen stirred passion in the poet, by his own admission:
"...that itching, and that tingling,

With all my purpose intermingling,
To your intrinsic merit true,
When call'd t'address myself to you..."

Mrs. Jones – sister to Lady Austen.
Rev. Morley Unwin – The father in the Unwin family who died in an accident in 1767.
Mrs. Unwin (Mary) – a good friend and support for William. The wife of Rev. Morley Unwin.

Mary Unwin

Cowper lodged with Rev. and Mrs. Unwin for two years in Huntingdon. When Rev. Unwin died, encouraged by the Reverend John Newton, Mrs. Unwin and Cowper moved to Olney, where they lived for 18 years. After that, they couple went to Weston Underwood to share a home there. Obviously, there was some apprehension about the respectability of this arrangement; and conceivably, for that reason the two became briefly engaged. Mary Unwin was a very virtuous woman. The idea that there might have been any sexual relationship between the two of them is unlikely. There seems little reason to doubt this. Their relationship was close, but like that of a mother and son, although Mrs. Unwin was but seven years older than Cowper.

Rev. William Cawthorne Unwin – The son in the Unwin family whom William first met. Educated at Cambridge.
Daughter Unwin – married Mr. Powley.
Mrs. Cowper – Sister of Rev. Martin Madan, wife of Major Cowper.
Rev. William Bull – a preacher of a neighboring town to Olney, called Newport Pagnell. He visited William weekly when Rev. Newton went to London.
William Hayley – Poet, translator, and essayist. Wrote *Life of William Cowper*. A friend and attendant in Cowper's final days.
John Johnson – The grandson of his mother's brother, Rev. Roger Donne. He wanted William to have a portrait of his mother. (Also called 'Johnny of Norfolk.')
Joseph Hill – A schoolfellow at Westminster.
Samuel Rose – an admirer of William's poetry.
Rev. Walter Bagot – interested in William's Homer translations.
Source:

http://curiosmith.com/index.php/authors/139-cowper-william

CHAPTER I.

His parentage—Loss of his mother—Verses to her Memory—First school—Cruelty he experienced there —First serious impressions—Entrance upon Westminster School—Character while there—Removal thence—Entrance upon an attorney's office—Want of employment there — Unfitness for his profession — Early melancholy impressions.

William Cowper was born at Great Berkhampstead, in Hertfordshire, November 15, 1731. His father, Dr. John Cowper, chaplain to King George the Second, was the second son of Spencer Cowper, who was Chief Justice of Chester, and afterwards a Judge in the Court of Common Pleas, and whose brother William, first Earl Cowper, was Lord High Chancellor of England. His mother was Anne, daughter of Roger Donne, Esq. of Ludham Hall, Norfolk, who had a common ancestry with the celebrated Dr. Donne, Dean of St. Paul's.

Dr. Johnson, his relative and biographer, remarked that the highest blood in the realm flowed in the veins of the modest and unassuming Cowper ... his mother having descended four different lines from Henry the Third, King of England ... royalty itself may be pleased and perhaps benefited, by discovering its kindred to such piety, such purity, and such talents as his.

Many distinguished literary characters have justly confessed themselves deeply indebted to the influence exerted over their minds by their mothers; and some of the most interesting records relate to the strength of their maternal attachments. Had Cowper's mother been spared, he would doubtless have been most ready to acknowledge his obligations to her tender and watchful care. Divine providence, however, for the best of reasons, permitted him only to enjoy the advantages of her maternal solicitude for a short season.

After giving birth to several children, this lady died in childbed in her thirty-seventh year, leaving only two sons, John the younger, and William the elder. Cowper was only six years old when he lost his mother; and how deeply he was affected by her early death, may be inferred from the following exquisitely

tender lines, and composed more than fifty years afterwards, on the receipt of her portrait from Mrs. Ann Bodham, a relation in Norfolk:

> O that those lips had language! Life has pass'd
> With me but roughly since I heard thee last.
> Those lips are thine—thine own sweet smile I see,
> The same that oft in childhood solaced me...

As revealed in a later poem, the maidservants in the Cowper home told the child that his mother had gone away on a long trip, but would return. However, Cowper had seen the hearse bearing her body away from his window. This likely left a traumatic mark upon the sensitive little boy.

He would later write:

> 'I heard the bell tolled on thy burial day,
> I saw the hearse that bore thee slow away,
> And turning from my nursery window, drew
> A long, long sigh, and wept a last adieu.'

Deprived thus early of his most affectionate parent, he was sent, at this tender age, to a large school at Market-street, Hertfordshire, under the care of Dr. Pitman. Here he had hardships of different kinds with which to deal. His chief sorrow arose from the cruel treatment he met with from a boy in the same school, about fifteen years of age, who persecuted him with unrelenting barbarity; and who never seemed pleased except when he was tormenting him. This savage treatment impressed upon Cowper's tender mind such a dread of this petty tyrant, (whose cruelty being subsequently discovered, led to his expulsion from the school) that he was afraid to lift his eyes higher than his knees; and he knew him better by his shoe buckles than by any other part of his dress. Some may ridicule young Cowper's feelings on this occasion, as symptomatic of his subsequent morbid depression; instances, however, may easily be found, in which boys have suffered greatly in a similar way, though there has not been the slightest constitutional tendency to melancholy.

Much may certainly be said in favour of public schools, but it cannot be denied and the opinion seems every day becoming more prevalent among well-informed Christians, that they are the sources of many great and serious evils; and that the habits of injustice, tyranny, and licentiousness, too often formed there.

It was at this school, and on one of these painful occasions, that the mind of Cowper, which was afterwards to become imbued with religious feelings of the highest order, received its first serious impressions;— a circumstance which cannot fail to be interesting to every Christian reader; and the more so as detailed in his own words:

'One day, as I was sitting alone on a bench in the school, melancholy, and almost ready to weep at the recollection of what I had already suffered, and expecting at the same time my tormenter every moment, these words of the Psalmist came into my mind—"I will not be afraid of what man can do unto me." I applied this to my own case, with a degree of trust and confidence in God that would have been no disgrace to a much more experienced Christian. Instantly I perceived in myself a briskness and a cheerfulness of spirit which I had never before experienced, and took several paces up and down the room with joyful alacrity. Happy had it been for me, if this early effort towards a dependence on the blessed God, had been frequently repeated. Alas! It was the first and the last, between infancy and manhood.'

From this school he was removed in his eighth year; and having at that time specks on both his eyes, which threatened to cover them, his father, alarmed for the consequences, placed him under the care of an eminent female oculist in London; in whose house he abode nearly two years. In this lady's family, religion was neither known nor practised; the slightest appearance of it, in any shape, was carefully guarded against; and even its outward forms were entirely unobserved. In a situation like this, it was not to be expected that young Cowper would long retain any serious impressions he might have experienced; nor is it surprising, that before his removal thence he should have lost them entirely.

In his ninth year, he was sent to Westminster School, then under the care of Dr. Nicholls; who, though an ingenious and learned man, was nevertheless a negligent tutor; and one that encouraged his pupils in habits of indolence, not a little injurious to their future welfare. Here he remained seven years, and had frequent reason to complain of the same unkind treatment from some of his schoolfellows, which he had experienced previously. We know but little of the progress he made while under the care of Dr. Nicholls; but his subsequent eminence as a scholar, proves that he must have been an attentive pupil, and must have made, at this period, a praiseworthy proficiency in his studies.

At this school he was roused a second time to serious consideration. Crossing a churchyard late one evening, he saw a glimmering light in rather a remote corner, which so excited his curiosity as to induce him to approach it. Just as he arrived at the spot, a gravedigger, who was at work by the light of his lantern, threw up a skull-bone, which struck him on the leg. This little incident alarmed his conscience, and gave rise to many fearful reflections. The impression, however, was only temporary, and in a short time, the event was entirely forgotten.

On another occasion, not long afterwards, he again, at this early age, became the subject of religious impressions. It was the laudable practice of Dr. Nicholls to take great pains to prepare his pupils for confirmation. The Doctor acquitted himself of this duty like one who had a deep sense of its importance, and young Cowper was struck by his manner, and much affected by his exhortations. He now, for the first time in his life, attempted prayer in secret, but being little accustomed to that exercise of the heart, and having very childish notions of religion, he found it a difficult task, and was then alarmed at his own insensibility. These impressions, like those made upon his mind before, soon wore off, and he relapsed into a forgetfulness of God. This was evidently the case with him, for on being afterwards seized with the smallpox, though he was in the most imminent danger, yet neither in the course of the disease, nor during his recovery from it, had he any sentiments of contrition, or any thoughts of God or eternity. He, however, derived one advantage from it;—it removed, to a great degree, if it did not entirely cure, the disease in his eyes; proving, as he afterwards observed in a letter to Mr. Hayley, 'a better oculist than the lady who had had him under her care.'

Such was the character of young Cowper, in his eighteenth year, when he left Westminster School. He had made a respectable proficiency in all his studies; but notwithstanding his previous serious impressions, he seems to have had hardly any more knowledge of the nature of religion, or concern about it. After spending six months at home, he was articled to a solicitor, with whom he was to remain three years. In this gentleman's family, he neither saw nor heard anything that could remind him of a single Christian duty; and here he might have lived ignorant of the God that made him, had he not been providentially situated near his uncle's in Southampton Row. At this favourite retreat, he was permitted to spend all his leisure hours, which indeed was almost the whole of his time, as he was scarcely ever employed. With his uncle's family, he passed nearly all his Sundays, and with some part of it he regularly attended public worship, which, probably, he would otherwise, have entirely neglected.

The choice of a profession for a youth is of supreme importance; if unwisely made, it lays the foundation for much future disappointment and sorrow. It would certainly have been difficult, and perhaps impossible, to have selected one more unsuitable to the mind of Cowper than that of the law. As Mr. Hayley observes, 'The law is a kind of soldiership, and, like the profession of arms, it may be said to require for the constitution of its heroes,

'A frame of adamant, a soul of fire.'

'The soul of Cowper had, indeed, its fire, but fire so refined and ethereal, that it could not be expected to shine in the gross atmosphere of worldly contention.' Reserved to an unusual and extraordinary degree, he was ill qualified to exhibit the activity unavoidably connected with this profession. Though he possessed superior powers of mind, and a richly cultivated understanding, yet were they combined with such extreme sensibility, as totally disqualified him for the bustle of the courts. An excessive tenderness, associated with a degree of shyness unfitted him for a profession that would often have placed him before the public, and brought him into contact with individuals unembarrassed by such weaknesses. His extreme modesty, however, while it precluded the possibility of his being successful in this profession, endeared him to all who had the happiness to enjoy his society. Never was there a mind more admirably formed for communicating to others, in private life, the richest sources of enjoyment; and yet, such were the peculiarities of his nature, that often while he delighted and interested all around him, he was himself extremely unhappy. The following lines, composed by him about this time reveal the state of his mind at this period. They are remarkable for their exquisite tenderness and poetic beauty.

> Doomed as I am in solitude to waste
> The present moments, and regret the past;
> Deprived of every joy I valued most,
> My friend torn from me, and my mistress lost;
> Call not this gloom I wear, this anxious mien,
> The dull effect of humour or of spleen.
> Still, still I mourn, with each returning day,
> Him, Sir William Russell* snatched by fate in early youth away;
> And her through tedious years of doubt and pain,
> Fix'd in her choice, and faithful—but in vain!
> Oh! Prone to pity, generous and sincere,
> Whose eye ne'er yet refused the wretch a tear;
> Whose heart the real claim of friendship knows,

Nor thinks a lover's are but fancied woes;
See me,—ere yet my destined course half done,
Cast forth a wanderer on a world unknown 1
See me neglected on the world's rude coast,
Each dear companion of my voyage lost t
Nor ask why clouds of sorrow shade my brow,
And ready tears wait only leave to flow!
Why all that soothes a heart from anguish free,
All that delights the happy, palls with me!'

Sir William was the contemporary of Cowper at Westminster, and his close friend. Sadly, young Russell died prematurely, while bathing in the Thames, amidst all the opening prospects of life, and with accomplishments and virtues that adorned his rank and station. This occurrence inflicted a great moral shock on the sensitive mind of Cowper. (*The Works of William Cowper: His life and Letters,* Vol. 5, page 307, by William Cowper, William Hayley, John William Cunningham London: Sanders and Otley, 1835.)

CHAPTER II. Entrance at the Temple—Employment there—Depression of his mind—Religious impressions—Visit to Southampton—Sudden removal of sorrow—Death of his father—Appointment to the office of reading clerk to the House of Lords—Dread of appearing in public —Consequent abandonment of the situation—Is pro-posed as Clerk of the Journals—Preparation for entering upon his office—Distressing sensations on the occasion—Is compelled to relinquish it—Serious attack of depression—Visit of his brother.

The Temple is a zone in central London, near Temple Church, one of the main legal districts of the capital and a famous centre for English law. The Temple region of the City of London comprises the Inner Temple and the Middle Temple, which are two of the four Inns of Court and act as local authorities in place of the City of London Corporation within their areas.

At the age of twenty-one, in 1752, Cowper left his late employer's house, and took possession of a set of chambers in the

Inner Temple. Here he remained nearly twelve years; but such was his dis like to his professional studies, and so entirely did he confine himself to literary pursuits, that it may be doubted whether, at the expiration of this lengthened period, he knew any more of the law than he did at its commencement. As this may be considered the most valuable part of life, it must ever be regretted that he suffered it to pass away so unprofitably. During the whole of this important period, he did scarcely anything more than compose a few essays and poems, either to gratify or to assist some literary friend. Prompted by benevolent motives, he became an occasional contributor to a work entitled, 'The Connoisseur,' edited by Robert Lloyd, Esq., a friend to whom he warmly attached. Three of these papers he subsequently pointed out to his friend Hayley; they appeared in the months of May, August, and September 1756, and are productions of more than ordinary interest.

The following extract from a playful poetic epistle, addressed to that gentleman, will be read with interest, as it shows that he began at that time to feel symptoms of the depressing malady, which afterwards became to him a source of so much misery.

> Tis not that I design to rob
> Thee of thy birthright, gentle Bob,
> For thou art born sole heir, and single,
> Of dear Mat Prior's easy jingle;
> Nor that I mean, while thus I knit
> My threadbare sentiments together,
> To show my genius or my wit,
> When God and you know I have neither;
> Or such as might be better shown,
> By letting poetry alone.
> 'Tis not with either of these views
> That I presume to address the muse;
> But to divert a fierce banditti
> (Sworn foes to everything that's witty)
> Who with a black infernal train,

Make cruel inroads on my brain,
And daily threaten to drive thence
My little garrison of sense;
The fierce banditti ^(outlaws), which I mean,
Are gloomy thoughts led on by spleen.

The speculation of Hayley seems highly probable that Cowper's friendship with Lloyd may have given rise to some early productions of his pen. The probability of this conjecture arises from the necessities of Lloyd, and the affectionate liberality of his friend. As the former was induced by his narrow finances to engage in periodical works, it is highly probable that the pen of Cowper, ever ready to second the charitable wishes of his heart, might be directed to the service of an indigent author, whom he appears to have loved with a very cordial affection.'

While Cowper remained in the Temple, he cultivated the friendship of the most distinguished writers of the day; and took a lively interest in their publications. Instead of applying himself to the composition of some original work, which he incidentally produced, his timid spirit contented itself only with occasional displays of its rich and varied capabilities. Translation from ancient and modern poets was one of his most favourite amusements. So far, however, was he from deriving any monetary benefit from these compositions, most of which were masterly productions, that he distributed them gratuitously among his friends. In this way, he assisted his friend Mr. Duncombe; for we find in the version of Horace, published by him in 1759, that two of the satires were translated by Cowper. In the same manner, he is said to have aided Bonnel Thornton in his literary engagements, and to have given him considerable help.

Whatever regret may be felt at the manner in which Cowper spent these twelve years, it must not be imagined that they were *wholly* lost and unimproved. Had he then concentrated his energies in some single work, though it might not, perhaps, have equalled the productions of his riper years, yet it would in no degree have impaired the powers of his mind, as some have ventured to assert; but would rather have been like the first fruits of the rich harvest which was to follow. Nature, however, had given him a contemplative mind, and during all this time he was perpetually accumulating those stores of information, which enabled him, when he subsequently poured them forth, to delight and instruct mankind.

When Cowper entered the Temple, he paid little or no attention to religion. The chilling atmosphere of the world had blighted all those serious impressions that he had once experienced, and he was left, at that dangerous and critical season of life, surrounded by many powerful temptations, without any other principles for his guide, than the corrupt affections of our common nature. It pleased God, however, at the very outset, to prevent him from pursuing that ruinous career of wickedness, into which many plunge with heedless insensibility. The feelings of his peculiarly sensitive mind about this period he thus describes:

'Not long after my settlement in the Temple, I was struck with such a dejection of spirits, as none but those who have felt the same can have the least conception of. Day and night, I was upon the rack, lying down in horror, and rising up in despair. I presently lost all relish for those studies to which I had before been closely attached; the classics had no longer any charms for me; I had need of something more beneficial than amusement, but I had no one to direct me where to find it.

'At length I met with *Herbert's Poems*; and, gothic and uncouth as they are, I found in them a strain of piety which I admired. This was the only author I had any delight in reading. I pored over him all day long; and though I found not in his work what I might have found—a cure for my malady, yet my mind never seemed so much alleviated as while I was reading it. At length I was advised, by a very near and dear relative, to lay it aside, for he thought such an author more likely to nourish my disorder than to remove it.

'In this state of mind I continued near a twelvemonth; when, having experienced the inefficacy of all human means, I at length betook myself to God in prayer. Such is the rank our Redeemer holds in our esteem, that we never resort to him but in the last instance, when all creatures have failed to succour us! My hard heart was at length softened, and my stubborn knees brought to bow. I composed a set of prayers, and made frequent use of them. Weak as my faith was, the Almighty, who will not break the bruised reed, nor quench the smoking flax, was graciously pleased to listen to my cry, instead of frowning me away in anger.

'A change of scene was recommended to me; and I went with some friends to Southampton, where I spent several months. Soon after our arrival, we walked to a place called Freemantle, about a mile from the town; the morning was clear and calm; the sun shone brightly upon the sea, and the country on the border of it was the most beautiful I had ever seen. Here it was, that suddenly, as if another sun had been created in the heavens on purpose to dispel sorrow and vexation of spirit, I felt the weight of all my misery taken off; my heart became light and joyful in a moment; I could have wept with transport had I been alone. I must believe that nothing less than the Almighty approval could have filled me with such delight; not by a gradual dawning of peace, but as if it were, with a flash of his life-giving countenance. I felt a glow of gratitude to the Father of mercies for this blessing, and ascribed it, at first, to his gracious acceptance of my prayers; but Satan, and my own wicked heart, persuaded me that I was indebted for my deliverance to nothing but a change of scene, and the amusing varieties of the place. By this means, he turned the blessing into a poison; teaching me to conclude that nothing but a continued circle of diversion, and indulgence of appetite, could secure me from a relapse. Acting upon this false and wicked principle, as soon as I returned to London, I burnt my prayers, and away went all my thoughts of devotion, and of dependence upon God my Saviour. Surely, it was of his mercy that I was not consumed. Glory be to his grace!

'I obtained, at length, so complete a victory over my conscience, that all remonstrances from that quarter were in vain, and in a manner silenced, though sometimes, indeed, a question would arise in my mind, whether it were safe to proceed any further in a course plainly condemned in the Scriptures. I saw that if the gospel were true, such a conduct must inevitably end in my destruction; but I see how I could change my Ethiopian complexion, or overcome such a chronic habit of rebelling against God.

'The next thing that occurred to me was a doubt whether the gospel were true or false. To this succeeded many an anxious wish for the decision of this important question. I foolishly thought that obedience would follow, were I but convinced that it was worthwhile to attend to it. Having no reason to expect a miracle, I acquiesced, at length, in favour of that impious conclusion, that the only course I could take to secure my present peace, was to wink hard against the prospects of future misery, and to resolve to banish all thoughts of a subject upon which I thought to so little purpose. Nevertheless, when I was in the company of deists, and heard the gospel blasphemed, I never failed to assert the truth of it with much vehemence of disputation, for which I was the better qualified, having been always a inquirer into the evidences by which it is supported. I think I once went so far into a controversy of this kind as to assert, that I would gladly submit to have my right hand cut off, so that I might but be enabled to live according to the gospel. Thus have I been employed in defending the truth of scripture, while in the very act of rebelling against its teachings. Lamentable inconsistency of a convinced judgment with an unsanctified heart! My inconsistency was evident to others as well as to myself.'

In 1756, Cowper sustained a heavy domestic loss, in the death of his excellent father, towards whom he had always felt the strongest parental regard. Such, however, was the depressed state of his mind at this season, that he was much less affected by the solemn event than he would probably have been had it occurred at any earlier or later period of his life. Perceiving that he should inherit but little fortune from his father, he now found it necessary to adopt some plan to augment his income. It became every day more apparent to his friends, as well as to himself, that his extreme hesitancy disallowed the possibility of his being successful in his profession.

After much anxiety, he mentioned it to a friend, who had two situations at his disposal, those of the Reading Clerk, and Clerk of the Journals in the House of Lords—which Cowper thought would suit him, and one of which he expressed a desire to obtain, should a vacancy occur. Quite unexpectedly to him, as well as to his friend, both these places, in a short time afterwards, became vacant; and as the Reading Clerk's was much the more valuable of the two, his friend offered it to him, which he gratefully accepted, and he was appointed to it in his thirty-first year.

All his friends were delighted with this providential opening. He himself, at first, looked forward to it with pleasure, intending, as soon as he was settled, to unite himself with an amiable and accomplished young lady, one of his first cousins, the daughter of Ashley Cowper, Esq., and youngest sister of his future favourite correspondent, Lady Hesketh, for whom he had long cherished a tender attachment. These fond hopes, however, were never realized. Annotation: This was his cousin, Theodora Cowper, who became the Delia of his love poems. They were engaged, but her father forbade the marriage, stating their close kinship. Apparently, Ashley Cowper saw what he considered weaknesses in William that persuaded him he would not have been a good husband. They never saw each other again after 1756, and neither ever married.

The situation required him to appear at the bar of the House of Peers; and the anxiety of this public exhibition overwhelmed his meek and gentle spirit. So severe were his distressing apprehensions, that, notwithstanding the previous efforts he made to qualify himself for the office, long before the day arrived that he was to enter upon it, such was the embarrassed and melancholy state of his mind, that he was compelled to relinquish it entirely. His harassed and dejected feelings on this occasion he thus affectingly describes:

'All the considerations by which I endeavoured to compose my mind to its former tranquillity, did but torment me the more. I returned to my chambers, thoughtful and unhappy; my countenance fell; and my friend was astonished to find an air of deep melancholy in all I said or did. Having been harassed in this manner for a week, perplexed between the apparent folly of casting away the only visible chance I had of being well provided for, and the impossibility of retaining it, I determined at length to write a letter to my friend, though he lodged next door, and we generally spent the day together. I did so, and begged him to accept my resignation of the Reading Clerk's place, and to appoint me to the other situation. I was well aware of the inconsistency between the value of the appointments, but my peace was gone: pecuniary advantages were not equivalent to what I had lost; and I flattered myself that the Clerkship of the Journals would fall, fairly and easily, within the scope of my abilities. Like a man in a fever, I thought a change of posture would relieve my pain, and, as the event will show, was equally disappointed. My friend, at length, after considerable reluctance, accepted my resignation, and appointed me to the least profitable office. The matter being thus settled, calm took place in my mind. I thought my path towards an easy maintenance was now plain and open, and, for a day or two, was tolerably cheerful; but behold; the storm was gathering all the while, and the fury of it was not the less violent from this gleam of sunshine.

'A strong opposition to my friend's right of nomination began to show itself. A powerful party was formed among the lords to thwart it, and it appeared plain, that if we succeeded at last, it could only be by fighting our ground by inches. Every advantage, I was told, would be sought for, and eagerly seized to disconcert us. I was led to expect an examination at the bar of the house, touching my adequacy for the post I had taken. It became expedient that I should visit the office daily, in order to qualify myself for the strictest scrutiny. All the horror of my fears and perplexities now returned; a thunderbolt would have been as welcome to me as this intelligence. I knew that, upon such terms, the Clerkship of the Journals was no place for me. In the meantime, the interest of my friend, the causes of his choice, and my own reputation and circumstances, all urged me forward, and

34

pressed me to undertake that which I saw to be impracticable. They whose spirits are formed as mine, to whom a public exhibition of themselves, on any occasion, is mortal poison, may have some idea of the horror of my situation—others can have none. My continual misery at length brought on a nervous fever; quiet forsook me by day, and peace by night; even a finger raised against me seemed more than I could bear.

'In this posture of mind, I attended regularly at the office, where, instead of a soul upon the rack, the most active spirits were essential to my purpose. I expected no assistance from any one there, all the inferior clerks being under the influence of my opponents; accordingly, I received none. The Journal books were thrown open to me, a thing that could not be refused, and from which, perhaps, a man in health with a head turned to business, might have gained all the information wanted. But it was not so with me. I read without perception, and was so distressed, that had every clerk in the office been my friend, it would have availed me little, for I was not in a condition to receive instruction, much less to elicit it from manuscripts, without direction.'

The following extract from a letter to his amiable cousin, Lady Hesketh, written 9th August, 1763, through which runs that happy mixture of playful seriousness, which distinguishes almost the whole of his epistolary productions, and imparts to them a charm superior to that of almost any other writer, will illustrate the state of his mind at that period.

'Having promised to write to you, I make haste to be as good as my word. I have a pleasure in writing to you at any time, but especially at the present, when my days are spent in reading the Journals, and my nights in dreaming of them. Oh! My good cousin! If I was to open my heart to you, I could show you strange sights; nothing, I flatter myself, that would shock you, but a good deal that would make you wonder. I am of a very singular temper, and very unlike all the men that I have ever conversed with. Certainly, I am not an absolute fool; but I have more weakness than the greatest of all fools I can recollect at present. In short, if I were as fit for the next world as I am unfit for this— and God forbid that I should speak it in vanity—I would not change conditions with any saint in Christendom. Ever since I was born, I have been good at disappointing the most natural expectations. Many years ago, cousin, there was a possibility that I might prove a very different thing from what I am at present. My character is now fixed, and riveted fast upon me; and, between friends, is not a very splendid one, or likely to be guilty of much fascination.'

Many months was Cowper thus employed, constant in the use of means to qualify himself for the office, yet despairing as to the issue. At length he says,

'The vacation being pretty far advanced, I repaired to Margate. There, by the help of cheerful company, a new scene, and the intermission of my painful employment, I presently began to recover my spirits; though even here, my first reflections when I awoke in the morning were horrible and full of wretchedness. I looked to the approaching winter, and regretted the flight of every moment that brought it nearer, like a man borne away, by a rapid torrent, into a stormy sea, whence he sees no possibility of returning, and where he knows he cannot subsist. By degrees, I acquired such a facility in turning away my thoughts from the ensuing crisis, that, for weeks together, I hardly adverted to it at all: but the stress of the tempest was yet to come, and was not to be avoided by any resolution of mine to look another way.

'How wonderful are the works of the Lord, and his ways past finding out! Thus was he preparing me for an event which I least of all expected; even the reception of his blessed gospel, working by means which, in all human contemplation, must needs seem directly opposite to that purpose, but which, in his wise and gracious disposal, have, I trust, effectually accomplished it.'

In October 1763, Cowper was again required to attend the office, and prepare for the final trial. This recalled all his fears, and produced a renewal of all his former misery. On revisiting the scene of his previous ineffectual labours, he felt himself pressed by difficulties on either side, with nothing before him but prospects of gloom and despair.

He realized that he must keep this appointment, thus exposing himself to failure, or relinquish it and lost the only opportunity he apparently had of having a comfortable living and being united to the one to whom he was most ardently attached.

A thought would sometimes cross his mind, that his sins perhaps had brought upon him this distress, and that the hand of divine vengeance was in it. Against this, however, the inherent pride of the human heart soon led him to revolt, and to acquit himself, tempting him to charge God with injustice, saying, 'What have I done to deserve this?' He perceived clearly that deliverance could only come from God, but being firmly persuaded that he would refuse his help, he omitted to ask it at his hands, seeking it only in the use of those means that were the least likely to heal his torn spirit. One effort of a devotional kind he made, for having found a prayer or two, he said them for a few nights, but with so little expectation of an answer that he soon laid aside the book, and with it all thoughts of God and hopes of a remedy.

His terrors on this occasion had become so overwhelming, as to induce that lamented abnormality of mind under which he suffered and which led him more than twice, in different ways, to attempt his own destruction. The dreadful apprehensions that had haunted him day and night, leaving him not a moment's peace, had wound him up to the highest pitch of mental agony. The idea of appearing in public was to him even more bitter than death. To his disordered perception, there appeared no possibility of escape from the horrors of his situation, but by an escape from life itself. Death, which he had always shuddered at before, he began ardently to wish for now. He could see nothing before him but overwhelming difficulties. The supposed ruined state of his pecuniary circumstances—the imagined contempt of his relations and acquaintance—and the apprehended prejudice he should do his patron, urged the fatal expedient upon his

37

shattered intellect, which he now meditated with inexpressible energy.

At this important crisis, when he needed the counsel of some judicious and kind friend, it so happened that he fell into the company of two most unhappy sophists, who both advanced claims to the right of self-destruction, and whose fallacious arguments won him over to their pernicious views. A sophism is an inaccurate argument for displaying ingenuity in reasoning or for deceiving someone. A sophist is a person who reasons with shrewd but misleading and false arguments.

The disordered state of Cowper's mind at this period will be seen by the following anecdote. Taking up a newspaper for the day, his eye caught a satirical letter that it happened to contain, and though it had no relation whatever to his case, he doubted not but the writer was fully acquainted with his purpose, and, in fact, intended to hasten its execution. Wrought up to a degree of anguish almost unbearable, he now experienced a convulsive agitation that deprived him of all his powers. Perceiving no possibility of escaping from his misery by any other means, all around him wearing only an aspect of gloom and despair, it will be no wonder to the reader that the day on which he would have to encounter an examination before the House of Lords, he made several attempts at the escape above alluded to. Suicide.

Most happily, indeed, and most mercifully, for himself and for others, though his attempts were of so determined a kind, that his deliverance was little less than miraculous. It was the will God, not only to preserve his life, but also to make that mind an instrument of incalculable benefit to his country and to the world, advancing and promoting the best interests of mankind, by aiding the cause of morality and religion.

The depths of affliction and sorrow that the amiable sufferer now endured were almost insupportable and were such that he might truly say with the Psalmist, "All thy waves and thy billows are gone over me. I am troubled: I am bowed down greatly, my heart is pained within me, my sorrow is continually before me; fearfulness and trembling are come upon me: I sink in deep mire where there is no standing: I am come into deep waters where the floods overflow me."

When at length the long dreaded day arrived, the approach of which he had feared more than he feared death itself, such were the melancholy results of his distress that all his friends immediately acquiesced in the propriety of his relinquishing the situation forever. Thus ended his connection with the House of Lords; unhappily, however, his sufferings did not end here. Despair still inflicted on him its deadliest sting, and he saw not how it could be extracted; Grief poured its spring tide of anguish into his heart, and he could perceive nothing before him but one interminable prospect of misery.

> O, Providence! Mysterious are thy ways.
> Inflexible thine everlasting plans!
> The finite power of man can ne'er resist
> The unseen hand which guides, protects, preserves,
> Nor penetrate the inscrutable designs
> Of Him, whose counsel is his sovereign will.

At this period of the poet's history, it appears desirable to remark, in confutation of those who attribute, or at least endeavour to attribute, his malady to his religious views, that viewed either as an originating cause, or in any other light, they can never be proved to have had any connection with it. It will not be denied, that those sacred truths, which, in all cases where they are properly received, prove an unfailing source of the most salutary contemplation to the non-deranged mind, were in his case, through the distorting medium of his malady, converted into a vehicle of intellectual poison. It is, as Dr. Johnson observes, a most erroneous idea to suppose, that those views of Christianity which Cowper adopted, and of which, when enjoying the intervals of reason, had in any degree contributed to excite the malady with which he was afflicted. It is capable of the clearest demonstration that nothing was further from the truth. On the contrary, all those alleviations of sorrow, those delightful anticipations of heavenly rest, those healing consolations to a wounded spirit, of which he was permitted to taste, were unequivocally to be ascribed to the operation of those very principles and views of religion, which, in the instance before us, have been charged with producing so opposite an effect. The primary aberration of his mental faculties was wholly to be attributed to other causes. There is abundant evidence of Cowper's melancholy prior to his conversion.

'To this moment I had felt no concern of a spiritual kind: ignorant of original sin; insensible of the guilt of actual transgression, I understood neither the law nor the gospel, the condemning nature of the one, nor the restoring mercies of the other. I was as much unacquainted with Christ in all his saving offices as if his name had never reached me. Now, therefore, a new scene opened upon me.

'My sins were set in array against me, and I began to see and feel that I had lived without God in the world. One moment I thought myself shut out from mercy by one chapter, and the next by another. The sword of the Spirit seemed to guard the tree of life against my touch, and to flame against me in every avenue by which I attempted to approach it. I particularly remember that the parable of the barren fig tree was to me an inconceivable source of anguish. I applied it to my case, with a strong persuasion that it was a curse pronounced on me by the Saviour.

'In every volume I opened I found something that struck me to the heart. I remember taking up one; and the first sentence I saw condemned me. Everything seemed to preach to me, not the gospel of mercy, but the curse of the law. In a word, I saw myself a sinner altogether; but I saw not yet a glimpse of the mercy of God in Christ Jesus.'

These convictions of sin were not in themselves delusions; for they were such as in their principle every Christian feels, and in some cases, where there has been no tinge of insanity, have been carried to such intensity of mental distress, that the penitent has really experienced what he expressed, that' the burden of his sins was intolerable.' The insanity in Cowper's case was shown in the sufferer's dwelling upon one truth, or rather one portion of a truth and never losing sight of it, but deriving from it the most inconsequential and unreasonable inferences, which he believed as firmly as the truth itself.

Some years after, when his reason was fully in exercise, he was mercifully permitted to enjoy those alleviations of sorrow, that sunshine of a conscience at peace with God, pardoned sin through the atonement of the Redeemer and those delightful anticipations of future rest. If religion is to be blamed because a lunatic happened to mix it up with his malady, we might blame every relationship of life, because brothers and sisters, and parents and children, and husbands and wives, have believed under the influence of delirium, that their most affectionate relatives were compassing their death. On the same principle, too we might abolish the House of Lords, as the cause of madness, because Cowper thrice attempted suicide to avoid an honourable invitation to appear at its bar. (*Christian Observer*, April, 1833.)

Cowper now wrote to his brother to inform him of the afflicting circumstances in which he was placed. His brother immediately paid him a visit, and employed every means in his power to alleviate his distress. All his efforts, however, proved unavailing; he found him almost overwhelmed by despair, maintaining, in spite of all remonstrances to the contrary, that he had been guilty of the unpardonable sin, in not properly improving the mercy of God towards him at Southampton. No favourable construction put upon his conduct in that instance by his brother, nor any argument he employed, afforded him a moment's alleviation of his distress. He rashly concluded that he had no longer any interest in the atonement, or in the gifts of the Spirit, and that nothing was left for him but the dismal prospect of eternally enduring the wrath of God. His brother, pierced to the heart at the sight of his misery, used every means to comfort him, but without the least effect; in fact, so deeply seated was his depression, that it rendered useless all the soothing reflections that were suggested.

At this trying period, Cowper remembered his friend and relative, the Rev. Martin Madan; and, though he had always considered him as an enthusiast, he was now convinced that, if there were any balm in Gilead for him, Mr. Madan was the only person who could administer it. His friend lost no time in paying him a visit; and perceiving the state of his mind, he began immediately to declare unto him the gospel of Christ. He spoke of original sin, of the corruption of every man born into the world; of the efficacy of the atonement made by Jesus Christ; of the Redeemer's compassion for lost sinners, and of the full salvation provided for them in the gospel. He then adverted to the Saviour's intercession; described him as a compassionate Redeemer, who felt deeply interested in the welfare of every true penitent, who could sympathize with those who were in distress, and who was able to save unto the uttermost all that came unto God by him.

To these statements, Cowper listened with the greatest attention. Hope seemed to dawn upon his disconsolate mind. His heart burned within him while he hearkened to the word of life; his soul was pierced with a sense of his great ingratitude to so merciful a Saviour; tears of contrition burst from his eyes; he saw clearly that this was the remedy his case required; and felt fully persuaded that this was indeed the gospel of salvation. He, however, still wanted that faith, without which he could not receive its blessings. He saw the suitability of this gospel to his circumstances, but saw not yet how one, as vile as he conceived himself to be, could hope to partake of its benefits.

Mr. Madan urged the necessity of a lively faith in the Redeemer, not as an assent of the understanding only, but as the cordial belief of the heart unto righteousness. Madan assured him that faith was the *gift* of God, a gift that our heavenly Father was most willing to bestow on all sought it by earnest and persevering prayer. Cowper deeply deplored the want of this faith, and could only reply to his friend's remarks, in a brief but very sincere petition, 'Most earnestly do I wish it would please God to bestow it on me.'

The reviewer quoted above, judiciously remarks, that these interviews with Mr. Madan still further show that his melancholy, or even that part of it which would be called religious melancholy, did not arise from those views of scripture doctrine which he afterwards embraced. His brother, whose opinions on these subjects were at that time widely different, admitted that Mr. Madan's counsels, instead of increasing, had reduced the sufferer's malady, and considerably alleviated his distress; and had not insanity intervened, his mind would have been set at ease.

The reasons of his fatherly chastisements, if such permitted afflictions are to be considered as intended for chastisements, are not always understandable by the most observant spectator, though they are sometimes obvious; and it may be, if we knew all, that the case of Cowper was not an exception.'

His brother, perceiving he had received some benefit from this interview, in his desire to relieve the poet's depressed mind, wisely overlooked the difference of religious sentiments which then existed between himself and Mr. Madan, and discovered the greatest anxiety that he should embrace the earliest opportunity to converse with him again. He now urged Cowper to visit Mr. Madan at his own house, and offered to accompany him thither. After much entreaty, Cowper consented and though the conversation was not then the means of affording him any permanent relief, it was not without its use. His mental anguish, though in some degree eased, was far from being removed; the wounded spirit within him was less in pain, but by no means healed. A long train of still greater terrors than any he had yet endured was at hand; and when he awoke the next morning, after a few hours' sleep, he seemed to feel a stronger alienation from God than ever. He was now again the subject of the deepest mental anguish. The sorrows of death seemed to encompass, and the pains of hell to get hold of him. His ears rang with the sound of the torments that seemed to await him. His terrified imagination presented to him many frightful visions, and led him to conceive that he heard many horrible sounds. His heart seemed at every pulse to beat its last; his conscience scared him; the avenger of blood seemed to pursue him; and he saw no city of refuge into which he could flee; in short, every moment he expected the earth would open and swallow him up.

He was now suddenly attacked with that nervous affection, of which the peculiar form of his mind seemed to have made him susceptible, which, on several subsequent occasions darkened his brightest prospects, and which ultimately overwhelmed his meek and gentle spirit, and caused him to end his days in circumstances the most gloomy and sorrowful. The attack was so violent that his friends instantly perceived the change, and consulted on the best manner to dispose of him.

Nathaniel Cotton

[Nathaniel Cotton (1707 1788) was an English physician and poet,] who then kept an establishment at St. Alban's for the reception of such patients. His skill as a physician, his well-known humanity and sweetness of temper, and the acquaintance which had formerly subsisted between him and the afflicted patient, slight as it was, determined them to place him under the doctor's care. No decision could have been more wisely taken. Subsequent events proved it to have been under His superintendence, who orders all things according to the counsels of His own will, and who, with the tenderest solicitude, watches over His people; managing those events which to us appear contingent, on principles of unerring wisdom; and overruling them for the accomplishment of his gracious and benevolent intentions.

CHAPTER III. His removal to St. Alban's—Painful state of his mind there—Receives a visit from his brother—Good effects of it—His recovery—How it was effected—His subsequent happiness—Pleasing conversation with Dr. Cotton — The delightful manner in which he now passed his time—Description of his experience—His gratitude to God—Employs his brother to look out for him a new residence—Leaves St. Albans—Feelings on the occasion.

ANNOTATION: Cowper had five major bouts of depression:
1. 1753 – First bout of severe depression happened when he moved to the Middle Temple.
2. 1763 – Occupational stress with suicide attempts.
3. 1773 – This occurrence stopped him from writing any more of the Olney Hymns.
4. 1787 – January, another round of deep depression (mostly 1786) which William hanged himself. Mrs. Unwin cut him down in time to save his life.
5. 1794 – Mrs. Unwin died and he was unable to work for a time.

On December 7, 1763, he was removed to St. Albans Asylum, and placed under the care of Dr. Cotton. Notwithstanding the skillful and judicious treatment pursued to effect his restoration, he remained in the same gloomy and desponding state for five months. Every means that ingenuity could devise, and that benevolence and tenderness could prompt, were resorted to for this protracted period in vain. To describe in lengthened detail the state of his mind during this long interval, would justly be deemed injudicious.

Without, however, entering minutely into particulars, on this painful subject, it will not be deemed improper to mention some of the leading facts respecting it, and here we shall allow the poet again to become his own biographer.

'The accuser of the brethren was ever busy with me night and day, bringing to my recollection the commission of long-forgotten sins, and charging upon my conscience things of an indifferent nature as atrocious crimes. Conviction of sin and despair of mercy, were the two prominent evils with which I was continually tormented from December 7, 1763, until the middle of the July following. But, blessed be the God of my salvation for every sigh I drew, and for every tear I shed, since thus it pleased him to judge me here, that I might not be judged hereafter.'

'After five months' continued expectation that the divine vengeance would plunge me into the bottomless pit, I became so familiar with despair, as to have contracted a sort of hardiness and indifference as to the event. I began to persuade myself, that while the execution of the sentence was suspended, it would be for my interest to indulge a less horrible train of ideas, than I had been accustomed to muse upon. I entered into conversation with the doctor, laughed at his stories, and told him some of my own to match them; still, however, carrying a sentence of irrevocable doom in my heart. He observed the seeming alteration with pleasure, and began to think my recovery well-nigh completed; but the only thing that could promote and effectuate my cure, was yet wanting; an experimental knowledge of the redemption which is in Christ Jesus.'

'About this time a diabolical species of regret found harbour in my wretched heart. I was sincerely sorry that I had not seized every opportunity of giving scope to my wicked appetites, and even envied those, who being departed to their own place before me, had the consolation to reflect, that they had well earned their miserable inheritance by indulging their sensuality without restraint. Oh, merciful God! What a Tophet ^{Hell} of pollution is the human soul, and wherein do we differ from evil spirits, unless thy grace prevent us.'

'About this time my brother came from Cambridge to pay me a visit. Dr. C. having informed him that he thought me better, he was disappointed at finding me almost as silent and reserved as ever. As soon as we were left alone, he asked me how I found myself; I answered, as much better as despair can make me. We went together into the garden. Here, on my expressing a settled assurance of sudden judgment, he protested to me that it was all a delusion; and protested so strongly, that I could not help giving some attention to him. I burst into tears, and cried out, If it be a delusion, then am I the happiest of beings. Something like a ray of hope was now shot into my heart; but still I was afraid to indulge it. We dined together, and I spent the afternoon in a more cheerful manner. Something seemed to whisper to me, every moment,—still there is mercy. Even after he left me, this change of sentiment gathered ground continually; yet my mind was in such a fluctuating state, that I can only call it a vague presage of better things at hand, without being able to assign any reason for it.'

'A few days after my arrival at St. Albans, I had thrown aside the Bible as a book in which I had no longer any interest or portion. The only instance in which I can recollect reading a single chapter was about two months before my recovery. I opened a Bible [I had] found on the bench in the garden at the 11th Chapter of John. [That is where] the miracle of Lazarus being raised from the dead is described. I saw so much benevolence, goodness, and mercy, in the Saviour's conduct; that I almost shed tears at the relation, little thinking that it was an exact type of the mercy which Jesus was on the point of extending towards myself. I sighed, and said, Oh, that I had not rejected so good a Redeemer; that I had not forfeited all his favours! Thus was my hard heart softened; and though my mind was not yet enlightened, God was gradually preparing me for the light of his countenance, and the joys of his salvation.'

'The next morning, having risen with somewhat of a more cheerful feeling, while 1 sat at breakfast I found the cloud of horror which had so long hung over my mind begin rapidly to pass away;—every moment came fraught with hopes. I felt persuaded that I was not utterly doomed to destruction. The way of salvation was hidden from my eyes. I did not see it clearer than before my illness. I only thought, that if it pleased God to spare me, I would lead a better life; and that I would yet escape hell, if a religious observance of my duty would secure me from it. Thus may the terror of the Lord make a Pharisee; only the sweet voice of mercy in the gospel can make a Christian.'

'But the happy period, which was to shake off my fetters, and afford me a clear discovery of the free mercy of God in Christ Jesus, was now arrived. I flung myself into a chair near the window, and seeing a Bible there, ventured once more to apply to it for comfort and instruction. The first verse I saw was the 25th of the 3rd of Romans: *Whom God hath set forth to be a propitiation, through faith in his blood, to declare his righteousness for the remission of sins that are past, through the forbearance of God.* Immediately I received strength to believe, and the full beams of the sun of righteousness shone upon me. I saw the sufficiency of the atonement he had made, for my pardon and complete justification. In a moment I believed, and received the peace of the gospel. Whatever my friend Madan had said to me long before, revived in all its clearness, with the demonstration of the Spirit, and with power.

'Unless the Almighty arm had been under me, I think I should have been overwhelmed with gratitude and joy. My eyes filled with tears, and my voice choked with transport. I could only look up to heaven in silent fear, overwhelmed with love and wonder. The work of the Holy Spirit is best described in his own words. It is "joy unspeakable and full of glory." Thus was my heavenly Father in Christ Jesus, pleased to give me the full assurance of faith; and, out of a stony, unbelieving heart, to raise up a child unto Abraham. How glad should I now have been to have spent every moment in prayer and thanksgiving! I lost no opportunity of repairing to a throne of grace; but flew to it with earnestness. Could I help it? Could I do otherwise than love and rejoice in my reconciled Father in Christ Jesus? The Lord had enlarged my heart, and I could now cheerfully run in the way of his commandments.'

'For many succeeding weeks tears would be ready to flow, if I did but speak of the gospel, or mention the name of Jesus. To rejoice day and night was all my employment; too happy to sleep much, I thought it but lost time that was thus spent. Oh, that the ardour of my first love had continued! But I have known many a lifeless and unhallowed hour since; long interval of darkness, interrupted by short returns of peace and joy in believing.'

His excellent physician, ever watchful and apprehensive for his welfare, now became alarmed, lest the sudden transition from despair to joy should wholly overpower his mind; but the Lord was his strength and his song, and had become his salvation. Christ was now formed in his heart the hope of glory. His fears were all dispelled. Despair, with its horrid train of evils, was banished from his mind and a new and delightful scene now opened before him. He became the subject of new affections, new desires, and new joys; in a word, old things were passed away, and all things were become new. God had brought him up out of the horrible pit, and out of the miry clay, and had put a new song into his mouth, even praise to his God. He felt the full force of that liberty, of which he afterwards so sweetly bore witness,

'A liberty unsung
By poets, and by senators unpraised;
E'en liberty of heart, derived from heaven;
Bought with his blood who gave it to mankind;
And sealed with the same token!'

The apprehensions of Dr. Cotton soon subsided; he saw with delight undoubted proofs of his patient's perfect recovery, became satisfied with the soundness of his cure, and subsequently had much sweet communion with him in conversing about the great things of salvation. He now visited him every morning, as long as he remained under his care, which was nearly twelve months after his recovery, and the gospel was invariably the delightful theme of their conversation. The patient and the physician became thus every day more endeared to each other: and Cowper often afterwards looked back upon this period, as among the happiest days he had ever spent.

His time no longer hung heavily upon his hands. Every moment of it that he could command was employed in seeking to acquire deeper views of the gospel. The Bible became his constant companion; from this pure fountain of truth, he drank of that living water, which was in him a well of water, springing up into everlasting life. Conversation on spiritual subjects afforded him a high degree of enjoyment. Many delightful seasons did he spend in these employments, while he remained with his beloved physician. His first transports of joy having subsided, a sweet serenity of spirit succeeded, uninterrupted by any of those distressing sensations, which he had before experienced; prayer and praise were his daily employment, his heart overflowed with love to his Redeemer, and his meditation of him was sweet. In his own expressive and beautiful lines, he felt:

'Ere yet mortality's fine threads gave way,
A clear escape from tyrannizing sin.
And full immunity from penal woe.*

His application to the study of the Scriptures was intense. In the short space of twelve months he acquired comprehensive and scriptural views of the great plan of redemption, and, in addition to this, his conceptions of real Christian experience, as distinguished from delusion and hypocrisy, were accurate and striking, and such as one would only have expected from an experienced Christian. He now composed two hymns, which exhibit an interesting proof of the scriptural character of those religious views he had then embraced. These hymns he himself styles specimens of his first Christian thoughts. Delightful specimens indeed they are; and the circumstances under which they were composed will greatly enhance their value in the minds of those to whom they have long been endeared by their own intrinsic excellence. The first is the 44th Hymn, 3rd Book, Olney Collection, upon Revelation xxi. 5; beginning—

How blest thy creature is, O God—

The second is entitled Retirement. The following lines of it are so touchingly beautiful, and so correctly descriptive of the overflowing of his heart in solitude while he walked with God, and was a stranger in the earth. He had left his old connections, and not yet found new ones in the church. He breathed throughout in strains so pure, tender, and unreserved, the language of the Christian's first love that they cannot fail to be read with deep interest.

The calm retreat, the silent shade,
With prayer and praise agree;
And seem by thy sweet bounty made
For those who follow thee.

There, if thy Spirit touch the soul,
And grace her mean abode,
Oh, with what peace, and joy, and love,
She communes with her God.

There like the nightingale she pours
Her solitary lays;
Nor asks a witness of her song,
Nor thirsts for human praise.

His letters, written about this period, as well as those of a subsequent date, abound with proofs of his deep acquaintance with Christian experience. The following remarks are taken from a letter to Mrs. Cowper.

'The deceitfulness of the natural heart is inconceivable. I know well that I passed among my friends for a person at least religiously inclined, if not actually religious. I thought of myself a Christian, when I had no faith in Christ. I saw no beauty in him that I should desire him, when I had neither faith, nor love, nor any Christian grace whatever, but a thousand seeds of rebellion instead, evermore springing up in enmity against him. Blessed be the God of my salvation, the hail of affliction and rebuke has swept away the refuge of lies. It pleased the Almighty, in great mercy, to set all my misdeeds before me. At length the storm being past, a quiet and peaceful serenity of soul succeeded, such as ever attends the gift of a lively faith in the all-sufficient atonement, and the sweet sense of mercy, and pardon purchased by the blood of Christ. Thus, did he break me and bind me up; thus, did he wound me and make me whole. This, however, is but a summary account of my conversion; neither would a volume contain the astonishing particulars of it. If we meet again in this world I will relate them to you; if not, they will serve for the subject of a conference in the next, where, I doubt not, we shall remember, and record them with a gratitude better suited to the subject.'

In another letter to his amiable and accomplished cousin, Lady Hesketh, he thus writes. 'Since the visit you were so kind as to pay me in the Temple, (the only time I ever saw you without pleasure) what have I not suffered? And since it has pleased God to restore me to the use of my reason, what have I not enjoyed. You know by experience how pleasant it is to feel the first approaches of health after a fever; but, oh! The fever of the brain! To feel the quenching of that fire is indeed a blessing, which I think it impossible to receive without the consummate gratitude. Terrible as this chastisement is, I acknowledge in it the hand of infinite justice. I am exceedingly thankful for it, and esteem it the greatest blessing, next to life itself, I ever received from the divine bounty. I pray God I may ever retain the sense of it, and then I am sure I shall continue to be, as I am at present, happy. My affliction has taught me a road to happiness, which, without it, I should never have found; and, I know, and have experience of it every day, that the mercy of God to the believer is more than sufficient to compensate for the loss of every other blessing. You will believe that my happiness is no dream, because I have told you the foundation on which it is built. What I have written would appear like enthusiasm to many, for we are apt to give that name to every warm affection of the mind in others, which we have not experienced ourselves; but to you, who have so much to be thankful for, and a temper inclined to gratitude, it will not appear so.'

To the same lady, a day or two afterwards, he writes: 'What could you think, my dear cousin, of my conduct the last time I saw you? I remember I neither spoke to you nor looked at you. The solution of the mystery, indeed, followed soon after; but at the time, it must have been inexplicable. The uproar within was even then begun, and my silence was only the sulkiness of a thunderstorm before it opens. I am glad, however, that the only instance, in which I knew not how to value your company, was when I was not in my senses. It was the first in my life, and I trust in God it will be the last. How naturally does affliction make us Christians! How impossible is it, when all human help is vain, and the whole earth too poor and trilling to furnish us with one moment's peace, how impossible is it then to avoid looking at the gospel. It gives me some concern, though at the same time it increases my gratitude to reflect, that a convert made in Bedlam is more likely to be an obstacle to others than to advance their faith. If it has that effect upon any, it is owing to their reasoning amiss, and drawing their conclusion from false premises. He, who can ascribe an amendment of life and manners and a reformation of the heart itself to madness, is guilty of an absurdity, which in any other case would fasten the imputation of madness upon himself. By so doing, he ascribes a reasonable effect to an unreasonable cause, and a positive effect to a negative. When Christianity only is to be sacrificed, he that stabs deepest is always the wisest man. You yourself, my dear cousin, will be apt to think I carry the matter too far; and that in the present warmth of my heart, I make too ample a concession in saying, that I am only now a convert. You think I always believed, and I thought so too; but you were deceived, and so was I. I called myself, indeed, a Christian, but he who knows my heart knows that I never did a right thing, nor abstained from a wrong one, because I was so; but if I did either, it was under the influence of some other motive. And it is such seeming Christians, such pretending believers, that do most mischief in the cause, and furnish the strongest arguments to support the infidelity of its enemies; unless profession and conduct go together, the man's life is a lie, and the validity of what he professes itself is called in question. The difference between a Christian and an unbeliever would be so striking if the treacherous allies of the church would go over at once to the other side that I am satisfied religion would be no loser by the bargain. You say, you hope it is not necessary for salvation, to undergo the same affliction that I have undergone. No, my dear cousin, God deals with his children as a merciful father; he does not, as he himself tells us, afflict willingly. Doubtless, there are many who, having been placed by his good providence out of the reach of evil, and the influence of bad example, have, from their very infancy, been partakers of the grace of his Holy Spirit, in such a manner, as never to allow themselves in any grievous offence against him. May you love him more and more, day by day, as every day while you think of him you will find him more worthy of your love, and may you be finally accepted by him for his sake, whose intercession for all his faithful servants cannot but prevail.'

In the same letter he thus expresses his gratitude to God for placing him under the care of Dr. Cotton:

'One instance of the providence of God, which has attended me through this whole event, was that I was not delivered into the hands of some London physician, but was carried to Dr. Cotton. I was treated by him with the greatest tenderness and utmost diligence while I was ill. When my reason was restored to me, and I had so much need of a religious friend to converse with, to whom I could open my mind upon the subject without reserve, I could hardly have found a better person for the purpose. My eagerness and anxiety to settle my opinions upon that long neglected point, made it necessary that while my mind was yet weak, and my spirits uncertain, I should have some assistance. The doctor was as ready to administer relief to me in this article likewise and as well qualified to do it, as in that which was more immediately his province. How many physicians would have thought this an irregular appetite, and a symptom of remaining madness! But if it were so, my friend was as mad as myself, and it is well for me that he was so. My dear cousin, you know not half the deliverances I have received; my brother is the only one in the family who does. My recovery is indeed a signal one, and my future life must express my thankfulness, for by words I cannot do it.'

He now employed his brother to seek out for him an abode somewhere in the neighbourhood of Cambridge, as he had determined to leave London, the scene of his former misery; and that nothing might induce him to return thither, he resigned the office of commissioner of bankrupts, worth about £60 per annum, which he still held. He relied upon the gracious promise of God, that bread should be given him, and water should be sure.

It may appear singular that Cowper did not, instead of hazarding his tender and scarcely convalescent spirit among strangers in the country, recline it on the bosom of his friends in London; and some persons may possibly imagine it was because his relations in town did not manifest for him that sympathy which his case required. Such, however, was far from being the case. The truth is, as Dr. Johnson in his sketch of the poet's life states, that 'no inducement to his return to them, which with a view to their mutual satisfaction, his affectionate relatives and most intimate friends could devise, was either omitted on their part, or declined without reluctance on his. But in the cultivation of the religious principle which, with the recovery of his reason he had lately imbibed, and which in so distinguished a manner it had pleased God to bless to the re-establishment of his peace, he had an interest to provide for, of a much higher order. This it was that inclined him to a life of seclusion: a measure in the adoption of which, though, in ordinary cases, he is certainly not to be quoted as an example, yet, considering the extreme peculiarity of his own, it seems equally certain that he is not to be censured. There can be no doubt, indeed, from the following passage of his poem on Retirement, that had his mind been the repository of less exquisitely tender sensibilities, he would have returned to his duties at the Temple.'

He was informed that his brother had made many unsuccessful attempts to procure him a suitable dwelling, so he one day poured out his soul in prayer to God. He beseeched him that wherever he should be pleased in his fatherly mercy to place him, it might be in the society of those who feared his name, and loved the Lord Jesus in sincerity. God was pleased graciously to answer. In the beginning of June 1765, he received a letter from his brother, to say that he had engaged such lodgings for him at Huntingdon as he thought would suit him. Though this was farther from Cambridge, where his brother then resided, than he wished, yet, as he was now in perfect health, and as his circumstances required a less expensive way of life than his present, he resolved to take them, and arranged his affairs accordingly.

On June 17, 1765, having spent more than eighteen months at St. Albans, partly in the bondage of despair, and partly in the liberty of the gospel, he took leave of the place, at four in the morning. He set out for Cambridge, taking with him the servant who had attended him while he remained with Dr. Cotton, and who had maintained an affectionate watchfulness over him during the whole of his illness, waiting upon him, on all occasions, with the utmost patience, and invariably treating him with the greatest kindness. The mingled emotions of his mind on leaving the place were painful and pleasing. He regarded it as the place of his second nativity. Here he had passed from death unto life. He had been favoured with much leisure to study the word of God and had enjoyed much happiness in conversing upon its great truths with his esteemed physician. He left it with considerable reluctance, offering up many prayers to God, that his richest blessings might rest upon its worthy manager, and upon all its inmates, especially those of them whose mental maladies had brought them there.

The state of his mind on this occasion he thus affectionately describes:

'I remembered the pollution which is in the world, and the sad share I had in it myself, and my heart ached at the thought of entering it again. The blessed God had endowed me with some concern for his glory, and I was fearful of hearing his name traduced by oaths and blasphemies, the common language of this highlyfavoured but ungrateful country; but the promise of God, "Fear not, I am with thee," was my comfort. I passed the whole of my journey in fervent prayer to God, earnestly but silently entreating him to be my guardian and counsellor in all my future journey through life, and to bring me in safety, when he had accomplished his purposes of grace and mercy towards me, to eternal glory.'

CHAPTER IV. Removal to Huntingdon—Sensations there—Engages in public worship for the first time after his recovery— Commences a regular correspondence with some of his friends—Pleasure he experienced in writing on religious subjects —Anxiety of his mind for the spiritual welfare of his former associates—Attributes their continuance in sin chiefly to infidelity—Absurdity of attributing events to second causes instead of to the overruling providence of God—Forms some connections—Becomes acquainted with the Unwin family—Happiness he experienced in their company.

After spending a few days with his brother at Cambridge, Cowper repaired to Huntingdon, and entered upon his new abode on Saturday, June 22, 1765; taking with him the servant he from St. Albans, to whom he had become strongly attached, from a sense of the great kindness he had shown him in his affliction. His brother, who had accompanied him hither, had no sooner left him, than, finding himself alone, surrounded by strangers, in a strange place, his spirits began to sink, and he felt like a traveller in the midst of an inhospitable desert without a friend to comfort, or a guide to direct him. He walked forth, towards the close of the day, in this melancholy frame of mind, and having wandered about a mile from the town, he found his heart so powerfully drawn towards the Lord, that on coming to a retired nook in the corner of a field, he kneeled down under a bank, and poured out his complaints unto God. It pleased his merciful Father to hear him; the load was removed from his mind, and he was enabled to trust in Him that careth for the stranger; to roll his burden upon him, and to rest assured, that wherever God might cast his lot, he would still be his guardian and shield.

The following day he went to church, for the first time after his recovery. Throughout the whole of the service, his emotions were so powerfully affecting, that it was with much difficulty he could restrain them, so much did he see of the beauty and glory of the Lord while thus worshipping him in his temple. His heart was full of love to the entire congregation. Such was the goodness of God to him that he gave him the oil of joy for mourning, and the garment of praise for the spirit of heaviness. Though he joined not with the congregation in singing the praises of his God, being prevented by the intenseness of his feelings, yet his soul sang within him and leaped for joy. The parable of the Prodigal Son was the portion of scripture read in the gospel appointed for the day. He saw himself in that glass so clearly, and the loving-kindness of his slighted and forgotten Lord, that the whole scene was realized by him, and acted over in his heart. He thus describes his feelings upon hearing it:

'When the gospel for the day was read, I was overwhelmed. Oh! What a word is the word of God, when the spirit quickens us to receive it, and gives the hearing ear, and the understanding heart!

Immediately after church, he repaired to the place where he bad prayed the day before, and found that the relief he had there received was but the earnest of a richer blessing. The Lord was pleased to visit him with his gracious presence; he seemed to speak to him face to face, as a man speaketh to his friend; he made all his goodness pass before him, and constrained him to say, with Jacob, not "how dreadful," but "how lovely is this place! This is the house of God, and the gate of heaven."

He remained four months in the lodgings procured for him by his brother, secluded from the bustling and active scenes of life, and receiving only an occasional visit from some of his neighbours. Though he had little intercourse with men, yet he enjoyed much fellowship with God in Christ Jesus. Living by faith, and thus tasting the joys of the unseen world, his solitude was sweet, his meditations were delightful, and he wanted no other enjoyments. He now regularly corresponded with all his friends and his letters furnish the clearest proofs of the happy, and indeed, almost enviable state of his mind, during this period. To Lady Hesketh, in a letter dated July 5, 1765, he thus discloses his feelings:

'I should have written to you from St. Albans long ago, but was willing to perform quarantine, as well for my own sake, as because I thought my letters would be more satisfactory to you from any other quarter. You will perceive I allowed myself a sufficient time for the purpose, for I date my recovery from the latter end of last July, having been ill seven, and well twelve months. About that time, my brother came to see me; I was far from well when he arrived, yet, though he only remained one day, his company served to put to flight a thousand deliriums and delusions, which I still laboured under.

'As far as I am acquainted with my new residence, I like it extremely. Mr. Hodgson, the minister of the parish, made me a visit yesterday. He is very sensible, a good preacher, and conscientious in the discharge of his duty: he is well known to Dr.

Newton, Bishop of Bristol, the author of the treatise on the Prophecies, the most demonstrative proof of the truth of Christianity, in my mind, that was ever published.'

In another letter, a few days afterwards, to the same lady, he thus writes:

'Mentioning Newton's treatise on the Prophecies brings to my mind an anecdote of Dr. Young, who you know died lately at Welwyn. Dr. Cotton paid him a visit about a fortnight before the good doctor was seized with his last illness. The old man was then in perfect health; the antiquity of his person, the gravity of his utterance, and the earnestness with which he discoursed about religion, gave him, in the doctor's eye, the appearance of a prophet.

Cowper now passed his time in the full enjoyment of religion. Its truths supported his mind, and furnished him with an ample field for meditation; its promises consoled him, freed him from every distressing sensation, and filled him with joy unspeakable and full of glory; its precepts regulated all his conduct, and his chief anxiety was to live entirely to the glory of God. The following beautiful lines of the poet are strikingly descriptive of his feelings at this period:

'I was a stricken deer, that left the herd
Long since, with many an arrow deep enfix'd
My panting side was charged, when I withdrew
To seek a tranquil death in distant shades.
There was I found by one who had himself
Been hurt by the archers: in his sides he bore,
And in his hands and feet, the cruel scars.
With gentle force soliciting the darts
He drew them forth, and healed, and bade me live.
Since then, with few associates, in remote
And silent woods I wander, far from those
My former partners of the peopled scene;
With few associates, and not wishing more,
Here much I ruminate, as much I may.

With other views of men and manners now
Than once; and others of a life to come.'

On all subjects connected with religion, Cowper now delighted to think and converse, and his best letters were those in which he could freely introduce them to his correspondents. In the close of the letter from which we made the above extract, he thus writes:

'My dear cousin, how happy am I in having a friend to whom I can open my heart upon these subjects! I have many intimates in the world, and have had many more than I shall have hereafter, to whom a long letter upon those most important articles would appear tiresome at least, if not impertinent. I am not afraid of meeting with that reception from you, who have never yet made it your interest that there should be no truth in the word of God. May this everlasting truth be your comfort while you live, and attend you with peace and joy in your last moments. I love you too well not to make this a part of my prayers; and when I remember my friends on these occasions, there is no likelihood that you can be forgotten.'

In another letter to Lady Hesketh, dated 1st of August, 1765, he thus adverts to the character of his former associates, and feelingly expresses his anxiety for their spiritual welfare:

I have great reason to lie thankful I have lost none of my acquaintance but those whom I determined not to keep; I am sorry this class is so numerous. What would I not give, that all my friends were Christians. My dear cousin, I am half-afraid to talk to you in this style, lest I should seem to indulge a censorious humour, instead of hoping, as I ought, the best of all men. But what can be said against ocular proof, and what is hope when built upon presumption? How dreadful to pass succeeding days, weeks, and months, and years, without one act of private devotion, one confession of our sins, or one thanksgiving for the numberless blessings we enjoy! How frightful to hear the word of God in public with a distracted attention, or with none at all—to absent ourselves voluntarily from the blessed communion, and to live in the total neglect of it! These are the common and ordinary liberties, which the generality of professors allow themselves: and what is this, but to live without God in the world. Many causes might be assigned for this antichristian spirit so prevalent among professors, but one of the principal I take to be their utter forgetfulness, that the Bible which they have in their possession, is, in reality, the *Word of God*. My friend, Sir William Russell was distantly related to a very accomplished man, who, though he never believed the gospel, admired the scriptures as the sublimest compositions in the world, and read them often. I have myself been friends with a man of fine taste, who has confessed to me, that though he in Christianity itself, yet he never could read St. Luke's account of our Saviour's appearance to his two disciples going to Emmaus, without being wonderfully affected by it. He bethought, that if the stamp of divinity was anywhere to be found in scripture, it was strongly marked and visibly impressed upon that passage. If these men, whose hearts were chilled with the darkness of infidelity, could find such charms in the mere style of scripture, what must those find whose eyes could penetrate deeper than the letter, and who firmly believed themselves interested in all the invaluable privileges of the gospel!" He that believeth on me is passed from death unto life," though it be as plain a sentence as words can form, has more beauties in it for such a person, than all the labours antiquity can boast of. If this poor man of taste searched a little further, he might have found other parts of the sacred history as strongly marked with the characters of divinity as that he mentioned. The parable of the Prodigal Son, the most beautiful fiction that ever was invented; our Saviour's speech to his disciples, with which he closes his earthly ministration, full of the sublimest dignity and tenderest affection, surpass everything that I ever read, and, like the spirit with which they were dictated, fly directly to the heart. If the scripture did not disdain all affectation of ornament, one should call such as these its ornamental parts; but the matter of it is that upon which it principally stakes its credit with us, and the style, however excellent, is only one of the many external evidences by which it recommends itself to our belief.'

The accuracy of Cowper's views, at this time, respecting the great importance of faith in the Christian system, will be seen by his remarks to his cousin, on *Pearsall's Meditations*, which she had kindly lent him:

'August 17, 1765. I shall do little more than thank you for your Meditations, which I admire exceedingly: the author of them manifestly loved the truth with an undissembled affection, had made great progress in the knowledge of it, and experienced all the happiness which naturally results from that noblest of all attainments. There is one circumstance which he gives us frequent occasion to observe in him, which I believe will ever be found in the philosophy of every true Christian. I mean the eminent rank, which he assigns to faith among the virtues, as the source and parent of them all. There is nothing more infallibly true than this, and doubtless it is with a view to the purifying and sanctifying nature of a true faith that our Saviour says, "He that believeth in me hath everlasting life," with many other expressions to the same purpose. Considered in this light, no wonder it has the power of salvation ascribed to it. Considered in any other, we must suppose it to operate like an oriental talisman, if it obtains for us the least advantage; which is an affront to him who insists upon our having it, and will admit us to his favour on no other terms. It forms the best distinction between the specious professor and the true believer; between him whose faith is in his Sunday-suit, and him who never puts it off at all—a distinction I am a little fearful sometimes of making, because it is a heavy stroke upon the practice of more than half the Christians in the world.'

The warmest expressions of his gratitude to God for his distinguishing goodness to him during his affliction were frequently employed in his letters. In one dated September 4, 1765, he thus writes to his cousin:

'Two of my friends have been cut off during my illness, in the midst of such a life as it is frightful to reflect upon, and here am I, in better health and spirits than I can remember to have ever enjoyed, after having spent months in the apprehension of instant death. How mysterious are the ways of Providence! Why did I receive grace and mercy? Why was I preserved, afflicted for my good, received, as I trust, into favour, and blessed with the greatest happiness I can ever know, or hope for in this life, while these were overtaken by the great arrest, unawakened, unrepenting, and every way unprepared for it! His infinite wisdom, to whose infinite mercy I owe it all, can solve these questions, and none else can. A freethinker, as many a man miscalls himself, would, without doubt, say, 'Sir, you were in great danger, and had, indeed, a most fortunate escape.' How excessively foolish, as well as shocking, is such language! As if life depended upon luck, and all that we are, or can be, all that we have now, or can hope for hereafter, could possibly be referred to accident. Fevers, and all diseases, are regarded as accidents; and long life, health, and recovery from sickness, as the gift of the physician. No man can be a greater friend to the use of means upon these occasions than I can, for it were presumption and enthusiasm to neglect them. God has endued them with salutary properties on purpose that we might avail ourselves of them. To impute our recovery to the medicine, and to carry our views no further, is to rob God of his honour. He that thinks thus, may as well fall upon his knees at once, and return thanks to the medicine that cured him, for it was certainly more immediately instrumental in his recovery than either the apothecary or the doctor.'

No one ever watched more carefully the providence of God than Cowper. His views of it were just and scriptural, as is abundantly evident by the above remarks, and if possible, more clearly evinced by the following extracts from the same excellent letter:

'My dear cousin, a firm persuasion of the superintendence of Providence over all our concerns, is absolutely necessary to our happiness. Without it we cannot be said to believe in the Scripture, or practice anything like resignation to his will. If I am convinced that no affliction can befall me without the permission of God, I am convinced likewise that he sees, and knows, that I am afflicted; believing this, I must, in the same degree, believe that, if I pray to him for deliverance, he hears me; I must needs know likewise, with equal assurance, that if he hears, he will also deliver me, should this be most conducive to my happiness! If he does not deliver me, I may rest well assured that he has none but the most benevolent intention in declining it. He made us, not because we could add to his happiness, which was always perfect, but that we might be happy ourselves. And will he not in all his dispensations towards us, even in the minutest, consult that end for which he made us? To suppose the contrary, is to affront every one of his attributes, and to renounce utterly our dependence upon him. In this view it will appear plainly, that the line of duty is not stretched too tight, when we are told that we ought to accept everything at his hands as a blessing, and to be thankful even when we smart under the rod of iron with which he sometimes rules us. Without this persuasion, every blessing, however we may think ourselves happy in the possession of it, loses its greatest recommendation, and every affliction is intolerable. Death itself must be welcome to him who has this faith; and he who has it not must aim at it, if he is not a madman.'

The excellence of these extracts from Cowper's correspondence will, it is hoped, be admitted by every reader as a sufficient apology for the interruption they may occasion to our narrative. They might be greatly enlarged; but it is not intended to admit any, except such as will, in some degree at least, serve to illustrate his character.

It was not to be expected that a person like Cowper could remain long unnoticed, how reserved soever was his conduct. Accordingly, he had been at Huntingdon only a short time before he was visited by several persons, and introduced into several families, all eminently distinguished for their respectability and general consistency of conduct. This soon endeared him to the place, and he thus communicated his sentiments respecting it to his correspondents:

'The longer I live here the better I like the place, and the people who belong to it. I am upon very good terms with five families, all of whom receive me with the utmost civility; and two in particular with as much cordiality as if their pedigree and mine had grown on the same sheepskin. You may recollect that I had but very uncomfortable expectations of the accommodations I should meet with at Huntingdon. How much better is it to take our lot where it shall please Providence to cast it, without anxiety? Had I chosen for myself, it is impossible I could have fixed upon a place so agreeable to me in all respects. I so much dreaded the thought of having a new acquaintance to make, with no other recommendation than that of being a perfect stranger that I heartily wished no creature here might take the least notice of me. Instead of which, in about two months after my arrival, I became known to all the people here, and do verily think it the most agreeable neighbourhood I ever saw. My brother and I meet every week, by an alternate reciprocation of intercourse, as Sam Johnson would express it. As to my own personal condition, I am much happier than the day is long; and sunshine and candle-light alike see me perfectly contented. I get books in abundance, as much company as I choose, a deal of comfortable leisure, and enjoy better health, I think, than for many years past. What is there wanting to make me happy? Nothing, if I can but be as thankful as 1 ought; and I trust that He, who has bestowed so many blessings on me, will give me gratitude to crown them all. I thank God for all the pleasing circumstances here, for my health of body, and perfect serenity of mind. To recollect the past, and compare it with the present, is all that I need to fill me with gratitude; and to be grateful is to be happy. I am far from thinking myself sufficiently grateful, or from indulging the hope that I shall ever be so in the present life. The warmest heart, perhaps, only feels by fits, and is often as insensible as the coldest. This, at least, is frequently the case with mine, and much oftener than it should be. But the mercy that can forgive iniquity will never be severe to mark our frailties. To that mercy, my dear cousin, I commend you.'

Among the families with whom Cowper was on terms of intimacy, there were none so entirely congenial to his taste as that of the Reverend Mr. Unwin. This worthy divine, who was now far advanced in years, had formerly been master of a free school in Huntingdon. On obtaining, however, from his college at Cambridge, the living of Grimston, he married Miss Cawthorne, the daughter of a very respectable draper in Ely, by whom he had two children, a son and a daughter. Disliking their residence at Grimston, they removed to Huntingdon, where they had now resided many years.

Cowper became acquainted with this remarkable family, which afterwards, almost to the close of his life, afforded him a source of comfort, in the following rather singular manner. The Unwins frequently noticed Mr. C. and remarked the degree of piety and intelligence he seemed to possess; this induced them to wish for a further acquaintance with the interesting stranger: but his manners were so reserved, that an introduction to him seemed wholly out of their reach. After waiting some time, with no apparent prospect of success, their eldest son, Mr. W. Unwin, though dissuaded from it by his mother, lest it should be thought too intrusive, ventured to speak to Mr. Cowper one day, when they were coming out of church, after morning prayers. Cowper soon found him to be one whose society was worth cultivating; he accordingly invited him to take tea with him that afternoon, to which Mr. U. gladly consented. This was perfectly agreeable to Cowper, who, in one of his letters, sometime afterwards, thus describes his new-made acquaintance:

'To my inexpressible joy, I found him one, whose notions of religion were spiritual and lively; one, whom the Lord had been training up from his infancy for the temple. We opened our hearts to each other at the first interview; and when he parted, I immediately retired to my chamber, and prayed the Lord, who had been the author, to be the guardian of our friendship, and to grant to it fervency and perpetuity, even unto death; and I doubt not that my gracious Father heard this prayer.' A friendship thus formed was not likely to be soon interrupted; accordingly it continued with unabated affection through life, and became to both parties a source of much real enjoyment. Well would it be for Christians, were they, in making choice of their friends, to follow the example of Cowper! Entering upon it by earnest prayer to God for his blessing, they might then hope to derive all those invaluable benefits from it, which it is adapted and designed to convey.

The following Sabbath Cowper dined with the Unwins, and was treated with so much cordiality and affection that he ever after felt warm attachment to this interesting family. In his letters on the subject, he thus writes:

"The last acquaintance I have made here is of the race of the Unwins, consisting of father and mother, son and daughter; they are the most agreeable people imaginable; quite sociable, and as free from the ceremonious civility of country gentlefolks as I ever met with. They treat me more like a near relation than a stranger, and their house is always open to me. The old gentleman carries me to Cambridge in his chaise; he is a man of learning and good sense, and as simple as parson Adams. His wife has a very uncommon understanding, has read much to excellent purpose, and is more polite than a duchess; she treats me with an affection so truly Christian, that I could almost fancy my own mother restored to life again, to compensate me for all my lost friends and broken connections. She has a son, in all respects worthy of such a mother, the most amiable young man I ever knew; he is not yet arrived at that time of life when suspicion recommends itself to us in the form of wisdom, and sets everything but our own dear selves at an immeasurable distance from our esteem and confidence. Consequently, he is known almost as soon as seen; and having nothing in his heart that makes it necessary for him to keep it barred and bolted, opens it to the perusal even of a stranger. His natural and acquired endowments are very considerable, and as to his virtues, I need only say that he is a Christian. Miss Unwin resembles her mother in her great piety, who is one of the most remarkable instances of it I ever knew. They are altogether the most cheerful and engaging family, it is possible to conceive. They see but little company, which suits me exactly; go when I will, I find a house full of peace and cordiality in all its parts, and am sure to hear no scandal, but such discourse instead of it as we are all the better for. Now I know them, I wonder that I liked Huntingdon so well before, and am apt to think I should find every place disagreeable that had not an Unwin belonging to it.

'This incident convinces me of the truth of an observation I have often made. When we circumscribe our estimate of all that is clever within the limits of our own acquaintance (which I at least have been always apt to do,) we are guilty of a very uncharitable censure upon the rest of the world, and of a narrowness of thinking disgraceful to ourselves. Wapping and Redriff may contain some of the most amiable persons living, and such as one would go to Wapping and Redriff to make acquaintance with. You remember Gray's stanza—

Full many a gem of purest ray serene,
The dark unfathom'd caves of ocean bear,
Full many a rose is born to blush unseen,
And waste its fragrance in the desert air.

The state of Cowper's mind at this period and the opinion he had formed of his new associates, will be seen by his remarks in reply to an affectionate and pressing invitation, which he appears to have received from his cousin. She was then about to fix her residence, for a time, at a villa called Freemantle, near Southampton, to pay her a visit there. Cowper seems first to have determined to accede to her kind request, remarking, 'You cannot think how glad I am to hear you are going to commence lady and mistress of Freemantle. I know it well, and could go to it from Southampton blindfold. You are kind to invite me to it, and I shall be so kind to myself as to accept the invitation, though I should not for a slight consideration be prevailed upon to quit my beloved retirement at Huntingdon.'

He appears afterwards however, to have changed his mind, and to have declined the visit. In a letter dated a month later, Oct. 18, 1765, we find him still at Huntingdon, congratulating her upon her safe arrival at Drayford, and himself upon the snugness of his own retreat. 'I wish you joy, my dear cousin, of being safely arrived in port from the storms of Southampton. For my own part, who am but as a Thames wherry in a world full of tempest and commotion, I know so well the value of the creek I have put into, and the snugness it affords me, that I have a sensible sympathy with you in the pleasure you find in being once more blown to Drayford. I am glad you think so favourably of my Huntingdon acquaintance; they are, indeed, a nice set of folks, and suit me exactly. They are altogether the most cheerful and most engaging family piece it is possible to conceive. It was my earnest request before I left St. Alban's, that wherever it might please Providence to dispose of me, I might meet with such an acquaintance as I find in Mrs. Unwin. How happy is it to believe with a steadfast assurance that our petitions are heard, even while we are making them; and how delightful to meet with a proof in the effectual and actual grant of them! Surely, it is a gracious finishing given to those means, which the Almighty has been pleased to make use of for my conversion.

My dear cousin, health and happiness, and, above all, the love of our great and gracious Lord attend you! While we seek it in spirit and in truth, we are infinitely more secure of it than we are of the next breath we expect to draw. Heaven and earth have their destined periods; ten thousand worlds will vanish at the consummation of all things; but the word of God standeth fast, and they who trust in him shall never be confounded.'

CHAPTER V. Cowper becomes an inmate with Mr. Unwin's family— Is much delighted with their society—His opinion respecting the knowledge which Christians will have of each other in heaven—Just views of Christian friendship—Strength of his religious affections—

Humbling views of himself—Melancholy death of Mr. Unwin—Cowper's reflections upon it—Mr. Newton's visit to Mrs. Unwin—Cowper's determination to remain with the family—Their removal from Huntingdon to Olney.

Towards the end of October 1765, Cowper began to fear that his solitary and lonely situation would not be agreeable to him during the winter. Finding his present method of living, though he was strictly economical, rather too expensive for his' reduced income, he judged it expedient to look out for a family in which he might become domesticated; where he might enjoy the advantage of social and familiar intercourse, and at the same time lessen the amount of his personal expenses. With this view, it occurred to him that he might probably be admitted, on such terms, into Mr. Unwin's family. He knew that a young gentleman who had lived with them as a pupil, had just left them for Cambridge, and it appeared not improbable, that he might be allowed to succeed him, not as a pupil, but as an inmate. This subject occasioned him a tumult of anxious solicitude, and for some days, it absorbed his entire attention. He at length made it the subject of earnest prayer to his Heavenly Father, that he would be pleased to bring this affair to such an issue as would be most calculated to promote his own glory; and he had the satisfaction, in a short time, to receive a gracious answer to his petitions. A few days afterwards, he mentioned the subject to Mrs. Unwin, a satisfactory arrangement was very speedily made with the family, and he entered upon his new abode on November 11, 1765.

The manner, in which he spent his time while associated with this exemplary family, and the high degree of enjoyment he there experienced, will be seen by the following extracts from his correspondence with his two amiable cousins, Lady Hesketh and Mrs. Cowper. To the former he thus writes:

'My dear Cousin,—the frequency of your letters to me, while I lived alone, was occasioned, I am sure, by your regard for my welfare, and was an act of particular charity. I bless God, however, that I was happy even then; solitude has nothing gloomy in it, if the soul points upwards. St. Paul tells his Hebrew converts, "Ye are come" (already come) "to Mount Sion, to an innumerable company of angels, to the general assembly of the first-born, which are written in heaven, and to Jesus the Mediator of the new covenant." When this is the case, as surely, it was with them, or the Spirit of truth would never have spoken it, there is an end to the melancholy and dullness of life at once. You will not suspect me, my dear cousin, of a design to understand this passage literally; but this, however, it certainly means, that a lively faith is able to anticipate, in some measure, the joys of that heavenly society which the soul shall actually possess hereafter.

'Since I have changed my situation, I have found still greater cause of thanksgiving to the Father of all mercies. The family with whom I live are Christians, and it has pleased the Almighty to bring me to the knowledge of them, that I may want no means of improvement in that temper and conduct which he requires of all his servants. One-half of the Christian world would call this madness, fanaticism, and folly; but are not these things warranted by the word of God. If we have no communion with God here, surely we can expect none hereafter. A faith that does not place our conversation in heaven, that does not warm the heart, and purify it. That does not govern our thoughts, words, and deeds, is not Christian faith, nor can we procure by it any spiritual blessing, here or hereafter. Let us therefore see that we do not deceive ourselves in a matter of such infinite moment. The world will be ever telling us that we are good enough, and the world will vilify us behind our backs: but it is not the world, which tries the heart. That is the prerogative of God alone. I have often prayed for you behind your back, and now I pray for you to your face. There are many who would not forgive me this wrong, but I have known you so long, and so well, that I am not afraid of telling you how sincerely I wish for your growth in every Christian grace, in everything that may promote and secure your everlasting welfare.'

To his cousin, Mrs. Cowper, he thus writes:

'I am obliged to you for the interest you take in my welfare, and for your inquiring so particularly after the manner in which my time passes here. As to amusements—I mean what the world calls such—we have none; the place, indeed, swarms with them, and cards and dancing are the professed business of almost all the gentle inhabitants of Huntingdon. We refuse to take part in them, or to be accessories to this way of murdering our time, and by so doing have acquired the name of Methodists. Having told you how we do not spend our time, I will next say how we do. We breakfast commonly between eight and nine; until eleven, we read either the scripture or the sermons of some faithful preacher; at eleven, we attend divine service, which is performed here every day; and from twelve to three, we separate, and amuse ourselves as we please. During that interval, I read in my own apartment, or walk, or ride, or work in the garden. We seldom sit an hour after dinner, but if the weather permits, adjourn into the garden, where, with Mrs. Unwin and her son, I have generally the pleasure of religious conversation until teatime. If it rains, or is too windy for walking, we either converse within doors, or sing some hymns of Martin's collection, and by the help of Mrs. Unwin's harpsichord, make up a tolerable concert, in which our hearts are the best and most musical performers. After tea, we sally forth to take a walk in good earnest, and we have generally travelled four miles before we see home again. At night, we read and converse until supper, and commonly finish the evening either with hymns, or with a sermon; and, last of all, the family are called to prayers. I need not tell you that such a life as this is consistent with the utmost cheerfulness; accordingly, we are all happy, and dwell together in unity as brethren. Mrs. Unwin has almost a maternal affection for me. I have something very like a filial one for her, and her son and I are brothers. Blessed be the God of our salvation for such companions, and for such a life; above all, for a heart to relish it.'

It was during his residence with this family, while they resided at Huntingdon, that he wrote some of those excellent letters to Mrs. Cowper, some extracts from which will enrich this part of his memoirs. Speaking of the knowledge that Christians will have of each other hereafter, he remarks:

'*Reason* is able to form many assumptions concerning the possibility of our knowing each other in a future state. S*cripture* has here and there favoured us with an expression that looks like a slight intimation of it, but a conjecture can never amount to a proof. A slight intimation cannot be construed into a positive assertion; therefore, I think we can never come to any absolute conclusion upon the subject. We may reason about the plausibility of our conjectures. We may discuss, with great industry and shrewdness of argument, those passages in the scripture that seem to favour this opinion. Still no certain means having been afforded us, no certain end can be attained; and after all that can be said, it will still be doubtful whether we shall know each other or not. Both reason and scripture, however, furnish us with a greater number of arguments on the affirmative side. In the parable of *The Rich Man and Lazarus*, the Rich Man is represented as knowing Lazarus and Abraham as knowing them both. The discourse between them is entirely concerning their respective characters and circumstances upon earth. Here, therefore, our Saviour seems to countenance the notion of a mutual knowledge and recollection; and if a soul that has perished shall know a soul that is saved, surely the heirs of salvation shall know and recollect each other.

'Paul, in the first epistle to the Thessalonians, encourages the faithful and laborious minister of Christ to expect that knowledge of those who had been converted by their instrumentality would contribute greatly to their felicity in a future state. "Here am I, with the children thou hast given me." This seems to imply, that the apostle should know the converts, and the converts the apostle, at least at the Day of Judgment, and if then, why not afterwards?'

In another letter, the following excellent remarks occur respecting the subjects that will engage our thoughts and form part of our communications in heaven:

'The common and ordinary occurrences of life, no doubt, and even the ties of kindred, and of all temporal interests, will be entirely discarded from that happy society, and possibly even the remembrance of them done away. However, it does not therefore follow that our spiritual concerns, even in this life, will be forgotten, neither do I think that they can ever appear trifling to us, in any even the most distant period of eternity. At present, whatever our convictions may be of the sinfulness and corruptions of our nature, we can make but an imperfect estimate of our weakness or our guilt. Then, however, we shall understand the full value of the wonderful salvation wrought out for us by our exalted redeemer. It seems reasonable to suppose, that in order to form a just idea of our redemption, we shall be able to form a just one of the danger we have escaped. When we know how weak and frail we were, surely we shall be more able to render due praise and honour to his strength who fought for us. When we know completely the hatefulness of sin in the sight of God, and how deeply we were tainted by it, we shall know how to value the blood by which we were cleansed, as we ought. The twenty-four elders, in the fifth chapter of the Revelation, give glory to God for their redemption out of every kindred, and tongue, and people, and nation. This surely implies a retrospect to their respective conditions on earth, and that each remembered out of what particular kindred and nation he had been redeemed; and if so, then surely the minutest circumstances of their redemption did not escape their memory. They, who triumph over the Beast in the fifteenth chapter, sing the song of Moses, the servant of God; and what was that song? A sublime record of Israel's deliverance, and the destruction of her enemies in the Red Sea; typical, no doubt, of the song, which the redeemed in Sion shall sing, to celebrate their own salvation and the defeat of their spiritual enemies. This again implies a recollection of the dangers they had before encountered, and the supplies of strength and ardour they had, in every emergency, received from the great deliverer out of all. These quotations do not, indeed, prove that their warfare upon earth forms part of their converse in heaven; but they prove that it is a theme not unworthy to be heard even before the throne of God, and therefore it cannot be unfit for reciprocal communication. I do not recollect any scripture that proves it directly; but reason seems to require it so peremptorily, that a society without social intercourse seems to be a solecism and contradiction in terms; and the inhabitants of those regions are called, you know, in scripture, an innumerable company, and an assembly, which seems to convey the idea of society as clearly as the word itself. Doddridge says, 'Our companions in glory may probably assist us by their wise and good observations, when we come to make the providence of God here upon earth, under the guidance of our Lord Jesus Christ, the subject of our mutual converse."

In the following letter to the same lady, he says:

'I am not sorry that what I have said concerning the knowledge of each other in a future state has a little inclined you to the affirmative. For though the redeemed of the Lord will be sure of being as happy in that state as infinite power, employed by infinite goodness, can make them; and therefore, it may seem immaterial, whether we shall, or shall not, recollect each other hereafter; yet, our present happiness, at least, is a little interested in the question. A parent, a friend, a wife, must needs, I think, feel a little heart-ache at the thought of an eternal separation from the objects of her regard: and not to know them when she meets them in another state, or never to meet them at all, amounts, though not altogether, yet nearly to the same thing. Remember and recognize them, I have no doubt we shall; and to believe that they are happy will, indeed, be no small addition to our own felicity; but to see them so, will surely be a greater. While friendship is necessary to our happiness here, and built upon Christian principles, upon which only it can stand, is a thing even of religious sanction — for what is that love which the Holy Spirit, speaking by St. John, so much inculcates, but friendship? The only love, which deserves the name, is a love that can enable the Christian to toil, and watch, and deny himself, and risk even exposure to death, for his brother. Worldly friendships are a poor weed compared with this; and even this union of the spirit in the bond of peace, would suffer, in my mind at least, could I think it were only coeval with our earthly mansions. It may possibly argue great weakness in me, in this instance, to stand so much in need of future hopes, to support me in the charge of present duty, but so it is. I am far, I know, very far from being perfect in Christian love, or any other divine attainment, and am, therefore, unwilling to forego whatever may help me on my progress. Thus, dear cousin, I have spread out my reasons before you for an opinion that, whether admitted or denied, affects not the state, or interest, of our soul.

May our Creator, Redeemer, and Sanctifier, conduct us into his own Jerusalem, where there shall be no night, nor any darkness at all, where we shall be free, even from innocent error, and perfect in the light and knowledge of God in the face of Jesus Christ.'

The anxiety of his mind respecting religion, and the progress he had made, and was still making in it, will appear from the following extract:

'You are so kind as to inquire after my health, for which reason I must tell you what otherwise would not be worth mentioning, that I have lately been just enough indisposed to convince me, that not only human life in general, but mine in particular, hangs by a slender thread. I am stout enough in appearance, yet a little illness demolishes me. I have had a serious shake, and the building is not as firm as it was. But I bless God for it, with all my heart. If the inner man is but strengthened day by day, as I hope, under the renewing influences of the Holy Spirit, it will be, no matter how soon the outward is dissolved. He who has, in a manner, raised me from the dead, in a literal sense, has given me the grace, I trust, to be ready, at the shortest notice, to surrender up to him that life, which I have twice received from him. Whether I live or die, I desire it may be to his glory, and then it must be to my happiness. I thank God that I have those amongst my kindred, to whom I can write, without reserve, my sentiments on this subject. A letter upon any other subject, is more insipid to me than ever my task was when a schoolboy. I say not this in vain glory, God forbid: but to show what the Almighty, whose name I am unworthy to mention, has done for me, the chief of sinners. Once he was a terror to me; and his service, oh, what weariness it was! Now I can say, I love him, and his holy name, and am never as happy as when I speak of his mercies to me.'

Feeling his heart dilated with love to Christ, it is no wonder he should wish publicly to exert himself in the Redeemer's cause, to which, it is likely, he was at times urged by the Unwins, or by some of his pious relatives. Much as some may wish that such had been the case, it may justly be doubted whether his natural timidity would not have prevented him almost entirely from doing much good in this way. Indeed there is some reason to think, from the following extract, that he attempted something of the kind, but with so little success, that he was perfectly satisfied it was not his duty thus to advocate the Redeemer's cause. 'I have had many anxious thoughts about taking orders, and I believe every new convert is apt to think himself called upon for that purpose. It has pleased God, by means which there is no need to particularize, to give me full satisfaction as to the propriety of declining it; indeed, they who have the least idea of what I have suffered from the dread of public exhibitions, will readily excuse my never attempting them hereafter. In the meantime, if it pleases the Almighty, I may be an instrument of turning many to the truth, in a private way, and hope that my endeavours, in this way, have not been entirely unsuccessful. Had I the zeal of a Moses, I should want an Aaron to be my spokesman.'

That Cowper inspected very closely, and watched very narrowly his own heart, will appear by the following extract from a letter to the same lady:

'You sent my friend, Unwin, home charmed with your kind reception of him, and with everything he saw at the Park. Shall I once more give you a peep into my rude and deceitful heart? What motive do you think lay at the bottom of my conduct, when I desired him to call on you! I did not suspect, at first, that pride and vainglory had any share in it; but quickly after I had recommended the visit to him, I discovered, in that fruitful soil, the very root of the matter. Oh, pride! Pride! It deceives with the subtlety of a serpent, and seems to walk erect, though it crawls upon the earth. How will it twist and twine itself about to get from under the cross, which it is the glory of our Christian calling to be able to bear with patience and good will! Those who can guess at the heart of a stranger, and you especially, who are of a compassionate temper, will be more ready to excuse me than I can be to excuse myself. I am too frequently guilty of the abominable vice. How should such a creature be admitted into those pure and sinless mansions where nothing shall enter that defileth; did not the blood of Christ, applied by faith, take away the guilt of sin, and leave no spot or stain behind it! O what continual need have I of an almighty, all-sufficient Saviour! I am glad you are acquainted so particularly with all the circumstances of my story, for I know that your secrecy and discretion may be trusted with anything. A thread of mercy ran through all the intricate maze of those afflictive providences, so mysterious to myself at the time, and which must ever remain so to all who will not see what was the great design of them; at the judgment-seat of Christ the whole shall be laid open. How is the rod of iron changed into a sceptre of love!

'I have so much cause for humility, and so much need of it too, and every little sneaking resentment is such an enemy to it, that I hope I shall never give quarter to anything that appears in the shape of sullenness or self-consequence hereafter. Alas! if my best Friend, who laid down his life for me, were to remember all the instances in which I have neglected him, and to plead them against me in judgment, where should I hide my guilty head in the day of recompense? I will pray, therefore, for blessings upon my friends, though they cease to be so, and upon my enemies, though they continue such.'

Cowper had now been an inmate with the Unwin family a little more than eighteen months; and the above extracts, taken from his confidential letters, describe the happy frame of his mind, and the great progress he made in divine knowledge, during this period. Living in the enjoyment of the divine presence himself, and associated with those who experienced the same invaluable privilege, he tranquilly pursued the even tenor of his Christian course with attention, and with holy zeal. He might fairly have calculated upon the uninterrupted continuance, for many years, of the same distinguished privileges; but the dispensations of Divine Providence are sometimes awfully mysterious. Events unforeseen, and unexpected, are often occurring, which give a turn to our affairs quite subversive of even our best-arranged plans. Such was the melancholy occurrence that happened in this family, about this time, and led, at no distant period, to Cowper's removal from Huntingdon.

Mr. Unwin, proceeding to his church one Sunday morning in July, 1767, was flung from his horse, and received a dreadful fracture on the back part of his skull, under which he languished till the following Thursday, and then died. Cowper, in relating this melancholy event to his cousin, remarks:

'This awful dispensation has left an impression upon our spirits which will not presently be worn off. May it be a lesson to us to watch, since we know not the day, nor the hour, when our Lord cometh. At nine o'clock last Sunday morning, Mr. Unwin was in perfect health, and as likely to live twenty years as either of us, and by the following Thursday he was a corpse. The few short intervals of sense that were vouchsafed him, he spent in earnest prayer, and in expressions of a firm trust and confidence in the only Saviour.'

His friend Mr. Hill, about this time, kindly invited Cowper to pay him a visit in London; probably imagining that he might now be weary of the monotony of the country; and perhaps, too, thinking this a favourable opportunity to attempt again bringing him into the active scenes of life. Cowper's reply shows how greatly he was mistaken. 'My dear friend, I am obliged to you for your invitation: but having been long accustomed to retirement, of which I was always fond, I am now more than ever unwilling to revisit those noisy and crowded scenes which I never loved, and which I now abhor. I remember you with all the friendship I ever professed, which is as much as I ever entertained for any man. The strange and uncommon incidents of my life have given an entirely new turn to my whole character and conduct, and rendered me incapable of receiving pleasure from the same employments and amusements of which I could readily partake in former days. The effect of the late very distressing event will only be a change of my abode; for I shall, by God's leave, continue with Mrs. Unwin, whose behaviour to me has always been that of a mother to a son. We know not yet where we shall settle, but we trust that the Lord, whom we seek, will go before us, and prepare a rest for us. We have employed our friends, Mr. Haweis, Dr. Conyers, and Mr. Newton, to look out a place for us, but at present are entirely ignorant under which of the three we shall settle, or whether under any one of them.'

Just after this melancholy event had occurred, and while the family were in the midst of their distress, Mr. Newton, then curate of Olney, while on his way home from Cambridge, was induced to call upon Mrs. Unwin. The late Dr. Conyers had learned from Mrs. Unwin's son, the change that had taken place in her mind, on the subject of religion; and he accordingly requested Mr. Newton to embrace the earliest opportunity of having some conversation with her on the subject. His visit could not possibly have been made at a more seasonable juncture. Mrs. Unwin was now almost overwhelmed with sorrow; and, though the strength of her Christian principles preserved her from losing that confidence in the Almighty, which can alone support the mind under such distressing circumstances, yet both she and Mr. Cowper stood in need of some judicious Christian friend, to administer to them the consolations of the gospel. Their Heavenly Father could not have sent them one more capable of binding up their wounds, and soothing their sorrow, than Mr. Newton. He knew when to pour the oil of consolation into their wounded spirits; and his visit, providentially ordered, proved as useful as it was seasonable. He invited them to fix their future abode at Olney, whither they repaired, in the following October, to a house he had provided for them, so near the vicarage in which he lived, that by opening a door in the garden wall, they could exchange mutual visits, without entering the street. Mrs. Unwin kept the house, and Cowper continued to board with her, as he had done during her husband's life.

CHAPTER VI. Commencement of Cowper's intimacy with Mr. Newton —Pleasure it afforded him—His charitable disposition —Means provided for its indulgence, by the munificence of the late J. Thornton, Esq.—Mr. Thornton's death—Cowper's poetic tribute to his memory— His great anxiety for the spiritual welfare of his correspondents — Consolatory remarks addressed to his cousin—Severe affliction of his brother—Cowper's great concern on his behalf—Happy change in his brother's sentiments on religious subjects —His death-Cowper's reflections on it—Deep impression it made upon his mind—Description of his brother's character—Engages with Mr. Newton to write the Olney Hymns—Cowper's severe indisposition.

Great as were the advantages enjoyed by Cowper, when boarding with the Unwin family at Huntingdon, they were not to be compared with those, which he experienced in his new situation at Olney. He spent his time nearly in the same manner as at Huntingdon, having the additional advantage of frequent religious intercourse with his friend, Mr. Newton, with whom he was now upon terms of the closest intimacy. The amiable manners and exemplary piety of Cowper greatly endeared him to all with whom he became acquainted. He gladly availed himself of the benefits of religious conversation with the pious persons in Mr. Newton's congregation, and was particularly attentive to those among them who were in circumstances of poverty. He regularly visited the sick, and to the utmost extent of his power, afforded them relief. He attended the social meetings for prayer established by Mr. Newton. At such seasons, when he was occasionally required to conduct the service, agitated as were his feelings before he commenced, he no sooner began, than he poured forth his heart unto God in earnest intercession, with a devotion equally simple, sublime, and fervent, affording to all who were present on these occasions, proofs of the unusual combination of elevated genius, exquisite sensibility, and profound piety, by which he was pre-eminently distinguished. His conduct in private was consistent with the solemnity and fervor of these social devotional engagements. Three times a day he prayed, and gave thanks unto God, in retirement, besides the regular practice of domestic worship. His familiar acquaintance with, and experimental knowledge of the gospel, relieved him from all terror and anxiety of mind; his soul was stayed upon God; the divine promise and faithfulness were his support; and he lived in the enjoyment of perfect peace.

His hymns, most of which were composed at this period, prove that he was no stranger to those corrupt dispositions, which the best of men have to bewail, and which have so strong a tendency to draw away the mind from God. Against these dispositions, however, he was constantly upon the watch, and by the gracious aid of the Divine Spirit, he restrained every irregular desire, mortified every corrupt inclination, and ultimately came off victorious in his spiritual warfare.

The first few years of his residence at Olney, may perhaps, he regarded as the happiest of his life. Associated intimately with his beloved friend, Mr. Newton, and availing himself of his valuable assistance, in his efforts to acquire divine knowledge, his heart became established in the truth, and he experienced that degree of confidence in God, which alone can ensure peace of mind and real tranquillity. There is every reason to believe, that in the following passage in his poem on Conversation, subsequently written, he alludes to the pleasures he now enjoyed:

'Thus souls that carry on a blest exchange
Of joys they meet with in their heavenly range,
And with a fearless confidence make known
The sorrows sympathy esteems its own;
Daily derive increasing light and force
From such communion; in their pleasant course
Feel less the journey's roughness and its length;

Meet their opposers with united strength;
And one in heart, in interest, and design,
Gird up each other to the race divine.'

    Aware of the pleasure which Cowper took in visiting the poor in his neighbourhood and contributing to their relief, Mr. Newton procured for him a liberal annual allowance, for distribution, from the late excellent John Thornton, Esq. It is almost needless to add, that becoming the almoner of this distinguished philanthropist, was to Cowper a source of the greatest enjoyment. No individual was ever more alive to the cry of distress; he seemed, indeed, to possess almost an excess of this amiable sensibility. Nothing gladdened his heart more than to be the means of drying up the widow's tears and assuaging the orphan's grief; which the liberality of this great philanthropist allowed him often to accomplish. The decease of Mr. Thornton took place in 1790, and Cowper has contributed to illustrate his memory by the following beautiful eulogy:

Thee, Thornton, worthy in some page to shine
As honest and more eloquent than mine,
I mourn; or, since thrice happy thou must be,
The world, no longer thy abode, not thee:
Thee to deplore were grief mis-spent indeed;
It were to weep, that goodness has its meed;
That there is bliss prepared in yonder sky,
And glory for the virtuous when they die.
What pleasure can the miser's fondled hoard,
Or spendthrift's prodigal excess afford,
Sweet as the privilege of healing woe,
Suffered by virtue, combating below!
That privilege was thine; Heaven gave thee means
To illumine with delight the saddest scenes,
Till thy appearance chased the gloom, forlorn
As midnight, and despairing of a morn.
Thou had'st an industry in doing good,

Restless as his who toils and sweats for food;
Avarice in thee was the desire of wealth,
By rust unperishable, or by stealth;
And if the genuine worth of gold depend
On application to its noblest end,
Thine had a value in the scales of heaven,
Surpassing all that mine or mint has given;
And though God made thee of a nature prone
To distribution, boundless, of thy own,
And still, by motives of religious force,
Impelled thee more to that heroic course,
Yet was thy liberality discreet,
Nice in its choice, and of a temperate heat;
And, though in act unwearied, secret still;
As, in some solitude, the summer rill
Refreshes, where it winds, the faded green,
And cheers the drooping flowers, unheard, unseen.
Such was thy charity; no sudden start,
After long sleep, of passion in the heart;
But steadfast principle, and in its kind
Of close alliance with the eternal mind;
Traced easily to its true source above,
To Him whose works bespeak his nature, love.
Thy bounties all were Christian, and I make
This record of thee for the gospel's sake;
That the incredulous themselves may see
Its use and power exemplified in thee.*

    Owing to some cause for which we are unable to account, Cowper's correspondence with his friends became much less frequent after his settlement at Olney than it had formerly been: probably it might be attributed, in some degree at least, to his close intimacy with Mr. Newton, for they were seldom seven waking hours apart from each other. The same vein of genuine and unaffected piety, however, runs through those letters, which he did write, and they abound with remarks of uncommon excellence. To his cousin, Mrs. Cowper, he thus expresses his feelings:

'You live in the centre of a world I know you do not delight in. Happy are you, my dear friend, in being able to discern the insufficiency of all it can afford, to fill and satisfy the desires of an immortal soul. That God, who created us for the enjoyment of himself, has determined in mercy that it shall fail us here, in order that the blessed result of all our inquiries after happiness in the creature, may be a warm pursuit, and a close attachment to our true interests, in fellowship with him through the mediation of our dear Redeemer. I bless his goodness and his grace, that I have any reason to hope I am a partaker with you in the desire after better things than are to be found in a world polluted by sin, and therefore devoted to destruction. May he enable us both to consider our present life in its only true light; as an opportunity put into our hands to glorify him amongst men, by a conduct suited to his word and will. I am miserably defective in this holy and blessed art. I hope there is, at the bottom of all my sinful infirmities, a desire to live just as long as I may be useful. Then may I cheerfully obey the summons and attend him in a world where they who are his servants here shall pay him obedience forever.

'Your dear mother is too good to me, and puts a more charitable construction upon my silence than the fact well warrants. I have that within which hinders me wretchedly in all that I ought to do; but is prone to trifle, and let time and every good thing run to waste. May God be with you, to bless you and do you good by all his dispensations. Don't forget me, when you are speaking to our best Friend, before his mercy-seat.'

The lively interest, which Cowper took in the spiritual welfare of his correspondents, will appear in the following letter to his esteemed friend, Joseph Hill, Esq., dated January 21, 1709:

'Dear Joe: I rejoice with you in your recovery, and that you have escaped from the hands of one, from whose hands you will not always escape. Death is either the most formidable or the most comfortable thing; we have in prospect on this side of eternity. To be brought near to him, and to discern neither of these features in his face, would argue a degree of insensibility of which I will not suspect my friend, whom I know to be a thinking man. You have been brought down to the sides of the grave, and you have been raised up again by him who has the keys of the invisible world; who opens, and none can shut; who shuts and none can open. I do not forget to return thanks to him on your behalf, and to pray that your life, which he has spared, may be devoted to his service. "Behold! I stand at the door, and knock," is the word of him, in whom both our mortal and immortal life depend; and blessed be his name, it is the word of one who wounds only that he may heal, and who waits to be gracious. The language of every such dispensation is, "Prepare to meet thy God." It speaks with the voice of mercy and goodness, for without such notices, whatever preparation we might make for other events, we should make none for this. My dear friend, I desire and pray, that when this last enemy shall come to execute an unlimited commission on us, we may be found ready; being established and rooted in a well-grounded faith in his name who conquered death, and triumphed over him on the cross. If I am ever enabled to look forward to death with comfort, which I thank God is sometimes the case, I do not take my view of it from the top of my own works; though God is witness, that the labour of my life is to keep a conscience void of offence towards him. Death is always formidable to me, but when I see him disarmed of his sting by having sheathed it in the body of Jesus Christ.'

To the same friend, on another occasion, he thus writes:

I take a friend's share in all your concerns, so far as they come to my knowledge, and consequently did not receive the news of your marriage with indifference. I wish you and your bride all the happiness that belongs to the state; and the still greater felicity of that state, of which marriage is only a type. All these connexions shall be dissolved; but there is an indissoluble bond between Christ and his church, the subject of derision to an unthinking world, but the glory and happiness of all his people.'

No one knew better how to administer consolation to those who were in distress, and no one ever took a greater delight in doing it, than Cowper. To his amiable cousin, Mrs. Cowper, who had been called to sustain a severe domestic affliction, he writes as follows:

'A letter from your brother brought me yesterday the most afflicting intelligence that has reached me these many years ;—I pray God to comfort you, and to enable you to sustain this heavy stroke with that resignation to his will, which none but himself can give, and which he gives to none but his own children. How blessed and happy is your lot, my dear friend, beyond the lot of the greater part of mankind; that you know what it is to draw near to God in prayer, and are acquainted with a throne of grace! You have resources in the infinite love of a dear Redeemer, which are withheld from millions: and the promises of God, which are yea and amen in Christ Jesus, are sufficient to answer all your necessities, and to sweeten the bitterest cup, which your heavenly Father will ever put into your hand. May he now give you liberty to drink at these wells of salvation, until you are filled with consolation and peace, in the midst of trouble. He has said, When thou passest through the fire, I will be with thee, and when through the floods, they shall not overflow thee. You have need of such a word as this, and he knows your need of it; and the time of necessity is the time when he will be sure to appear in behalf of those who trust in him. I bear you and yours upon my heart before him, night and day; for I never expect to hear of distress that shall call upon me with a louder voice to pray for the sufferer. I know the Lord hears me for myself, vile and sinful as I am; and I believe and am sure, that he will hear me for you also. He is the friend of the widow and the father of the fatherless, even God in his holy habitation; and in all our afflictions he is afflicted; and when he chastens us, it is in mercy. Surely, he will sanctify this dispensation to you. O that comfortable word!" I have chosen thee in the furnace of affliction;" so that our very sorrows are evidences of our calling, and he chastens us because we are his children. My dear cousin, I commit you to the word of his grace, and to the comforts of his Holy Spirit. Your life is needful for your family; may God, in mercy to them, prolong it, and may he preserve you from the dangerous effects that a stroke like this might have upon a frame as tender as yours. I grieve for you, I pray for you; could I do more I would, but God must comfort you.'

Cowper had scarcely forwarded this consolatory and truly Christian letter, when he was himself visited with a trial so severe as to call into exercise all that confidence in the Almighty, which he had endeavoured to excite in the mind of his amiable relative. He received a letter from his brother, then residing as a fellow in Corpus Christi College, Cambridge, between whom and himself there had always existed affection truly fraternal, stating that he was seriously indisposed. No brothers were ever more warmly interested in each other's welfare. At the commencement of Cowper's affliction, which led to his removal to St. Alban's, his brother had watched over him with the tenderest solicitude; and it was owing to his tenderness, that Cowper was placed under the care of Dr. Cotton. While he remained at St. Alban's, his brother visited him, and, as has been related above, became the means of contributing materially to his recovery.

When William Cowper moved to Huntingdon, these affectionate brothers adopted a plan for a frequent and regular interchange of visits. The distance between their places of abode was fifteen miles; and, even after Cowper's removal to Olney, his brother, during the first two years, paid him several visits. They seemed, indeed, mutually delighted with an opportunity of being in each other's company.

Cowper, on hearing of his brother's illness, immediately repaired to Cambridge. To his inexpressible grief, he found him in a condition, which left little or no hopes of his recovery. He had taken cold on his return from a journey into Wales; and, lest he should be laid up at a distance from home, had pushed forward as fast as he could from Bath with a fever upon him. This, with the previous state of his health, produced a complication of most dangerous complaints. In this state of extreme peril, he seemed to have no more concern about his spiritual interests than when in perfect health.

His couch was strewed with volumes of plays, to which, at first, except when there seemed but little prospect of his recovery, he had frequent recourse for amusement. In a letter to his cousin, Cowper thus describes the case:

'My brother continues much as he was. His case is a very dangerous one—an imposture of the liver, attended by an asthma and dropsy. The physician has little hopes of his recovery; indeed, I might say none at all, only, being a friend, he does not formally give him over by ceasing to visit him, lest it should sink his spirits. For my own part, I have no expectation of it, except by a signal interposition of Providence in answer to prayer. His case is clearly out of the reach of medicine, but I have seen many a sickness healed, where the danger has been equally threatening, by the only Physician of value. I doubt not he will have an interest in your prayers, as he has in the prayers of many. May the Lord incline his ear, and give an answer of peace. I know it is good to be afflicted; I trust you have found it so, and that under the teaching of the Spirit of God, we shall both be purified. It is the desire of my soul to seek a better country, where God will wipe away all tears from the eyes of his people, and where, looking back upon the ways by which he has led us, we shall be filled with everlasting wonder, love, and praise.'

Conversion of his brother, John Cowper:

Finding his brother on the verge of the grave, Cowper discovered the greatest anxiety respecting his everlasting welfare. He knew that his sentiments on some of the most important truths of religion had long been unsettled. William worked to impart to him those views of the gospel, which he had himself found so singularly beneficial. His work was not in vain. He had the unspeakable gratification of witnessing the complete triumph of the truth and its consolatory influence upon the mind of his beloved brother in his dying moments.

Writing to Mr. Hill, he says:

'It pleased God to cut short my brother's connections and expectations here, yet, not without giving him lively and glorious views of a better happiness than any he could propose to himself in such a world as this. Notwithstanding his great learning, (for he was one of the chief men in the university in that respect) he was candid and sincere in his inquiries after truth. He could not agree to my sentiments when I first acquainted him with them, nor in many conversations, which I afterwards had with him upon the subject. Yet I had no sooner left St. Albans than he began to study, with the deepest attention, those points on which we differed, and to furnish himself with the best writers upon them. His mind was kept open to conviction for five years, during all which time he laboured in this pursuit with unwearied diligence, whilst leisure and opportunity were afforded. Amongst his dying words were these, "Brother, I thought you wrong, yet wanted to believe as you did. I found myself not able to believe, yet always thought I should be one day brought to do so." From the study of books he was brought, upon his deathbed, to the study of himself, and there learnt to renounce all reliance on his own righteousness or on his own most amiable character, and to submit himself to the righteousness which is of God by faith. With these views, he was desirous of death: satisfied of his interest in the blessing purchased by the blood of Christ, he prayed for death with earnestness, felt the approaches of it with joy, and died in peace.'

It afforded Cowper inexpressible delight, to witness, in his brother's case, the consoling and animating power of those principles that he had himself found to be so highly beneficial. From that time, he took constant occasion to declare to his brother what God had done for his soul; and neglected no opportunity of attempting to engage him in conversation of a spiritual kind. On his first visit to him at Cambridge, after he left St. Alban's, his heart being then full of the subject, he poured it out to his brother without reserve, taking care to show him, that what he had received was not merely a new set of notions, but a real impression of the truths of the gospel. His brother listened to his statements at first with some attention, and often laboured to convince him that the difference in their sentiments was much less real than verbal. Subsequently, however, he became more reserved; and though he heard patiently, he never replied, nor ever discovered a desire to converse on the subject. This, he afterwards, confessed was the effect of a resolution he had made to that effect, in order to avoid disputes, and to secure the continuance of that peace that had always subsisted between them. The natural goodness of his temper enabled him strictly to adhere to the rule he had thus prescribed to himself, never remarking upon anything he heard or saw, if it was the least likely to introduce the discussion of serious subjects. At the commencement of his affliction, little as was the concern he then felt for his spiritual interests, the thoughts of God and of eternity would sometimes force themselves upon his mind; at every little prospect of recovery, however, he found it no difficult matter to thrust them out again. It was evident that his mind was very far from being set on things spiritual and heavenly; as on almost every subject but that of religion, he would converse fluently. At every suitable opportunity, Cowper endeavoured to give a serious turn to the discourse, but without any apparent success. Having obtained his permission, he prayed with him frequently; still, however, he seemed as careless and unconcerned as ever.

On one occasion, after his brother had survived a severe paroxysm of his disorder, he observed to him, as he sat by his bedside, 'that, though it had pleased God to visit him with great afflictions, yet mercy was mingled with the dispensation. You have many friends that love you, and are willing to do all they can to serve you, and so, perhaps, have many others in the like circumstances; but it is not the lot of every sick man, how much soever he may be beloved, to have a friend that can pray for him.' He replied, 'That is true; and I hope God will have mercy upon me.' His love to Cowper, from that time, became very remarkable; there was tenderness in it more than was merely natural; and he generally expressed it by calling for blessings upon him in the most affectionate terms, and with a look and manner not to be described. One afternoon, a few days before he died, he suddenly burst into tears, and said, with a loud cry, 'O forsake me not!'

Cowper went to the bedside, grasped his hand, and tenderly inquired why he wished him to remain.

'O, brother,' said he, 'I am full of what I could say to you; if I live, you and I shall be more like one another than we have been. But, whether I live or not, all is well, and will be so; I know it will; I have felt that which I never felt before; and am sure that God has visited me with this sickness, to teach me what I was too proud to learn in health. I never had satisfaction till now, having no ground to rest my hopes upon; but now I have a foundation which nothing can shake. The doctrines I have confided in, referred me to myself, or the foundation of my hopes, and there I could find nothing to rest upon; the anchor of my soul was wanting. I have now peace in myself; and if I live, I hope it will be that I might be a messenger of peace to others. I have learned that in a moment, which I could not have learned by reading many books for many years. I have often studied these points, and studied them with great attention; but was blinded by prejudice; and unless he, who alone is worthy to unloose the seals, had opened the book to me, I had been blind still. Now they appear so plain, that though I am convinced no comment could ever have made me understand them, I wonder 1 did not see them before. Yet, great as my doubts and difficulties were, they have only served to pave the way; and, being solved, they make it plainer. The light I have received comes late, but not too late, and it is a comfort to me that I never made the gospel truths a subject of ridicule. This bed is to me a bed of misery, but it is likewise a bed of joy and a bed of discipline. Were I to die this night, I know I should be happy. This assurance, I hope, is quite consistent with the word of God. It is founded upon a sense of my own utter insufficiency, and the all sufficiency of Christ. 1 have been building my glory on a sandy foundation. I have laboured night and day, to perfect myself in things of no profit; I have sacrificed my health to these pursuits, and am now suffering the consequences of my mis-spent labour. But how contemptible do some of the writers I once highly valued now appear to me!" Yea, doubtless, I count all things but loss, for the excellency of the knowledge of Christ Jesus my Lord." I succeeded in my former pursuits. I wanted to be highly applauded, and I was so, even to the height of my wishes; but now I have learned a new lesson. What a scene is passing before me! Ideas upon these subjects crowd upon me faster than I can give them utterance. How plain do many texts appear, to which, after consulting all the commentators, I could hardly before affix any meaning. Now I have their true signification, without any comment at all. There is but one key to the New Testament; there is but one interpreter. I cannot describe to you, nor shall I ever be able to describe to you, what I felt when this was given to me. May I make a good use of it! How I shudder when I think of the danger I have just escaped! How wonderful is it that God should look upon me! Yet he sees me, and takes notice of all that I suffer. I see him too, and can hear him say, "Come unto me, all ye that labour and are heavy laden, and I will give you rest." I can never be sufficiently thankful for the mercy I have received. Perhaps I may ascribe some part of this insensibility to my great weakness of body. I hope, at least, that if I were better in health, it would be better with me in these respects also. Have I not cause to praise him, when I feel that I have an interest in Christ, in his blood and sufferings, and that my sins are forgiven me? I will confess to you, brother, what I never confessed before, that my function and the duties of it were beginning to be weariness to me that I could not bear. Yet, base as I am, I have no doubt, now, that God has accepted me, and blotted out all my iniquities.' For a few days, during his affliction, there appeared some prospect of his recovery, and while such was the case, he was deeply sensible of the difficulties he should have to encounter, were he again raised up. He knew that he must expect great opposition, but was determined to be faithful. The souls committed to his care were much upon his mind; and, under the weight of these impressions, he one day, when Cowper was with him alone, prayed aloud:

'O Lord, thou art light, and in thee is no darkness at all. Thou art the fountain of all wisdom; it is essential to thee to be good and gracious. I am weak and foolish as a child; O Lord, teach me how I shall conduct myself. Give me the wisdom of the serpent, and the harmlessness of the dove. Bless the souls thou hast committed to the care of thy helpless, miserable creature, and make me faithful to them for thy name and mercies' sake.' He survived this change only a few days, and died happily, rejoicing in hope of the glory of God.

An event like this could not fail to make a deep impression upon the tender spirit of Cowper, and his feelings on the occasion were such as are not experienced by ordinary minds. The following letter to his amiable cousin shows clearly the state of his mind:

'You judge rightly of the manner in which I have been affected by the Lord's late dispensation towards my brother. I found it a cause of sorrow that I lost so near a relation and one so deservedly dear to me, and that he left me just when our sentiments upon the most interesting of subjects became the same. But it was also a cause of joy, that it pleased God to give me a clear and evident proof that he had changed his heart, and adopted him into the number of his children. For this I hold myself peculiarly bound to thank him, because he might have done all that he was pleased to do for him, and yet have afforded him neither strength nor opportunity to declare it. He told me, that from the time he was first ordained, he began to be dissatisfied with his religious opinions, and to suspect that there were greater things revealed in the Bible, than were generally believed or allowed to be there. From the time when I first visited him, after my release from St. Alban's, be began to read upon the subject. It was at that time I informed him of the views of divine truth, which I had received in that school of affliction. He laid what I said to heart, and began to furnish himself with the best writers on the controverted points, whose works he read with great diligence and attention, carefully comparing them with the scriptures. None ever truly and ingenuously sought the truth, but they found it. A spirit of earnest inquiry is the gift of God, who never says to any, " Seek ye my face in vain." Accordingly, about ten days before his death, it pleased the Lord to dispel all his doubts, to reveal in his heart the knowledge of the Saviour, and to give him that firm and unshaken confidence in the ability and willingness of Christ to save sinners, which is invariably followed by a joy that is unspeakable and full of glory.'

On another occasion, adverting to his brother's case, Cowper very properly remarks:

'There is that in the nature of salvation by grace, when it is truly and experimentally known, which prompts every person to think himself the most extraordinary instance of its power. Accordingly, my brother insisted upon the precedence in this respect; and, upon comparing his case with mine, would by no means allow my deliverance to be so wonderful as his own. He observed that from the beginning his manner of life had been such, as had a natural tendency to blind his eyes, and to confirm and rivet his prejudices against the truth. His acquaintance had been of that stamp who had trusted in themselves that they were righteous, though they despised the doctrines of the cross.'

Of the character of his much-beloved brother, whose death filled him with mingled emotions of joy and grief, Cowper has given the following interesting description:—He was a man of a most candid and ingenuous spirit; his temper remarkably sweet, and in his behaviour to me he had always manifested an uncommon affection. His outward conduct, so far as it fell under my notice, or I could learn it by the report of others, was perfectly decent and un-blamable. There was nothing vicious in any part of his practice, but being of a studious, thoughtful turn, he placed his chief delight in the acquisition of learning, and made such progress in it, that he had but few rivals. He was critically skilled in the Latin, Greek, and Hebrew languages; was beginning to make himself master of the Syriac, and perfectly understood the French and Italian, the latter of which he could speak fluently. Learned, however, as he was, he was easy and cheerful in his conversation, and entirely free from the stiffness that is generally contracted by men devoted to such pursuits. The following poetic tribute to his memory, from Cowper's pen, deserves a place in this memoir:

'I had a brother once;
Peace to the memory of a man of worth!
A man of letters and of manners too!
Of manners sweet as virtue always wears.
When gay good humour dresses her in smiles!
He grac'd a college, in which order yet
Was sacred, and was honoured, lov'd, and wept
By more than one, themselves conspicuous there.

Notwithstanding the cheerfulness with which Cowper bore up under this painful bereavement, when it first occurred, owing to the happy circumstances related above, by which it was attended, yet there is reason to believe that it made an impression upon his peculiarly sensitive mind, more deep than visible; and that was not soon to be effaced. It unquestionably diminished his attachment to the world, and made him less unwilling to leave it. Writing to his friend, Mr. Hill, at this time, who had kindly given him another pressing invitation to visit London, perhaps hoping that the loss of his brother might thereby be less sensibly felt, he says:

'I have not done conversing with terrestrial objects, though I should be happy were I able to hold more continual converse with a friend above the skies. He has my heart, but he allows a corner of it for all who show me kindness, and therefore one for you. The storm of 1763 made a wreck of the friendships I had contracted, in the course of many years, yours only excepted, which has survived the tempest.'

About this time, a considerable change took place in Mrs. Unwin's domestic establishment. Her son had recently settled at Stock, in Essex, and her daughter was on the eve of marriage to the Rev. Mr. Powley, an excellent and evangelical clergyman. The cordial esteem, which Cowper had always felt for Mrs. Unwin, had gradually assumed the similitude of conjugal attachment. There was now no prospect of a separation through life, this, Cowper deemed it advisable to propose marriage to Mrs. Unwin. The difference of their ages, though considerable, was far less than that which had subsisted in the case of a Johnson, or a Howard, who had both, probably, for similar reasons to those that influenced Cowper, chosen for their companions through life, females much older than themselves. The time for the consummation of this union was fixed, and there seemed no prospect of its being frustrated. Divine providence, however, did not permit it to be accomplished; the tender spirit of Cowper became again enveloped in the deepest gloom, occasioned, perhaps, partly by the deep regret he felt at the loss of his brother, and partly by the excitement connected, in a mind like his, with the change he now contemplated.

It appears not improbable that his friend Mr. Newton might have witnessed, in the morbid tendency of his mind to melancholy, of which he then discovered symptoms, some traces of the deep and extensive wound, which his mind had received by this event, though his efforts to conceal it were incessant. Hence, he wisely engaged him in a literary undertaking, congenial with his taste, suited to his admirable talents, and, perhaps, more adapted to alleviate his distress than any other that could have been selected. Mr. Newton had felt the want of a volume of evangelical hymns, on experimental subjects, suited for public and private worship; he mentioned the subject to Cowper, and pressed him to undertake it, and the result was, a friendly compact to supply the volume between them, with an understanding that Cowper was to be the principal composer. He entered upon this work with great pleasure, and though he does not appear, previous to this, to have employed his poetical talents for a considerable time, yet the admirable hymns he composed, show with what ease he could write upon the doctrinal, experimental, or practical parts of Christianity.

One of our best living poets, whose writings more frequently remind us of Cowper's than any we have ever read, in an essay on the poet's productions, remarks:

'Of these hymns it must suffice to say, that, like all his best compositions, they are principally the communing with his own heart, or avowals of personal Christian experience. As such, they are frequently applicable to every believer's feelings, and touch, unexpectedly, the most secret springs of joy and sorrow, faith, fear, hope, love, trial, despondency, and triumph. Some allude to infirmities, the most difficult to be described, but often the source of excruciating anguish to the tender conscience. The 72nd Hymn, Book I. is written with the confidence of inspiration, and the authority of a prophet. The 96th Hymn, of the same Book, is a perfect allegory in miniature, without a failing point, or confusion of metaphor, from beginning to end. Hymn 51, Book III. presents a transformation, which, if found in Ovid, might have been extolled as the happiest of his fictions. Hymn 12, Book II. closes with one of the hardiest figures to be met with out of the Hebrew Scriptures. None but a poet of the highest order could have written it; verses cannot go beyond it, and painting cannot approach it. Hymn 38, Book II. is a strain of noble simplicity, expressive of confidence the most remote from presumption, and such as a heart at peace with God alone could enjoy or utter. Who can read the 55th Hymn, Book II. without feeling as if he could, at that moment, forsake all, take up his cross, and follow his Saviour? The 19th Hymn, Book III. is a model of tender pleading of believing, persevering prayer in trouble; and the following one is a brief parody of Bunyan's finest passage, and is admirable of its kind. The reader might almost imagine himself Christian on his pilgrimage, the triumph and the trance are brought so home to his bosom. Hymn 15, of the same book, is a lyric of high tone and character, and rendered awfully interesting, by the circumstances under which it was written—in the twilight of departing reason." Essay on Cowper's Productions, by James Montgomery.

The benevolent heart of Cowper was delighted to a high degree to co-operate with a man of Mr. Newton's talents and piety, in promoting the advancement of religion in his neighbourhood. It is deeply to be regretted, that when he had only composed sixty-eight hymns, all of which were uncommonly excellent, he was laid aside from the interesting employment by serious indisposition. It pleased God, for reasons inscrutable to us, and which it would be impious to arraign, to visit the afflicted poet with a renewed attack of his former hypochondriacal complaint, more protracted, and not less violent than the one he had before experienced. Just on the eve of the attack he composed the following sublime hymn—

God moves in a mysterious way
His wonders to perform;
He plants His footsteps in the sea
And rides upon the storm.

Deep in unfathomable mines
Of never failing skill
He treasures up His bright designs
And works His sov'reign will.

Ye fearful saints, fresh courage take;
The clouds ye so much dread
Are big with mercy and shall break
In blessings on your head.

Judge not the Lord by feeble sense,
But trust Him for His grace;
Behind a frowning providence
He hides a smiling face.

His purposes will ripen fast,
Unfolding every hour;

The bud may have a bitter taste,
But sweet will be the flow'r.

Blind unbelief is sure to err
And scan His work in vain;
God is His own interpreter,
And He will make it plain.

CHAPTER VII. Great severity of Cowper's mental depression—His presentiment of it—Its consequences—Remarks upon its probable cause—Absurdity of attributing it, in any degree, to religion—Mrs. Unwin's great attention to him—His aversion to the company of strangers— Symptoms of his recovery—Domesticates three leverets—Amusement they afforded him—Mr. Newton's removal from Olney—Introduction of Mr. Bull to Cowper—His translation of Madame de la Guyon's poems, at Mr. Bull's request—Commences his original productions, at the suggestion of Mrs. Unwin— Renews his correspondence with Mr. and Mrs. Newton—Describes the state of his mind.

We are again arrived at another of those melancholy periods of Cowper's life, over which it must be alike the duty of the biographer, and the wish of the reader, to cast a veil. Mental aberration, whoever may be the subject of it, excites the tenderest commiseration of all; but if there be one time when it may be contemplated with emotions more truly distressing than another, it is when it attacks those who are endowed with talents the most brilliant, with dispositions the most amiable, and with piety the most ardent and unobtrusive. Such was eminently the case in the present instance. To see a mind like Cowper's, enveloped in the thickest gloom of despondency, and for several years in the prime of life, remaining in a state of complete inactivity and misery, must have been distressing in no ordinary degree.

A short time before this afflictive visitation, Cowper appears to have received some presentiment of its approach, and during a solitary walk in the fields, as was hinted above, he composed that beautiful hymn in the Olney collection with which we closed our last chapter. On this occasion, acute as may have been his feelings, he must have experienced an unshaken confidence in God; for it is scarcely possible to read this admirable production, however dark and distressing the dispensations of Divine Providence towards us may be, without enjoying the same delightful emotions. About the same time, he composed the hymn entitled *Temptation*, the following lines from which will show how powerfully his mind was then exercised.

The billows swell, the winds are high,
Clouds overcast my wintry sky;
Out of the depths to thee I call,
My fears are great, my strength is small.
O Lord, the pilot's part perform,
And guide and guard me through the storm;
Defend me from each threatening ill;
Control the waves; say, 'Peace, be still.'
Amidst the roaring of the sea,
My soul still hangs her hope on thee;
Thy constant love, thy faithful care,
Is all that saves me from despair.'

He now relapsed into a state, very much resembling that which had previously occasioned his removal to St. Alban's. The second attack occurred in 1773; and he remained in the same painful and melancholy condition, without even a single alleviation of his sufferings, for the protracted period of five years: and it was five years more, before he wholly recovered the use of his admirable powers. His mind, which could formerly soar on the wings of faith and love, to the utmost limits of Christian knowledge and enjoyment, now sunk into the lowest depths of depression; and here seemed as if it would remain immovably fixed; rejecting, with deplorable firmness, every species of consolation that was attempted to be administered.

'Children of pity, who for other's woe,
In secret shed the sympathetic tear;
And ye, who in life's ocean wave serene,
Ply the smooth oar, and spread the silken sail,
Here gently pausing o'er the solemn shrine,
One generous drop bestow; where he, adorn'd
With purest gifts of science, and of truth;
Amidst the pressure of severe disease.
Stood,—like the oak assail'd by wintry storms,
Leafless and shudd'ring at the rude attack;
A spectacle to angels and to men.
'Twas then, all earthly honours quick became
Obscure and faded in his wounded sight.
His intellectual and colloquial powers,
Ere while so brilliant, suffered sore eclipse;
Social endearments could delight no more;
The sweet companion and the friend sincere
Had lost their powers of pleasing, and unheard
Strove to divert his pangs, and whisper peace:
Viewed by his joyless eye, the once-lov'd face
Of beauteous nature wore a general gloom.
—*Tribute to Cowper's Memory*, by I. I. Shewell, Esq.

Various causes have been assigned by different writers for the melancholy aberration of mind of which Cowper was now, and at other seasons of his life, the subject; but none are so irreconcilable to everything like just and legitimate reasoning, as the attempt to ascribe it to religion. That unjust views of the character of God, and of the nature of the gospel, may occasionally have been the predisposing causes of great and severe mental depression, we are not disposed to deny; though we think this a case of infrequent occurrence, and one in which the individual must be in a state of great ignorance respecting the fundamental truths of religion. Ought this, however, when it does happen, to be identified with religion, of which, at the best, it can only be regarded as a mere distortion? There was evidently, in the case of Cowper, nothing that bore the slightest resemblance to this. Making some allowances for peculiar expressions occasionally employed by him, perhaps it will not be saying too much to affirm, that no individual ever entertained more scriptural views of the gospel dispensation, in all its parts, and of the perfections and attributes of its great Author, than this excellent man. Indeed, all that is alleged as being involved in the most rigid system of religion, would have produced no dismay in the mind of Cowper: for the faith he possessed would have dispelled or irradiated the darkness of the gloomiest speculative creed. His views of religion were not sombre; he had experienced their cheering efficacy, and dispensed to others the consolation he had proved them to be adapted to impart. The impression, which haunted his imagination, during the partial derangement which closed the latter period of his life, was not simply erroneous or unscriptural; it was wholly out of the line of religious belief. It had no relation to anyone proposition of theology; it was an assumption built upon premises completely fictitious; all was unreal but the anguish and despair which the delusion of his reason produced. The letters he wrote to his correspondents, and the hymns he composed, prior to this second attack, prove unquestionably that his views of religion were at the remotest distance from what can be termed visionary and enthusiastic: on the contrary they were perfectly scriptural and evangelical, and were, therefore, infinitely more adapted to support, than to depress his mind.

Strange as it may appear, it is evident that Cowper now, and indeed for the greater part of his future life, laboured under that peculiar species of hypochondriasis which left him, except when suffering under the severest paroxysms of his malady, the entire command of his faculties, in reference to every subject but one, and that one, in his case, was religion. He had not been led into it by any mental process, nor was it a conclusion at which he had arrived by the operation of either reason or conscience, for it was wholly unconnected with any tenet he held; but it had come upon him as a visitation, not as a judgment, from God, for reasons to us inscrutable, but unquestionably in entire harmony with His infinite benevolence. The sensation, however, was real; it could not be reasoned away, any more than the headache, or any other physical disorder. It was as clearly a case of hypochondriasis as those instances in which the patient imagines himself transformed into a block, a tree, or any other material object. If in this case the impression seemed more rational, it was far from being so in reality, as it is evident from the specific nature of the idea on which he fixed, that he was excluded from salvation for not having complied with a suggestion to extinguish his own life, which his hallucination led him to imagine was the command of God. It is impossible that religion could have given birth to a notion thus unnatural and monstrous; and yet that it was mainly this, which produced his melancholy, none who have considered the nature of his case can deny.

Between this prominent feature of Cowper's hypochondriasis, and the notions ever entertained of religion by himself or by others, there was the utmost incompatibility. The unalterable persuasion which had taken fixed possession of his mind, that he was doomed to everlasting perdition, not only opposed the doctrine which he admitted to be true, but led him to regard his own case as a solitary exception to the general laws of the Divine Government, in which isolated case, an individual, though he believed with the heart unto righteousness, would be lost. The supposed cause of his exclusion from divine mercy, was his having neglected, what he called a known duty, in disobeying the command of God to commit that tragic act, at which nature itself revolts, but which he conceived was specially enjoined upon him as a trial of his obedience to the will of God; but which, through weakness and irresolution, he had resisted: thus placing himself beyond the reach of redemption. 'Never neglect a known duty,' was the injunction, which he pressed upon a young friend, in reference to his own condition; to such neglect he attributed all his hopeless agony of mind. So consistent, so blameless had been his own conduct since he had embraced the truths of

Christianity, that it should seem that there was no one act of mental disobedience which furnished occasion for remorse; no stain upon his conscience, which in his melancholy broodings supplied the tempter with an accusation: all that he could find to fix upon was an imaginary crime. Nor was there any one doctrine in his creed, which his disordered mind could convert into an instrument of self-inflicted condemnation.

The living poet whom we have before quoted, remarks with regard to Cowper's malady, there scarcely needs any other proof that it was not occasioned by his religion than that the error on which he stumbled was in direct contradiction to his creed. He believed that he had been predestined to life, yet under his delusion he imagined that God, who cannot lie, repent, or change, had, in *his sole instance,* reversed His own decree, which had been in force from all eternity.

The remarks of Mr. Hayley, in his life of the poet, page 144, vol. 1, are, we think, exceedingly reprehensible and unfounded. He says:

'So fearfully and wonderfully are we made, that man in all conditions ought, perhaps, to pray that he never may be led to think of his Creator and his Redeemer, either too little or too much, since human misery is often seen to arise equally, from an utter neglect of all spiritual concerns, and from a wild extravagance of devotion.'

It is surely needless to observe, that the devotion of Cowper was as much unlike what could, with any degree of propriety, be termed wild or extravagant, as can well be imagined. To what description of devotion Mr. Hayley would apply these epithets we cannot tell, but surely not to that which is scripturally evangelical, which was eminently the character of Cowper's, and which is of a nature so heavenly and spiritual, so perfectly adapted to the circumstances of mankind, and withal so soothing and consoling, that it can never be carried to excess. The more powerfully its influence is felt upon the mind, the more extensive must be the enjoyment it produces, unless when it pleases God, as in the case of Cowper, to disorganize the mental powers, and thereby unfit it for the reception of that comfort which it would otherwise experience. Mental disorganization may undoubtedly arise from an almost infinite variety of causes, many of which, as in the poet's case, must forever elude our search, though they are all under the control of that God who is the giver of life, and its preserver. Real religion, however, which consists in a cordial reception of the truth in the heart, can never produce it in the remotest degree: evangelical devotion cannot be too intense, nor can we know too much of our Creator and Redeemer. Contemplating the Divine Being apart from the gospel of Christ, or through the distorting medium of our own fancies, may possibly, in some cases, produce depression; while viewing him as he is presented to our minds in the scriptures, in all the plentitude of his goodness and benevolence, is sure to be productive of consequences directly opposite. Instead of there being any danger likely to arise from having our thoughts too much employed upon the character of God, we think a scripturally comprehensive view of his perfections the best possible preservative from despair. To represent an excess of devotion as the cause of Cowper's malady, in however slight a degree, is obviously opposed to every consistent view of religion, and is assigning that for its cause which was infinitely more likely to become its effectual cure.

 To investigate the influence which physical causes often have on the operation of the moral faculties, and to enter into the nice and delicate subject of physiological speculation, interesting as might be the inquiry, would lead to no certain result. After all that might be said, it could only be regarded as matter of speculation, owing to the extreme difficulty of determining at all times, with anything like accuracy or certainty, what in each separate case are the real causes of despondency. So exquisite does the sympathy exist between the body and the mind, especially in some constitutions, that the slightest variation in the temperature of the frame communicates itself to the imagination and the feelings, with such force, that almost every breath and pulsation seem to be regulated by the thoughts.

Cowper's imagination was evidently subject to a degree of morbid excitement, which rendered him at some periods unable to judge between what was real and what was illusive, between the impressions received from external objects and those that proceeded from the reflux operations of his own mind. Had it not been so he could never have imagined that the Almighty would have made his case an exception to all others, nor could he have supposed that God would have made it his duty to destroy his life, which he knew involved the commission of a most serious crime in every other case, justly exposing the delinquent to the righteous displeasure of God.

It has been judiciously remarked, 'had Cowper never become a convert to religion, in his own acceptation of the phrase, the only difference in the character of his dejection would have been, its being less irrational, less obviously at variance with his own creed and with the dictates of Revealed Truth. It may be imagined, that religion had at least a share in determining the direction of his disorder. But this, we think, is extremely questionable. As no one can pretend to believe that the return of his hypochondriacal attack would have been prevented, had his opinions undergone no change on the subject of religion, in other words, had he never been converted, so there is small reason to conclude that the dejection into which he eventually sunk, would, in that case, have assumed a different aspect. It must be recollected, that in the attacks of depression to which he was subject in his youth, what is falsely called religious melancholy, gave the character to the morbid affection of his spirits. Accident and, we believe, the last impression, often determine the complexion of the patient's anxiety, under the influence of physical melancholy; and it is notorious that in by far the larger proportion of cases, the morbid symptoms exhibit a contrariety to the disposition and character of the individual when he is in health. If then any persons still resolutely maintain that Cowper's religion made him mad, what can be said in reply, but that they are certainly themselves, as it respects right reason, insane; and it is to be feared, belong to that class which will ever remain incurable.'

The melancholy condition to which Cowper was now reduced, afforded Mrs. Unwin an opportunity of proving the warmth of her affection for, and the sincerity of her attachment to, the dejected poet. He now required to be watched with the greatest care, vigilance, and perseverance; and it pleased God to endow her with all that tenderness, fortitude, and firmness of mind, which were requisite for the proper discharge of duties so important. Her incessant care over him, during the long continuance of his depressive malady, could only be equalled by the pleasure she experienced, on seeing his richly endowed mind gradually emerge from that awful state of darkness in which it had been enveloped, into the clear sunshine of liberty and peace: she hailed his approach to convalescence, slowly as it advanced, with the mingled emotions of gratitude and praise.

Cowper, throughout the whole of this severe attack, was inaccessible to all, except his friend Mr. Newton, who, during the whole of its continuance, watched over him with the greatest tenderness, and was indefatigable in his efforts to administer consolation to his depressed spirit. During a period of no less than fourteen months, he retained him at the vicarage and with untired perseverance laboured incessantly to dissipate the dark cloud that had gathered over his mind; but to every consolatory suggestion he was utterly deaf, concluding that God had rejected him, and that, consequently, it was sinful for him even to wish for mercy. How awful are the effects of mental disorganization; how easily does it convert that into poison which was designed for solid food! How highly should we prize, and how thankfully ought we to appreciate, the uninterrupted enjoyment of our mental powers!

After enduring an accumulation of anguish almost inconceivable, for the long space of five years, unalleviated by a single glimpse of comfort, the interesting sufferer began at length to recover. He listened to the advice of Mrs. Unwin, and allowed her, occasionally at least, to divert his mind from those melancholy meditations by which it had so long been occupied. It now occurred to this friend that he might probably find it beneficial to be employed in some amusing occupation. She suggested this to some of her neighbours, who all deplored the poet's case, felt a lively interest in his welfare, and would gladly have done anything in their power that was in the least likely to mitigate his distress.

The children of one of his neighbours had recently received, as a plaything, a young leveret; which was at that time about three months old. Understanding better how to tease the poor creature than to feed it, and soon becoming weary of their charge, they readily consented that their father, who saw it pining and growing leaner every day, should offer it to Cowper's acceptance. Beginning then to be glad of anything that would engage his attention without fatiguing it, he was willing enough to take the prisoner under his protection, perceiving that, in the management of such an animal, and in the attempt to tame it, he should find just that sort of employment which his case required. It was soon known among his neighbours that he was pleased with the present; and the consequence was that in a short time, he had as many leverets offered him as would have stocked a paddock. He undertook the care of three, which he named Puss, Tiney, and Bess. The choice of their food, and the diversity of their dispositions, afforded him considerable amusement, and their occasional diseases excited his sympathy and tenderness. One remained with him during the whole of his abode at Olney, and was afterwards celebrated in his unrivalled poem, the Task; and at its decease was honoured with a beautiful epitaph from his pen; another lived with him nearly nine years; but the third did not long survive the restraints of its confined situation. An admirably written narrative of these animals, from his own pen, was inserted in the *Gentleman's Magazine* of that day, which has since been published at the end of almost every edition of his works.

Besides the amusement which attention to these animals afforded him, he now devoted much of his time to various mechanical pursuits. In a letter subsequently written to Mrs. King, thanking her for some presents she had been kind enough to make him, he thus amusingly adverts to his employment at this time: "You are perfectly secure from all danger of being overwhelmed with presents from me. There was a time when I amused myself in a way somewhat similar to yours; allowing, I mean, for the difference between masculine and female operations. The scissors and the needle are your chief implements; mine were the chisel and the saw. _{Cowper was a talented carpenter.} In those days, you might have been in some danger of too plentiful a return for your favours. Tables such as they were, and joint-stools such as never were, might have travelled to Pertenhall in most inconvenient abundance. Many arts I have thus exercised, for which nature never designed me, though among them were some in which I arrived at considerable proficiency, by mere dint of the most heroic perseverance. There is not a squire in all the country who can boast of having made better squirrel-houses, hutches for rabbits, or birdcages, than me; and in the article of cabbage-nets I had no superior. I even had the hardihood to take in hand the pencil, and studied a whole year the art of drawing. Many figures were the fruit of my labours, which had at least the merit of being unparalleled by any production either of art or nature.'

In 1774, he was given three young hares, known as leverets, as companion animals by the children of a neighbor who had grown tired of the animals. Although all three were males, Cowper always referred to them as "she." He had written to a friend that he had been seeking something that would 'engage his attention without fatiguing it,' and the hares met that demand perfectly. Cowper immediately set about making them each a house within his home!

Each house had separate sleeping quarters for each of the hares, and had a tray underneath to catch the droppings. Cowper writes that by this means their quarters were kept "sweet and clean."

Puss, Tiney and Bess, as they were named, were as entertaining as any rabbit could be. Bess, unfortunately, died shortly after reaching adulthood. The hares went out to play in the garden (a backyard) with Cowper daily, and he wrote that Puss would tug on his pants leg when he wanted to frolic outside. They danced for him in the evening, and he said that they often brought him out of his depression simply by being there. In the epitaph to Tiney, Cowper wrote,

"A Turkey carpet was his lawn,
whereon he loved to bound,
to skip and gambol like a fawn,
And swing his rump around."

Puss was a "lap rabbit," and Cowper wrote that he often licked his hand and leap into his lap for attention. Tiney had a retractable personality that was well loved anyway, because he made Cowper smile often with his antics. Cowper writes, in *The Task*: "I describe these animals as each having a character of his own. Such they were, in fact, and their countenances were so expressive of that character, that when I looked on the face of either, I immediately knew who it was."

In 1785, Cowper published his first book of poems, called *The Task*. In it, he wrote the touching poem, "The Garden," to his beloved hares, then nearly ten years old. Lines such as this pull on the heartstrings: "For I have pledged all that is human in me to protect thine unsuspecting gratitude and love. If I survive thee, I will dig thy grave; and when I place thee in it, sighing say, I knew at least one hare that had a friend."

Tiney was almost nine years old when he died. Cowper wrote at his death, "Old Tiney, surliest of his kind...was still a wild jack-hare. Though duly from my hand he took his pittance every night, He did it with a jealous look, and when he could, would bite." Cowper's most beloved companion Puss lived to be eleven years and eleven months old.

The Task was well received by the public, including the royal family. Mary Unwin and Cowper moved to Weston Underwood a year later and Cowper's poetry flourished. Although they had been in an on-again, off-again engagement, when Mary died in 1791, Cowper lost both her and his living arrangement. However, King George III gave Cowper a stipend for the remainder of his life.

The story of Cowper's hares and hare keeping continues to captivate people today.

(Sandy Coi, http://www.rabbit.org/journal/4-8/cowper.html)

>Well – one at least is safe. One shelter'd hare
>Has never heard the sanguinary yell
>Of cruel man, exulting in her woes.
>Innocent partner of my peaceful home,
>Whom ten long years' experience of my care
>Has made at last familiar; she has lost
>Much of her vigilant, instinctive dread.
>Not needful here, beneath a roof like mine.
>Yes – thou may'st eat thy bread, and lick the hand
>That feeds thee; thou may'st frolic on the floor
>At evening, and at night retire secure
>To thy straw couch, and slumber unalarm'd.
>For I have gain'd the confidence, have pledg'd
>All that is human in me to protect
>Thine unsuspecting gratitude and love.
>If I survive thee, I will dig thy grave
>And, when I place thee in it, sighing, say,
>I knew at least one hare that had a friend.

William Cowper, from *The Task*, Book III, "The Garden".

In a letter to Mr. Unwin, he facetiously adverts to the same subject. '*Amico mio*, be pleased to buy me a glazier's diamond pencil. I have glazed the two frames designed to receive my pine plants, but I cannot mend the kitchen windows until by the help of that implement I can reduce the glass to its proper dimensions. If I were a plumber, I should be a complete glazier, and possibly the happy time may come when I shall be seen trudging away to the neighbouring towns, with a shelf of glass hanging at my back. If government should impose another tax upon that commodity, I hardly know a business in which a gentleman might more successfully employ himself. A Chinese, often times my fortune, would avail himself of such an opportunity without scruple; and why should not I, who want money as much as any mandarin in China? I would recommend it to you to follow my example. You will presently qualify yourself for the task, and may not only amuse yourself at home, but may even exercise your skill in mending the church windows; which, as it would save money to the parish, would conduce, together with your ministerial accomplishments, to make you extremely popular in the place.'

For a considerable period, Cowper's only companions were Mrs. Unwin, Mr. and Mrs. Newton, and his three hares. About this time, it pleased God to remove Mr. Newton to another scene of labour. Deeply interested in the welfare of his afflicted friend, and aware of his aversion to the visits of strangers, Mr. Newton thought it advisable, before he left Olney, to introduce to his interesting but most afflicted friend, the Rev. Mr. Bull, of Newport Pagnel. After some difficulty, Mr. Newton triumphed over Cowper's extreme reluctance to see strangers, and Mr. Bull visited him regularly once a fortnight, and gradually acquired his cordial and confidential esteem.

Of this gentleman, Cowper, in one of his letters, gives the following playful and amusing description:

'You are not acquainted with the Rev. Mr. Bull, of Newport—perhaps it is as well that you are not. You would regret still more than you do, that there are so many miles interposed between us. He spends part of the day with us to-morrow. A dissenter, but a liberal one; a man of letters and of genius; master of a fine imagination, or rather not master of it; an imagination which, when he finds himself in the company he loves, and can confide in, runs away with him into such fields of speculation, as amuse and enliven every other imagination that has the happiness to be of the party. At other times, he has a tender and delicate sort of melancholy in his disposition, not less agreeable in its way. No men are better qualified for companions in such a world as this, than men of such a temperament. Every scene of life has two sides, a dark and a bright one; and the mind that has an equal mixture of melancholy and vivacity, is best of all qualified for the contemplation of either. He can be lively without levity, and pensive without dejection. Such a man is Mr. Bull; but nothing is perfect—he smokes tobacco,'

In another letter, in reply to one from Mr. Bull, in which he attempted to convince the depressed poet that it was both his duty and his privilege to engage in acts of divine worship, in which Cowper now refused to take any part, we find him writing in a manner that proves the strength of his affection for his new-made companion, at the same time that it displays the depth of his own depression, and the peculiarity of his feelings:

'Mon aimable tres cher ami. My very dear friend. It is not in the power of chariots or horses to carry you where my affections will not follow you. If I heard that you were gone to finish your days in the moon, I should not love you the less. I should contemplate the place of your abode as often as it appeared in the heavens, and say, Farewell, my friend, forever; lost, but not forgotten: live happily in thy lantern, and smoke the remainder of thy pipes in peace, thou art rid of earth at last, and all its cares. So far I can rejoice in thy removal, and as to the cares that are to be found in the moon, I am resolved to suppose them lighter than those below; heavier they can hardly be. Both your advice, and your manner of giving it, are gentle and friendly, and like yourself. I thank you for them, and do not refuse your counsel because I dislike it, but because it is not for me. There is not a man upon earth that might not be the better for it—myself only excepted. Prove to me that I have a right to pray, and I will pray without ceasing; yes, and pray too, even in the belly of this hell, compared with which Jonah's was a palace, a temple of the living God. But let me add, there is no encouragement in the scripture so comprehensive as to include my case, nor any consolation so effectual as to reach it. I do not relate it to you because you could not believe it; you would agree with me if you could; and yet the sin by which I am excluded from the privileges I once enjoyed, you would account no sin. You would even tell me it was my duty. This is strange; you will think me mad—but I am not mad, most noble Festus, I am only in despair; and those powers of mind which I possess are only permitted me for my amusement sometimes, and to accumulate and enhance my misery at others.'

Mr. Bull, who probably regarded the want of some regular employment as one of the predisposing causes of Cowper's malady, prevailed upon him to translate several spiritual songs, from the poetry of Madame de la Mothe Guion, the friend of the mild and amiable Fenelon. The devotion of these songs is not of that purely unexceptionable character which might be wished; and if devotional excitement had been the cause of Cowper's malady, no recommendation could have been more injudicious. The result, however, was beneficial to the poet, instead of being injurious; proving irresistibly, that devotion had a soothing, rather than an irritating, effect upon his mind.

Mrs. Unwin, who still watched over her patient with the tenderest anxiety, saw, with inexpressible delight, the first efforts of his mind, after his long and painful depression: and perceiving that translation had a good effect, she wisely urged him to employ himself in the composition of some original poem, which she thought still more likely to become beneficial. Cowper now listened to her advice, and felt so powerfully the obligations under which he was laid to her, for her continued attention and kindness, that he cheerfully complied with her request. The result exceeded her most sanguine expectations. A beautiful poem was produced, entitled Table Talk; another, called the Progress of Error, was shortly composed; Truth, as a pleasing contrast, followed it; this was succeeded by others of equal excellence, proving that the poet's mind had now completely emerged from that darkness in which it had so long been confined by his depressing malady.

It is interesting to observe, that Cowper's poems were almost invariably composed at the suggestion of his friends. He wrote hymns to oblige Mr. Newton; translated Madam Guion's songs to gratify his friend Mr. Bull, and composed the greater part of his poems to please Mrs. Unwin. The influence of friendship on his tender mind, was powerfully affecting; and he ever regarded it as his happiest inspiration. It kindled the warmth of his heart into a flame, intense and ardent; stimulated into activity the rich but dormant powers of his mind, and produced those bursts of poetic feeling and beauty, which abound in his unrivalled compositions.

Cowper regained his admirable talent for composition, both in poetry and prose, and renewed his correspondence with some of his more intimate friends, long before his mind was wholly convalescent; and his letters, written at this period, afford the best clue to the painful peculiarities of his case. On every subject but that of his own feelings, his remarks were in the highest degree pleasing; and there was often a sprightliness and vivacity about them, which seemed to indicate a state of mind at the remotest distance from painful; but whenever he adverted to his own case, it was in a tone the most plaintive and melancholy.

Immediately after the removal of his esteemed friends, Mr. and Mrs. Newton, he commenced a correspondence with them, which he regularly kept up during almost the whole of his life. To Mrs. Newton, soon after this event, he thus describes his feelings on the occasion:

'The vicarage-house became a melancholy object as soon as Mr. Newton had left it; when you left it, it became more melancholy; now it is actually occupied by another family, I cannot even look at it without being shocked. As I walked in the garden last evening, I saw the smoke issue from the study chimney, and said to myself, 'That used to be a sign that Mr. Newton was there; but it is so no longer. The walls of the house know nothing of the change that has taken place, the bolt of the chamber door sounds just as it used to do, and when Mr. P. goes upstairs, for aught I know, or ever shall know, the fall of his foot can hardly perhaps be distinguished from that of Mr. Newton. Mr. Newton's foot will never be heard upon that staircase again. These reflections and such as these occurred to me on this occasion. If I were in a condition to leave Olney, I certainly would not stay in it. It is no attachment to the place that binds me to it, but rather unfitness for every other. I lived in it once, but now I am buried in it, and have no business with the world on the outside of my sepulchre; my appearance would startle them, and theirs would be shocking to me.'

In a letter to Mr. Newton, 3rd May, 1780, he thus writes, ' You indulge me in such a variety of subjects, and allow me such a latitude of excursion in this scribbling employment, that I have no excuse for silence. I am much obliged to you for swallowing such boluses as I send you, for the sake of my gilding, and verily believe I am the only man alive from whom they would be welcome to a palate like yours. I wish I could make them more splendid than they are, more alluring to the eye at least, if not more pleasing to the taste. But my leaf-gold is tarnished, and has received such a tinge from the vapours that are ever brooding over my mind, that I think it no small proof of your partiality to me, that you will read my letters. I am not fond of longwinded metaphors. I have always observed that they halt at the latter end of their progress, and so does mine. I deal much in ink, indeed, but not such ink as is employed by poets and writers of essays. Mine is a harmless fluid and guilty of no deceptions but such as may prevail without the least injury to the person imposed on. I draw mountains, valleys, woods, and streams, and ducks, and dab chicks. I admire them myself, and Mrs. Unwin admires them; and her praise and my praise put together, are fame enough for me. Oh! I could spend whole days, and moonlight nights, in feeding upon a lovely prospect? My eyes drink the rivers as they flow. If every human being upon earth could think for one quarter of an hour, as I have thought for many years, there might perhaps be many miserable men among them, but not one unawakened one would be found, from the Arctic to the

Antarctic Circle. At present, the difference between them and me, is greatly to their advantage. I delight in baubles, and know them to be so; for rested in, and viewed without a reference to their author, what is the earth, what are the planets, what is the sun itself, but a bauble? Better for a man never to have seen them, or to see them with the eyes of a brute, stupid and unconscious of what he beholds, than not to be able to say, 'The Maker of all these wonders is my friend!' Their eyes have never been opened to see that they are trifles; mine have, and will be, till they are closed for ever.'

In reply to a letter from the same correspondent, which seems to have contained some complaint that the poet had been more liberal in the bestowment of his poetic favours to others, than to him, he writes:

'You may think, perhaps, that I deal more liberally with Mr. Unwin, in the way of poetical export, than I do with you, and I believe you have reason. The truth is this: If I walked the streets with a fiddle under my arm, 1 should never think of performing before the window of a privy-councillor or a chief-justice, but should rather make free with ears more likely to be open to such amusement. The trifles I produce in this way are indeed such trifles, that I cannot think them seasonable presents for you. Mr. Unwin himself would not be offended, if I were to tell him there was this difference between him and Mr. Newton—that the latter is already an apostle, while he himself is only undergoing the process of incubation, with a hope that he may be hatched in due time. When my muse comes forth arrayed in sables, at least in a robe of a graver cast, I make no scruple to direct her to my friend at Hoxton.'

To Mr. Newton he again plaintively discloses his feelings. 'I live in a world abounding with incidents, upon which many grave, and perhaps some profitable observations might be made; but these incidents never reaching my unfortunate ears, both the entertaining narrative, and the reflections it might suggest, are to me annihilated and lost. I look back on the past week, and say, "What did it produce?" I ask the same question of the week preceding, and duly receive the same answer from both, — Nothing! A situation like this, in which I am as unknown to the world, as I am ignorant of all that passes in it, in which I have nothing to do but to think, would exactly suit me, were my subjects of meditation as agreeable as my leisure is uninterrupted. My passion for retirement is not at all abated, after so many years spent in the most sequestered state, but rather increased. Providence, who appoints the bounds of our habitations, chooses for us. Thus, I am both free and a prisoner at the same time. The world is before me. I am not shut up in the Bastille. There are no moats about my castle, no locks upon my gates, of which I have not the keys; but an invisible, uncontrollable agency, a local attachment, an inclination, more forcible than ever I felt, even to the place of my birth, serves me for prison-walls, and for bounds, which I cannot pass. In former years, I have known sorrow, and before I had ever tasted of spiritual trouble. The effect was an abhorrence of the scene in which I had suffered so much, and a weariness of those objects that I had so long looked at with an eye of despondency and dejection. But it is otherwise with me now. The same cause subsisting, and in a much more powerful degree, fails to produce its natural effect. The very stones in the garden walls are my intimate acquaintance. I should miss almost the minutest object, and be disagreeably affected by its removal. I am persuaded, that were it possible I could leave this incommodious nook for a twelvemonth, I should return to it again with raptures, and be transported with the sight of objects, which, to all the world beside, would be at least indifferent; some of them, perhaps, such as the ragged thatch and the tottering walls, disgusting. So it is; and it is so, because here is to be my abode, and because such is the appointment of Him who placed me in it. It is the place of the entire world I love the most, not for any happiness it affords me, but because here I can be miserable with most convenience to myself, and with least disturbance to others. My mind has always a melancholy cast, and is like some pools I have seen, which though filled with a black and putrid water, will nevertheless, on a bright day, reflect the sun-beams from their surface.'

The deep depression of Cowper's mind did not make him insensible to the afflictions of his friends. To his cousin, Mrs. Cowper, who had recently sustained a heavy loss in the death of a beloved and amiable brother, who died in America, he thus pathetically discloses his feelings:

'I do not write to comfort you. That office is not likely to be well performed by one who has no comfort for himself; nor to comply with an impertinent ceremony, which in general might well be spared upon such occasions: but because I would not seem indifferent to the concerns of those I have so much reason to esteem and love. If I did not sorrow for your brother's death, I should expect that nobody would for mine. When I knew him he was much beloved, and I doubt not continued to be so. To live and die together, is the lot of a few happy families; who hardly know what a separation means, and one sepulchre serves them all; but the ashes of our kindred are dispersed indeed. Whether the American gulf has swallowed up any other of my relations 1 know not; it has made many mourners. Believe me, my dear cousin, though after a long silence, which perhaps nothing less than the present concern could have prevailed with me to interrupt, as much as ever, Your affectionate kinsman,— W. C.

In a letter to Mrs. Unwin's son, he thus describes his feelings:

'So long as I am pleased with an employment, I am capable of unwearied application, because my feelings are all of the intense kind. I never received pleasure from anything in my life; if I am delighted, it is in the extreme. The unhappy consequence of this temperature is that my attachment to my occupation seldom outlives the novelty of it. That nerve of my imagination that feels the touch of any particular amusement, twangs under the energy of the pressure with so much vehemence, that it soon becomes sensible of weariness and fatigue.'

Writing to Mr. Newton, 12th July, 1780, he thus again adverts to his own case.

'Such nights as I frequently spend are but a miserable prelude to the succeeding day, and indispose me, above all things, to the business of writing. Yet, with a pen in my band, if I am able to write at all, I find myself gradually relieved; and as I am glad of any employment that may serve to engage my attention, so especially I am pleased with an opportunity of conversing with you, though it be but on paper. This occupation, above all others, assists me in that self-deception, to which I am indebted for all the little comfort I enjoy; things seem to be as they were, and I almost forget that they can never be so again. If I have strength of mind, I have not strength of body for the task that you say some would impose upon me. I cannot bear much thinking. The meshes of that fine network, the brain, are composed of such mere spinner's threads in me, that when a long thought finds its way into them, it buzzes, and twangs, and bustles about at such a rate, as seems to threaten the whole contexture.

'I thank you for your offer of Robertson, but I have now more reading upon my hands than I shall get rid of in a twelvemonth; and this moment I recollect I have read him before; he is an author that I admire much, with one exception—that I think his style is too laboured-. Hume, as an historian, pleases me more. I have read just enough of the Biographia Britannica, to say, that I have no doubt I shall like it. I am pretty much in the garden at this season of the year, so read but little. In summer time, I am as giddy-headed as a boy. Winter condenses me, and makes me lumpish and sober; and then I can read all day long.'

To the same correspondent he writes on another occasion:

'Your sentiments, with respect to me, are exactly like Mrs. Unwin's. She, like you, is perfectly sure of my deliverance, and often tells me so; I make her but one answer, and sometimes none at all. That answer gives her no pleasure, and would give you as little; therefore, at this time I suppress it. It is better on every account that they who interest themselves so deeply in that event, should believe the certainty of it, than that they should not. It is a comfort to them at least, if it be none to me, and as I could not, if I would, so neither would I, if I could, deprive them of it. If human nature may be compared to a piece of tapestry, (and why not?) then human nature, as it subsists in me, though it is sadly faded on the right side, retains its entire colour on the wrong. At this season of the year, and in this gloomy and uncomfortable climate, it is no easy matter for the owner of a mind like mine, to divert it from sad subjects, and fix it upon such as may administer to its amusement. Poetry, above all things, is useful to me in this respect. While I am held in pursuit of pretty images, or a pretty way of expressing them, I forget everything that is irksome, and, like a boy that plays truant, determine to avail myself of the present opportunity to be amused, regardless of future consequences. It will not be long, perhaps, before you will receive a poem called the Progress of Error; that will be succeeded by another, in due time, called Truth. Do not be alarmed; I ride Pagasus with a curb. He will never run away with me again. I have even convinced Mrs. Unwin that I can manage him, and make him stop when I please.'

On another occasion, he gives the following curious and playful description of himself. 'I can compare this mind of mine to nothing that resembles it more, than to a board that is under the carpenter's plane: (I mean while I am writing to you) the shavings are my uppermost thoughts; after a few strokes of the tool, it acquires a new surface; this again, upon a repetition of his task, he takes off, and a new surface still succeeds. Whether the shavings of the present day will be worth your acceptance, I know not; I am, unfortunately, made neither of cedar nor of mahogany, but *truncus ficulnus, inutile lignum*; tree stump, a useless piece of wood consequently, though I should be planed till I am as thin as a wafer, it will be but rubbish at last.'

To his cousin, Mrs. Cowper, he thus plaintively describes his feelings:

'You will see me sixteen years older than when I saw you last; but the effects of time seem to have taken place rather on the outside of my head than within it. What was brown is become grey, but what was foolish remains foolish still. Green fruit must rot before it ripens, if the season is such as to afford it nothing but cold winds and dark clouds that interrupt every ray of sunshine. My days steal away silently, and march on, (as poor mad Lear would have made his soldiers march) as if they were shod with felt; not so silently but that I hear them, yet were it not that I am always listening to their flight, having no infirmity that I had not when I was much younger, I should deceive myself with an imagination that I am still young. I am fond of writing, as an amusement, but do not always find it one. Being rather scantily furnished with subjects that are good for anything, and corresponding only with those who have no relish for such as are good for nothing, I often find myself reduced to the necessity, the disagreeable necessity, of writing about myself. This does not mend the matter much; for though, in a description of my own condition, I discover abundant materials to employ my pen upon, yet as the task is not very agreeable to me, so, I am sufficiently aware, that it is likely to prove irksome to others. A painter who should confine himself, in the exercise of his art, to the drawing of his own picture, must be a wonderful coxcomb indeed, if he did not soon grow sick of his occupation, and be peculiarly fortunate if he did not make others as sick as himself.'

It must not be imagined that Cowper wrote invariably to his correspondents in a melancholy or mournful strain; some of his letters, even at this time, contain admirable criticism, conveyed always in a style the most elegant and sprightly. The following remarks on letter writing, in which he so much excelled, will be read with no ordinary interest, especially as they were so happily illustrated in his own practice. 'You like to hear from me: this is a good reason why I should write. I have nothing to say—this seems equally a good reason why I should not. Yet if you had alighted from your horse at our door this morning, and at the time I am now writing to you, five o'clock in the afternoon, had found occasion to say to me, ' Mr. Cowper, you have not spoken since I came in, have you resolved never to speak again?'—it would be but a poor reply if in answer I were to plead my inability, as my best and only excuse. And this, by the way, suggests to me a seasonable piece of instruction, and reminds me of what I am very apt to forget, when I have any epistolary business in hand, that a letter may be written upon anything or nothing, just as that anything or nothing happens to occur. A man that has a journey before him twenty miles in length, which he is to perform on foot, will not hesitate and doubt whether he shall set out or not, because he does not readily conceive how he is to reach the end of it, for he knows that by the simple operation of moving one foot forward first, and then the other, he shall be sure to accomplish it. So it is in the present case, and so it is in every similar case. A letter is written as a conversation is maintained or a journey is performed; not preconcerted, or by premeditated means, a new contrivance, or an invention never heard of before; hut merely by maintaining a progress, and resolving, as a postilion does, having once set out, never to stop till we reach the appointed end. If a man may talk without thinking, why may he not write upon the same terms?' Notwithstanding Cowper's depressing malady, yet his views of religion, even at that period, remained unaltered, and were as much distinguished for their excellence as ever. Writing to his friend Mr. Unwin, the following judicious remarks occur, on the observance of the Sabbath:

'With respect to the advice you are required to give to a young lady, that she may be properly instructed in the manner of keeping the Sabbath, I just subjoin a few hints that have occurred to me on the occasion. I think the Sabbath may be considered, first, as a commandment, no less binding upon Christians than upon Jews. The spiritual people among them did not think it enough merely to abstain from manual occupations on that day, but entering more deeply into the meaning of the precept, allotted those hours they took from the world, to the cultivation of holiness in their own souls; which ever was, and ever will be, incumbent upon all who have the scriptures in their hands, and is of perpetual obligation, both upon Jews and Christians. The commandment enjoins it, and the prophets have enforced it; and, in many instances, the breach of it has been punished with a providential severity which has made bystanders tremble. Secondly, it may be considered as a privilege, which you will know how to dilate upon better than I can; thirdly, as a sign of that covenant by which believers are entitled to a rest that yet remaineth; fourthly, as the *sine qua non* of the Christian character, and, upon this head, I should guard against being misunderstood to mean no more than two attendances upon public worship, which is a form observed by thousands who never kept a Sabbath in their lives. Consistency is necessary to give substance and solidity to the whole. To sanctify the day at church, and to trifle it away out of church, is profanation, and vitiates all. After all, 1 should say to my catechumen, Do you love the day, or do you not? If you love it, you will never inquire how far you may safely deprive yourself of the enjoyment of it. If you do not love it, and you find yourself in conscience obliged to acknowledge it, that is an alarming symptom, and ought to make you tremble. If you do not love it, then it is a weariness to you, and you wish it over. The two ideas of labour and of rest are not more opposite to each other than the idea of a Sabbath, and that dislike and disgust with which it fills the souls of thousands; and which is worse than bodily labour.'

To his cousin, Mrs. Cowper, he again writes:

'It costs me not much difficulty to suppose that my friends who were already grown old, when I saw them last, are old still; but it costs me a good deal sometimes to think of those, who were at that time young, as being older than they were. Not having been an eye-witness of the change that time has made in them, and my former idea not being corrected by observation, it remains the same; my memory presents me with this image unimpaired, and while it retains the resemblance of what they were, forgets that by this time the picture may have lost much of its likeness, through the alteration that succeeding years have made in the original. I know not what impressions time may have made upon your person, for while his claws, strike deep furrows in some faces, he seems to sheath them with much tenderness, as if fearful of doing injury, to others. But, though an enemy to the body, he is a friend to the mind, and you have doubtless found him so. Though, even in this respect, his treatment of us depends upon what he meets with at our hands; if we use him well, and listen to his admonitions, he is a friend indeed; but otherwise, the worst of enemies, who takes from us daily something that we valued, and gives us nothing better in its stead. It is well with them, who like you, can stand a tip-toe on the mountain-top of human life, look down with pleasure upon the valley they have passed, and sometimes stretch their wings in joyful hope of a happy flight into eternity. Yet a little while, and your hope will be accomplished. The course of a rapid river is the justest of all emblems, to express the variableness of our scene below. Shakespeare says, none ever bathed himself twice in the same stream; and it is equally true, that the world upon which we close our eyes at night, is never the same as that upon which we open them in the morning.'

CHAPTER VIII. Makes preparation for publishing his first volume—Reasons assigned for it—Beneficial effects of composition on his mind—His comparative indifference to the success of his volume—Great care, nevertheless, with which he composed it—His readiness to avail himself of the assistance and advice of his friends— The interest which Mr. Newton took in his publication — Writes the preface for the volume—Cowper's judicious reply to some objections that had been made to it — Publication of the volume—Manner in which it was received—Continuance of Cowper's depression—State of his mind respecting religion—Ardent desires to make his volume the means of usefulness to others.

More than seven years had now elapsed since the commencement of Cowper's distressing malady; and though he was not yet perfectly recovered, he had, at length, gradually acquired the full exercise of those mental powers for which he was so highly distinguished. Having now employed his muse, with the happiest effect, for nearly two years, he had composed a sufficient number of lines to form a good-sized volume. Mrs. Unwin had witnessed with delight the productions of his pen, and she now wisely urged him to make them public. He was, at first, exceedingly averse to the measure; but, after some consideration, he at length yielded to her suggestions, and prepared to appear as an author. His letters to his correspondents on the subject are highly interesting; and afford a full development of the design he had in view in appearing before the public.

To Mr. Unwin he thus writes:

'Your mother says I must write, and must admits of no apology; I might otherwise plead that I have nothing to say, that I am weary, that I am dull, that it would be more convenient for you, as well as for myself, that I should let it alone. But all these pleas, and whatever pleas besides, either disinclination, indolence, or necessity might suggest, are overruled, as they ought to be, the moment a lady adduces her irrefragable argument, you must. Urged by her entreaties, I have at length sent a volume to the press; the greater part of which is the produce of the last winter. Two-thirds of the volume will be occupied by four pieces. It contains, in all, about two thousand five hundred lines: and will be known, in due time, by the names of *Table Talk, The Progress of Error, Truth, Expostulation*, with an addition of some smaller poems, all of which, I believe, have passed under your notice. Altogether they will furnish a volume of tolerable bulk, which need not be indebted to an intolerable breadth of margin, for the importance of its figure.'

In this undertaking he was encouraged by his friend, Mr. Newton, with whom he corresponded on the subject, and to whom he thus discloses his mind: —' If a board of inquiry were to be established, at which poets were to undergo an examination respecting the motives that induced them to publish, and I were to be summoned to attend, that I might give an account of mine, I think I could truly say, what perhaps few poets could, that though I have no objection to lucrative consequences, if any such should follow, they are not my aim; much less is it my ambition to exhibit myself to the world as a genius. 'What then,' says Mr. President, 'can possibly be your motive?' I answer, with a bow,'

Amusement.' There is no occupation within the compass of my small sphere, poetry excepted, that can do much towards diverting that train of melancholy forebodings, which, when I am not thus employed, are forever pouring themselves in upon me. If I did not publish what I write, I could not interest myself sufficiently in my own success to make an amusement of it. My own amusement, however, is not my sole motive. I am merry that I may decoy people into my company, and grave that they may be the better for it. Now and then, I put on the garb of a philosopher, and take the opportunity that disguise procures me, to drop a word in favour of religion. In short, there is some froth, and here and there a bit of sweet-meat, which seems to entitle it justly to the name of a certain dish the ladies call 'a trifle.' I did not choose to be more facetious, lest I should consult the taste of my readers at the expense of my own approbation; nor more serious than I have been, lest I should forfeit theirs. A poet in my circumstances has a difficult part to act; one minute obliged to bridle his humour, if he has any, the next, to clap a spur to the sides of it. Now ready to weep, from a sense of the importance of his subject, and on a sudden constrained to laugh, lest his gravity should be mistaken for dullness.'

Writing to his amiable correspondent Mrs. Cowper, 19th October, 1781, he says:

'I am preparing a volume of poems for the press, which I imagine will make its appearance in the course of the winter. It is a bold undertaking at this time of day, when so many writers of the greatest abilities have gone before, who seem to have anticipated every valuable subject, as well as all the graces of poetical embellishment, to step forth into the world in the character of a bard; especially when it is considered that luxury, idleness, and vice, have debauched the public taste, and that scarcely anything but childish fiction, or what has a tendency to excite a laugh, is welcome. I thought, however, that I had stumbled upon some subjects that had never been poetically treated, and upon some others, to which I imagined it would not be difficult to give an air of novelty, by the manner of treating them. My sole drift is to be useful: a point at which, however, I knew I should in vain aim, unless I could be likewise entertaining. I have therefore fixed these two strings to my bow; and by the help of both, have done my best, to send my arrow to the mark. My readers will hardly have begun to laugh, before they will be called upon to correct that levity, and peruse me with a more serious air. I cast a sidelong glance at the good liking of the world at large, more for the sake of their advantage and instruction than their praise. They are children; if we give them physic, we must sweeten the rim of the cup with honey. As to the effect, I leave that in his hands, who alone can produce it; neither prose, nor verse, can reform the manners of a dissolute age, much less can they inspire a sense of religious obligation, unless assisted and made efficacious by the power who superintends the truth he has vouchsafed to impart.'

To his warm friend Mr. Hill, he thus amusingly adverts to his publication:

'I am in the press, and it is in vain to deny it. My labours are principally the production of the last winter; all, indeed, except a few of the minor pieces. When I can find no other occupation, I think, and when I think, I am very apt to do it in rhyme. Hence, it happens that the season of the year, which generally pinches off the flowers of poetry, unfolds mine, such as they are, and crowns me with a winter garland. In this respect, therefore, my contemporary bards and I are by no means upon a par. They write when the delightful influences of fine weather, fine prospects, and a brisk motion of the animal spirits, make poetry almost the language of nature; and I, when icicles depend from all the leaves of the Parnassian laurel, and when a reasonable man would as little expect to succeed in verse, as to hear a blackbird whistle. This must be my apology to you for whatever want of fire and animation you may observe in what you will shortly have the perusal of. As to the public, if they like me not, there is no remedy. A friend will weigh and consider all disadvantages, and make as large allowances as an author can wish, and larger, perhaps, than he has any right to expect, but not so the world at large; whatever they do not like, they will not, by an apology, be persuaded to forgive; it would be in vain to tell them that I wrote my verses in January, for they would immediately reply, Why did you not write them in May? A question that might puzzle a wiser head than we poets are generally blessed with.'

To Mr. Unwin, on the same subject, he writes thus playfully:

'If a writer's friend has need of patience, how much more the writer? Your desire to see my muse in public, and mine to gratify you, must both suffer the mortification of delay. I expected that my trumpeter would have informed the world by this time of all that is needful for them to know upon such an occasion; and that an advertising blast, blown through every newspaper, would have said, 'The Poet is coming;' but man, especially man that writes verse, is born to disappointments, as surely as printers and booksellers are born to be the most dilatory and tedious of all creatures. The plain English of this magnificent preamble is, that the season of publication is just elapsed; that the town is going into the country every day, and that my book cannot appear till they return, that is to say, not till next winter. This misfortune, however, comes not without its attendant advantages. I shall now have, what I should not otherwise have had, an opportunity to correct the press myself; no small advantage upon any occasion, but especially important where poetry is concerned. A single erratum may knock out the brains of a whole passage, and that perhaps; which of all others, the unfortunate poet is the most proud of. Add to this, that now and then there is to be found in the printing-house a presumptuous intermeddler, who will fancy himself a poet too, and what is still worse, a better than he that employs him. The consequence is, that with cobbling and tinkering, and patching on here and there a shade of his own, he makes such a difference between the original and the copy, that an author cannot know his own work again. Now as I choose to be responsible for nobody's dullness but my own, I am a little comforted when I reflect that it will be in my power to prevent all such impertinence.'

It might have been supposed, that the vigorous exercise of the mental powers, which the composition of poetry, like, that of Cowper's, required, would have increased his oppressive malady, instead of diminishing it. His, however, was a peculiar case, and he found the employment of great advantage, as we learn in a letter to Mr. Newton, where he says:

'I have never found an amusement, among the many I have been obliged to have recourse to, that so well answered the purpose for which I used it, as composition. The quieting and composing effect of it was such, and so totally absorbed have I sometimes been in my rhyming occupation, that neither the past, nor the future, (those themes that to me are so fruitful in regret at other times) had any longer a share in my contemplation. For this reason I wish, and have often wished since the fit left me, that it would seize me again, but hitherto I have wished it in vain. I see no want of subjects, but I feel a total disability to discuss them. Whether it is thus with other writers or not, I am ignorant, but I should suppose my case, in this respect, a little peculiar. The voluminous writers at least, whose vein of fancy seems always to have been rich in proportion to their occasions, cannot have been so unlike, and so unequal to themselves. There is this difference between my poetship and the generality of them; they appear to have been ignorant how much they stood indebted to an Almighty power for the exercise of those talents they supposed to be their own. Whereas I know, and know most perfectly, that my power to think, whatever it be, and consequently my power to compose, is, as much as my outward form, afforded to me by the same hand that makes me, in any respect, to differ from a brute.'

The commencement of authorship is generally a period of much painful anxiety; few persons have ventured on such an undertaking without experiencing considerable excitement; and in a mind like Cowper's, it might have been supposed that such would have been the case in a remarkable degree. No person, however, ever ventured before the public in the character of an author, with less anxiety. Writing to Mr. Unwin, he says:

'You ask me how I feel on the occasion of my approaching publication? Perfectly at ease. If I had not been well assured beforehand that my tranquillity would be but little endangered by such a measure, I would never have engaged in it, for I cannot bear disturbance. I have had in view two principal objects; first, to amuse myself, and then to compass that point in such a manner, that others might possibly be the better for my amusement. If I have succeeded, it will give me pleasure; but if I have failed, I shall not be mortified to the degree that might perhaps be expected. The critics cannot deprive me of the pleasure I have in reflecting, that so far as my leisure has been employed in writing for he public, it has been employed conscientiously, and with a view to their advantage. There is nothing agreeable, to be sure, in being chronicled for a dunce; but I believe there lives not a man upon earth who would be less affected by it than me.'

Indifferent as he was to the result of his publications, he was far from being careless in their composition. Perhaps no author ever took more pains with his productions, or sought more carefully to make them worthy of public approbation. In one of his letters, adverting to this subject, he says, 'To touch, and retouch, is, though some writers boast of negligence, and others would be ashamed to show their foul copies, the secret of almost all good writing, especially in verse. I am never weary of it myself, and if you would take as much pains as I do, you would not need to ask for my corrections. With the greatest indifference to fame, which you know me too well to suppose me capable of affecting, I have taken the utmost pains to deserve it. This may appear a mystery, or a paradox, in practice, but it is true. I considered that the taste of the day is refined and delicate to excess. To disgust that delicacy of the taste by a slovenly inattention to it, would be to forfeit at once all hope of being useful; and for this reason, though I have written more verse this year than any man in England, I have finished, and polished, and touched and retouched, with the utmost care. Whatever faults I may be chargeable with as a poet, I cannot accuse myself of negligence; I never suffer a line to pass till I have made it as good as I can; and though some may be offended at my doctrines, I trust none will be disgusted by slovenly inaccuracy in the numbers, the rhymes, or the language. If, after all, I should be converted into waste paper, it may be my misfortune, but it will not be my fault; and I shall bear it with perfect serenity.'

In the character of Cowper there was nothing like an overweening confidence in his own powers. No person was ever more willing to avail himself of the advice of his friends, nor did anyone ever receive advice more gratefully. Not satisfied with bestowing upon his productions the greatest pains himself, he occasionally submitted them to the correction of others, and his correspondence affords many proofs of his readiness to profit by the slightest hint. To Mr. Newton he thus writes:

'I am much obliged to you for the pains you have taken with my poems, and for the manner in which you have interested yourself in their appearance. Your favourable opinion affords me a comfortable presage with respect to that of the public; for though I make allowance for your partiality to me, yet I am sure you would not suffer me, unadmonished, to add myself to the number of insipid rhymers with whose productions the world is already too much pestered. I forgot to mention, that Johnson uses the discretion my poetship has allowed him, with much discernment. He has suggested several alterations, or rather marked several defective passages, which I have corrected; much to the advantage of the poems. In the last sheet he sent me, he noticed three such, which I reduced to better order. In the foregoing sheet I assented to his criticisms in some instances, and chose to abide by the original expression in others; whenever he has marked such lines as did not please him, I have, as often as I could, paid all possible respect to his animadversions. *Animadversions* is the third of John Milton's antiprelatical tracts, in the form of a response to the works and claims of Bishop Joseph Hall. The tract was published in July 1641. Thus we jog on together comfortably enough; and perhaps it would be as well for authors in general, if their booksellers, when men of some taste, were allowed though not to tinker the work themselves, yet to point out the flaws, and humbly to recommend an improvement. I have also to thank you, and ought to have done it in the first place, for having recommended to me the suppression of some lines, which I am now more than ever convinced would at least have done me no honour.'

Adverting to the same subject, to his esteemed friend Mr. Unwin, who appears to have had some delicacy about forwarding a letter he had written, containing some criticisms on the poet's productions, he writes:

'The letter you withheld so long, lest it should give me pain, gave me pleasure. Horace says the poets are a waspish race; and from my own experience of the temper of two or three, with whom I was formerly connected, I can readily subscribe to the character he gives them. For my own part, I have never yet felt that excessive irritability which some writers discover, when a friend, to use the words of Pope, 'Just hints a fault, or hesitates dislike.'

Least of all, would I give way to such an unreasonable ebullition, merely because a civil question is proposed to me with such gentleness, and by a man whose concern for my credit and character I verily believe to be sincere. I reply, therefore, not peevishly, but with a sense of the kindness of your intentions, that I hope you may make yourself very easy on a subject which I can perceive has occasioned you some solicitude.'

The great interest Mr. Newton took in Cowper's publication, induced the poet to request him to compose the preface; and his correspondence with Mr. Newton on the subject is alike honourable to his judgment and his feelings; and affords a striking display of the strong hold which religion had upon his affections. He thus introduces the subject to Mr. Newton, 'With respect to the poem called *Truth*, it is so true that it can hardly fail of giving offence to an unenlightened reader. I admit that it will require much delicacy, but am far from apprehending that you will find it difficult to succeed. You can draw a hair-stroke where another man would make a blot as broad as a sixpence.'

The preface composed by Mr. Newton, though it was in the highest degree satisfactory to Cowper, and was admitted by him to be everything that he could wish, was nevertheless thought by others to be of too sombre a cast to introduce a volume of poems, pre-eminently distinguished for their vivacity and eloquence. Adverting to this objection, and to the suggestion of the publisher to suppress it, Cowper thus writes:

'If the men of the world are so merrily disposed, in the midst of a thousand calamities, that they will not deign to read a preface of three or four pages because the purport of it is serious, they are far gone, indeed, in the last stage of a frenzy. I am, however, willing to hope that such is not the case; curiosity is an universal passion. Few persons think a book worth reading, but feel a desire to know something about the writer of it. This desire will naturally lead them to peep into the preface, where they will soon find that a little perseverance will furnish them with some information on the subject. If, therefore, your preface finds no readers, I shall take it for granted that it is because the book itself is accounted not worth their notice. It is quite sufficient that I have played the antic myself for their diversion ; and that, in a state of dejection such as they are absolute strangers to, I have sometimes put on an air of cheerfulness and vivacity, to which I myself am in reality a stranger, for the sake of winning their attention to more useful matter. I cannot endure the thought, for a moment, that you should descend to my level on the occasion, and court their favour in a style suitable to your function, than to the constant and consistent strain of your whole character and conduct. Though your preface is of a serious cast, it is free from all offensive peculiarities, and contains none of those obnoxious doctrines at which the world is too apt to be angry. It asserts nothing more than every rational creature must admit to be true—that divine and earthly things can no longer stand in competition with each other in the judgment of any man, than while he continues ignorant of their respective value; and that the moment the eyes are opened, the latter are always cheerfully relinquished for the former. It is impossible for me, however, to be so insensible to your kindness in writing the preface, as not to be desirous of defying all contingencies, rather than entertain a wish to suppress it. It will do me honour, indeed, in the eyes of those whose good opinion is worth having, and if it hurts me in the estimation of others, I cannot help it; the fault is neither yours nor mine, but theirs. If a minister's is a more splendid character than a poet's, and I think nobody that understands their value can hesitate in deciding that question, then, undoubtedly, the advantage of having our names united in the same volume, is all on my side.'

Mr. Newton's Preface, much as it may be undervalued by those who dislike the truth, will ever be esteemed by the enlightened Christian, as a production of unusual excellence, every way worthy of his pen, and written with the elegance of a scholar and the piety of a saint. This devoted and useful Christian minister undertook, no doubt, to perform this service for his afflicted friend, with the greatest pleasure. He had seen him living in the full enjoyment of that peace which passeth all understanding, and had himself spent many months of delightful communion and Christian fellowship with the poet, while he was thus walking in the love of God, and living in the light of his countenance. He had afterwards seen him plunged into the lowest depths of despair, and had, at length, after years of painful apprehension and suspense, seen him gradually emerge out of the cloud, so far at least, as to be enabled to produce some of the most striking descriptions of true piety that are any where to be found; and now that the pen of his long-afflicted friend had been so successfully employed, he could not but feel highly gratified at the opportunity afforded him of introducing these productions to the world. It was an act of the purest friendship, undertaken from motives of the most sincere regard.

Cowper's first volume was published in the spring of 1782. Its success, at first, fell far short of what might have been anticipated from its extraordinary merit. It was not long, however, before the more intelligent part of the reading public appreciated its value. It soon found its way into the hands of all lovers of literature. Abounding with some of the finest passages that are to be met with, either in ancient or modern poetry, it was impossible that it should remain long unnoticed. By mere readers of taste, it was read for the beauty and elegance of its composition; by others, it was eagerly sought after for the sprightliness, vivacity, and wit with which it abounded ;—while by Christians of all denominations it was read with unfeigned pleasure, for the striking and beautiful descriptions it contained, of Christianity, both as assented to by the judgment, and as enthroned in the heart.

It would scarcely be supposed that the author of a volume of poems like this, exhibiting such a diversity of powers as could not fail to charm the mind, delight the imagination, and improve the heart, could have remained, during the whole time he was composing it, in a state of great and painful depression. Such however was the peculiarity of Cowper's malady, that a train of melancholy thoughts seemed ever to be pouring themselves upon his mind, for which neither himself nor his friends were ever able satisfactorily to account. Writing to his friend Mr. Newton, who had recently paid him a visit, he thus discloses the state of his mind:

'My sensations at your departure were far from pleasant. When we shall meet again, and in what circumstances, or whether we shall meet or not, is an article to be found nowhere but in that providence which belongs to the current year, and will not be understood till it is accomplished. This I know, that your visit was most agreeable to me, who, though I live in the midst of many agreeables, am but little sensible of their charms. But when you came, I determined, as much as possible, to be deaf to the suggestions of despair; that if I could contribute but little to the pleasure of the opportunity, I might not dash it with unseasonable melancholy, and like an instrument with a broken string, interrupt the harmony of the conceit.'

It is gratifying to observe, that neither the attention, which Cowper paid to his publication, nor the depressive malady with which he was afflicted, could divert his attention from the all-important concerns of religion. A tone of deep seriousness and genuine Christian feeling pervades many of his letters written about this time. To Mr. Newton he thus writes:

'You wish you could employ your time to better purpose, yet are never idle, in all that you do: whether you are alone, or pay visits, or receive them: whether you think, or write, or walk, or sit still, the state of your mind is such as discovers even to yourself, in spite of all its wanderings, that there is a principle at the bottom, whose determined tendency is towards the best things. I do not at all doubt the truth of what you say, when you complain of that crowd of trifling thoughts that pesters you without ceasing; but then you always have a serious thought standing at the door of your imagination, like a justice of the peace, with the *Riot Act* in his hand, ready to read it and disperse the mob. Here lies the difference between you and me. "You wish for more attention, I for less. Dissipation itself would be welcome to me, so it were not a vicious one; but however earnestly invited, it is coy and keeps at a distance. Yet with all this distressing gloom upon my mind, I experience, as you do, the slipperiness of the present hour, and the rapidity with which time escapes me. Everything around us, and everything that befalls us, constitute a variety, which, whether agreeable or otherwise, has still a thievish propensity; and steals from us days, months, and years, with such unparalleled suddenness, that even while we say they are here, they are gone. From infancy to manhood is rather a tedious period; chiefly, I suppose, because at that time we act under the control of others, and are not suffered to have a will of our own. But thence downward into the vale of years, is such a declivity, that we have just an opportunity to reflect upon the steepness of it and then find ourselves at the bottom.'

The accuracy of Cowper's views respecting the opinion which the Christian should form of the present life, and the degree of importance he should attach to its blessings, were not in the least degree affected by his malady, as will be seen by the following critical remarks, made on a work that he had about that time been reading. 'When a person tells us, in order to depreciate earthly riches, that gold and diamonds are only matter modified in a particular way, and thence concludes them not more valuable in themselves than the dust under our feet, his assertion is false, and his cause is hurt by the assertion. It is that very modification that gives them both a beauty and a value; a value and a beauty recognised in Scripture, and by the universal consent of all well-informed and civilized nations. It is in vain to tell men that gold and dirt are equal, so long as their experience convinces them to the contrary. It is necessary, therefore, to distinguish between the thing itself and the abuse of it. Wealth is in fact a blessing, when honestly acquired and conscientiously employed: and when otherwise, the man is to be blamed and not his treasure. How does the Scripture combat the vice of covetousness? Not by asserting that gold is only earth, exhibiting itself to us under a particular modification, and therefore not worth seeking: but by telling us that covetousness is idolatry—that the love of money is the root of all evil—that it has occasioned in some even the shipwreck of their faith—and is always, in whomsoever it obtains, an abomination.

'When, speaking of sumptuous edifices, a writer calls a palace an assemblage of sticks and stones, which a puff of wind may demolish, or a spark of fire consume; and thinks he has thus reduced a magnificent building and a cottage to the same level, so that the latter, viewed through an optic glass, may be made to appear as large as the former, and the former, by inverting the glass, reduced to the pitiful dimensions of the latter, has he indeed carried his point? is he not rather imposing on the judgment of his readers, just as the glass would impose on their senses? How is it possible to deduce a substantial argument in this case, from an acknowledged deception of the sight? The objects continue what they were, the palace is still a palace, and the cottage is not at all ennobled in reality, though we contemplate them ever so long through an elusive medium. There is in fact a real difference between them, and such an one as the Scripture itself takes very emphatical notice of; assuring us that in the last day much shall be required of him, to whom much is given; that every man shall be then considered as a steward, and render a strict account of the things with which he was intrusted. This consideration, indeed, may make the dwellers in palaces tremble, who, living for the most part in the continued abuse of their talents, squandering, and wasting, and spending upon themselves their Master's treasure, will have reason enough to envy the cottager, whose accounts will be more easily settled. To tell mankind, that a palace and a hovel are the same thing, is to affront their senses, to contradict their knowledge, and to disgust their understandings.

'Herein seems to consist one of the principal differences between philosophy and Scripture, or the wisdom of men and the wisdom of God; the former endeavours, indeed, to convince the judgment, but is frequently obliged to have recourse to unlawful means, such as misrepresentation and the play of fancy; the latter addresses itself to the judgment likewise, but it carries its point by awakening the conscience, by enlightening the understanding, and by appealing to our experience. As philosophy, therefore, cannot make a Christian, so a Christian ought to take care that be be not too much a philosopher. It is mere folly, instead of wisdom, to forego those arguments, and to shut our eyes upon those motives which truth itself has pointed out to us.'

The following extracts from his correspondence with Mr. Unwin, who at that time, was on a visit at Brighton, will show the degree of piety which constantly pervaded his mind: ' I think with you, that the most magnificent object under heaven is the great deep; and cannot but feel an non polite species of astonishment, when I consider the multitudes that view it without emotion, and even without reflection. In all its varied forms, it is an object, of all others, the most suitable to affect us with lasting impressions of the awful power that created and controls it. I am the less inclined to think this negligence excusable, because, at a time of life when I gave as little attention to religion as any man, I yet remember that the waves would preach to me, and that in the midst of worldly dissipation I had an ear to hear them. In the fashionable amusements which you will probably witness for a time, you will discern no signs of sobriety, or true wisdom. But it is impossible for a man who has a mind like yours, capable of reflection, to observe the manners of a multitude without learning something. If he sees nothing to imitate, he is sure to see something to avoid. If nothing to congratulate his fellow-creatures upon, at least much to excite his compassion. There is not, I think, so melancholy a sight in the world, (an hospital is not to be compared to it), as that of a multitude of persons, distinguished by the name of gentry, who, gentle perhaps by nature, and made more gentle by education, have the appearance of being innocent and inoffensive, yet being destitute of all religion, or not at all governed by the religion they profess, are none of them at any great distance from an eternal state, where self-deception will be impossible, and where amusements cannot enter. Some of them we may hope will be reclaimed, it is most probable that many will, because mercy, if one may be allowed the expression, is fond of distinguishing itself by seeking its objects among the most desperate class; but the Scripture gives no encouragement to the warmest charity to expect deliverance for them all. When I see an afflicted and unhappy man, I say to myself, there is perhaps a man, whom the world would envy, if they knew the value of his sorrows, which are possibly intended only to soften his heart, and to turn his affections towards their proper centre. But when I see or hear of a crowd of voluptuaries, who have no ears but for music, no eyes but for splendour, and no tongues but for impertinence and folly—I say, or at least I see occasion to say, this is madness—this, persisted in, must have a tragical conclusion. It will condemn you, not only as Christians, unworthy of the name, but as intelligent creatures—you know by the light of nature, if you have not quenched it, that there is a God, and that a life like yours cannot be according to his will. I ask no pardon of you for the gravity and gloominess of these reflections, which, with others of a similar complexion, are sure to occur to me when I think of a scene of public diversion like that you have witnessed.'

To the same correspondent, who was still at Brighton, he writes:

'What a world are you daily conversant with, which I have not seen these twenty years, and shall never see again! The arts of dissipation, I suppose, are nowhere practised with more refinement and success than at the place of your present residence. By your account of it, it seems to be just what it was when I visited it—a scene of idleness and luxury. Though my life has long been that of a recluse, I have not the temper of one, nor am I in the least an enemy to cheerfulness and good humour; but I cannot envy you your situation; I even feel myself constrained to prefer the silence of this nook, and the snug fireside in our own diminutive parlour, to all the splendour and gaiety of Brighton.'

Writing to his cousin, who was called to sustain another painful bereavement in the loss of a very highly esteemed friend, Cowper remarks:

'You made my heart ache with a sympathetic sorrow, when you described the state of your mind on occasion of your late loss. Had I been previously informed of it, I should have been able to have foretold all your feelings with the most unerring certainty of prediction. You will never cease to feel upon that subject; but with your principles of resignation and acquiescence in the divine will, you will always feel as becomes a Christian. We are forbidden to murmur, but we are not forbidden to regret; and whom we loved tenderly while living, we may still pursue with an' affectionate remembrance, without having any occasion to charge ourselves with rebellion against the sovereignty that appointed a separation. A day is coming, when, I am confident, you will see and know, that mercy to both parties was the principal agent in a scene, the recollection of which is still painful.'

The following remarks, extracted from a letter to Mr. Unwin, while they serve to display the state of his mind respecting religion, exhibit at the same time, the high value that he set upon the leading truths of the gospel:

'When I wrote the poem on 'Truth,' it was indispensably necessary that I should set forth that doctrine which I know to be true; and that I should pass what I considered to be a just censure, upon opinions and persuasions that stand in direct opposition to it; because, though some errors may be innocent, and even religious errors are not always dangerous, yet in a case where the faith and hope of a Christian are concerned, they must necessarily be destructive; and because, neglecting this, I should have betrayed my subject; either suppressing what in my judgment is of the last importance, or giving countenance by a timid silence, to the very evils it was my design to combat. That you may understand me better, I will add, that I wrote that poem on purpose to inculcate the eleemosynary character of the gospel, as a dispensation of mercy, in the most absolute sense of the word, to the exclusion of all claims of merit on the part of the receiver; consequently to set the brand of invalidity upon the plea of works, and to discover, upon scriptural ground, the absurdity of that notion which includes a solecism in the very terms of it, that man by repentance and good works may deserve the mercy of his Maker. I call it a solecism, because mercy deserved ceases to be mercy, and must take the name of justice. This is the opinion which I said, in my last, the world would not acquiesce in; but except this, I do not recollect that I have introduced a syllable into any of my pieces that they can possibly object to; and even this I have endeavoured to deliver from doctrinal dryness, by as many pretty things in the way of trinket and plaything, as I could muster upon the subject. So that if I have rubbed their gums, I have taken care to do it with a coral, and even that coral embellished by the ribbon to which it is attached, and recommended by the tinkling of the bells which I contrived to annex to it.'

The following beautiful lines convey sentiments so much in unison with this extract, that we cannot forbear to insert them at the close of this chapter:

'I am no preacher; let this hint suffice,
The cross once seen is death to every vice;
Else he that hung there suffered all his pain,
Bled, groaned, and agonized, and died in vain.
There, and there only, (though the deist rave,
And atheist, if earth bear so base a slave,)
There, and there only, is the power to save;
There no delusive hope invites despair,
No mockery meets you, no deception there;
The spells and charms that blinded you before,
All vanish there, and fascinate no more.'
—*Progress of Error.*

CHAPTER IX. Commencement of Cowper's acquaintance with Lady Austen—Poetic epistle to her ladyship—Beneficial influence of her conversational powers on Cowper's mind—Occasion of his writing John Gilpin—Lines composed at Lady Austen's request—Induced by her to commence writing The Task—Principal object he had in view in composing it—Sudden and final separation from Lady Austen—Occasional severity of his depressive malady—Hopes entertained by his friends of his ultimate recovery—His own opinion of it—Pleasing proofs of the power of religion on his mind—Tenderness of his conscience—Aversion to religious deception and pretended piety—Sympathy with the sufferings of the poor—Enviable condition of such of them as are pious, compared with the rich who disregard religion.

> ANNOTATION: Women apparently were quite attracted to Cowper. When he was not in a depressive state, he was an entertaining companion. He was witty, congenial, but perhaps most important to the ladies was his attentiveness to them. Some might interpret his concentration as flirtations. His charm lay in his knack of paying detailed attention to people. His many letters to both men and women, affirm this. — *Editor.*

Cowper with Mrs. Unwin and Lady Austen.

In the autumn of 1781, Cowper became acquainted with Lady Austen, whose brilliant wit and unrivalled conversational powers were admirably adapted to afford relief to a mind like his. This lady was introduced to the retired poet by her sister, the wife of a clergyman who resided at Clifton, a mile distant from Olney, and who occasionally called upon Mrs. Unwin. Lady Austen came to pass some time with her sister, in the summer of 1781, and Mrs. Unwin, at Cowper's request, invited the ladies to tea.

ANNOTATION: It has been recounted that Cowper saw Lady Austen in the street from his Olney window, thought she was very pretty, and had Mrs. Unwin invite to tea so he could meet her properly.

So much, however, was he averse to the company of strangers, that after he had occasioned the invitation, it was with considerable reluctance he was persuaded to join the party. Having at length overcome his feelings, he entered freely into conversation with Lady Austen, and derived so much benefit from her sprightly and animating discourse, that he from that time cultivated her acquaintance with the greatest interest.

The opinion Cowper formed of this accomplished and talented lady, may be ascertained by the following extracts from his letters:

'Lady Austen has paid us her first visit, and not content with showing us that proof of her respect, made handsome apologies for her intrusion. She is a lively, agreeable woman; has seen much of the world, and accounts it a great simpleton, as it is. She laughs, and makes laugh, without seeming to labour at it. She has many features in her character, which you must admire, but one in particular, because of the rarity of it, will engage your attention and esteem. She has a degree of gratitude in her composition, so quick a sense of obligation, as is hardly to be found in any rank of life. Discover but a wish to please her, and she never forgets it; not only thanks you, but the tears will start into her eyes at the recollection of the smallest service. With these fine feelings she has the most harmless vivacity you can imagine: half an hour's conversation with her will convince you that she is one of the most intelligent, pious, and agreeable ladies you ever met with.'

Lady Austen was delighted with her new acquaintance than Cowper and Mrs. Unwin were with her. She had previously determined to leave London, and had been looking out for a residence in the country, not far distant from her sister's. The house immediately adjoining that in which Cowper resided was at liberty; she accordingly hired it, and took possession of it in the course of the ensuing summer. Cowper thus adverts to this circumstance, in a letter to Mr. Newton:

'A new scene is opening upon us, which, whether it perform what it promises, or not, will add fresh plumes to the wings of time, at least while it continues to be a subject of contemplation. Lady Austen, very desirous of retirement, especially of a retirement near her sister, an admirer of Mr. Scott, as a preacher, and of your two humble servants, Mrs. Unwin, and myself is come to a determination to settle here; and has chosen the house formerly occupied by you, for her future residence. I am highly pleased with the plan, upon Mrs. Unwin's account, who, since Mrs. Newton's departure, has been nearly destitute of female connection, and has not, in any emergency, a woman to speak to. It has, in my view, and I doubt not it will have the same in yours, strong marks of a providential interposition. A female friend, who bids fair to prove herself worthy of the appellation, comes, recommended by a variety of considerations, to such a place as Olney. Since your removal, there was not in the kingdom a retirement more absolutely such than ours. We did not covet company, but when it came we found it agreeable. A person that understands the world well and has high spirits, a lively fancy, and great readiness of conversation, introduces a sprightliness into such a scene as this, which, if it was peaceful before, is not the worse for being a little enlivened. In case of illness too, to which we are all liable, it was rather a gloomy prospect, if we allowed ourselves to advert to it, that there was hardly a woman in the place from whom it would have been reasonable to have expected either comfort or assistance.'

    Both Cowper and Mrs. Unwin were so charmed with her society, and she was so delighted with theirs, that it became their custom to dine together at each other's houses every alternate day. The effect of Lady Austen's almost irresistible conversational powers proved highly beneficial to the poet's mind, and contributed greatly to remove that painful depression of which he still continued to be the subject; and which would sometimes seize him so violently, even when he was in her company. With all her unrivalled talents, she was scarcely able to remove the deep and melancholy gloom that still shed its darkening influence over his mind. On one occasion, when she observed him to be sinking into rather an unusual depression, she exerted, as she was invariably accustomed to do, her utmost ability to afford him immediate relief. It occurred to her that she might then probably accomplish it by telling him a story of John Gilpin, which she had treasured up in her memory from her childhood. The amusing incidents of the story itself, and the happy manner in which it was related, had the desired effect. It dissipated the gloom of the passing hour, and he informed Lady Austen the next morning, that convulsions of laughter, brought on by the recollection of her story, had kept him awake during the greater part of the night, and that he had composed a poem on the subject. Hence arose the fascinating and amusing ballad of John Gilpin, which rapidly found its way into all the periodical publications of the day, and was admired by readers of every description.

An illustrated book presenting the poem may be found at
https://www.mirrorservice.org/sites/gutenberg/2/3/7/5/23753/23753-h/23753-h.htm

Its happy influence on his own mind on subsequent occasions is adverted to in the following letter to Mr. Unwin:

'You tell me that John Gilpin made you laugh tears, and that the ladies at court are delighted with my poems. Much good may they do them; may they become as wise as the writer wishes them, and they will then be much happier than he! I know there is, in the greater part of the poems, which make up the volume, that wisdom which cometh from above, because it was from above that I received it. May they receive it too; for whether they drink it out of the cistern, or whether it falls upon them immediately from the clouds, as it did on me, it is all one. It is the water of life, which whosoever drinketh shall thirst no more. As to the famous horseman above mentioned, he and his feats are an inexhaustible 'source of amusement. At least we find them so; and seldom meet without refreshing ourselves with the recollection of them. You are perfectly at liberty to do with them as you please, and when printed send me a copy.'

The following anecdote respecting the first perusal of this facetious ballad by Cowper's friends in London, will shew the irresistible power over the risible faculties, which the poet here contrived to exert. A lady now living (1833), was one of a party at the house of the Rev. John Newton, in London. After tea, Mr. Thornton took a written paper from his pocket, and, looking round the company, said, 'Here is something I received this morning from Mr. Cowper.' He then addressed the Rev. H. Foster, saying, 'Mr. F., I think you are the gravest amongst us, and I will get you to read this paper, as you are the most likely to do so without laughing. 'Mr. F. took the paper, and began to read the 'Adventures of John Gilpin.' The whole party was soon convulsed with laughter, but the reader proceeded until Gilpin arrived at Edmonton, when he could no longer refrain from joining in the merriment around him.

He managed to proceed, but with some difficulty. *John Gilpin* has been read to many a party since that time, but it probably never has been read to any that were more amused by it than this circle of Mr. Newton, who were much pleased to find the mental powers of Cowper thus rising above the gloom, which oppressed him.

Lady Austen's association with Mrs. Unwin and Cowper continued, without interruption, till near the close of 1784; and during all this time, by her sprightly, judicious, and captivating conversation, she was often the means of rousing him from his depression. To console him, she would frequently exert her musical talents on the harpsichord; and at her request, he composed, among others, the following beautiful song, suited to an air she was accustomed to play:

'No longer I follow a sound;
No longer a dream I pursue;
O, happiness! not to be found,
Unattainable treasure, adieu.

I have sought thee in splendour and dress,
In the regions of pleasure and taste;
I have sought thee, and seemed to possess,
But have proved thee a vision at last.

An humble ambition and hope
The voice of true wisdom inspires;
'Tis sufficient, if peace be the scope
And the summit of all our desires.

Peace may be the lot of the mind
That seeks it in meekness and love;
But rapture and bliss are confined
To the glorified spirits above!

During the winter of 1783-4, Cowper spent the evenings in reading to these ladies, taking the liberty himself, and affording the same to them, of making occasional remarks on what came under their notice. On these interesting occasions, Lady Austen displayed her enchanting and almost magical powers with singular effect. The conversation happened one evening to turn on blank verse, of which she had always expressed herself to be passionately fond. Persuaded that Cowper was able to produce, in this measure, a poem that would eclipse anything he had hitherto written, she urged him to try his powers in that species of composition. He had hitherto written only in rhyme, and he felt considerable reluctance to make the attempt. After repeated solicitations, however, he promised her, if she would furnish the subject, he would comply with her request. 'Oh!' she replied, 'you can never be in want of a subject, you can write upon anything—write upon this sofa.'

The poet obeyed her command, and the world is thus indebted to this lady for *The Task*, a poem of matchless beauty and excellence. It embraces almost every variety of style and every description of subject, combining elegance and ease with sublimity and grandeur, adapted to impress the heart with sentiments of the most exalted piety, and to make its readers happy in the present life, while it excites in them earnest and longing desires after the felicity and glory of heaven.

In composing this exquisite poem, however, it ought to be observed that Cowper had a higher object in view than merely to please Lady Austen. His great aim was to be useful; and, indeed, this was his leading motive in all his productions, as is evident from the following extract from a letter to Mr. Unwin:

'In some passages of the enclosed poem, which I send for your inspection, you will observe me very satirical, especially in my second book. Writing on such subjects, I could not be otherwise. I can write nothing without aiming at least at usefulness. It were beneath my years to do it, and still more dishonourable to my religion. I know that a reformation of such abuses as I have censured, is not to be expected from the efforts of a poet; but to contemplate the world, its follies, its vices, its indifference to duty, and its strenuous attachment to what is evil, and not to reprehend it, were to approve it. From this charge, at least, I shall be clear, for I have neither tacitly nor expressly flattered either its characters or its customs. My principal purpose has been to allure the reader by character, by scenery, by imagery, and other poetical embellishments, to the reading of what may profit him. Subordinately to this, to combat that predilection in favour of a metropolis that beggars and exhausts the country, by evacuating it of all its principal inhabitants; and collaterally, and as far as is consistent with this double intention, to have a stroke at vice, vanity, and folly, wherever I find them. What there is of a religious cast in the volume, I have thrown towards the end of it, for two reasons; first, that I might not revolt the reader at his entrance; and, secondly, that my best impressions might be made last.

The close of the year 1784 witnessed the completion of this extensive performance, and the commencement of another of greater magnitude, though of a different description, and less adapted for general usefulness,—the translation of Homer; undertaken less from choice than necessity, being almost driven to it by a desire to escape from his melancholy forebodings. This was a remarkable period in Cowper's life.

> ANNOTATION: The following lines, part of a poetical epistle addressed by Cowper to Lady Austen, will show how much he was delighted with his new friend:
>
> 'Dear Anna,—between friend and friend
> Prose answers every common end;
> Serves in a plain and homely way,
> To express the occurrence of the day;
> Our health, the weather, and the news;
> What walks we take, what books we choose;
> And all the floating thoughts we find
> Upon the surface of the mind:

> But when the poet takes the pen,
> Far more alive than other men,
> He feels a gentle tingling come
> Down to his fingers and his thumb,
> Deriv'd from nature's noblest part,
> The centre of a glowing heart!

ANNOTATION: [Almost any lady would assume that if a man tingled in her presence, he must be in love with her, or at least have passionate feelings.] Furthermore, Lady Austen was encouraged by these lines that Cowper wrote about her wearing his hair in a brooch piece of jewellery.

It would appear that Lady Austen excited in Cowper feelings of passion. In short, William seems to have given Lady Austen romantic encouragement, but then would change his mind. Obviously, she would have married him. Why was he so vacillating? Why was he reluctant to commit to marriage?

There is the theory that he was still too much in love with Theodora. Some postulate that he was an effeminate man, or asexual. However, good sources indicate that this is not true. By his own admission in his younger days he would comment approvingly on any shapely and attractive woman he chanced to meet on the street. He wrote of himself:

> "He eyed the women, and made free
>   To comment on their shapes;
> So that there was, or seem'd to be,
>   No fear of a relapse."

Writing to his friend, John Newton in 1783, he says, "It [Olney] is the place of all the world I love the most, not for any happiness if affords me, but because here I can be miserable with most convenience to myself and with the least disturbance to others."

This would give us illumination on his reluctance to marry. He knew of his mental problems. He feared a protracted return. He felt he might become a burden and did not wish to impose this burden on someone with whom he was *in love*.

Lady Austen apparently "gave up" on any hope of marrying Cowper and left Olney. — *Editor*.

He had been so greatly benefitted by Lady Austen's company when suffering under the influence of his depressing malady, and had received such repeated proofs of her affability and kindness, that he could not entertain the thought of separation without considerable disquietude. Immediately, however, on perceiving that this step became requisite for the maintenance of his own peace, as well as to ensure the tranquillity of his faithful and long-tried friend, Mrs. Unwin, he wisely and unhesitatingly adopted such measures as were necessary, though it was at the expense of considerable anxiety and mental suffering.

Some of Cowper's biographers have unjustly and without the slightest foundation, attempted to cast considerable odium upon the character of Mrs. Unwin, for her conduct in this affair, as if all the blame of Cowper's separation from Lady Austen were to be laid at her door. One has even gone so far as to state, that her mind was of such a sombre hue, that it rather tended to foster than to dissipate Cowper's melancholy. An assertion utterly incapable of proof, and which, were the poet living, he would be the first to deny. The fact is, that Cowper never felt any other attachment to Lady Austen than that of pure friendship, though he usually addressed her by the affectionate appellation of' Dear Sister;' and much as he valued her society, when it became necessary for his own peace, to decide whose personal attentions he would choose to retain, he could not hesitate for a moment to prefer the individual who had watched over him with so much tenderness, probably to the injury of her own health; and to whom he would, long before then, have been united by the tenderest ties, had the state of his health permitted it. The whole of his conduct in this affair, and indeed the manner in which he has everywhere spoken of his faithful inmate, proves this indubitably.

Aware of the influence which she had obtained over the poet, and unacquainted with the matrimonial engagement existing between him and Mrs. Unwin, there is nothing surprising that Lady Austen should have wished to carry her point still further, until she had completely gained the affections of an individual to whom any woman must have felt it an honour to be united.

Had she known that a pledge of union had been given by Cowper to Mrs. Unwin, much as she might perhaps have regretted it, her conduct in the whole affair would undoubtedly have differed in many respects, while her society would not have been less beneficial to the poet, and might perhaps have been enjoyed by him much longer. It is a little surprising, and excites much regret, that neither Cowper nor Mrs. Unwin, after Lady Austen's intimacy with them had become so close, did not convey to her, by some delicate allusion, the truth of this secret pledge. It most certainly would have spared subsequent painful feeling.

Many of Cowper's friends now became apprehensive that the removal of Lady Austen would be attended with consequences seriously injurious to the poet. Deep, however, as was the impression, which it made upon his mind, he bore it with much more fortitude than could have been expected, as will be seen by the manner in which he adverted to it in a letter to Mr. Hill:

'We have, as you say, lost a lively and sensible neighbour in Lady Austen, but we have been so long accustomed to a state of retirement, within one degree of solitude, and being naturally lovers of still life, we can relapse into our former duality without being unhappy in the change. To me, indeed, a third individual is not necessary, while I can have the faithful companion I have had these twenty years.' They parted to meet no more. Lady Austen was subsequently married to a Mons. de Tardif, a French gentleman of poetical talents, and died at Paris on the 19th of August 1802, somewhat more than two years after Cowper.

It might be imagined, from the production of Cowper's pen at this period, that he was entirely recovered from his depressing malady, but such was far from the case. His letters to his correspondents prove that whatever gaiety and vivacity there was in his writings, there was nothing in his own state of mind that bore any resemblance to such emotions; but that, on the contrary, his fits of melancholy were frequent, and often painfully acute. To his friend, Mr. Newton, he thus feelingly discloses his peculiarly painful sensations:

My heart resembles not the heart of a Christian, mourning and yet rejoicing; pierced with thorns, yet wreathed about with roses: I have the thorn without the rose. My brier is a wintry one; the flowers are withered, but the thorn remains. My days are spent in vanity, and it is impossible for me to spend them otherwise. No man upon earth is more sensible of the unprofitableness of such a life as mine than I am, or groans more heavily under the burden; but this too is vanity; my groans will not bring me the remedy, because there is no remedy for me.'

To many individuals, not labouring under any mental alienation, dreams have often proved a source of the greatest distress. It is said that Bloomfield used to complain of the unutterable horror of his dreams, reiterated night after night, from which he awoke more exhausted than when he retired to rest; and the dread of which would sometimes pursue him through the day. So it was with Cowper: hence he writes:

'I have been lately more dejected and more distressed than usual; more harassed by dreams in the night, and more deeply poisoned by them in the following day. I know not what is portended by an alteration for the worse after eleven years of misery; but firmly believe that it is not designed as the introduction of a change for the better. You know not what I have suffered while you were here, nor was there any need you should. Your friendship for me would have made you in some degree a partaker of my woes, and your share in them would have been increased by your inability to help me. Perhaps, indeed, they took a keener edge, from the consideration of your presence. The friend of my heart, the person with whom I had formerly taken sweet counsel, no longer useful to me as a minister, no longer pleasant to me as a Christian, was a spectacle that must necessarily add the bitterness of mortification to the sadness of despair. I now see a long winter before me, and am to get through it as I can; I know the ground before I tread upon it. It is hollow; it is agitated; it suffers shocks in every direction; it is like the soil of Calabria—all whirlpool and undulation; but I must reel through it, at least if I be not swallowed up by the way.'

At the commencement of 1784, looking back on what he had already suffered, and foreboding a continuance of his distress, he thus pours forth the anguish of his mind:

'I have taken leave of the old year, and parted with it just when you did, but with very different sentiments and feelings upon the occasion. I looked back upon all the passages and occurrences of it as a traveller looks back upon a wilderness, through which he has passed with weariness and sorrow of heart, reaping no other fruit of his labour than the poor consolation, that, dreary as the desert was, he left it all behind him. The traveller would find even this comfort considerably lessened, if, as soon as he passed one wilderness, he had to traverse another of equal length, and equally desolate. In this particular, his experience and mine would exactly tally. I should rejoice indeed that the old year is over and gone, if I had not every reason to expect a new one similar to it. Even the new year is already old in my account. I am not, indeed, sufficiently second-sighted, to be able to boast, by anticipation, an acquaintance with the events of it yet unborn, but rest assured that, be they what they may, not one of them comes a messenger of good to me. If even death itself should be of the number, he is no friend of mine; it is an alleviation of the woes, even of an unenlightened man, that he can wish for death, and indulge a hope, at least, that in death he shall find deliverance. But, loaded as my life is with despair, I have no such comfort as would result from a probability of better things to come, were it once ended. I am far more unhappy than the traveller I have just referred to; since, pass through whatever difficulties, dangers, or afflictions I may, I am not a whit nearer home, unless a dungeon be called so. This is no very agreeable theme, but in so great a dearth of subjects to write upon, and especially impressed as I am at this moment with a sense of my own condition, I could choose no other.'

The melancholy ingenuity with which he would sometimes baffle the arguments of his friends, who attempted to inspire him with hope of better days, and the facility with which he could convert an ordinary incident into an illustration of his own case, and deduce from it an argument against his recovery, will be seen in the following extract:— 'The weather is an exact emblem of my mind in its present state. A thick fog envelopes every thing, and at the same time it freezes intensely. You will tell me, that this cold gloom will be succeeded by a cheerful spring, and endeavour to encourage me to hope for a spiritual change resembling it, but it will be lost labour. Nature revives again; but a soul once slain lives no more. The hedge that has been apparently dead is not so; it will burst into leaf, and blossom at the appointed time, but no such revival is appointed for the stake that stands in it. It is as dead as it seems, and will prove itself no dissembler. The latter end of next month will complete a period of eleven years, in which I have spoken no other language. It is a long time for a man, whose eyes were once opened, to spend in darkness; long enough to make despair an inveterate habit; and such it is in me. My friends, I know, expect that I shall yet enjoy health again. They think it necessary to the existence of divine truth, that he who once had possession of it should never finally lose it. I admit the solidity of this reasoning in every case but my own : And why not in my own? For causes which to them it appears madness to allege, but which rest upon my mind, with a weight of immoveable conviction.'

The depth of Cowper's depression led him to suppose that his life was useless; and though he had written a volume of poems eminently calculated to promote the best interests of mankind, yet such were the humbling views he had of himself, that he remarks:

If I am recoverable, why am I thus? Why crippled, and made useless in the church, just at the time of life when my judgment and experience, being matured, I might be more useful? Why cashiered, and turned out of service, till, according to the course of years, there is not life enough left in me to make amends for the years I have lost;—till there is no reasonable hope left that the fruit can ever pay the expense of the fallow? I forestall the answer—God's ways are mysterious, and he giveth no account of his matters—an answer that would serve my purpose as well as theirs that use it. There is a mystery in my destruction, and in time it will be explained.'

In reply to a letter from Mr. Newton, in which, with a view to encourage Cowper with the hope of a speedy deliverance, he had mentioned the case of an individual who had recently recovered from severe and protracted mental hallucination, after suffering great distress,—Cowper, with all the dexterity of the acutest disputant, remarks:

'I could easily, were it not a subject that would make us melancholy, point out to you some essential difference between the state of the person you mentioned and my own, which would prove mine to be by far the most deplorable of the two. I suppose no man would despair if he did not apprehend something singular in the circumstances of his own story; something that discriminates it from that of every other man, and that induces despair as an inevitable consequence. You may encounter his unhappy persuasion with as many instances as you please, of persons who, like him, having renounced all hope, were yet restored, and may thence infer that he, like them, shall meet with a season of restoration—but it is in vain. Every such individual accounts himself an exception to all rules, and, therefore, the blessed reverse that others have experienced, affords no ground of comfortable expectation to him. But you will say, it is reasonable to conclude that as all your predecessors in this vale of misery and horror have found themselves delightfully disappointed, so may you. I grant the reasonableness of it; it would be sinful, perhaps, as well as uncharitable to reason otherwise; but an argument hypothetical in its nature, however rationally conducted, may lead to a false conclusion; and in this instance so will yours. But I forbear, and will say no more, though it is a subject on which I could write more than the mail could carry. I must deal with you as I deal with poor Mrs. Unwin, in all our disputes about it;—cutting all controversy short by the event.'

To a request from Mr. Newton that Cowper would favour the editor of the *Theological Magazine* with an occasional essay, he thus writes:

'I converse, you say, upon other subjects than that of despair, and may therefore write upon others. Indeed, my friend, I am a man of very little conversation upon any subject. From that of despair, I abstain as much as possible, for the sake of my company, but I will venture to say that it is never out of my mind one minute in the whole day. I do not mean to say that I am never cheerful. I am often so; always, indeed, when my nights have been undisturbed for a season. But the effect of such continual listening to the language of a heart hopeless and deserted, is, that I can never give much more than half my attention to what is started by others, and very rarely start anything myself. You will easily perceive that a mind thus occupied, is but indifferently qualified for the consideration of theological matters. The most useful, and the most delightful topics of that kind, are to me forbidden fruit: I tremble as I approach them. It has happened to me sometimes that I have found myself imperceptibly drawn in and made a party in such discourse. The consequence has been dissatisfaction and self-reproach. You will tell me, perhaps, that I have written upon those subjects in verse, and may therefore in prose. But there is a difference. The search after poetical expression, the rhymes and the numbers, are all affairs of some difficulty, they amuse indeed, but are not to be attained without study, and engross, perhaps, a larger share of the attention than the subject itself.'

In the spring of 1785, his friends became more sanguine in their expectations of his ultimate recovery, and they felt persuaded, that it would take place at no very distant period. It appears also, by the following extract, that Cowper was not himself wholly destitute of hope, on the subject. Writing to Mr. Newton, he says:

'I am sensible of the tenderness and affectionate kindness with which you recollect our past intercourse, and express your hopes of my future restoration. I too, within the last eight months, have had my hopes, though they have been of short duration,—cut off, like the foam upon the waters. Some previous adjustments, indeed, are necessary before a lasting expectation of comfort can take place in me. There are two persuasions in my mind, which either entirely forbid the entrance of hope, or, if it enter, immediately eject it. They are incompatible with any such inmate, and must be turned out themselves before so desirable a guest can possibly have secure possession. This you say will be done. It may be; but it is not done yet; nor has a single step in the course of God's dealings with me been taken towards it. If I mend, no creature ever mended so slowly, that recovered at last. I am like a slug, or a snail, that has fallen into a deep well; slug as he is, he performs his descent with a velocity proportioned to his weight; but he does not crawl up again quite so fast. Mine was a rapid plunge; but my return to daylight, if I am indeed returning, is leisurely enough.'

One symptom of Cowper's case, was an impression that so complete a transformation had taken place in his character, since he had been attacked, as to make him utterly unworthy the notice of his friends. Hence, he writes:

'Were I such as I once was, I should say that I have a claim upon your particular notice, which nothing ought to supersede. Most of your other connections you may fairly be said to have formed by your own act; but your connection with me was the work of God. The kine that went up with the ark from Bethshemesh, left what they loved behind them, in obedience to an impression, which to them was perfectly dark and unintelligible. Your journey to Huntingdon was not less wonderful. He, indeed, who sent you, knew well wherefore, but you knew not. That dispensation, therefore, would furnish me as long as we can both remember it, with a plea for some distinction at your hands, had I occasion to use and urge it, which I have not. But I am altered since that time; and if your affection for me had ceased, you might very reasonably justify your change by mine. I can say nothing for myself at present; but this I can venture to foretell, that should the restoration, of which my friends assure me, ever take place, I shall undoubtedly love those who have continued to love me, even in a state of transformation from my former self, much more than ever.'

It is gratifying to know, that, while such was the melancholy state of Cowper's mind, and while he steadily refused all religious comfort, come whence it might, he nevertheless afforded the most pleasing proofs, by his amiable and consistent conduct, of the firm hold which religion still had of his affections. The excellent remarks that are to be found in his letters, written at this period, show that he had some lucid intervals, and that occasional gleams of light shot across the darkened horizon of his mind.

'It strikes me,' (he says on one occasion), 'as a very observable instance of providential kindness to man, that such an exact accordance has been contrived between his ear and the sounds with which, at least in a rural situation, it is almost every moment visited. All the world is sensible of the uncomfortable effect that certain sounds have upon the nerves, and consequently upon the spirits; and if a sinful world had been filled with such as would have curdled the blood, and have made the sense of hearing a perpetual inconvenience, I do not know that we should have a right to complain. But now the fields, the woods, and the gardens, have each their concerts, and the ear of man is forever regaled by creatures, who, while they please themselves, at the same time delight him. Even the ears that are deaf to the gospel, are continually entertained, though without appreciating it, by sounds, for which they are solely indebted to its Author. There is somewhere in infinite space, a world that does not roll within the precincts of mercy, and as it is reasonable, and even scriptural to suppose, that there is music in heaven, in these dismal regions perhaps the reverse of it is found; tones so dismal, as to make woe itself more insupportable, and even to acuminate despair.'

In a letter to Mr. Newton, the following serious reflections occur:

'People that are but little acquainted with the terrors of divine wrath, are not much afraid of trifling with their Maker. But for my own part, I would sooner take Empedocles' leap, _{Empedocles was born in Acragas, Sicily around 492 B.C. He believed he was a divine being exiled by the gods. He finally jumped into the crater at Mt. Aetna, a symbolic descent into the underworld, a prelude his celestial ascent.} and fling myself into Mount Aetna, than I would do it in the slightest instance, were I in circumstances to make an election. In the scripture, we find abroad and clear exhibition of mercy; it is displayed in every page. Wrath is in comparison but slightly touched upon, because the gospel is not so much a discovery of wrath as of forgiveness. But had the displeasure of God been the principal subject of the book, and had it circumstantially set forth that measure of it only which may be endured in this life, the Christian world would, perhaps, have been less comfortable; but I believe presumptuous meddlers with the gospel would have been less frequently met with.'

To Mr. Unwin he writes:

'Take my word for it (the word of a man singularly qualified to give his evidence in this matter, who having enjoyed the privilege some years, has been deprived of it more, and has no hope that he shall live to recover it)— those that have found a God, and are permitted to worship him, have found a treasure of which, highly as they may prize it, they have but very scanty and limited conceptions. These are my Sunday morning speculations—the sound of the bells suggested them, or rather gave them such an emphasis, that they forced their way into my pen in spite of me; for though I do not often commit them to paper, they are never absent from my mind.'

There is, perhaps, no criterion by which we can so correctly estimate the degree of true piety an individual may possess, as by the warmth of his attachment to his Saviour: where there is little or no love to Him, there can be but little or no religion. Aware of this, Cowper writes, 'You express sorrow, that your love of Christ was excited in you by a picture. Could the most insignificant thing suggest to me the thought that Christ is precious, I would not despise the thought. The meanness of the instrument cannot debase the nobleness of the principle. He that kneels to a picture of Christ is an idolater; but he in whose heart the sight of such a picture kindles a warm remembrance of the Saviour's suffering, must be a Christian. Suppose that I dream as Gardiner did, that Christ walks before me, that he turns and smiles upon me, and fills my soul with ineffable love and joy. Will a man tell me that I am deceived, that I ought not to love or rejoice in him for such a reason, because a dream is merely a picture drawn upon the imagination? I hold not with such divinity. To love Christ is the greatest dignity of man, be that affection wrought-in him how it may.'

No person ever formed more correct views of what really constitutes Christianity than Cowper; nor could anyone ever feel a greater aversion to a mere profession of it. In a letter to one of his correspondents, the following remarks occur:

'I say amen, with all my heart, to your observations on religious characters. Men who profess themselves adepts in mathematical knowledge, in astronomy, or jurisprudence, are generally as well qualified as they would appear. The reason may be, that they are always liable to detection should they attempt to impose upon mankind and therefore take care to be what they pretend. In religion alone, a profession is often slightly taken up, and slovenly carried on, because, forsooth, candour and charity require us to hope the best, and to judge favourably of our neighbour; and because it is easy to deceive the ignorant, who are a great majority, upon this subject. Let a man attach himself to a particular party, contend furiously for what are properly called evangelical doctrines, and enlist himself under the banner of some popular preacher, and the business is done. Behold a Christian! a saint! a phoenix! In the meantime perhaps his heart, his temper, and even his conduct, is unsanctified: possibly less exemplary than that of some avowed infidels. No matter, he can talk, he has the Bible in his pocket, and a head well stored with notions. But the quiet, humble, modest, and peaceful person, who is in his practice what the other is only in his profession, who hates a noise about religion, and therefore makes none, who knowing the snares that are in the world, keeps himself as much out of it as he can, and never enters it but when duty calls, and even then with fear and trembling,—this is the Christian that will always stand highest in the estimation of those who bring all characters to the test of true wisdom, and judge of the tree by its fruits.'

In another letter, he depicts with glowing colours, and deplores most deeply, the evils that have arisen from the unhappy spirit of discord and strife, which has too often rent asunder the Christian church. 'It is indeed a melancholy consideration, that the gospel, whose direct tendency is to promote the happiness of mankind, in the present as well as in the life to come, and which so effectually answers the design of its author, whenever it is well understood and sincerely believed, should, through the ignorance, the bigotry, the superstition of its professors, and the ambition of popes and princes, have produced incidentally so much mischief; only furnishing the world with a plausible pretext to worry each other, while they sanctified the worst cause with the specious pretext of zeal for the furtherance of the best. Angels descend from heaven to publish peace between man and his Maker—the Prince of Peace himself comes to confirm and establish it: and war, hatred, and desolation are the consequence. Thousands quarrel about the interpretation of a book, which none of them understand. He that is slain dies firmly persuaded that the crown of martyrdom awaits him; he that slew him, is equally convinced that he has done God service. In reality, they are both mistaken, and equally unentitled to the honour they have arrogated to themselves. If a multitude of blind men should set out for a certain city, and dispute about the right road till a battle ensued between them, the probable effect would be, that none of them would ever reach it; and such a fray, preposterous and shocking in the extreme, would exhibit a picture in some degree resembling the original of which we have been speaking. And why is not the world thus occupied at present? Only because they have exchanged a zeal that was no better than madness for an indifference equally pitiable and absurd.'

In the same letter he reprehends, with great severity, that unhappy spirit of indifference to the leading and prominent truths of Christianity, which has superseded the intolerance of past ages, and which, under the imposing but often delusive appellation of philosophy, deprives religion of all its interest and value; remarking with great propriety, that the preservation of the Christian faith from the attacks of its enemies and the perfidy of its friends, can hardly be regarded as otherwise than miraculous.

'The holy sepulchre has lost its importance in the eyes of nations called Christian, not because the light of true wisdom has delivered them from a superstitious attachment to the spot, but because he that was buried in it is no longer regarded by them as the Saviour of the world. The exercise of reason, enlightened by philosophy, has cured them indeed of the misery of an abused understanding, but together with the delusion they have lost the substance, and for the sake of the lies that were grafted upon it, have quarrelled with the truth itself. Here then we see the ne plus ultra of human wisdom, at least in affairs of religion. It enlightens the mind with respect to non-essentials, but with respect to that in which the essence of Christianity consists, leaves it perfectly in the dark. It can discover many errors which in different ages have disgraced the faith, but it is only to make way for one more fatal than them all, which represents that faith as a delusion. Why those evils have been permitted will be known hereafter. One thing, in the meantime, is certain, that the folly and frenzy of the professed disciples of the gospel have been more dangerous to its interests, than all the avowed hostilities of its adversaries, and perhaps for this cause these mischiefs might be suffered to prevail for a season, that its divine original and nature might be the more illustrated, when it should appear that it was able to stand its ground for ages, against that most formidable of all dangers—the indiscretion of its friends. The outrages that have followed this perversion of the truth have proved, indeed, a stumbling-block to individuals; the wise of this world, with all their wisdom, have not been able to distinguish between the blessing and the abuse of it. Voltaire was offended, and Gibbon has turned his back, but the flock of Christ is still nourished, and still increases, notwithstanding the unbelief of a philosopher is able to convert bread into a stone, and fish into a serpent.'

The following very serious reflections occur in a letter to Mr. Newton about this time, adverting to the sufferings of the poor at Olney, whose distressing circumstances on all occasions excited the tenderest sympathies of the poet:

'The winter sets in with great severity. The rigour of the season, and the advanced price of provisions, are very threatening to the poor. It is well with those that can feed upon a promise, and wrap themselves up warm in the robe of salvation. A good fire-side and a well-spread table are but indifferent substitutes for these better accommodations; so very indifferent, that I would gladly exchange them both for the rags and the unsatisfied hunger of the poorest creature, that looks forward with hope to a better world, and weeps tears of joy in the midst of penury and distress. What a world is this! How mysteriously governed, and, in appearance, left to itself. One man, having squandered thousands at a gaming table, finds it convenient to travel; gives his estate to somebody to manage for him; amuses himself a few years in France and Italy; returns, perhaps, wiser than he went, having acquired knowledge, which, but for his follies, he would never have acquired; again makes a splendid figure at home, shines in the senate, governs his country as its minister, is admired for his abilities, and if successful, adored, at least by a party. When he dies he is praised as a demigod, and his monument records everything but his vices. The exact contrast of such a picture is to be found in many cottages at Olney. I have no need to describe them; you know the characters I mean; they love God, they trust him, they pray to him in secret, and though he means to reward them openly, the day of recompense is delayed.

In the meantime they suffer everything that infirmity and poverty can inflict upon them. Who would suspect, that has not a spiritual eye to discern it, that the fine gentleman might possibly be one whom his Maker had in abhorrence; and that the wretch last mentioned was dear to him as the apple of his eye?'

CHAPTER X. Publication of Cowper's second volume of poems—Manner in which it was received by the public—His feelings on the occasion—Great self-abasement—Renewal of his correspondence with Lady Hesketh— Acceptance of her proffered assistance—Her projected visit to Olney—Cowper's pleasing anticipations of its results—Her arrival—Cowper's removal from Olney to Weston—His intimacy with the Throckmortons— Happiness it afforded him.

Cowper's second volume of poems, the publication of which had been delayed much longer than was expected, appeared, at length, in the summer of 1785. His first volume, though it had not met with that success which might have been expected had nevertheless been extensively circulated, and was spoken of highly by some of the first literary characters of the age. It had thus made way for its successor, which no sooner made its appearance than it was eagerly sought after, and met with a rapid and an extensive sale. High as had been the expectations of his friends, they fell far short of what he had accomplished in that brilliant display of poetical talent, which appeared in the *Task*. The singularity of the title made its first appearance somewhat repulsive; its various and matchless beauties were however soon discovered, and it speedily raised the reputation of Cowper's genius to the highest summit, and placed him in the first rank of poets.

In a letter to Mr. Newton, he describes his feelings on this occasion in such a manner, as proves him to have been influenced by nothing like selfish or ambitious motives; but by principles far more noble and exalted:

'I found your account of what you experienced in your state of maiden authorship very entertaining, because very natural. I suppose no man ever made his first sally from the press without a conviction that all eyes and ears would be engaged to attend him, at least without a thousand anxieties lest they should not. Arduous and interesting such an enterprise may be in the first instance, it seems to me that our feelings on the occasion soon become obtuse. I can answer at least for one. Mine are what they were when I published my first volume. I am even so very indifferent to the matter, that I can truly assert myself guiltless of the very idea of my book sometimes for whole days together. God knows that my mind having been occupied more than twelve years in the contemplation of the most distressing subjects, the world, and its opinion of what I write, is become as unimportant to me as the whistling of a bird in a bush. Despair made amusement necessary, and I found poetry the most agreeable amusement. Had I not endeavoured to perform my best, it would not have amused me at all. The mere blotting of so much paper would have been but indifferent sport. God gave me grace also to wish that I might not write in vain. Accordingly, I have mingled much truth with some trifle; and such truths as deserved at least to be clad as well and as handsomely as I could clothe them.'

To the influence, which the applause that might be conferred upon him for his productions might have upon his mind, he writes in a strain of piety and humility:

'As to the commendations, if I should chance to win them, I feel myself invulnerable there. The view that I have had of myself, for many years, has been so truly humiliating, that I think the praises of all mankind could not hurt me. God knows that I speak my present sense of the matter, at least, most truly, when I say, that the admiration of creatures like myself seems to me a weapon the least dangerous that my worst enemy could employ against me. I am fortified against it by such solidity of real self-abasement, that I deceive myself most egregiously, if I do not heartily despise it. Praise belongeth to God; and I seem to myself to covet it no more than I covet divine honours.'

While Cowper looked upon his publication with so much indifference, his friends regarded it with opposite feelings. Its rapid and extensive circulation not only delighted those who were intimately associated with him, and had been witnesses to the acute anguish of his mind during this afflicting malady, but it also gratified several of his former associates and correspondents, and induced them to renew their communications with the poet. Among these was Lady Hesketh, who was so charmed with the productions of his pen, that on her return from the continent, where she had spent several years with her husband, she renewed her correspondence with Cowper; and as she was now a widow, and was in opulent circumstances, she generously offered to render him any assistance he might want. Cowper's reply to an interesting letter she wrote him, shows the warmth of his affection towards those whom he loved. He thus writes:

'My dear Cousin, It is no new thing for you to give pleasure. I will venture to say that you do not often give more than you gave me this morning. When I came down to breakfast, and found on the table a letter franked by my uncle, and when, on opening that frank, I found that it contained a letter from you, I said within myself, *this is just as it should be.* We are all grown young again, and the days that I thought, I should see no more are actually returned. You perceive, therefore, that you judged well when you conjectured that a line from you would not be disagreeable to me. It could not be otherwise than, as in fact it has proved, a most agreeable surprise. I can truly boast of affection for you that years have at all abated. I need only recollect how much I valued you once, and with how much cause, immediately to feel a revival of the same value; if that can be said to revive, which at the most was only dormant for want of employment. I slander it when I say that it has slept. A thousand times have I recollected a thousand scenes, in which our two selves have formed the whole of the drama, with the greatest pleasure at times too, when I had no reason to suppose that I should ever hear from you again. The hours that I have spent with you were among the pleasantest of my former days, and are therefore chronicled in my mind so deeply as to fear no erasure.'

In reply to one part of his cousin's letter, in which she congratulated him on the happiness that she had been informed he enjoyed in his retired situation, he briefly and feelingly glances at the anguish he had endured, describing, at the same time, the actual condition in which he was then placed. 'You say that you have often heard of me; that puzzles me. I cannot imagine from what quarter; but it is no matter. I must tell you, however, my dear cousin, that your information has been a little defective. That I am happy in my present situation is true; I live, and have lived these twenty years, with Mrs. Unwin, to who has affectionately cared for me. But I do not account myself happy in having been for thirteen of those years in a state of mind which has made all that care and attention necessary; an attention and a care that have injured her health, and which, had she not been uncommonly supported, must have brought her to the grave. But I will pass to another subject; it would be cruel to particularize only to give pain, neither should I by any means wish to give a sable hue to the first letter of a correspondence so unexpectedly renewed. Dejection of spirits, which I suppose may have prevented many a man from becoming an author, has made me one. I find constant employment necessary, and therefore take care to be constantly employed. Manual occupations do not engage the mind sufficiently, as I know by experience, having tried many. Composition, especially of verse, absorbs it wholly. I write therefore generally three hours in the morning, and in the evening, I transcribe. I read also, but less than I write, for I must have bodily exercise, and therefore never pass a day without it.

'I do not seek new friends, not being altogether sure that I should find them, but have unspeakable pleasure in being beloved by an old one. I hope that our correspondence has now suffered its last interruption, and that we shall go down together to the grave, chattering and chirping as happily as such a scene as this will permit. I am happy that my poems have pleased you. My volume has afforded me no such pleasure at any time, either while I was writing it, or since its publication, as I have derived from yours and my uncle's favourable opinion respecting it. I make certain allowances for partiality, and for that peculiar quickness of taste, with which you both relish what you like, and after all drawbacks upon those accounts, duly made, find myself rich in the measure of your approbation that still remains. I honour John Gilpin, since it was he who first encouraged you to write. I made him on purpose to laugh at, and he served his purpose well; but I am now indebted to him for a more valuable acquisition that all the laughter in the world amounts to, the recovery of my intercourse with you, which is to me inestimable.'

The interesting manner, in which Cowper referred to his cousin's generous and unsolicited offer of pecuniary aid, shows that he possessed that true delicacy of feeling that is sure to render an individual amiable:

'I am glad that I always loved you as I did. It releases me from any occasion to suspect that my present affection for you is indebted for its existence to any selfish considerations. No, I am sure I love you disinterestedly, and for your own sake, because I never thought of you with any other sensations than those of the truest affection, even while I was under the persuasion that I should never hear from you again. I perceive myself in a state of mind similar to that of the traveller described in Pope's *Messiah*, who, as he passes through a sandy desert, starts at the sudden and unexpected sound of a waterfall. Your very generous offer of assistance has placed me in a situation new to me, and in which I feel myself somewhat puzzled how to behave. When I was once asked if I wanted anything, and given delicately to understand that the inquirer was ready to supply all my occasions, I thankfully and civilly but positively declined the favour. I know you thoroughly, and the liberality of your disposition, and have that consummate confidence in the sincerity of your wish to serve me, that delivers me from all awkward constraint, and from all fear of trespassing by acceptance. To you, therefore, I reply, *Yes; whensoever and whatsoever, and in what manner soever you please; and add moreover, that my affection for the giver is such as will increase to me tenfold the satisfaction I shall have in receiving.*'

The happiest consequences resulted from the renewal of Cowper's correspondence with this accomplished and excellent lady. After an interchange of some of the most interesting letters that were ever written, she proposed at length to pay the sequestered poet a visit at Olney, and made arrangements accordingly. The following extracts from Cowper's letters to her on this occasion will be read with pleasure, as a faithful record of the delight he anticipated from this interview:

'I have been impatient to tell you that I am impatient to see you again. Mrs. Unwin partakes with me in all my feelings. Let me assure you that your kindness in promising us a visit has charmed us both. I shall see you again; I shall hear your voice. We shall take walks together. I will show you my prospects—the hovel, the alcove, the Ouse and its banks, everything that I have described. I anticipate the pleasure of those days not very far distant, and feel a part of it at this moment. My dear, I will not let you come until the end of May or the beginning of June, because before that time, my greenhouse will not be ready to receive us, and it is the only pleasant room belonging to us. When the plants go out, we go in. I line it with nets, and spread the floor with mats; and there you shall sit, with a bed of mignonette at your side, and a hedge of honeysuckles, roses, and jasmine; and I will make you a bouquet of myrtle every day. We now talk of nobody but you—what we will do with you when we get you; where you shall walk, where you shall sleep, in short everything that bears the remotest relation to your well-being at Olney, occupies all our talking-time, which is all that I do not spend at Troy. Mrs. Unwin has already secured for you an apartment, or rather two, just such as we could wish. The house in which you will find them is within thirty yards of our own, and opposite to it. The whole affair is thus commodiously adjusted; and now I have nothing to do but to wish for June; and June, my cousin, was never so wished for since June was made. I shall have a thousand things to hear, and a thousand to say, and they will all rush into my mind together, until it will be so crowded with things impatient to be said, that for some time I shall say nothing. Sooner or later they will all come out. After so long a separation, a separation which of late seemed so likely to last for life, we shall meet each other as alive from the dead; and, for my own part, I can truly say, that I have not a friend in the other world whose resurrection would give me greater pleasure.'

Anticipating, rather impatiently, this promised visit, he thus pleasantly records his feelings on the occasion:

'If you will not quote Solomon, my dearest cousin, I will. He says, and as beautifully as truly, "Hope deferred maketh the heart sick; but when the desire cometh, it is a tree of life." I feel how much reason he had on his side when he made this observation, and am myself sick of your delay. Well, the middle of June will not always be a thousand years off; and when it comes, I shall hear you, and see you too, and shall not care a single farthing if you do not touch a pen for a month. From this very morning, May 15, 1786, I begin to date the last month of our long separation; and confidently and most comfortably hope, that before June 15 shall present itself we shall have seen each other. Is it not so? Will it not be one of the most extraordinary eras of my extraordinary life? A year ago, we neither corresponded nor expected to meet in this world. This world is a scene of marvellous events, many of them more marvellous than fiction itself, blessed be God! They are not all of the distressing kind. Now and then, in the course of an existence whose hue is for the most part sable, a day turns up that makes amends for many sighs, and many subjects of complaint. Such a day shall I account the day of your arrival at Olney.'

Referring to the same subject, he depicts beautifully those mingled emotions of pain and pleasure often experienced by sensitive minds, strongly and affectionately attached to each other, when they meet after the endurance of a long separation:

'Wherefore is it (canst thou tell me) that, together with all these delightful sensations, to which the sight of a long absent dear friend gives birth, there is a mixture of something painful, fluttering and tumults, and I know not what accompaniments of our pleasure, that are in fact perfectly foreign from the occasion?

Such I feel when I think of our meeting, and such, I suppose, feel you; and the nearer the crisis approaches, the more I am sensible of them. I know beforehand that they will increase with every turn of the wheels that shall convey you to Olney; and when we actually meet, the pleasure and this unaccountable pain together, will be as much as I shall be able to support. I am utterly at a loss for the cause, and can only resolve it into that appointment, by which it has been foreordained that all human delights shall be qualified and mingled with their contraries. A fig for them all! Let us resolve to combat with, and to conquer them. They are dreams; they are illusions of the judgment. Some enemy that hates the happiness of human kind, and is ever industrious to dash, if he cannot destroy it, works them in us, and their being so perfectly unreasonable as they are, is a proof of it.'

The poet then delicately alludes to his depression, in terms that would lead us to suppose there were times when he was himself persuaded that his delusion was entirely imaginary:

'Nothing that is such can be the work of a good agent. I know, too, by experience, that, like all other illusions, they exist only by force of imagination, are indebted for their prevalence to the absence of their object, and in a few moments after their appearance cease. So then, this is a settled point, and the case stands thus. You will tremble as you draw near to Olney, and so shall I; but we will both recollect that there is no reason why we should, and this recollection will, at least, have some little effect in our favour. We will likewise both take the comfort of what we know to be true, that the tumult will soon cease, and the pleasure long survive the pain, even as long, I trust, as we ourselves shall survive it. Assure yourself, my dear cousin, that both for your sake, since you make a point of it, and for my own, I will be as philosophically careful as possible, that these fine nerves of mine shall not be beyond measure agitated when you arrive. In truth, there is a much greater probability that they will be benefitted and greatly too. Joy of heart, from whatever occasion it may arise, is the best of all nervous medicines; and I should not wonder if such a turn given to my spirits should have even a lasting effect of the most advantageous kind upon them. You must not imagine either, that I am, on the whole, in any great degree, subject to nervous affections: occasionally I am, and have been these many years, much liable to dejection; but, at intervals, and sometimes for an interval of weeks, no creature would suspect it. For I have not that which commonly is a symptom of such a case belonging to me,—I mean occasional extraordinary elevation. When I am in the best health, my tide of animal sprightliness flows with great equality, so that I am never, at any time, exalted in proportion as I am sometimes depressed. My depression has a cause, and if that cause were to cease, I should be as cheerful thenceforth, and perhaps forever, as any man need be.

'Your visit is delayed too long, to my impatience at least it seems so, who find this spring, backward as it is, too forward, because many of its beauties will have faded before you will have an opportunity to see them. We took our customary walk yesterday, and saw, with regret, the laburnums, syringas, and roses, some of them blown, and others just upon the point of blowing, and could not help observing, that all these will be gone before Lady Hesketh comes. Still, however, there will be roses, and jasmine, and honeysuckle, and shady walks, and cool alcoves, and you will partake them with us. I want you to have a share of everything that is delightful here, and cannot bear that the advance of the season should steal away a single pleasure before you come to enjoy it. I will venture to say, that even you were never so much expected in your life.'

'I regret that I have made your heart ache so often, my dear cousin, with talking about my fits of dejection. Something has happened that has led me to the subject, or I would have mentioned them more sparingly. But the tale is too long for a letter; I will only add, for your present satisfaction, that the cause is not exterior, that it is not within the reach of human aid, and that yet I have a hope myself, and Mrs. Unwin a strong persuasion, of its removal. I am indeed even now, and have been for a considerable time, sensible of a change for the better, and expect, with good reason, a comfortable lift from you. Guess then, my beloved cousin, with what wishes I look forward to the time of your arrival, from whose coming I promise myself not only pleasure, but also peace of mind, at least an additional share of it. At present, it is an uncertain and transient guest with me. The joy, with which I shall see and converse with you at Olney, may perhaps make it an abiding one.

It is seldom that pleasure, anticipated with such warmth of feeling, fully answers our expectations. Human enjoyments almost invariably seem much more valuable in prospect than in possession, but Cowper's interview with his cousin was altogether an exception, and proved a source of more real delight to both parties than either of them had expected. As might naturally be supposed on meeting after a separation of three-and-twenty years, they both experienced the full force of those emotions. Their first interview was, indeed, painfully pleasing; every sensation, however, that was in any degree painful, soon subsided, and gave place to such only as were pure and delightful. Mrs. Unwin was pleased with the sweetness of temper, agreeable manners, and cheerful conversation of Lady Hesketh, and her ladyship was no less delighted with the mild, amiable, and affectionate conduct of her new companion; while Cowper's heart was gladdened to have the advantage of daily interaction with another highly cultivated mind.

The happy effect of this change upon Cowper's spirits will be seen by the following extracts from his correspondence:

My dear cousin's arrival has made us happier than we ever were at Olney. Her great kindness, in giving us her company, is a cordial that I shall feel the effect of, not only while she is here, but while I live. She has been with us a fortnight. She pleases everybody, and is, in her turn, pleased with everything she finds here; is always cheerful and good-tempered; and knows no pleasure equal to that of communicating pleasure to us and to all around her. This disposition in her is the more comfortable, because it is not the humour of the day, a sudden flash of benevolence and goodness, occasioned merely by a change of scene; but it is her natural turn, and has governed all her conduct ever since I first knew her. We are consequently happy in her society, and shall be happier still to have you partake with us in our joy. I am fond of the sound of bells, but was never more pleased with those of Olney than when they rang her into her new habitation. She is, as she ever was, my pride and my joy, and I am delighted with everything that means to do her honour. Her first appearance was too much for me; my spirits, instead of being gently raised, broke down with me, under the pressure of too much joy, and left me flat, or rather melancholy, throughout the day, to a degree that was mortifying to myself, and alarming to her. I have made amends for this torture since; and, in point of cheerfulness, have far exceeded her expectations, for she knew that sable had been my suit for many years. By her help we get change of air and scene, though still resident at Olney; and by her means have intercourse with some families in this country, with whom, but for her, we could never have been acquainted. Her presence here would at any time, even in her happiest days, have been a comfort to me; but in the present day, I am doubly sensible of its value. She leaves nothing unsaid, nothing undone, that she thinks will be conducive to our well-being; and so far as she is concerned, I have nothing to wish, but that I could believe her sent hither in mercy to myself; then I should be thankful.'

 Lady Hesketh had not long been at Olney before she became dissatisfied with the poet's residence. She thought it a situation altogether unsuitable for a person subject to depression. Cowper himself had often entertained the same opinion respecting it; and both he and Mrs. Unwin had frequently wished for a change, and had indeed been looking out for a house more agreeable to their taste. At that time a very commodious cottage, pleasantly situated in the village of Weston Underwood, a mile and a half distant from Olney, belonging to Sir John Throckmorton, was unoccupied. It occurred to Cowper, that this would be a very agreeable summer residence for his cousin; and on his mentioning it to her, she immediately engaged it, not for herself only, but for the future residence of the poet and his amiable companion, with whom she had now made up her mind to become a frequent, if not a constant associate. The following extracts will best describe Cowper's feelings on this occasion:

'I shall now communicate news that will give you pleasure. When you first contemplated the front of our abode, you were shocked. In your eyes, it had the appearance of a prison, and you sighed at the thought that your mother lived in it. Your view of it was not only just, but prophetic. It had not only the aspect of a place built for the purposes of incarceration, but has actually served that purpose, through a long, long period, that we have been the prisoners; but a gaol delivery is at hand. The bolts and bars are to be loosed, and we shall escape. A very different mansion, both in point of appearance and accommodation, expects us; and the expense of living in it will not be much greater than we are subjected to in this. It is situated at Weston, one of the prettiest villages in England, and belongs to Mr. Throckmorton,' afterwards Sir John Throckmorton. 'We all three dine with him to-day by invitation, and shall survey it in the afternoon, point out the necessary repairs, and finally adjust the treaty. I have my cousin's promise that she will never let another year pass without a visit to us, and the house is large enough to accommodate us three and any guest she might wish to bring. The change will I hope prove advantageous, both to your mother and to me, in all respects. Here we have no neighbourhood; there we shall have most agreeable neighbours in the Throckmortons. Here we have a bad air in the winter, impregnated with the fishy smelling fumes of the marsh mist; there we shall breathe in an atmosphere untainted. Here we are confined from September to March, and sometimes longer; there we shall be upon the very verge of pleasure grounds, upon which we can always ramble, and shall not wade through almost impassable dirt to get at them. Both your mother's constitution and mine have suffered materially by such close and long confinement; and it is high time, unless we intend to retreat into the grave, that we should seek out a more wholesome residence. So far is well; the rest is left to heaven.'

To his friend Mr. Newton, he thus writes:

'You have heard of our intended removal. The house that is to receive us is in a state of preparation, and when finished, will be both smarter and more commodious than our present abode. But the circumstance that recommends it chiefly is its situation. Long confinement in the winter, and indeed, for the most part in the autumn too, has hurt us both. A gravel walk, thirty yards long, affords but indifferent scope to the locomotive faculty; yet it is all that we have had to move in for eight months in the year, during thirteen years that I have been a prisoner. Had I been confined in the Tower, the battlements of it would have furnished me with a larger space. You say well, that there was a time when I was happy at Olney; and I am now as happy at Olney, as I expect to be anywhere, without the presence of God. Change of situation is with me no otherwise an object, than as both Mrs. Unwin's health and my own happen to be concerned in it. We are both, I believe, partly indebted for our respective maladies, to an atmosphere encumbered with raw vapours, issuing from flooded meadows, and we have perhaps fared the worse for sitting so often, and sometimes for several successive months, over a cellar filled with water. The ills we shall escape in the uplands; and as we may reasonably hope, of course, their consequences. But as for happiness, he that once had communion with his Maker, must be more frantic than ever I was yet, if he can dream of finding it at a distance from him. I no more expect happiness at Weston than here, or than I should expect it in company with felons and outlaws in the hold of a ballast-lighter. Animal spirits, however, have their value, and are especially desirable to him who is condemned to carry a burthen which at any rate will tire him, but which, without their aid, cannot fail to crush him.'

On November 15, 1786, Cowper entered upon his new abode. The following extracts from his letters describe his sensations on the occasion:

'There are some things that do not exactly shorten the life of man, yet seem to do so, and frequent removals from place to place are of that number. For my own part, at least, I am apt to think, if I had been stationary, I should seem to myself to have lived longer. My many changes of habitation have divided my time into many short periods; and when I look back upon them, they appear only as the stages of a day's journey, the first of which is at no great distance from the last. I lived longer at Olney than anywhere. There indeed I lived until mouldering walls and a tottering house warned me to depart. I have accordingly taken the hint, and two days since arrived, or rather took up my abode, at Weston. You perhaps have never made the experiment, but I can assure you that the confusion that attends a transmigration of this kind is infinite, and has a terrible effect in deranging the intellect. When God speaks to a chaos, it becomes a scene of order and harmony in a moment; but when his creatures have thrown one house into confusion by leaving it, and another by tumbling themselves and their goods into it, not less than many days' labour and contrivance are necessary to give them their proper places. It belongs to furniture of all kinds, however convenient it may be in its place, to be a nuisance out of it. We find ourselves here in a comfortable house. Such it is in itself; and my cousin, who has spared no expense in dressing it up for us, has made it a genteel one. Such, at least, it will be, when its contents are a little harmonized. She left us on Tuesday, and on Wednesday, Mrs. Unwin and I took possession of our new abode. I could not help giving a last look to my old prison, and its precincts; and though I cannot easily account for it, having been miserable there so many years, felt something like a heartache, when I took my leave of a scene, that certainly in itself had nothing to engage affection. I recollected that I had once been happy there, and could not, without tears in my eyes, bid adieu to a place in which God had so often found me. The human mind is a great mystery; mine, at least, appears to be such upon this occasion. I found that I not only had a tenderness for that ruinous abode, because it had once known me happy in the presence of God, but that even the distress I had there suffered, for so long a time, on account of his absence, had endeared it to me as much. I was weary of every object, had long wished for a change, and yet could not take leave without a pang at parting. What consequences are to attend our removal, God only knows. I know well that it is not in the power of situation to effect a cure of melancholy like mine. The change, however, has been entirely a providential one; for much as I wished it, I never uttered that wish, except to Mrs. Unwin. When I learned that the house was to be let, and had seen it, I had a strong desire that Lady Hesketh should take it for herself, if she should happen to like the country. That desire, indeed, is not exactly fulfilled, and yet, upon the whole, is exceeded. We are the tenants; but she assures us that we shall often have her for a guest, and here is room enough for us all. You, I hope, my dear friend, and Mrs. Newton, will want no assurances to convince you that you will always be received here with the sincerest welcome; more welcome than you have been you cannot be, but better accommodated you may and will be.'

CHAPTER XI. Extracts from his correspondence—Description of the deep seriousness generally pervading his mind— His remarks to justify his removal from Olney— Vindicates himself and Mrs. Unwin from unjust aspersions—Reasons for undertaking the translation of Homer— Immense pains he bestowed upon it— His readiness to avail himself of the assistance of others — Vexation he experienced from a multiplicity of critics—Just remarks upon criticism— Determination to persevere in his work — Justifies himself for undertaking it — Pleasure he took in relieving the poor—Renewal of his correspondence with General Cowper and the Rev. Dr. Bagot—Consolatory letter to the latter.

The extracts we have already made from Cowper's correspondence prove, unquestionably, that the bent of his mind was towards the all-important affairs of religion. As an exhibition, however, of his feelings in this respect at least, up to the close of 1786, the period of his removal to Weston, we think the following extracts cannot fail to be interesting. To Mr. Newton he writes:

'Those who enjoy the means of grace and know how to use them well will thrive anywhere. My experiences, however, of this latter kind are rare and transient. The light that reaches me cannot be compared to that of the sun, or of the moon, [which shine steadily.] It is a flash in a dark night, during which the heavens seem to open only to shut again.'

Owing to the poet's peculiar depression, though there were in his conduct and experience the most convincing proofs that he was entitled to every Christian privilege, and had a right to avail himself of every means of instruction that God had provided, yet could he never be persuaded to engage in any, lest he should thereby displease God. On this subject, he writes:

'I should be happy. When I say this, I mean to be understood in the fullest and most emphatic sense of the word. [Would that] my frame of mind were such as to permit me to study the important truths of religion. But Adam's approach to the tree of life, after he had sinned, was not more effectually prohibited by the flaming sword that turned every way, than mine to its great Antitype has been now almost these thirteen years, a short interval of three or four days, which passed about this time twelvemonth, alone excepted. For what reason I am thus long excluded, is known to God only. For though others have suffered desertion, yet few, I believe, for so long a time, and perhaps none a desertion accompanied with such experience. They have this belonging to them; that as they are not fit for recital, being made up merely of infernal ingredients, so neither are they susceptible of it, for I know no language in which they could be expressed. They are as truly things, which it is not possible for man to utter, as those were which Paul heard and saw in the third heaven. If the ladder of Christian experience reaches, as I suppose it does, to the very presence of God, it has nevertheless its foot in the abyss. And if Paul stood, as no doubt he did, on the topmost stave of it, I have been standing, and still stand, on the lowest, in this thirteenth year that has passed since I descended.'

The incidents that have brought different individuals before the public in the character of authors, are, no doubt, exceedingly various: very few, however, if any, have been driven to it by distress, as was Cowper. Referring to this, he writes:

'In such a situation of mind, as I have so long had to experience, encompassed by the midnight of absolute despair, and a thousand times filled with unspeakable horror, I first commenced an author. Distress drove me to it; and the impossibility of existing without some employment, still recommends it. I am not, indeed, so perfectly hopeless as I was, but I am equally in need of an occupation, being often as much, and sometimes even more, worried than ever. I cannot amuse myself as I once could, with carpenters' or with gardeners' tools, or with squirrels and guinea pigs. At that time, I was a child; but since it has pleased God, whatever else he withholds from me, to restore to me a man's mind, I have put away childish things. '

As to the peculiarity of his case and to the great severity of his distress, not in a complaining or impatient spirit, but in perfect submission to the Divine will, he writes:

'The dealings of God with me are to myself unintelligible. I have never met, either in books, or in conversation, with an experience at all similar to my own. More than twelve months have now passed since I began to hope, that having walked the whole breadth of the bottom of this Red Sea, I was beginning to climb the opposite shore, and I prepared to sing the song of Moses. I have been disappointed; those hopes have been blasted; those comforts have been wrested from me. I could not be so duped even by the archenemy himself, as to be made to question the divine nature of them, but I have been made to believe (which you will say is being duped still more) that God gave them to me in derision, and took them away in vengeance. Such, however, is, and has been my persuasion many a long day; and when I shall think on this subject more comfortably, or, as you will be inclined to tell me, more rationally and scripturally, I know not. In the meantime I embrace, with alacrity, every alleviation of my case, and with the more alacrity, because whatever proves a relief of my distress is a cordial to Mrs. Unwin, whose sympathy with me, through the whole of it, has been such, that, despair excepted, her burden has been as heavy as mine.'

Some of his friends, and Mr. Newton among the rest, on being apprised of his intended removal from Olney, expressed apprehensions that it would introduce him to company uncongenial to his taste, if not detrimental to his piety. Regarding these objections, he thus writes to his esteemed correspondent:

'If in the course of such an occupation as I have been driven to by despair, or by the inevitable consequence of it, either my former connections are revived, or new ones occur, these things are as much a part of the dispensation of Providence as the leading points themselves. If his purposes in thus directing me are gracious, he will take care to prove them such in the issue; and, in the meantime, will preserve me (for he is able to do that in one condition of life as well as in another,) from all mistakes that might prove pernicious to myself, or give reasonable offence to others. I can say it, as truly as it was ever spoken, *here I am; let him do with me as seemeth to him good*. At present, I have no connections at which either you, or any who love me and wish me well, have occasion to conceive alarm. Much kindness, indeed, I have experienced at the hands of several, some of them near relations, others not related to me at all, but I do not know that there is among them a single person from whom I am likely to catch contamination. I can say of them all, with more truth than Jacob uttered, when he called kid venison, "The Lord thy God brought them unto me." I could shew you among them two men, whose lives, though they have but little of what we call evangelical light, are ornaments to a Christian country, men who fear God more than some who profess to love him. I will not particularize further on such a subject. Be "they what they may, our situations are so distant, and we are likely to meet so seldom, that were they, as they are not, persons even of exceptionable manners, their manners would have little to do with me. We correspond, at present, only on the subject of what passed at Troy three thousand years ago; and they are matters that, if they can do no good, will at least hurt nobody.'

In reply to an undesirable report made to Mr. Newton by some spiteful and officious individual, casting some severe reflections on Cowper and Mrs. Unwin for associating with individuals not decidedly pious, he remarks:

'Your letter to Mrs. Unwin concerning our conduct, and the offence taken at it in our neighbourhood, gave us both a great deal of concern, and she is still deeply affected by it. Of this, you may assure yourself, that if our friends in London have been grieved, it is because they have been misinformed. The bearers of intelligence hence to London are not always very scrupulous concerning the truth of their reports; and that if any of our serious neighbours have been astonished; they have been so without the slightest occasion. Poor people are never well employed even when they judge one another; but when they undertake to scan the motives, and estimate the behaviour, of those whom Providence has raised a little above them, they are utterly out of their province and their depth. They often see us get into Lady Hesketh's carriage, and rather uncharitably suppose that it always carries us into a scene of dissipation, which, in fact, it never does. We visit, indeed, at Mr. Trockmorton's, and at Gayhurst, rarely however at the latter, because of the great distance; frequently, though not very frequently, at Weston, both because it is nearer, and because our business in the house which is making ready for our reception, often calls us that way. What good we can get or can do in these visits, is another question that they, I am sure, are not qualified to solve. Of this we are both sure, that under the guidance of Providence we have formed these connections; that we should have hurt the Christian cause rather than have served it, by a prudish abstinence from them; and that St. Paul himself, conducted to them as we have been, would have found it expedient to have done as we have done.

I speak a strict truth as in the sight of God, when I say that we are neither of us at all more addicted to gallivanting than heretofore. We both naturally love seclusion rather than company, and never go into society without putting a force upon our own dispositions; at the same time, I will confess, and you will easily conceive, that the melancholy resulting from such close confinement as we have long endured, finds itself a little relieved by such amusements as a society so innocent affords. You may look round the Christian world and find few I believe, of our station, who have so little association as we with the world that is not Christian. We place all the uneasiness that you have felt for us on the subject, to the account of that cordial friendship of which you have long given us a proof. But you may be assured, that notwithstanding all rumours to the contrary, we are exactly what we were when you saw us last—I, miserable on account of God's departure from me, which I believe to be final: and she seeking his return to me in the path of duty, and by continual prayer.'

After the publication of Cowper's second volume of poems, and for some considerable time before its actual appearance, he was diligently engaged in producing a new translation of the unrivalled works of Homer. His reasons for undertaking a work of so great magnitude, and which required such immense labour, and the spirited manner in which he ended it, shall be related as nearly as possible in his own words. Writing to Mr. Newton, he thus describes the commencement of this great undertaking:

'I am employed in writing a narrative, but not as useful as that you have published. Employment, however, with the pen, is, through habit, become essential to my well-being; and to produce original poems, especially of considerable length, is not so easy. For some weeks after I had finished the *Task*, and sent away the last sheet corrected, I was through necessity idle, and suffered not a little in my spirits from being so. One day, being in such distress of mind as was hardly supportable, I took up the Iliad; and merely to divert attention, and with no more preconception of what I was then entering upon, than I have at this moment of what I shall be doing this day twenty years hence, translated the first twelve lines of it. The same necessity pressed me again; I had recourse to the same expedient, and translated more. Every day bringing its occasion for employment with it, every day consequently added something to the work; until at last I began to reflect thus—the *Iliad and the Odyssey* together consist of about forty thousand verses. To translate these forty thousand verses will furnish me with occupation for a considerable time. I have already made some progress, and find it a most agreeable amusement. Homer, in point of purity, is a blameless writer; and though he was not an enlightened man, has interspersed many great and valuable truths throughout both his poems. I will try, therefore, whether I cannot copy him more happily myself. I have at least the advantage of Pope's faults and failings, which, like so many beacons upon a dangerous coast, will serve me to steer by, and will make my chance for success more probable. These, and many other considerations, but especially a mind which abhorred a vacuum as its chief bane, impelled me so effectually to the work, that ere long I mean to publish proposals for a subscription to it, having advanced so far as to be warranted in doing so.'

In another letter to the same correspondent, the following just and critical remarks on Pope's translation occur:

Your sentiments of Pope's *Homer* agree perfectly with those of every competent judge with whom I have conversed about it. I never saw a copy so unlike the original. There is not, I believe, to be found in the entire world, an uninspired poem as simple as are both those of *Homer*; nor in the entire world, a poem more bedizened with ornaments than Pope's translation of them. Accordingly, the sublime of Homer in the hands of Pope becomes bloated and tumid, and his description tawdry. Neither had Pope the faintest conception of those exquisite discriminations of character for which Homer is so remarkable. All his persons, and equally upon all occasions, speak in an inflated and strutting phraseology, as Pope has managed them; although in the original, the dignity of their utterance, even when they are most majestic, consists principally in the simplicity of their sentiments, and of their language. Another censure I must pass upon our Anglo-Grecian, out of many that obtrude themselves upon me, but for which I have now neither time nor room to spare, which is, that with all his great abilities, he was defective in his feelings to a degree that some passages in his own poems make it difficult to account for. No writer is more pathetic than *Homer*, because none more natural; and because none less natural than Pope, in his version of *Homer*, therefore, than he, none less pathetic. One of the great faults of Pope's translation is that it is licentious. To publish, therefore, a translation that should be at all chargeable with the same fault would be useless. Whatever will be said of mine, when it does appear, it shall never be said that it is not faithful. I thank you heartily both for your wishes and prayers, that should a disappointment occur, I may not be too much hurt by it. Time will show to what it ultimately tends. I am inclined to think that it has a tendency to which I myself am at present a perfect stranger. Be that as it may, he knows my frame, and will consider that I am dust, and dust too that has been so trampled underfoot, and beaten, that a storm less violent than an unsuccessful issue of such a business might occasion, would be sufficient to blow me quite away. As I know not to what end this my present occupation may finally lead, so neither did I know when I wrote it, or at all suspect, one valuable end, at least, that was to be answered by the *Task*. It has pleased God to prosper it. Being composed in blank verse, it is likely to prove as seasonable an introduction to a blank verse of Homer. '

Having undertaken a work that required so much labour, he bestowed upon it the utmost pains, and allowed nothing to divert his attention from it. In his correspondence the following remarks occur:

'The little time that I can devote to any other purpose than that of poetry, is stolen. Homer is urgent; much is done, and much still remains undone. No schoolboy is more attentive to the performance of his daily task than I am. In truth, my time is very much occupied; and the more so, because I not only have a long and laborious work in hand,—for such it would prove at any rate,—but because I make it a point to bestow my utmost attention to it, and to give it all the finishing that the most scrupulous accuracy can command. As soon as breakfast is over, I retire to my nutshell of a summerhouse, which is my verse manufactory, and here I abide seldom less than three hours, and not often more. In the afternoon, I return to it; and all the daylight that follows, except what is sometimes devoted to a walk, is given to Homer. It is well for me, that a course that is now become necessary is so much my choice. Assure yourself, therefore, that when at any time it happens that I am in arrears in my correspondence with you, neither neglect nor idleness is the cause, I have a daily occupation of forty lines to translate, a task that I never excuse myself from, when it is possible to perform it. Equally sedulous am I in the matter of transcribing, so that between both, my mornings and evenings are completely engaged. Add to this, that though my spirits are seldom so bad but I can write verse, they are often at so low an ebb as to make the production of a letter impossible. I am now in the twentieth book of Homer, and shall assuredly proceed, because the further I go the more I find myself justified in the undertaking, and in due time, if I live, shall assuredly publish. In the whole I shall have composed about forty thousand verses, about which forty thousand verses I shall have taken great pains, on no occasion suffering a slovenly line to escape me. I leave you to guess, therefore, whether such a labour once achieved, I shall not determine to turn it to some account, and to gain myself profit by it if I can; if not, at least, some credit for my reward. Till I had made such a progress in my present undertaking as to put it out of all doubt, that, if I lived, I should proceed in, and finish it, I kept the matter to myself. It would have done me little honour to tell my friends, that I had an arduous enterprise, if afterwards I must have told them that I had dropped it.

 I wish that all English readers had an unsophisticated and unadulterated taste, and could relish real simplicity. But I am well aware that in this respect I am under a disadvantage, and that many, especially many ladies, missing many pretty turns of expression that they have admired in Pope, will account my translation, in those particulars, defective. But, I comfort myself with the thought that in reality it is no defect; on the contrary, that the want of all such embellishments as do not belong to the original, will be one of its principal merits, with persons really capable of relishing Homer. He is the best poet that ever lived, for many reasons, but for none more than that majestic plainness that distinguishes him from all others. As an accomplished person moves gracefully without thinking of it, in like manner the dignity of Homer seems to have cost him no labour. It was natural to him to say great things, and to say them well, and little ornaments were beneath his notice.'

The following extract will show that no person ever appeared before the public in a work of any literary importance, with more correct views of its legitimate claims under such circumstances.

'I thank you for your friendly hints and precautions, and shall not fail to use them in the guidance of my pen. I respect the public, and I respect myself, and had rather want bread than expose myself wantonly to the condemnation of either. I hate the affectation so frequently found in authors, of negligence and slovenliness, and in the present case am sensible, how necessary it is to shun them, when I undertake the vast and invidious labour of doing better than Pope has done before me. I thank you for all that you have said and done in my cause, and, beforehand, for all that you shall say and do hereafter. I am sure that there will be no deficiency on your part. On my own part, I assure you that no pains shall be wanted to make the work as complete as possible. I am now in a scene of perfect tranquillity and the profoundest silence, kicking up the dust of heroic narrative, and besieging Troy again. I told you that I had almost finished the translation of the Iliad, and I verily thought so. I was never more mistaken. By the time when I had reached the end of the poem, the first book of my version was a twelvemonth old. When I came to consider it, after having laid it by so long, it did not satisfy me; I set myself to mend it, and did so. Still it appeared to me improvable, and that nothing would so effectually secure that point as to give the whole book a new translation. With the exception of a very few lines, I have so done, and was never in my life so convinced of the soundness of Horace's advice to publish nothing in haste; so much advantage have I derived from doing that twice which I thought I had accomplished notably at once. He, indeed, recommends nine years' imprisonment of your verses before you send them abroad; but the ninth part of that time is, I believe, as much as there is need of to open a man's eyes upon his own defects, and to secure him from the danger of premature self-approbation. Neither ought it to be forgotten, that nine years make so wide an interval between the cup and the lip that a thousand things may fall out between. New engagements may occur, which may make the finishing of that which a poet has begun impossible. In nine years, he may rise into a situation, or he may sink into one, utterly incompatible with his purpose. His constitution may break in nine years, and sickness may disqualify him for improving what he enterprized in the days of his health. His inclination may change, and he may find some other employment more agreeable; or another poet may enter upon the same work, and get the start of him. Therefore, my friend Horace, though I acknowledge your principle to be good, I must confess the practice you would ground upon it is carried to an extreme. The rigour that I exercised upon the first book, I intend to exercise upon all that follow, and have now actually advanced into the middle of the seventh, nowhere admitting more than one line in fifty of the first translation. You must not imagine that I had been careless and hasty in the first instance. In truth, I had not; but, in rendering so excellent a poet as Homer into our language, there are so many points to be attended to, in respect of both language and numbers, that a first attempt must be fortunate if it does not call aloud for a second. You saw the specimen, and you saw one great fault in it; I mean the harshness of some of the elisions. I do not altogether take the blame of these to myself, for into some of them I have been absolutely driven and hunted by a series of reiterated objections, made by a critical friend, whose scruples and delicacies teased me almost out of all patience.'

With a view to make his translation as perfect as possible, Cowper, before he committed it to the press, availed himself of the assistance of several eminent critics, from some of whom he derived considerable assistance, which, at every convenient opportunity, he very readily and gratefully acknowledged. The remarks of others, however, to whose notice he had been persuaded to submit parts of his manuscript, were so frivolous and perfectly hypercritical, as to occasion him considerable vexation. Of this, the closing remarks of the last, and the whole of the following extract will afford ample proof.

'The vexation and perplexity that attends a multiplicity of criticisms by various hands, many of which are sure to be futile, many of them unfounded, and some of them contradictory to others, is inconceivable, except by the author whose ill-fated work happens to be the subject of them. This also appears to me self-evident, that if a work have passed under the review of one man of taste and learning, and have had the good fortune to please him, his approbation gives security for that of all others qualified like himself. I speak thus, after having just escaped such a storm of trouble, occasioned by endless remarks, hints, suggestions, and objections, as drove me almost to despair, and to the very verge of a resolution to drop my undertaking forever. With infinite difficulty, I at last sifted the chaff from the wheat, availed myself of what appeared to be just, and rejected the rest, but not till the labour and anxiety had nearly undone all that one judicious critic had been doing for me. I assure you I can safely say that vanity and self-importance had nothing to do in all distress that I suffered. It was merely the effect of an alarm that I could not help taking, when I compared the great trouble I had with a few lines only, thus handled, with that which I foresaw such handling of the whole must necessarily give me. I felt beforehand that my constitution would not bear it. Though Johnson's friend has teased me sadly, I verily believe that I shall have no more such cause to complain of him. We now understand each other, and I firmly believe that I might have gone the world through before I had found his equal in an accurate and familiar acquaintance with the original. Though he is a foreigner, he has a perfect knowledge of the English language, and can consequently appreciate its beauties, as well as discover its defects.

'The animadversions of the critic you sent me, hurt me more than they would have done, had they come from a person from whom I might have expected such treatment. In part they appeared to me unjust, and in part ill-natured; and, the man himself being an oracle in almost every body's account, I apprehended that he had done me much mischief. Why he says that the translation is far from exact is best known to himself. For I know it to be as exact as is compatible with poetry; and prose translations of Homer are not wanted. The world has one already. I am greatly pleased with the amendments of a friend, to whom I sent a specimen, which he has returned amended with so much taste and candour, and accompanied with so many expressions of kindness, that it quite charmed me. He has chiefly altered the lines encumbered with elisions, and I will just take this opportunity to tell you, because I know you to be as much interested in what I write as myself, that some of the most offensive of these elisions were occasioned by mere criticism. I was fairly hunted into them by vexatious objections, made without end by and his friends, and altered, and altered, till at last I scarcely cared how I altered. The power of a critic freezes my poetical powers, and discourages me to such a degree, as to make me ashamed of my own weakness. Yet I presently recover my confidence again, especially when I have every reason to believe, as in the case you refer to, that the critic's censures are harsh and unreasonable, and arise more from his own wounded and mortified feelings, than from any defect in the work itself.'

To Lady Hesketh he thus discloses the state of his mind in this respect.

'Your anxious wishes for my success delight me, and you may rest assured that I have all the ambition on the subject that you can wish me to feel. I more than admire my author. I often stand astonished at his beauties. I am forever amused with the translation of him, and I have received a thousand encouragements: these are all so many happy omens, which I hope will be verified by the event. I am not ashamed to confess that, having commenced author, I am most abundantly desirous to succeed as such. I have in my nature (what perhaps you little suspect me of,) an infinite share of ambition. With it I have at the same time, as you well know, an equal share of diffidence. To this combination of opposite qualities it has been owing that, till lately, I stole through life without undertaking anything, yet always wishing to distinguish myself. At last I ventured, ventured too in the only path that, at so late a period, was yet open to me, and am determined, if God have not determined otherwise, to work my way through the obscurity that has been so long my portion, into notice. Everything, therefore, that seems to threaten this favourite purpose with disappointment affects me severely. I suppose that all ambitious minds are in the same predicament. He who seeks distinction must be sensible of disapprobation, exactly in the same proportion, as he desires applause. I have thus, my dear cousin, unfolded my heart to you in this particular, without a speck of dissimulation. Some people and good people too, would blame me, but you will not; and they, I think, would blame without just cause. We certainly do not honour God when we bury, or when we neglect to improve, so far as we can, whatever talent he may have bestowed upon us, whether it be little or much. Set me down, therefore, my dear cousin, for an industrious rhymer, so long as I shall have ability. For in this only way is it possible for me, so far as I can see, either to honour God, or to serve men, or even to serve myself.'

This attention to Homer, though it took up a great portion of Cowper's time, was not allowed to absorb it wholly. His letters prove him to have been an attentive observer of every passing event, and afford innumerable proofs of the purity of his taste, the accuracy of his judgment, and the depth of his piety. On the subject of style, he remarks, in a letter to Mr. Newton:

'You wonder, and (I dare say) unfeignedly, because you do not think yourself entitled to such praise, that I prefer your style, as an historian, to that of the two most renowned writers of history the present day has seen. That you may not suspect me of having said more than my real opinion will warrant, I will tell you why. In your style, I see no affectation; in every line of theirs, I see nothing else. They disgust me always—Robertson with his pomp and his strut, and Gibbon with his finical and French manners. You are as correct as they; you express yourself with as much precision; your words are ranged with as much propriety; but you do not set your periods to a tune. They discover a perpetual desire to exhibit themselves to advantage; whereas your subject engrosses you. They sing, and you say; which, as history is a thing to be said, and not sung, is, in my judgment, very much to your advantage. A writer that despises these tricks, and is yet neither inelegant nor inharmonious, proves himself, by that single circumstance, a man of superior judgment and ability to them both.'

On the same subject, speaking of the French writer Caraccioli, Marquis Louis-Antoine Caraccioli (1719 –1803) was a productive French writer, poet, historian, and biographer he remarks:

'There is something in his style that touches me exceedingly, and which I do not know how to describe. I should call it pathetic, if it were occasional only, and never occurred but when his subject happened to be particularly affecting. It is universal; he has not a sentence that is not marked with it. Perhaps, therefore, I may describe it better by saying, that his whole work is full of pious and tender melancholy, which, to me at least, is extremely agreeable. This property of it, which depends perhaps altogether upon the arrangement of his words and the modulation of his sentences, it would be very difficult to preserve in a translation. I do not know that our language is capable of being so managed, and rather suspect that it is not; and that it is peculiar to the French, because it is not infrequent among their writers, and I never saw anything like it in our own.'

It was Cowper's intention to have translated this writer's treatise on the subject of self-knowledge, a work that, in many respects, he much admired.

'Though I think no book more calculated to teach the art of pious meditation, or to enforce a conviction of the vanity of all pursuits that have not the soul's interests for their object, I can yet see a flaw in his manner of instructing, which, in a country so enlightened as ours, would escape nobody's notice. Allowing for these defects, he is a charming writer, and, by those who know how to make such allowances, may be read with great delight and improvement. But with these defects in his manner, though I believe no man ever had a heart more devoted to God, he does not seem to be dressed with sufficient exactness to be fit for the public eye, among those with whom man is known to be nothing, and Jesus to be all in all.'

The following just criticisms will show that, on literary subjects, equally with others, the poet possessed the nicest discrimination:

'I have lately been employed in reading Beattie and Blair's Lectures. I find the former the more agreeable of the two, and the most entertaining writer upon dry subjects I ever met with. His imagination is highly poetical, his language easy and elegant, and his manner so familiar that we seem to be conversing with an old friend, upon terms of the most sociable intercourse, while we read him. Blair is, on the contrary, rather stiff; his language is, except Swift's, the least figurative I remember to have seen. I take him to be a critic very little animated by what he reads; who rather reasons about the beauties of an author than really tastes them, and who finds that a passage is praiseworthy, not because it charms him, but because it is accommodated to the laws of criticism made and provided. He is a sensible man, and understands his subject, but is too conscious that he is addressing the public, and too solicitous about his success, to indulge himself for a moment in that play of fancy which makes the other so agreeable. In Blair we find a scholar—in Beattie both a scholar and an amiable man. Having never in my life perused a page of Aristotle, I am glad to have had an opportunity of learning more than I suppose he would have taught me, from the writings of two modern critics. I felt myself, too, a little disposed to compliment my own acumen upon the occasion: for though the art of writing and composing was never much my study, I did not find that they had any great news to tell me. They have assisted me in putting my observations into some method; but have not suggested many of which I was not by some means previously apprised. In fact, critics did not originally beget authors, but authors made critics. Common sense dictated to writers the necessity of method, connection, and thoughts congruous to the nature of their subject; genius prompted them with embellishments, and thence came the critics.'

Of Johnson's *Lives of the Poets*, which he had recently read, he remarks:

I am very much the biographer's humble admirer. His uncommon share of good sense, and his forcible expression, secures to him that tribute from all his readers. He has a penetrating insight into character, and a happy talent of correcting the popular opinion where it is erroneous. This he does with the boldness of a man who will think for himself, but at the same time, with a justness of sentiment that convinces us be does not differ from others through affectation, but because he has a sounder judgment. '

There were few, if any, works perused by Cowper, which, if he made any comments upon them at all, did not serve to develop the pious tendency of his mind, affording proofs that he ever looked upon religion as a far more important subject than all others do. Thus, in reference to the *Lives of the Poets*, he writes:

'It is a melancholy observation, which it is impossible not to make, after having run through this series of poetical lives, that where there were such shining talents there should be so little virtue. These luminaries of our country seem to have been kindled into a brighter blaze than others, only that their spots might be more noticed! So much can nature do for our intellectual part, and so little for our moral part. What vanity, what petulance, in Pope! How powerfully sensible of censure, and yet how restless in provocation! To what mean artifices could Addison stoop, in hopes of injuring the reputation of his friend! Savage, how sordidly vicious, and the more condemned for the pains that are taken to palliate his vices! Offensive as they appear through a veil, how would they disgust without one? What a sycophant to the public taste was Dryden, sinning against his feelings, lewd in his writings, though chaste in his conversation! I know not but one might search these eight volumes with a candle, as the prophet says, to find a man, and not find one, unless Arbuthnot ^{John Arbuthnot (April 1667 – 1735), was a Scottish physician, satirist and polymath in London.} were he. I shall begin Beattie this evening, and propose to myself much satisfaction in reading him. In him, at least, I shall find a man whose faculties have now and then a glimpse from heaven upon them; a man, not indeed in possession of much evangelical light, but faithful to what he has, and never neglecting an opportunity to use it. How much more respectable is such a character, than thousands who would call him blind.'

The following admirable remarks in a letter to Mr. Newton, on the subject of ministerial addresses, will show that on men, as well as on books and things, Cowper's judgment was equally correct:

'To be angry with his congregation, hurts a Christian minister; and had he the understanding and eloquence of Pascal himself, would still hurt him. Warmth of temper, indulged to a degree that may be called scolding, defeats the end of preaching. No man was ever scolded out of his sins. The heart, corrupt as it is, and because it is so, grows angry if it be not treated with some management and good manners, and scolds again. A surly mastiff will bear perhaps to be stroked, though he will growl even under that operation; but if you touch him roughly, he will bite. There is no grace that the spirit of self can counterfeit with more success than this sort of religious zeal. A man thinks he is fighting for Christ, when he is only fighting for his own notions. He thinks that he is skillfully searching the hearts of others, when he is only gratifying the malignity of his own; and charitably supposes his hearers destitute of all grace, that he may shine the more in his own eyes by comparison. When he has performed this notable task, he wonders that his hearers are not converted. *He has given it them soundly; and if they do not tremble, and confess that God is in him of a truth, he gives them up as reprobate, incorrigible, and lost forever.* A man that loves me, if he sees me in an error, will pity me, and endeavour calmly to convince me of it, and persuade me to forsake it: and if he has great and good news to tell me, he will not do it angrily, and in much heat and discomposure of spirit. A people will always love a minister, if a minister seems to love his people; therefore you were beloved at Olney, and if you preached to the Chickasaws and Choctaws, [Native American tribes] would be equally beloved by them.'

During the whole of Cowper's residence at Olney, he retained the same sentiments of affectionate sympathy for the sufferings of the poor that he had evinced when he first came among them. Though he had experienced some painful proofs of their insensibility, ingratitude, and even unkindness, yet his heart had often been made to rejoice with those, whom either his own liberality or the liberality of his friends had enabled him to relieve. Aware that it afforded him so much pleasure to be employed in communicating happiness to others, his friends often placed at his disposal such things, as they felt inclined to distribute. The following interesting extract from a letter to Mr. Unwin, proves how highly he was gratified in being thus benevolently employed:

'I have thought with pleasure of the summer that you have had in your heart, while you have been employed in softening the severity of winter, in behalf of so many who must otherwise have been exposed to it. You never said a better thing in your life than when you assured Mr.— of the expediency of a gift of bedding to the poor at Olney. There is no article of this world's comforts, with which, as Falstaff says, they are so heinously unprovided. When a poor woman, and an honest one, whom we know well, carried home two pair of blankets, a pair for herself and husband, and a pair for her six children, which you kindly placed at my disposal, as soon as the children saw them, they jumped out of their straw, caught them in their arms, kissed them, blessed them, and danced for joy. An old woman, a very old one, the first night that she found herself so comfortably covered, could not sleep a wink, being kept awake by the contrary emotions of transport on the one hand, and the fear of not being thankful enough on the other.'

A short time before this, Cowper's intimacy with the Rev. S. Greatheed commenced, which continued with mutually unabated affection through life. This eminently pious and excellent clergyman visited the depressed poet at regular and stated intervals, employing invariably, on these occasions, all the ingenuity that Christian sympathy could inspire, to alleviate, if he could not remove, the distress under which his afflicted friend laboured. Cowper had now become less averse to society, and Mr. Bull and Mr. Greatheed frequently met him by appointment at the same time, in hopes that by their edifying conversation they might divert his mind, in some degree at least, from his desponding thoughts. It was not, however, by arguing against his delusion, that they could promote his relief; as the most distant allusion to the subject, would frequently bring on its worst symptoms. His conversation on these occasions, though it was less sprightly and cheerful than would have been expected from his poems, was always serious, sensible, and affectionate.

After the publication of Cowper's second volume, and before his removal from Olney, he had renewed his correspondence with some relatives and friends, with whom he had formerly been on terms of intimacy, but who seemed almost to have forgotten him, until the popularity of his publications arrested their attention. Among these were General Cowper and the Rev. Walter Bagot. Cowper's letters to the latter prove that his attachment to him was not slight and superficial, but deep and fervent. In February 1786, it pleased God to deprive Mr. Bagot of his amiable and accomplished wife, who was respected and beloved by all who knew her. On this melancholy occasion, Cowper wrote to him as follows:

'Alas! Alas! My dear, dear friend, may God himself comfort you! I will not be so absurd as to attempt it. By the close of your letter, it should seem that in this hour of great trial, he withholds not his consolations from you. I know by experience that they are neither few nor small; and though I feel for you as I never felt for man before, yet do I sincerely rejoice in this, that, whereas there is but one Comforter in the universe, under afflictions such as yours, you both know him, and know where to seek him. I thought you a man the most happily mated that I had ever seen, and had great pleasure in your felicity. Mrs. Unwin also sympathizes with you most sincerely, and you neither are, nor will be soon forgotten, in such prayers as we can make. I will not detain you longer now, my poor afflicted friend, than to commit you to the mercy of God, and to bid you a sorrowful *adieu*. May God be with you my friend, and give you a just measure of submission to his will, the most effectual remedy for the evils of this changing scene. I doubt not that he has granted you this blessing already, and may he still continue it.'

The interest that Cowper took in the spiritual welfare of his correspondents, and the sympathy he felt for them under their domestic bereavements, frequently elicited from his pen such remarks as prove the state of his mind to have been decidedly serious. On one occasion, in a letter to Mr. Unwin, adverting to the state of an individual recently deceased, he writes:

'What an inquiry does the thought of a departed spirit suggest, and how impossible is it to make it to any purpose! What are the employments of the departed spirit? And where does he subsist? Has it any cognizance of earthly things? Is it transported to an immeasurable distance; or is it still, though imperceptible to us, conversant with the same scene, and interested in what passes here! How little do we know of a state to which we are destined! And how does the obscurity that hangs over that undiscovered country, increase the anxiety we sometimes feel as we are journeying towards it? It is sufficient, however, for such as you, and a few more of my acquaintance, to know that in your separate state you will be happy. Provision is made for your reception, and you will have no cause to regret aught that you have left behind.'

CHAPTER XII. Pleasure he enjoyed in his new residence—Sudden death of Mrs. Unwin's son—Cowper's distress on the occasion—Experiences a severe attack of illness—Is compelled to relinquish, for a time, his labours of translation—Mr. Rose's first visit to him—His sudden recovery—Manner of spending his time—Peculiarities of his case—Is dissuaded from resuming his translation—His determination to persevere in it—Applies to it with the utmost diligence—Great care with which he translated—His admiration of the original—Providential preservation of Mrs. Unwin—His painful depression unremoved.

By the end of November 1786, Cowper was comfortably settled in his new residence at Weston. The house was delightfully situated, very near that of his friendly and accomplished landlord, Sir John Throckmorton, with whom he was now on terms of intimacy, and who had given him the full use of his spacious and agreeable pleasure grounds. This afforded him an opportunity, at almost all seasons, of taking that degree of exercise in the open air, which he always found so conducive to his health. The following extracts from his first letter to Lady Hesketh, after entering on his new abode, describe the state of his feelings, and prove how truly he enjoyed the change.

'November 26, 1786. It is my birthday, my beloved cousin, and I determine to employ a part of it that is not destitute of festivity in writing to you. The dark thick fog that has obscured it, would have been a burden to me at Olney, but here I have hardly attended to it. The neatness and snugness of our abode compensates for all the dreariness of the season, and whether the ways are wet or dry, our house at least is always warm and commodious. Oh! For you to partake these comforts with us! I will not begin already to tease you upon that subject, but Mrs. Unwin remembers to have heard from your own lips, that you hate London in the spring. Perhaps, therefore, by that time, you may be glad to escape from a scene, which will be every day growing more disagreeable, that you may enjoy the comforts of the Lodge. You well know that the best house has a desolate appearance unfurnished. This house accordingly, since it has been occupied by us, is as much superior to what it was when you saw it as you could imagine; the parlour is even elegant. When I say that the parlour is elegant, I do not mean to insinuate that the study is not so. It is neat, warm, and silent, and a much better study than I deserve, if I do not produce in it an incomparable translation of Homer. I think every day of those lines of Milton, and congratulate myself on having obtained, before I am quite superannuated, what he seems not to have hoped for sooner.

> And may at length my weary age
> Find out some peaceful hermitage.

For if it is not a hermitage, at least it is a much better thing, and you must always understand, my dear, that when poets talk of cottages and hermitages, they mean a house with six sashes in front, two comfortable parlours, a smart staircase, and three bedchambers of convenient dimensions; in short, exactly such a house as this.'

'The Throckmortons continue the most obliging neighbours in the world. I thought I had known these brothers long enough to have found out all their talents and accomplishments, but I was mistaken. Some men may be estimated at a first interview, but the Throckmortons must be seen often and known long before one can understand all their value. One morning last week, they both went with me to the cliff;—a scene, my dear, in which you would delight beyond measure, but which you cannot visit except in the spring or autumn. The heat of summer and clinging dirt of winter would destroy you. What is called the cliff, is no cliff, nor at all like one, but a beautiful terrace, sloping gently down to the base, and from the brow of which, though it is not lofty, you have a view of such a valley, as makes that which you saw from the hills near Olney, and which I have had the honour to celebrate, an affair of no consideration at all.

'Wintry as the weather is, do not suspect that it confines me. I ramble daily, and every day changes my ramble. Wherever I go, I find short grass under my feet, and when I have travelled, perhaps, five miles, come home with shoes not at all too dirty for a drawing-room.'

Cowper was scarcely settled in his new abode, and had hardly had time to appreciate its enjoyments, before an event occurred, which plunged both him and Mrs. Unwin in the deepest distress. It pleased God, who does everything according to his will, to remove from this scene of toil and labour to the regions of peace and happiness, Mrs. Unwin's son, in the prime of life, and in a manner the most sudden and unexpected. Cowper had always loved him as a brother, and had most unreservedly communicated his mind to him, on all occasions. Their attachment to each other was mutually strong, cordial, and affectionate. The loss of such a friend could not fail to make a deep impression on the poet's mind, and the following extracts will show how much he felt on the occasion.

'I find myself here situated exactly to my mind. Weston is one of the prettiest villages in England; the walks about it are at all seasons of the year delightful. We had just begun to enjoy the pleasantness of our new situation, and to find at least as much comfort in it as the season of the year would permit, when affliction found us out in our retreat, and the news reached us of the death of Mr. William Unwin. He had taken a western tour with Mr. Henry Thornton. On his return, at Winchester, was seized with a putrid fever, which sent him to his grave. He is gone to it, however, though young, as fit for it as age itself could have made him. Regretted indeed, and always to be regretted, by those who knew him; for he had everything that makes a man valuable, both in his principles and in his manners, but leaving still this consolation to his surviving friends; that he was desirable in this world, chiefly because he was so well prepared for a better.'

'The death of one whom I valued as I did Mr. Unwin, is a subject on which I could say much, and with much feeling. Habituated as my mind has been these many years to melancholy themes, I am glad to excuse myself the contemplation of them as much as possible. I will only observe that the death of so young a man, whom I saw so lately in good health, and whose life was so desirable on every account, has something in it peculiarly distressing. I cannot think of the widow and the children he has left without a heartache that I do not remember to have felt before. We may well say that the ways of God are mysterious: in truth, they are so, and to a degree that only such events can give us any conception of Mrs. Unwin's life has been so much a life of affliction, that whatever occurs to her in that shape has not, at least, the terrors of novelty to embitter it. She is supported under this, as she has been under a thousand others, with a submission of which I never saw her deprived for a moment.'

'Though my experience has long since taught me that this world is a world of shadows, and that it is the more prudent, as well as the more Christian course, to possess the comforts that we find in it, as if we possessed them not, it is no easy matter to reduce this doctrine to practice. We forget that that God who gave them, may, when he pleases, take them away; and that, perhaps, it may please him to take them away at a time when we least expect it, and are least disposed to part with them. Thus, it has happened in the present case. There never was a moment in Unwin's life when there seemed to be more urgent want of him than the moment in which he died. He had attained to an age, when, if they are at any time useful, men become more useful to their families, their friends, and the world. His parish began to feel, and to be sensible of the value of his ministry; his children were thriving under his own tuition and management. The removal of a man in the prime of life, of such a character, and with such connections, seems to make a void in society that can never be filled. God seemed to have made him just what he was, that he might be a blessing to others, and when the influence of his character and abilities began to be felt, removed him. These are mysteries that we cannot contemplate without astonishment, but which will nevertheless be explained hereafter, and must, in the meantime, be revered in silence. It is well for Mrs. Unwin that she has spent her life in the practice of an habitual acquiescence in the dispensations of providence, else I know that this stroke would have been heavier, after all that she has suffered upon another account, than she could have borne. She derives, as she well may, great consolation from the thought that be lived the life, and died the death of a Christian. The consequence is, if possible, more certain than the most mathematical conclusion, that therefore he is happy. "The shock that attended this event,' writes Cowper, 'was the more severe, as till within a few hours of his decease there seemed to be no very alarming symptoms. But an unexpected turn to his distemper dashed all our hopes, and deprived us almost immediately of a man whom we must ever regret. His mind, having been from his infancy deeply tinctured with religious sentiments, he was always impressed with a sense of the vast importance of the great change of all, and on former occasions, when at any time he found himself indisposed, was consequently subject to distressing alarms and apprehensions. But in this last instance his mind was from the first composed and easy; his fears were taken away, and succeeded by such a resignation as warrants us in saying that God made all his bed in his sickness. I believe it is always thus where the heart, though upright towards God, as Unwin's assuredly was, is yet troubled with the fear of death. When death indeed comes, he is either welcome or has lost his sting. The virtues and amiable qualities of our friends are the things for which we most wish to keep them: but they are, on the other hand, the very things that in particular ought to reconcile us to their departure. We find ourselves sometimes connected with, and engaged in affections too, to a person of whose readiness and fitness for another life, we cannot have the highest opinion. The death of such a man has bitterness in it, both to themselves and survivors, which, thank God! is not to be found in the death of Unwin.'

Cowper had scarcely given vent to his feelings on the melancholy occurrence of Mr. Unwin's decease, when he was himself again visited by severe indisposition. His depressing malady returned, with all its baleful consequences, and prevented him, for more than six months, from either doing anything with his translation of Homer, or carrying on his correspondence with his friends, or even from enjoying the conversation of those with whom he was most intimately associated, and whom he loved most affectionately. It is highly probable that the painful feelings occasioned by a too frequent recurrence to the apparently disastrous consequences that must be the result of his friend's removal, occasioned this attack. His mind bore up under the first shock with comparative firmness, but his intense feelings, perhaps, pictured its remote effects in colours much more gloomy than were ever likely to be realized. Such seems to have been the case with him at the death of his brother. He attended him in his dying hours, saw him gradually sink into the arms of death, arranged all the affairs of his funeral, and then, when other persons less susceptible of feeling, would in all probability have forgotten the event, his apprehensive mind invested it with imaginary horrors that were to him insupportable.

This affliction of Cowper's commenced in the early part of January, 1787. In a letter to his cousin, he thus adverts to its first symptoms:

'I have had a little nervous fever lately that has somewhat abridged my sleep; and though 1 find myself better to-day than I have been since it seized me, yet I feel my head *light-ish*, and not in the best order for writing.'

In the next letter to the same correspondent, written about a week afterwards—the last he wrote to any of his correspondents until his recovery, he again adverts to the progress of his complaint.

'I have been so much indisposed with the nervous fever which I told you in my last had seized me, that my nights, during the whole week, may be said to have been almost sleepless. The consequence has been that, except the translation of about thirty lines at the conclusion of the thirteenth book, I have been forced to abandon Homer entirely. This was a sensible mortification to me, as you may suppose, and felt the more, because my spirits of course failing with my strength, I seemed to have peculiar need of my old amusement. It seemed hard, therefore, to be forced to resign it, just when I wanted it most. Homer's battles cannot be fought by a man who does not sleep well, and who has not some little degree of animation in the day time. Last night, however, quite contrary to my expectation, the fever left me entirely, and I slept soundly, quietly, and long. If it please God that it return not, I shall soon find myself in a condition to proceed. I walk constantly, that is to say, Mrs. Unwin and I together; for at these times I keep her continually employed, and never suffer her to be absent from me many minutes. She gives me all her time, and all her attention, and forgets that there is another object in the world beside myself.'

Imagining that much of Cowper's distress arose from his dreams of which he frequently complained during the whole of his life, Lady Hesketh attempted to dissuade him from regarding them as affairs of any importance. For this purpose, she sent him the opinion of an eminently pious lady on the subject, on whose judgment she conceived the poet would place much confidence. In reply, he writes:

'Mrs. Carter thinks on the subject of dreams as everybody else does, that is to say, according to her own experience. She has had no extraordinary ones, and therefore accounts them only the ordinary operations of the fancy. Mine are of a texture that will not suffer me to ascribe them to so inadequate a cause, or to any cause but the operation of an exterior agency. I have a mind, my dear, (and to you I will venture to boast of it,) as free from superstition as any man living; neither do I give heed to dreams in general as predictive, though particular dreams I believe to be so. Some very sensible persons will acknowledge that in old times God spoke by dreams, but affirm, with much boldness, that he has since ceased to do so. If you ask them why: they answer, Because he has now revealed his will in the Scripture, and there is no longer any need that he should instruct or admonish by dreams. I grant, that with respect to doctrines and precepts, he has left us in want of nothing; but has he thereby precluded himself in any of the operations of his providence? Surely not. It is perfectly a different consideration; and the same need that there ever was of his interference in this way, there is still, and ever must be, while man continues blind and fallible, and a creature beset with dangers, which he can neither foresee nor obviate. His operations, however, of this kind are, I allow, very rare; and as to the generality of dreams, they are made of such stuff, and are in themselves so insignificant, that though I believe them to be the manufacture of others, and not our own, I account it not a farthing matter who manufactures them. So much for dreams.'

About this time, that intimacy between Cowper and Samuel Rose, Esq., which subsequently ripened into a friendship, which nothing but death could dissolve, commenced. At the close of the letter from which we made our last extract, Cowper thus discusses the circumstance.

'A young gentleman called here yesterday, who came six miles out of his way to see me. He was on a journey from Glasgow to London, having just left the university there. He came, I suppose, partly to satisfy his own curiosity, but chiefly, as it seemed, to bring me the thanks of some of the Scotch professors for my two volumes. His name is Rose, an Englishman. Your spirits being good, you will derive more pleasure from this incident than I can at present, therefore I send it.' Notwithstanding the depression of mind which Cowper was beginning again to experience, when this unexpected interview between him and Mr. Rose took place, and his consequent aversion to the visits of any one, but especially of strangers, yet he was so highly pleased with his new friend, that he commenced a correspondence with him immediately on recovering his health; and he ever regarded it as a providential circumstance, and a token of the goodness of God towards him, in giving him a friend, who, as a literary correspondent, in some measure, at least, supplied the loss he had experienced by the death of Mr. Unwin.

In February 1787, Cowper's mental malady had so greatly increased that his mind became again enveloped in the deepest gloom. The following extracts from his letters, written after his recovery, which took place in the ensuing autumn, will best describe the painful and distressing state to which he was reduced:

'My indisposition could not be of a worse kind. Had I been afflicted with a fever, or confined by a broken bone, neither of these cases would have made it impossible that we should meet. 1 am truly sorry that the impediment was insurmountable while it lasted, for such, in fact, it was. The sight of any face, except Mrs. Unwin's, was to me an insupportable grievance; and when it has happened, that by forcing himself into my hiding place, some friend has found me out; he has had no great cause to exult in his success, as Mr. Bull could tell you. From this dreadful condition of mind, I emerged suddenly; so suddenly that Mrs. Unwin, having no notice of such a change herself could give none to anybody and when it obtained, how long it might last, and how far it might be depended upon, was a matter of the greatest uncertainty. It affects me on the recollection with the more concern, because it has deprived me of an interview with you, and has prevented you from visiting others who would have been very glad to see you.'

In the midst of Cowper's severe attack, his friend Mr. Rose paid him another visit, and was greatly distressed to find him reduced to such a degree of wretchedness, that he could not be prevailed upon to converse with him on any subject. Cowper, as soon as he began to feel the slightest symptoms of recovery, recollected the great sympathy and disinterested kindness of his new friend, and he took care to present him with the first productions of his pen. In the last week of July 1787, he thus addressed him:

'This is the first time I have written these six months; and nothing but the constraint of obligation could induce me to write now. I cannot be so wanting to myself as not to endeavour at least to thank you, both for the visits with which you have favoured me, and the poem that you have sent me. In my present state of mind I taste nothing, nevertheless I read, partly from habit, and partly because it is the only thing I am capable of.'

A month afterwards, he again writes to the same correspondent:

'I have not yet taken up my pen, except to write to you. The little taste that I have had of your company, and your kindness in finding me out, make me wish that we were nearer neighbours, and that there were not so great a disparity in our years; that is to say, not that you were older, but that I was younger. Could we have met early in life, I flatter myself that we might have been more intimate than now we are likely to be. You shall not find me slow to cultivate such a measure of your regard as your friends of your own age can spare me. I hope the same kindness which has prompted you twice to call on me, will prompt you again; and I shall be happy, if, on a future occasion, I shall be able to give you a more cheerful reception than can be expected from an invalid. My health and spirits are considerably improved, and I once more associate with my neighbours. My head, however, has been the worst part of me, and continues so, It is subject to giddiness and pain, maladies very unfavourable to poetical employment: but I feel some encouragement to hope that I may possibly, before long, find myself able to resume the translation of Homer. When I cannot walk I read, and read perhaps more than is good for me. I cannot be idle. The only mercy that I show myself in this respect is, that I read nothing that requires much closeness of application.'

Cowper was now recovered sufficiently to resume his correspondence with Lady Hesketh, and the following extracts will throw some additional light on the gradually improving state of his health, and on the manner in which he then spent his time:

'My dear cousin, though it costs me something to write, it would cost me more to be silent. My intercourse with my neighbours being renewed, I can no longer forget how many reasons there are why you especially should not be neglected; no neighbour, indeed, but the kindest of my friends, and ere long, I hope, an inmate. My health and spirits seem to be mending daily. To what end I know not, neither will conjecture, but endeavour, as far as I can, to be content that they do so. I use exercise, and take the air in the park; I read much; have lately read Savary's *Travels in Egypt*; Memoirs of Baron du Tott; Fenn's *Original Letters*; the *Letters of Frederick of Bohemia*; and am now reading *Memoires d'Henri de Lorraine, Due de Guise*. I have also read Barclay's *Argenis*, a Latin romance, and the best romance that was ever written. All these, together with Madan's Letters to Priestley, and several pamphlets, I have read within these two months. So that you will see that, I am a great reader. I, however, write but little, because writing is become new to me; but I shall come on by degrees, and hope to regain the use of my pen before long. Our friends at the Hall make themselves more and more amiable on our account, by treating us rather as old friends, than as friends newly acquired. I am now almost as much at home in their house as in my own. I have the free use of their library, an acquisition of great value to me, as I cannot live without books. By this means I have been so well supplied, that I have not yet even looked at the Lounger, which you were so kind as to send me. His turn comes next, and I shall probably begin him tomorrow.'

Cowper's correspondence with Mr. Newton had now been suspended for some months. In the beginning of the ensuing October he renewed it; and the following extracts will afford some interesting information respecting the peculiarity of his case.

'My dear Friend—After a long but necessary interruption of our correspondence, I return to it again, in one respect, at least, better qualified for it than before; I mean by a belief of your identity, which, for thirteen years, strange and unaccountable as it may appear, I did not believe. The acquisition of this light, if light it may be called, which leaves me as much in the dark as ever on the most interesting subjects, releases me, however, from the most disagreeable suspicion that I am addressing myself to you as the friend whom I loved and valued so highly in my better days, while in fact you are not that friend, but a stranger. I can now write to you without seeming to act a part, and without having any need to charge myself with dissimulation; a charge from which, in that state of mind, and under such an uncomfortable persuasion, I knew not how to exculpate myself, and which, as you will easily conceive, often made my correspondence with you a burden. Still, indeed, it wants, and is likely to want, that best ingredient, which alone can make it truly pleasant, either to myself or you—that spirituality which once enlivened all our intercourse. You will tell me, no doubt, that the knowledge I have gained is an earnest of more, and more valuable information too; and that the dispersion of the clouds in part promises, in due time, their complete dispersion. I should be happy to believe it; but the power to do so is at present far from me. Never was the mind of man benighted to the degree in which mine has been. The storms that have assailed me would have overset the faith of every man that ever had any; and the very remembrance of them, even after they have been long passed by, makes hope impossible.

'Mrs. Unwin, whose poor bark is still held together, though much shattered by being tossed and agitated so long at the side of mine, does not forget yours and Mrs. Newton's kindness on this last occasion. Mrs. Newton's offer to come to her assistance, and your readiness to have rendered us the same service, could you have hoped for any salutary effect of your presence, neither Mrs. Unwin nor I undervalue, nor shall presently forget. But you judged right when you supposed that even your company would have been no relief to me; the company of my father or my brother, could they have been returned from the dead to visit me, would have been none. We are now busied in preparing for the reception of Lady Hesketh, whom we expect here shortly. Mrs. Unwin's time has, of course, been lately occupied to a degree that made writing impracticable; and she excused herself the rather, knowing my intentions to take her office. It does not suit me to write much at a time. This last tempest has left my nerves in a worse condition than it found them; my head especially, though better informed, is more infirm than ever; I will therefore only add, that I rejoice to hear Mrs. Cowper has been so comfortably supported under her heavy trial. She must have severely felt the loss of her son. She has an affectionate heart towards her children, and could not but be sensible of the bitterness of such a cup. God's presence sweetens every bitter. Desertion is the only evil that a Christian cannot bear.'

Cowper's friends were all delighted to see him again vigorously and usefully employing his mental powers; and, as many of them attributed his last attack to the irritation and fatigue occasioned by his translation of Homer, they endeavoured to dissuade him from pursuing it, and recommended him to confine his attention to original poetry.

'I have many kind friends, who, like yourself, wish that, instead of turning my endeavours to a translation of Homer, I had proceeded in the way of original poetry. I can truly say, that it was ordered otherwise, not by me, but by that God who governs all my thoughts, and directs all my intentions as he pleases. It may seem strange, but it is true, that after having written a volume, in general, with great ease to myself, I found it impossible to write another page. The mind of man is not a fountain, but a cistern; and mine, God knows, a broken one. It is my creed that the intellect depends as much, for both the energy and the multitude of its exertions, upon the operations of God's agency upon it, as the heart does for the exercise of its graces, upon the influence of the Holy Spirit. According to this persuasion, I may very reasonably affirm, that it was not God's good pleasure that I should proceed in the same track, because he did not enable me to do it. A whole year I waited, and waited in circumstances of mind that made a state of new employment peculiarly irksome to me. I longed for the pen as the only remedy, but I could find no subject; extreme distress at last drove me as, if I mistake not, I told you some time since, to lay Homer before me, and translate for amusement. Why it pleased God that I should be hunted into such a business, of such enormous length and labour, by miseries for which he did not see good to afford me any other remedy, I know not. '

Ten months had now elapsed since Cowper had laid aside his translation, and as Johnson, the publisher, had been informed of his recovery, he wrote to beg of him to persevere in the work with as little delay as possible. Cowper immediately recommenced the undertaking, and again entered upon it with all his former spirit and activity. The following extracts will show that his affliction had not deprived him of the vigour of his mind, or produced in him the slightest disinclination to engage in this laborious work:

'I am as heretofore, occupied with Homer; my present occupation is the revisal of all I have done, which is the first fifteen books. I stand amazed at my own increasing dexterity in the business, being verily persuaded that as far as I have gone, I have improved the work to double its value. I will assure you that it engages unavoidably my whole attention. The length of it, the spirit of it, the exactness requisite to its due performance, are so many most interesting subjects of consideration to me, who find that my best attempts are only introductory to others, and, that what to-day I supposed finished, to-morrow I must begin again. Thus, it fares with a translator of Homer.

They say of poets, that they must be born such; so must mathematicians, so must great generals, so must lawyers, and so indeed must men of all denominations, or it is not possible that they should excel. With whatever faculties we are born, and to whatever studies our genius may direct us, studies they must still be. I am persuaded that Milton did not write his *Paradise Lo*st, nor Homer his *Iliad,* nor Newton his *Principia,* without immense labour. Nature gave them a bent to their respective pursuits, and that strong propensity, I suppose, is what we mean by genius. The rest they gave themselves.'

'My first thirteen books of Homer have been criticised in London; have been by me accommodated to these criticisms; returned to London in their improved state, and sent back to Weston with an imprimatur. This would satisfy some poets less anxious than I am about what they expose in public, but it has not satisfied me. I am now revising them again, by the light of my own critical taper, and make more alterations than at the first. But are they improvements? Is not the spirit of the work endangered by all this correctness? I think and hope that it is not. Being well aware of the possibility of such a catastrophe, I guard particularly against it. Where I find a servile adherence to the original would render the passage less animated than it ought to be, I still, as at the first, allow myself a liberty. On all other occasions I prune with an unsparing hand, determined that there shall not be found in the whole translation an idea that is not Homer's. My ambition is, to produce the closest copy possible, and, at the same time, as harmonious as I can possibly make it. This being my object, you will no longer think, if indeed you have thought it at all, that I am unnecessarily and overmuch industrious. The original surpasses everything; it is of an immense length, is composed in the best language ever used upon earth, and deserves, indeed demands, all the labour that any translator, be he who he may, can possibly bestow upon it. At present, mere English readers know no more of Homer in reality, than if he had never been translated. That consideration indeed it was, which mainly induced me to the undertaking; and if, after all, either through idleness or dotage upon what I have already done, I leave it chargeable with the same incorrectness as my predecessors, or, indeed, with any other that I may be able to amend, I had much better have amused myself otherwise. I am now in the nineteenth book of the Iliad, and on the point of displaying such feats of heroism, performed by Achilles, as make all other achievements trivial. I may well exclaim, Oh, for a muse of fire! especially, having not only a great host to cope with, but a great river also; much, however, may be done when Homer leads the way. What would I give if he were now living, and within my reach? I, of all men living, have the best excuse for indulging such a wish, unreasonable as it may seem, for I have no doubt that the fire of his eyes, and the smile of his lips, would put me, now and then, in possession of his full meaning more effectually than any commentator!'

This close application of Cowper's to the translation of Homer, was not allowed to suspend, though it in some measure interrupted, his correspondence with Mr. Newton. To him he still opened the state of his mind without the least reserve, and it will appear from the following extracts, that he had lost in no degree his relish for the enjoyments of religion, though his mind still continued under the influence of his depressing malady. 'Your last letter informed us that you were likely to be much occupied for some time in writing on a subject that must be interesting to a person of your feelings—the Slave Trade.

'A few days ago, Providence interfered to preserve me from the heaviest affliction that I could now suffer—the loss of Mrs. Unwin, and in a way the most shocking imaginable. Having kindled her fire in the room where she dresses (an office that she always performs for herself), she placed the candle on the hearth, and kneeling, addressed herself to her devotions; a thought struck her while thus occupied, that the candle, being short, might possibly catch her clothes, she pinched it out with the tongs, and set it on the table. In a few moments the chamber was so filled with smoke, that her eyes watered, and it was hardly possible to see across it. Supposing that it proceeded from the chimney, she pushed the billets backward, and while she did so, casting her eye downward, perceived that her dress was on fire. In fact, before she extinguished the candle, the mischief that she apprehended had begun; and when she related the matter to me, she showed me her clothes, with a hole burnt in them as large as this sheet of paper. It is not possible, perhaps, that so tragic a death should occur to a person actually engaged in prayer, for her escape seems almost a miracle. Her presence of mind, by which she was enabled, without calling for help, or waiting for it, to gather up her clothes, and plunge them, burning as they were, in water, seems as wonderful a part of the occurrence as any. The very report of fire, though distant, has rendered hundreds torpid and incapable of self-succour; how much more was such a disability to be expected, when the fire had not seized a neighbour's house, or begun its devastations in our own, but was actually consuming the apparel that she wore, and seemed in possession of her person.'

In a letter to Mr. Rose, we find him with all his accustomed humility, when adverting to himself, regretting the manner in which he had spent his early life, and pointing out the importance of a due improvement of time at that season:

'You are in possession of the best security imaginable for the due improvement of your time, which is a just sense of its value. Had I been, at your age, as much affected by the important consideration as I am at present, I should not have devoted, as I did, all the earliest parts of my life to amusements only. I am now in the predicament into which the thoughtlessness of youth betrays nine-tenths of mankind, who never discover that the health and good spirits which generally accompany it, are in reality blessings only according to the use we make of them; until advanced years begin to threaten them with the loss of both. How much wiser would thousands have been than now they ever will be, had a puny constitution, or some occasional infirmity, constrained them to devote those hours to study and reflection, which, for want of some such cheek, they have given entirely to dissipation! I therefore account yon happy, who, young as you are, need not be informed that you cannot always be so; and who already know, that the materials upon which age can alone build its comfort, should be brought together at an earlier period.'

The continued pressure upon Cowper's mind will be seen by the following extract from a letter to his cousin, Lady Hesketh, with whom he corresponded, as nearly as possible, at stated and regular intervals, January 30, 1788, he thus writes:

'It is a fortnight since I heard from you, that is to say, a week longer than you have been accustomed to make me wait for a letter. I do not forget that you have recommended to me, on occasions somewhat similar, to banish all anxiety, and to ascribe your silence only to the interruptions of company. Good advice, my dear, but not easily taken by a man circumstanced as I am. I have learned in the school of adversity, a school from which I have no expectations that I shall ever be dismissed, to apprehend the worst, and have ever found it the only course in which I can indulge myself, without the least danger of incurring a disappointment. This kind of experience, continued through many years, has given me such an habitual bias to the gloomy side of everything, that I never have a moment's ease on any subject to which I am not indifferent. How then can I be easy, when I am left afloat upon a sea of endless conjectures, of which you furnish the occasion. Write, I beseech you, and do not forget that I am now a battered actor upon this turbulent stage; that what little vigour of mind I ever had, of the self-supporting kind I mean, has long since been broken, and that though I can bear nothing well, yet anything better than a state of ignorance concerning your welfare. I have spent hours in the night, leaning upon my elbow, and wondering what your silence can mean. I entreat you once more to put an end to these speculations, which cost me more animal spirits than I can spare. I love you, my cousin, and cannot suspect, either with or without cause, the least evil in which you may be concerned, without being greatly troubled! O trouble! The portion of mortals—but mine in particular. Would I had never known thee, or could bid thee farewell forever!

CHAPTER XIII. Pressing invitations of his friends to write a poem on the Slave Trade—Reasons for declining it—Correspondence with Mrs. King—Particular description of his feelings—Death of Sir Ashley Cowper—Description of his character—Great severity of Cowper's depression—Is again urged to write on the Slave Trade —Again declines it—Assigns particular reasons for it—His indefatigable application to Homer—Notice he took of passing events—Mr. and Mrs. Newton's visit to Weston—The pleasure it afforded Cowper— Lady Hesketh's visit—Completion of the *Iliad*, and commencement of the *Odyssey*—His unwearied application to Homer not allowed to divert his attention from religion—Occasional composition of original poetry —Readiness to listen to any alteration that might be suggested in his productions.

Many of Cowper's friends were anxious to have him employ his admirable powers on a poem on the abolition of slavery, and Lady Hesketh wrote him several pressing invitations on the subject, to which he gave the following reply:

'I have now three of your letters, my dearest cousin, before me, all written in the space of a week, and must be, indeed, insensible of kindness, did I not feel yours on this occasion. I cannot describe to you, neither could you comprehend it if I could, the manner in which my mind is sometimes impressed with melancholy on particular subjects. Your late silence was such a subject. I heard, saw, and felt, a thousand terrible things, which had no real existence, and was haunted by them night and day, till they at last extorted from me that doleful epistle, which I have since wished had been burnt before I sent it. But the cloud has passed, and, as far as you are concerned, my heart is once more at rest. Before you gave the hint contained in your last letters, I had once or twice, ruminated on the subject, which you kindly recommended to me. Slavery such as the poor Negroes have endured appeared to me a theme so important at the present juncture that I more than once perceived myself ready to start in that cause, could I have allowed myself to desert Homer for so long a time as it would have cost me to do them justice. While I was pondering these things, the public prints informed me that Miss More was on the point of publication, having actually finished what I had not begun. The sight of her advertisement convinced me that my best course would be that to which I felt myself most inclined; to persevere, without turning aside to attend to any other call, however alluring, in the business I have in hand. It occurred to me likewise, that I had lately borne my testimony in favour of my black brethren, and that I was one of the earliest, if not the first, of those who have expressed their detestation of the diabolical trade in question. On all these accounts, I judged it best to be silent. I shall be glad to see Hannah More's poem; she is a favourite writer with me, and has more nerve and energy, both in her thoughts and language, than half the rhymers in the kingdom.'

The testimony, to which the poet here refers, consisted of three excellent ballads he had composed on the subject, to which he playfully adverts in a letter to Mr. Rose:

'If you hear ballads sung in the streets, on the hardships of the Negroes in the islands, they are probably mine. It must be an honour to any man to have given a blow to that chain, however feeble. Woe be to us, if we refuse the poor captives the redress to which they have so clear a right; and prove ourselves, in the sight of God and men, indifferent to all considerations but those of gain.'

Lest it should be thought singular that Cowper should have written ballads, it may be desirable to record his opinion on this sort of composition, of which he declared himself to be very fond, stating, that as he inherited a taste for it from his father, who succeeded well in it himself, he should have addicted himself to it more than to any other, had not his attention been called from it by graver subjects. 'The ballad,' he remarks, 'is a species of poetry, 1 believe, peculiar to this country, equally adapted both to the drollest and the most tragic subjects. Simplicity and ease are its proper characteristics. Our forefathers excelled in it, but we moderns have lost the art. So much for ballads and ballad-writers; a worthy subject, you will say, for a man whose head might be filled with better things; and it is filled with better things, but I thrust into it all manner of topics that may prove more amusing.'

It will be seen by the last extract made from Cowper's letters to Mr. Newton that he had now commenced a correspondence with Mrs. King, and as his letters to that lady are highly interesting, we shall make such use of them as will be descriptive of the state of his mind at that period. 'A letter from a lady who was once intimate with my brother, could not fail of being most acceptable to me. I lost him just at a moment when those truths which have recommended my volumes to your approbation, were become his daily sustenance, as they had long been mine. The will of God was done. I have sometimes thought that had his life been spared, being made brothers by a closer tie than ever, in the bonds of the same faith, hope, and love, we should have been happier in each other than it was in the power of mere natural affection to make us. But it was his blessing to be taken from a world in which he had no longer any wish to continue; and it will be mine, if, while I live in it, my time may not be altogether wasted: in order to effect that good end, I wrote what I am happy to find has given you pleasure to read. For that pleasure, Madam, you are indebted neither to me nor to my muse; but (as you are well aware) to Him who alone can make divine truths palatable, in whatever vehicle conveyed. A man himself destitute of all spiritual consolation may be the occasion of imparting it to others. Thus I, it seems, who wrote those very poems to amuse a mind oppressed with melancholy, and who have myself derived from them no other benefit (for mere success in authorship will do me no good,) have nevertheless, by so doing, comforted others, at the same time that they administer to me no consolation. I will proceed no further in this strain, lest my prose should damp a pleasure that my verse has happily excited. On the contrary, I will endeavour to rejoice in your joy, and especially because I have myself been the instrument of conveying it.' 'I owe you many acknowledgments, dear madam, for that unreserved communication both of your history and of your sentiments, with which you honoured me in your last: it gives me great pleasure to learn that you are so happily circumstanced, both in respect of situation and frame of mind. With your view of religious subjects, you could not, indeed, speaking properly, be pronounced unhappy in any circumstances; but to have received from above, not only that faith which reconciles the heart to affliction, but many outward comforts also, and especially that greatest of all earthly comforts, a comfortable home, is happiness indeed. May you long enjoy it! As to health or sickness, you have learned already their true value, and know well that the former is no blessing, unless it be sanctified, and that the latter is one of the greatest we can receive, when we are enabled to make a proper use of it.

'The melancholy that I have mentioned to you, and concerning which you are so kind as to inquire, is of a kind, so far as I know, peculiar to myself. It does not at all affect the operations of my mind, on any subject to which I can attach it, whether serious or ludicrous, or whatever it may be; for which reason I am usually employed in either reading or writing, when I am not engaged in conversation. A vacant hour is my abhorrence; because, when I am not occupied, I suffer under the whole influence of my unhappy temperament. I thank you for your recommendation of a medicine from which you have derived benefit yourself; but there is hardly anything that I have not proved, however beneficial it may have been found to others, to be in my own case, utterly useless.

The world in which we live is, indeed, as you say, a foolish world, and is likely to continue such, until the Great Teacher himself shall vouchsafe to make it wiser. I am persuaded that time alone will never mend it.

'You must think me a tardy correspondent. My silence has been occasioned by a malady to which I have all my life been subject—an inflammation of the eyes. The last sudden change of weather, from excessive heat to a wintry degree of cold, occasioned it, and at the same time gave me a pinch of the rheumatic kind, from both which disorders I have but just recovered.'

The following extract from a letter to Mr. Newton, June 5, 1788, in reply to an inquiry which he appears to have made, why Cowper did not associate more with Mr. Bean, an evangelical and truly pious minister, who had recently come to reside at Olney. While it shows the elegance of the poet's taste on the subject of manners, proves, at the same time, that he much enjoyed the conversation of holy and consistent characters:

'It is certain that we do not live far from Olney, but small as the distance is, it has too often the effect of a separation between Mr. Bean and us. He is a man with whom, when I can converse at all, I can converse on terms perfectly agreeable to myself; who does not distress me with forms, nor yet disgust me by the neglect of them; whose manners are easy and natural, and his observations always sensible. I often, therefore, wish him a nearer neighbour.'

In the beginning of June 1788, an event occurred, which, though it had been long expected by Cowper and by all his friends, made a deep impression upon his sensitive mind. This was the death of his esteemed and venerable relation Ashley

Cowper, Esq., Clerk of the Parliaments, and brother to Cowper's father, the last moments of whose life his daughter, Lady Hesketh, had watched over with the tenderest solicitude. In reply to an affectionate letter from his friend Mr. Hill, apprizing him of the event, he thus writes:

'Your letter brought me the first intelligence of the event it mentions. My last from Lady Hesketh gave me reason enough to expect it; but the certainty of it was unknown to me until I learned it by your information. If gradual decline, the consequence of great age, be a sufficient preparation of the mind to encounter such a loss, our minds were certainly prepared to meet it: yet to you I need not say that no preparation can supersede the feelings of the heart on such occasions. While our friends yet live, inhabitants of the same world with ourselves, they seem still to live to us— we are sure that they often think of us; and, however improbable it may seem, it is never impossible that we may see each other once again. But the grave, like a great gulf, swallows all such expectations, and in the moment when a beloved friend sinks into it, a thousand tender recollections awaken a regret that will be felt in spite of all reasonings, and let our warnings have been what they may. Thus it is I take my leave of poor Ashley, whose heart towards me was ever truly parental, and to whose memory I owe a tenderness and respect that will never leave me.'

The following remarks on his uncle's character, in a letter to Lady Hesketh, will show how justly Cowper had appreciated the merits of his esteemed relative, who was himself an elegant poet, and was beloved by all who knew him for his amiable and virtuous conduct. 'My dear uncle's death awakened in me many reflections, which, for a time, sunk my spirits. A man like him would have been mourned, had he doubled the age he reached. The consciousness that he still lived was a comfort to me. Let it comfort us now, that we have lost him only at a time when nature could afford him to us no longer; that as his life was blameless, so was his death without anguish, and that he is gone to heaven. I know not that human life, in its most prosperous state, can present anything to our wishes half so desirable as such a close of it.'

In another letter, he again writes:

'We have indeed lost one who has not left his like in the present generation of our family; and whose equal, in all respects, no future generation of it will probably produce. My memory retains so perfect an impression of him, that, had I been painter instead of poet, I could, from those youthful traces, have perpetuated his face and form with the most minute exactness; and this I the rather wonder at, because some, with whom I was equally conversant five-and-twenty years ago, have almost faded out of all recollection with me. He made an impression not soon to be effaced, and was in figure, in temper, and manner, and in numerous other respects, such as I shall never behold again. I often think what a joyful interview there has been between him and some of his friends who went before him. The truth of the matter is, my dear, they are happy ones, and we shall never be entirely so ourselves till we have joined the party. Can there be anything so worthy of our warmest wishes as to enter on an eternal, unchangeable state, in blessed fellowship and communion with those whose society we valued most, and for the best of reasons, while they continued with us? A few steps more through a vain, foolish world and this happiness will be yours. I earnestly hope the end of thy journey is not near. For of all that live, thou art one whom I can least spare; for thou also art one who shall not leave thy equal behind thee.'

The state of Cowper's mind at this period will be discovered by the following extract from a letter to his friend, Mr. Bull, who appears to have solicited him for some original hymns, to be used by him, probably, on some public occasion.

'Ask possibilities, and they shall be performed; but ask not hymns from a man suffering with despair as I do. I would not sing the Lord's song were it to save my life, banished as I am, not to a strange land, but to remoteness from his presence, in comparison with which the distance from east to west is no distance—is vicinity and cohesion. I dare not, either in prose or verse, allow myself to express a frame of mind which I am conscious does not belong to me; least of all can I venture to use the language of absolute resignation, lest, only counterfeiting, I should, for that very reason, be taken strictly at my word, and lose all my remaining comfort. Can there not be found, among the translations of Madame Guion somewhat that might serve the purpose? I should think there might. Submission to the will of Christ, my memory tells me, is a theme that pervades them all. If so, your request is performed already; and if any alteration in them should be necessary, I will, with all my heart, make it. I have no objection to giving the graces of a foreigner an English dress, but insuperable ones to all false pretences and affected exhibitions of what I do not feel.'

Several of Cowper's correspondents, at this time, again strongly urged him to write a poem on the slave trade. The following extracts will show that he was unwilling to give a refusal, though he could by no means prevail upon himself to accede to their wishes. 'Twice or thrice, before your request came, have I been solicited to write a poem on the cruel, odious, and disgusting subject of Negro slavery. But besides that it would be in some sort treason against Homer to abandon him for any other matter, I felt myself so much hurt in my spirits the moment I entered on the contemplation of it, that I have at last determined, absolutely, to have nothing more to do with it. I shall rejoice if your friend, influenced by what you told him of my present engagements, shall waive his application to me for a poem on this revolting subject. I account myself honoured by his intention to solicit one, and it would give me pain to refuse him, which inevitably I shall be constrained to do. The more I have considered it, the more I have convinced myself that it is not a promising theme for verse, at least to me. General censure on the iniquity of the practice will avail nothing. The world has been overwhelmed with such remarks already, and to particularize all the horrors of it, were an employment for the mind, both of the poet and of his readers, of which they would necessarily soon grow weary. For my own part, I cannot contemplate the subject very nearly, without a degree of abhorrence that affects my spirits, and sinks them below the pitch requisite for success in verse. Lady Hesketh recommended it to me some months since, and then I declined it for these reasons, and for others which I need not now mention.'

The summer of 1788 was remarkably hot and dry, and to show the manner in which it affected Cowper's mind, we give the following extract from a letter to one of his correspondents:

'It has pleased God to give us rain, without which, this part of the country at least, must soon have become a desert. The goodness and power of God are never, (I believe,) so universally acknowledged as at the end of a long drought. Man is naturally a self-sufficient animal, and in all concerns that seem to be within the sphere of his own ability, thinks little, or not at all, of the need he always has of protection and furtherance from above.

The summer is leaving us at a rapid rate, as indeed do all the seasons, and though I have marked their flight often, I know not which is the swiftest. Man is never so deluded as when he dreams of his own duration. The answer of the old patriarch to Pharaoh may be adopted by every man at the close of the longest life. "Few and evil have been the days of the years of my pilgrimage." Whether we look back from fifty, or from twice fifty, the past appears equally a dream; and we can only be said truly to have lived, while we have been profitably employed.'

In the latter part of July 1788, Mr. and Mrs. Newton paid Cowper a visit at Weston; and the pleasure it afforded him, with the state of his mind on the occasion, will be seen by the following extract from a letter addressed to Mr. Newton, after his return.

'I rejoice that you and yours reached London safe, especially when I reflect that you performed your journey on a day so fatal, as I understand, to others travelling the same road. I found those comforts in your visit, which have formerly sweetened all our interviews, in part restored. I knew you, knew you for the same shepherd who was sent to lead me out of the wilderness into the pasture, where the Chief Shepherd feeds his flock, and felt my sentiments of affectionate friendship for you the same as ever... [I feel at this time] a firm persuasion that I can never durably enjoy a comfortable state of mind, but must be depressed in proportion as I have been elevated, withers my joys in the bud, and, in a manner, entombs them before they are born: for I have no expectation but of sad vicissitude, and ever believe that the last shock of all will be fatal.'

It might be supposed, from the gloomy state of Cowper's mind, as described by his letters, that no person could feel any real enjoyment in his society; and that his friends who visited him, did so, not so much for their own sake as for his. Referring to this, in a letter to Mr. Rose, he remarks:

'It seems almost incredible to myself that my company should be at all desirable to you, or to any man. I know so little of the world as it goes on at present, and labour generally under such a depression of spirits, especially at those times when I could wish to be most cheerful, that my own share in every conversation appears to me to be the most insipid thing imaginable. But yesterday you found it otherwise, and I will not, for my own sake, doubt your sincerity.'

The fact was, that all who had once been favoured with his company, were particularly anxious to enjoy it again; for though he was never what might be termed brilliant in conversation, yet he was always interesting; and his amiable, polite, and unaffected manners, associated with his rich intellectual acquirements, which he had the happy talent of displaying in a manner perfectly unobtrusive, made him the charm of the social circle. His anxiety to promote the happiness of those with whom he might happen to be associated, gave to his conversation an air of cheerfulness, and sometimes even of sprightliness and vivacity, altogether different from that which generally pervaded his correspondence: and the same amiable solicitude for the welfare of others, caused him sometimes to write to his correspondents in a style the most playful and agreeable.

During the time that Mr. and Mrs. Newton were on their visit at Weston, Cowper's friend, Mr. Samuel Rose, arrived there also. Cowper was highly pleased with this circumstance, as it served to enliven his social circle, and afforded him an opportunity to introduce his young friend to Mr. Newton, whose advice and influence might probably be of considerable advantage to him at a future period. To a person easily diverted from his purpose, the company of friends whom he so highly esteemed, would have been thought a sufficient excuse for the suspension of every literary engagement. Cowper, however, laboured indefatigably at his translation, and instead of laying it aside because of his friends' visits, he gladly availed himself of their advice and assistance. We learn from the following remarks, extracted from a letter to his cousin, written about this time, that Cowper would not allow his friend Rose to pay him an idle visit:

'My dear cousin, the Newtons are still here, and will continue with us, I believe, till the 15th of the month. Here is also my friend, Mr. Rose, a valuable young man, who, attracted by the effluvia of my genius, found me out in my retirement last January twelvemonth. I have not permitted him to be idle, but have made him transcribe for me the twelfth book of the *Iliad*. He brings me the compliments of several of the *literati*, with whom he is acquainted in town; and tells me that from Dr. MacLaine, whom he saw lately, he learns that my book is in the hands of sixty different persons at the Hague, who are all enchanted with it; not forgetting the said Dr. MacLaine himself, who tells him that he reads it every day, and is always the better for it. I desire to be thankful for this encouraging information, and am willing to ascribe it to its only legitimate cause, the blessing of God upon my feeble efforts.'

Shortly after Mr. Rose and Mr. and Mrs. Newton left Weston, the vacuum which the absence of their agreeable company made in Cowper's enjoyments was supplied by the arrival of his cousin, Lady Hesketh, whose cheerful conversation contributed greatly to his comfort, and who diminished much of the labour of his translation by transcribing the manuscript, so that a fair copy might be forwarded to the printer. In September,

1788, he finished the Iliad, and thus describes his feelings on the occasion, in a letter to his friend, Mr. Rose:

'The day on which you shall receive this, I beg you will remember to drink one glass at least, to the success of the *Iliad*, which I finished the day before yesterday, and yesterday began the *Odyssey*. It will be some time before I shall perceive myself "travelling in another road.

Cowper's time was now so much employed in his translation, that he had but little opportunity for keeping up his correspondence, and the letters he wrote at this period, abound with apologies for his apparent neglect. He still, however, found time to advert to passing events, sufficiently to prove that the bent of his mind remained decidedly serious.

Lady Hesketh remained at Weston through the greater part of the winter of 1788-9, and contributed much to revive Cowper's drooping spirits, and to cheer and animate him in his important undertaking; which seemed to engage more of his time the nearer it approached to a finish. The close attention that he found it indispensably necessary to bestow upon it compelled him almost entirely to relinquish his correspondence. We find him thus excusing himself for his apparent neglect:

'The post brings me no letters that do not grumble at my silence. Had not you, therefore, taken me to task as roundly as others, I should perhaps have concluded that you were more indifferent to my epistles than the rest of my correspondents; of whom one says, 'I shall be glad when you have finished Homer; then possibly you will find a little leisure for an old friend.' Another says, 'I don't choose to be neglected, unless you equally neglect everyone else.' Thus I hear of it with both ears, and shall, till I appear in the shape of two large quarto volumes, the composition of which, I confess, engrosses me to a degree that gives my friends, to whom I feel myself much obliged for their anxiety to hear from me, but too much reason to complain. But be it known to you, that I have still two books of the Odyssey before me, and when they are finished, shall have almost the whole eight-and-forty to revise. Judge then, my dear Madam, if it is yet time for me to play, or gratify myself with scribbling to those I love. No, it is necessary that waking I should be all absorbed in Homer, and that sleeping I should dream of nothing else.'

Busily engaged, however, as Cowper was with his translation, he found time to compose several short and beautiful poems, on various subjects, which happened to occur to his mind. These were eagerly sought after by his correspondents, and were forwarded to them respectively, as opportunities offered, accompanied generally with the poet's acknowledgments of their comparative insignificance, at least in his own esteem. Several of these productions were written to oblige his friends, for whom Cowper always had the highest regard, and whom he felt pleased on all occasions to accommodate; others were written at the request of strangers, whom he was willing, when it lay fairly in his way, to oblige. On one occasion, the parish clerk of Northampton applied to him for some verses, to be annexed to some bills of mortality, which he was accustomed to publish at Christmas. This singular incident, so illustrative of Cowper's real kindness of heart, he relates in the following most interesting and sprightly manner:

On Monday morning last, Sam brought me word that there was a man in the kitchen, who desired to speak with me. I ordered him in. A plain, decent, elderly-looking figure made its appearance, and being desired to sit, spoke as follows: ' Sir, I am clerk of the parish of All Saints, in Northampton; brother of Mr. C. the upholsterer. It is customary for the person in my office to annex to a bill of mortality, which he publishes at Christmas, a copy of verses. You would do me a great favour, Sir, if you would furnish me with one.'

To this, I replied: 'Mr. C. you have several men of genius in your town, why have you not applied to some of them? There is a namesake of yours in particular, Mr. C. the statuary, who everybody knows is a first-rate maker of verses. He surely is the man, of all the world, for your purpose.'

'Alas! Sir,' replied he, 'I have heretofore borrowed help from him, but he is a gentleman of so much reading, that the people of our town cannot understand him.' I confess I felt all the force of the compliment implied in this speech, and was almost ready to answer, 'Perhaps, my good friend, they may find me unintelligible for the same reason.' But on asking him whether he had walked over to Weston on purpose to implore the assistance of my muse, and on his replying in the affirmative, I felt my mortified vanity a little consoled, and pitying the poor man's distress, which appeared to be considerable, promised to supply him. The wagon has accordingly gone this day to Northampton, loaded in part with my effusions in the mortuary style. A fig for poets who write epitaphs upon individuals, I have written one that serves two hundred persons.'

On another occasion, Cowper thus writes to Mr. Hill about the numerous entreaties he sometimes received for the assistance of his muse:

'My muse were a vixen, if she were not always ready to fly in obedience to your commands. But what can be done? I can write nothing in the few hours that remain to me of this day, that will be fit for your purpose; and, unless I could despatch what I write by to-morrow's post, it would not reach you in time. I must add, too, that my friend, the vicar of the next parish, engaged me, the day before yesterday, to furnish him by next Sunday with a hymn to be sung on the occasion of his preaching to the children of the Sunday school; of which hymn I have not yet produced a syllable. If I could split myself into as many poets as there are muses, I could find employment for them all.'

These numerous engagements, however, did not prevent the poet from recording his sentiments respecting any circumstance that occurred which be thought deserving of notice. About this time the following melancholy event happened, which drew from him lines expressive of his entire abhorrence of cruelty upon the lower order of animals.

John A—, Esq. a young gentleman of large fortune, who was passionately fond of cockfighting, came to his death in the following awful manner. He had a favourite cock, upon which he had won many large sums. The last bet he laid upon it he lost, which so enraged him, that he had the bird tied to a spit, and roasted alive before a large fire. The screams of the suffering animal were so affecting, that some gentlemen who were present attempted to interfere, which so exasperated Mr. A— , that he seized the poker, and with the most furious vehemence declared that he would kill the first man who interfered. However, in the midst of his rage and imprecations, awful to relate, he fell down dead upon the spot.

Cowper was so deeply affected by the circumstance, that he composed a poetic obituary on the occasion, which was inserted in the *Gentleman's Magazine* for May 1789, and has since been published in the additional volume of his works, compiled and edited by his kinsman Dr. Johnson.

Although Cowper's literary engagements compelled him now to write fewer letters than formerly, and obliged him to make those he did write much shorter, yet, on every subject that came under his notice he made many judicious and excellent remarks.

Concerning that constitutional timidity, which occasioned him so much bitterness of feeling, he thus writes to his friend Rose, who was studying for the bar, and who seemed to have been harassed with similar apprehensions:

'I pitied you for the fears which deprived you of your uncle's company, and the more from having suffered so much by those fears myself. Fight against that vicious fear, for such it is, as strenuously as you can. It is the worst enemy that can attack a man destined to the forum. It ruined me. To associate as much as possible with the most respectable company, for good sense and good breeding, is, I believe, the only—at least, I am sure, it is the best—remedy. The society of men of pleasure will not cure it, but rather leaves us more exposed to its influence in company of better persons.'

On another occasion, referring to the injurious effects of talent, when not associated with piety, he remarks, "Ability, therefore, is not wisdom, and an ounce of grace is a better guard against gross absurdity, than the brightest talents in the world."

The watchful eye with which Cowper regarded providential events, will be seen by the following remarks in a letter cursorily written on the subject of his cousin's return to London, January, 1789. 'My cousin reached home safely. An observation here suggests itself, which, though I have but little time for observation making, I must allow myself time to mention. Accidents, as we call them, generally occur when there seems least reason to expect them. If a friend of ours travels far, over indifferent roads, and at an unfavourable season, we are reasonably alarmed for the safety of one in whom we take such interest; yet how seldom do we hear a tragic account of such a journey! It is, on the contrary, at home, in our own yard or garden, perhaps in our parlour, that disaster finds us out; in any place, in short, where we seem perfectly out of the reach of danger. The lesson inculcated by such a procedure on the part of Providence towards us, seems to be that of perpetual dependence.'

It was Cowper's intention, after finishing his translation, to publish a third volume of original poems, which was to contain, in addition to a poem he intended to compose, similar to the *Task*, entitled *The Four Ages*, all the minor unpublished productions of his pen. It is deeply to be regretted that he was not permitted to carry this design into completion, as the interesting subject of the different stages of man's existence would have been admirably adapted for a complete development of his poetic talents.

CHAPTER XIV. Mrs. Unwin much injured by a fall—Cowper's anxiety respecting her—Continues incessantly engaged on his Homer—His regret that it should have suspended his correspondence with his friends—Revises a small volume of poems for children—State of his mind —Receives as a present from Mrs. Bodham, a portrait of his mother—Feelings on the occasion— Interesting description of her character—Translates a series of Latin letters from a Dutch minister of the gospel—Continuance of his depression—Is attacked with a nervous fever—Completion of his translation— Death of Mrs. Newton—His reflections on the occasion—Again revises his Homer—His unalterable attachment to religion.

In the commencement of 1789, a circumstance occurred, which occasioned Cowper considerable uneasiness. Mrs. Unwin, his amiable inmate and faithful companion, received so severe an injury by a fall, when walking on a gravel path covered with ice, that she was confined to her room for several weeks. Though she neither dislocated any joint, nor broke any bones, yet such was the effect of the fall that it crippled her completely, and rendered her utterly incapable of assisting herself. It happened providentially that Lady Hesketh was at Weston when this painful event occurred. By her kind attention to Mrs. Unwin, and her no less tender care over her esteemed relative, lest his mind should be too deeply affected by this afflicting occurrence, she contributed greatly to the recovery of the former, and to the support of the latter. It was, however, several weeks before Mrs. Unwin recovered her strength sufficiently to attend to her domestic concerns. Her progress, too, when she began to amend, was so slow as to be almost imperceptible, and her lengthened affliction, notwithstanding the precautionary measures adopted by herself and by Lady Hesketh to prevent that effect, tended in a great degree to depress the mind of Cowper.

Early in the ensuing spring, Lady Hesketh was compelled to return to town. Mrs. Unwin had not then wholly recovered her strength, she was, however, so far convalescent as to resume the management of her domestic concerns, and to pay the same kind attention to the poet's comfort which had distinguished all her former conduct towards him. During the greater part of the year 1789, Cowper was incessantly engaged, principally in translating Homer, but occasionally, and indeed frequently, in composing original poems for the gratification of his friends, or in the more difficult employment of revising the productions of less-gifted poets. The few letters he wrote at this time abound with apologies for his seeming negligence, and with descriptions of the manner in which he employed his time. To one of his correspondents he thus writes:

'I know that you are too reasonable a man to expect anything like punctuality of correspondence from a translator of Homer, especially from one who is also a doer of many other things at the same time. I labour hard, not only to acquire a little fame for myself, but to win it for others, men of whom I know nothing, not even their names, who send me their poetry, that, by translating it out of prose into verse, I may make it more like poetry than it was. I begin to perceive that if a man will be an author, he must live neither to himself nor to his friends, so much as to others whom he never saw nor shall see. I feel myself in no small degree unworthy of the kind solicitude, which you express concerning my welfare, and me after a silence so much longer than you had reason to expect. I should indeed account myself inexcusable, had I not to allege in my defence, perpetual engagements of such a kind as could by no means be dispensed with. Had Homer alone been in question, Homer should have made room for you; but I have had other work at the same time, equally pressing and more laborious. Let it suffice to say, that I have not willfully neglected you for a moment, and that you have not been out of my thoughts for a day together. Having heard all this, you will feel yourself disposed not only to pardon my long silence, but to pity me for the causes of it. You may, if you please, believe likewise, for it is true, that I have a faculty of remembering my friends even when I do not write to them, and of loving them not one jot the less, though I leave them to starve for want of a letter from me.'

Some months afterwards, to John Newton, Cowper thus writes:

'On this fine first of December, under an unclouded sky, and in a room full of sunshine, I address myself to the payment of a debt, long in arrear, but never forgotten by me, however I may have seemed to forget it. I will not waste time in apologies. I have but one and that one will suggest itself unmentioned. I will only add, that you are the first to whom I write, of several to whom I have not written many months, who all have claims upon me , and who, I flatter myself, are all grumbling at my silence. In your case, perhaps I have been less anxious than in the case of some others; because, if you have not heard from myself, you have heard from Mrs. Unwin. From her you have learned that I live; that I am as well as usual; and that I translate Homer; three short items, but in which is comprised the whole detail of my present history. Thus I fared when you were here; thus I have fared ever since you were here; and thus, if it please God, I shall continue to fare for some time longer; for, though the work is done, it is not finished; a riddle which you, who are a brother of the press, will solve easily. I have been the less anxious on your behalf, because I have had frequent opportunities to hear from you; and have always heard that you are in good health, and happy. Of Mrs. Newton, too, I have heard more favourable accounts of late, which has given us both the sincerest pleasure. Mrs. Unwin's case is, at present, my only subject of uneasiness that is not immediately personal, and properly my own. She has almost constant headaches; almost a constant pain in her side, which nobody understands; and her lameness, within the last half-year, is very little amended. But her spirits are good, because supported by comforts which depend not on the state of the body; and I do not know that with all her pain, her appearance is at all altered since we had the happiness to see you here, unless indeed it be altered a little for the better. I have thus given you as circumstantial an account of ourselves as I could; the most interesting matter, I verily believe, with which I could have filled my paper, unless I could have made spiritual mercies to myself the subject. In my next, perhaps, I shall find time to bestow a few lines on what is doing in France, and in the Austrian Netherlands; though, to say the truth, I am much better qualified to write an essay on the siege of Troy, than to descant on any of these modern revolutions. I question if in either of the countries just mentioned, full of bustle and tumult as they are, there be a single character whom Homer, were he living, would deign to make his hero. The populace are the heroes now, and the stuff of which gentlemen heroes are made seems to be all expended.'

The year 1790 found Cowper still indefatigably engaged in preparing his translation for the press. In a letter to Mrs. King, 4th January, he thus writes:

'Your long silence has occasioned me a thousand anxious thoughts about you. So long has it been, that whether I now write to a Mrs. King at present on earth, or already in heaven, I know not. I have friends whose silence troubles me less, though I have known them longer; because, if I hear not from themselves, I yet hear from others, that they are still living, and likely to live. But if your letters cease to bring me news of your welfare, from whom can I gain the desirable intelligence? The birds of the air will not bring it, and third person there is none between us by whom it might be conveyed. Nothing is plain to me on this subject, but that either you are dead, or very much indisposed, or—which would, perhaps, affect me with as deep a concern, though of a different kind,—very much offended. The latter of those suppositions I think the least probable, conscious as I am of an habitual desire to offend nobody, especially a lady, and a lady too who has laid me under so many obligations. But all the three solutions above-mentioned are very uncomfortable; and, if you live, and can send me one that will cause me less pain than either of them, I conjure you, by the charity and benevolence which I know influence you on all occasions, to communicate it without delay. It is possible, notwithstanding appearances to the contrary, that you are not become perfectly indifferent to me, and to what concerns me. I will, therefore, add a word or two on the subject which once interested you, and which is, for that reason, worthy to be mentioned, though truly for no other. I am well, and have been so (uneasiness on your part excepted) both in mind and body ever since I wrote to you last. I have still the same employment; Homer in the morning, and Homer in the evening, as constant as the day goes round. In the spring, I hope to send the Iliad and the Odyssey to the press. So much for me and my occupations.'

It would scarcely be supposed that a person performing such an Herculean task as that of translating Homer, would have troubled himself to compose, or even to revise, a volume of hymns for children. The following extract, however, will show that, anxious as Cowper was to finish his Homer, he could nevertheless allow his attention to be, in a great measure, diverted from it, at least for a time, when he thought he could employ his talents usefully. 'I have long been silent, but you have had the charity, I hope and believe, not to ascribe my silence to a wrong cause. The truth is, I have been too busy to write to anybody, having been obliged to give my early mornings to the revisal and correction of a little volume of hymns for children, written by I know not whom. The late Rev. Rowland Hill was their author, of which Cowper was afterwards apprized. This task I finished yesterday, and while it was in hand, wrote only to my cousin, and to her rarely. From her, however, I knew that you would hear of my well-being, which made me less anxious about my debts to you than I should have been otherwise. The winter has been mild; but our winters are in general such, that when a friend leaves us in the beginning of that season, I always feel in my heart a perhaps, importing that we may possibly have met for the last time, and that the robins may whistle on the grave of one of us before the return of summer.'

Relating to the difficulties he found in rendering some parts of his translation to please his taste, he remarks:

'Though I have been employed as described above, I am still thrumming Homer's lyre; that is to say, I am still employed in my last revisal; and to give you some idea of the intenseness of my toils, I will inform you that it cost me all the morning yesterday, and all the evening, to translate a single simile to my mind. The transitions from one member of the subject to another, though easy and natural in the Greek, turn out often so intolerably awkward in an English version, that almost endless labour, and no little address, are requisite to give them grace and elegance. The under parts of the poem, (those, I mean, which are merely narrative) I find the most difficult. These can only be supported by the diction, and on these, for that reason, I have bestowed the most abundant labour. Fine similes, and fine speeches, are more likely to take care of themselves; but the exact process of slaying a sheep and dressing it, it is not so easy in our language and in our measure to dignify. I shall have the comfort, as I before said, to reflect, that whatever may be hereafter laid to my charge, the sin of idleness will not,—justly, at least, it never will. In the meantime, I must be allowed to say, that not to fall short of the original in any respect, is impossible. I thank you for your German clavis, which has been of considerable use to me; I am indebted to it for a right understanding of the manner in which Achilles prepared pork, mutton, and goats' flesh, for the entertainment of his friends, on the night when they came deputed by Agamemnon to negotiate a reconciliation:—a passage of which nobody in the world is perfectly master, myself only and Schaulfelbergerus excepted, nor ever was, except when Greek was a living language.'

About this time, Mrs. King appears to have been informed that it was Cowper's intention to leave Weston, and that Mrs. Unwin had been making inquiries after a house at Huntingdon. Adverting to this report, in a letter to that lady, he thus writes:

The report that informed you of inquiries made by Mrs. Unwin after a house at Huntingdon was unfounded. We have no thought of quitting Weston, unless the same Providence that led us hither should lead us away. It is a situation the most eligible, perfectly agreeable to us both and to me in particular, who write much, and walk much, and, consequently, love silence and retirement. If it has a fault, it is, that it seems to threaten us with a certainty of never seeing you. May we hope that when a milder season shall have improved your health, we may yet, notwithstanding the distance, be favoured with Mr. King's and your company? A better season will likewise improve the roads, and exactly in proportion as it does so, will, in effect, lessen the interval between us. I know not if Mr. King be a mathematician, but most probably he is a good one, and he can tell you that this is a proposition mathematically true, though rather paradoxical in appearance.

In a letter to Mr. Newton, February 5, 1790, Cowper again plaintively describes the state of his mind.

Your kind letter deserved a speedier answer, but you know my excuse, which were I to repeat always, my letters would resemble the fag end of a newspaper, where we always find the price of stocks, detailed with little or no variation. When January returns, you have your feelings concerning me, and such as prove the faithfulness of your friendship. I have mine also concerning myself, but they are of a cast different from yours. Yours have a mixture of sympathy and tender solicitude, which makes them pleasant. Mine, on the contrary, are of an unmixed nature, and consist simply and merely of the most alarming apprehensions. Twice has that month returned upon me, accompanied by horrors. I number the nights as they pass, and in the morning bless myself that another night is gone, and no harm has happened. This may argue, perhaps, some imbecility of mind, and, indeed, no small degree of it; but it is natural, I believe, and so natural as to be necessary and unavoidable. I know that God is not governed by secondary causes in any of his operations; and that, on the contrary, they are all so many agents, in his hand, which strike only when he bids them. I know, consequently, that one month is as dangerous to me as another; and that in the middle of summer, at noonday, and in the clear sunshine, I am in reality, unless guarded by Him, as much exposed as when fast asleep at midnight, and in midwinter. We are not always wiser for our knowledge, and I can no more avail myself of mine, in this case, than if it were in the head of any other man, and not in my own. I have heard of bodily aches and ails, that have been particularly troublesome when the season returned in which the hurt that occasioned them was received. The mind, I believe, (with my own, however, I am sure it is so,) is liable to similar periodical affections. But February is come; January, my terror, is passed; and some shades of the gloom that attended his presence have passed with him. I look forward, with a little cheerfulness, to the buds and the leaves that will soon appear, and say to myself; *Till they turn yellow I will make myself easy.* The year will go round, and January will approach; I shall tremble again, and I know it; but in the meantime I will be as comfortable as I can.'

Towards the end of this month, Cowper received as a present from Anne Bodham, a cousin of his, then residing in Norfolk, his mother's portrait. The following extracts will show the powerful impression which this circumstance made upon his tender mind: 'My dearest Rose, Mrs. Bodham's name was Anne, but Cowper always called her Rose whom I thought withered and fallen from the stalk, but whom I found still alive: nothing could give me greater pleasure than to know it, and to learn it from yourself. I loved you dearly when you were a child, and love you not a jot the less for having ceased to be so. Every creature that bears any affinity to my mother is dear to me, and you, the daughter of her brother, are but one remove distant from her. I love you, therefore, and love you much, both for her sake, and for your own. The world could not have furnished you with a present so acceptable to roe as the picture you have so kindly sent me. I received it the night before last, and received it with foreboding of nerves and spirits, somewhat akin to what I should have felt had the dear original presented herself to my embraces. I kissed it, and hung it where it is the last object that I see at night, and, of course, the first that I open my eyes upon in the morning. She died when I had completed my sixth year, yet I remember her well, and am an ocular witness of the great fidelity of the copy. I remember too, a multitude of the maternal tenderness which I received from her, and which have endeared her memory to me beyond expression. There is, I believe, in me, more of the Donne than of the Cowper, and though I love all of both names, and have a thousand reasons to love those of my own name, yet I feel the bond of nature draw me vehemently to your side. I was thought, in the days of my childhood, much to resemble my mother, and in my natural temper, of which, at the age of fifty-eight, I must be supposed a competent judge, can trace both her, and my late uncle, your father. Somewhat of his irritability, and a little, I would hope, both of his, and of her , I know not what to call it, without seeming to praise myself, which is not my intention; but speaking to you, I will even speak out, and say, good nature. Add to all this, I deal much in poetry, as did our venerable ancestor, the Dean of St. Paul's, and I think I shall have proved myself a Donne at all points. The truth is, whatever I am, and wherever I am, I love you all.'

To Lady Hesketh he thus adverts to the circumstance.—' I am delighted with Mrs. Bodham's kindness in giving me the only picture of my mother that is to be found, I suppose, in all the world. I had rather possess it than the richest jewel in the British crown, for I loved her with an affection that her death, fifty years since, has not in the least abated.

I remember her too, young as I was when she died, well enough to know that it is a very exact resemblance of her, and as such, it is to me invaluable.— Everybody loved her, and with an amiable character so impressed on all her features, everybody was sure to do so.'

To John Johnson, Esq., 28th February, 1790, he thus records his feelings on this occasion. 'I was never more pleased in my life than to learn, and to learn from herself, that my dearest Rose is still alive. Had she not engaged me to love her by the sweetness of her character when a child, she would have done it effectually now, by making me the most acceptable present in the world, my own dear mother's picture. I am perhaps the only person living who remembers her, but I remember her well, and can attest on my own knowledge, the truth of the resemblance. Amiable and elegant as the countenance is, such exactly was her own; she was one of the tenderest of parents, and so just a copy of her is therefore to me invaluable. I wrote yesterday to my Rose, to tell her all this, and to thank her for her kindness in sending it! Neither do I forget your kindness, who intimated to her that I should be happy to possess it. She invites me into Norfolk, but alas! She might as well invite the house in which I dwell: for, all other considerations and impediments apart, how is it possible that a translator of Homer should lumber to such a distance. But though I cannot comply with her kind invitation, I have made myself the best amends in my power, by inviting her, and all the family of Donnes, to Weston.'

To Mrs. King, on the same interesting occasion he writes,

'I have lately received from a female cousin of mine in Norfolk, whom I have not seen these five-and-twenty years, a picture of my own mother. She died when I wanted two days of being six years old; yet I remember her perfectly, find the picture a strong resemblance of her, and because her memory has been ever precious to me, I have written a poem on the receipt of it; a poem which, one excepted, I had more pleasure in writing, than any that I ever wrote. That one was addressed to a lady whom I expect in a few minutes to come down to breakfast, and who has supplied to me the place of my own mother—my own invaluable mother—these six-and-twenty years. Some sons may be said to have many fathers, but a plurality of mothers is not common.'

In May of this year, 1790, Cowper thus describes the manner in which he was employed. 'I am still at my old sport—Homer all the morning, and Homer all the evening. Thus have I been held in constant employment, I know not exactly how many, but I believe these six years, an interval of eight months excepted. It is now become so familiar to me to take Homer from my shelf at a certain hour, that I shall, no doubt, continue to take him from my shelf at a certain time, even after I have ceased to want him. That period is not far distant. I am now giving the last touches to a work, which had I foreseen the difficulty of it, I should never have meddled with; but which, having at length nearly finished it to my mind, I shall discontinue with regret.'

Such was the activity of Cowper's mind, and so desirous was he of turning every incident to advantage, that though harassed by his depressing malady, and closely occupied with his translation, he still found time to compose a number of small poems, on such subjects as happened to attract his notice. To Mrs. King, who, like all the poet's friends, was anxious to see these lighter original productions, and who promised to send her servant to Weston for conveying some to her that Cowper had kindly offered to send, he writes:

'Observe, madam, I do not wish to hasten your messenger hither, for it is probable that the later he arrives the more he will receive when he comes; for I never fail to write when I think I have found a suitable subject.' Perhaps no one was ever better qualified to give sound and judicious advice to persons in various conditions in life than Cowper was, and no one certainly ever gave it more cheerfully, or in a manner more perfectly unassuming. An instance of this occurred in a letter, which he wrote in June of this year, to his cousin, Mr. Johnson, who was then pursuing his studies at Cambridge, who had recently been introduced to him, and for whom he entertained the most affectionate regard. 'You never pleased me more than when you told me you had abandoned your mathematical pursuits. It grieved me to think that you were wasting your time merely to gain a little Cambridge fame; not scarcely worth having. I cannot be contented that your renown should thrive nowhere but on the banks of the Cam. Conceive a nobler ambition, and never let your honour be circumscribed by the paltry dimensions of a University. It is well that you have already acquired sufficient information in that science to enable you to pass creditably such examinations as I suppose you must hereafter undergo. Keep what you have gotten, and be content; more is needless. You could not apply to a worse than I am to advise you concerning your studies. I was never a regular student myself, but lost the most valuable part of my life in an attorney's office, and in the Temple. I will not therefore give myself airs, and affect to know what I know not. The affair is of great importance to you, and you should be directed by a wiser than I. To speak, however, in very general terms on the subject, it seems to me that your chief concern is with history, natural philosophy, logic, and divinity; as to metaphysics, I know but little about them, but the very little I do know has not taught me to admire them. Life is too short to afford time even for serious trifles; pursue what you know to be attainable, make truth your object, and your studies will make you a wise man. Let your divinity, if I may advise you, be the divinity of the glorious Reformation. I mean in contradiction to Arminianism, and all the isms that were ever broached in this world of error and ignorance. The divinity of the Reformation is called Calvinism, but injuriously. It has been that of the Church of Christ in all ages. It is the divinity of St. Paul, and of St. Paul's master, who met him on his way to Damascus.'

In the summer of 1790, much as Cowper's time was occupied in giving the final edit to his Homer, he nevertheless, at the request of Mr. Newton, undertook to translate six Latin letters, which he had received from a Dutch minister of the gospel at the Cape of Good Hope. This occupation, though it left him but little time for writing to his numerous correspondents, afforded him considerable pleasure. There was a congeniality in it to the prevailing disposition of his mind, and in a letter to Mr. Newton, who requested him to publish these letters, he thus writes.—' I have no objection at all to be known as the translator of Van Leer's letters, when they shall be published. Rather, I am ambitious of it as an honour. It will serve to prove that if I have spent much time to little purpose in the translation of Homer, some small portion of my time has, however, been well disposed of.'

These letters were afterwards published by Mr. Newton, under the title of The Power of Grace Illustrated. They contain an affecting and most interesting narrative of the author's conversion to God, from a state of darkness truly deplorable, through the means of reading Mr. Newton's writings, and the writings of some other English divines. Mr. Van Leer was a student of theology at a Dutch university; but like too many other young men in similar situations on the continent, he was avowedly opposed to Christianity. It pleased God, by some afflictive events, to lead him to serious consideration; and afterwards, in a sudden and wonderful manner, effectually to change his heart, and to give him joy and peace in believing; so that, being justified by faith, he had peace with God through our Lord Jesus Christ. He was removed early in life, dying when he was about thirty years of age, in the midst of his usefulness, to the great regret of all who knew him: leaving behind him many proofs of the beneficial results of his labours. Cowper executed the translation of these letters with his accustomed fidelity and elegance; deriving from them, notwithstanding the continuance of his depression, some degree of pleasure, while he traced the striking operations of grace upon the author's mind.

It will have been perceived, from the extracts we have already made that Cowper's gloomy peculiarity of mind still prevailed, at least occasionally, to a painful extent. It is true, he adverts to it in his letters at this time less frequently than formerly; he introduces it, however, often enough to show, that it had undergone no diminution, and that it was suppressed only by the intense application which his engagements required. The following extracts from his letters written towards the close of 1790, will describe the state of his mind in this respect, at that period. 'I have singularities of which I believe at present you know nothing; and which would fill you with wonder if you knew them. I will add, however, in justice to myself, that they would not lower me in your good opinion; though perhaps they might tempt you to question the soundness of my upper story. I have been thus unhappily circumstanced twenty years and the remedy is in the hands of God only. That I make you this partial communication on the subject, conscious at the same time that you are well worthy to be entrusted with the whole, is merely because the recital would be too long for a letter, and would be painful to you and me. All this may vanish in a moment, and if it please God, it shall. In the meantime, my dear Madam, remember me in your prayers, and mention me at those times, as one whom it hath pleased God to afflict with singular visitations.'

Cowper's great caution lest he should engage in anything that would furnish him with matter of reproach, and his extreme anxiety to avoid even the appearance of evil, will be seen by the following reply to a letter from Mr. Newton, who had informed him that Mr. Holloway had kindly offered to initiate the poet into the secrets of animal magnetism: [Animal magnetism, also known as mesmerism,] was the name given by the German doctor Franz Friedrich Anton Mesmer in the 18th century to what he believed to be an invisible natural force exerted by animals. He believed that the force could have physical effects, including healing.

'With respect to my initiation into this art I have a thousand doubts. Twice I have been overwhelmed with the blackest despair; and at those times, everything in which I have been at any time of my life concerned, has afforded to the enemy a handle against me. I tremble, therefore, almost at every step I take, lest on some future similar occasion, it should yield him opportunity, and furnish him with means to torment him. Decide for me if you can, and in the meantime present, if you please, my respectful compliments, and very best thanks to Mr. Holloway for his most obliging offer. I am, perhaps, the only man living who would hesitate a moment, whether, on such easy terms, he should or should not accept it. But if he finds another like me, he will make a greater discovery than even that which he has already made, of the principles of his art.' Here, Cowper shows greater discernment than Newton.-*Editor.*

On another occasion, he thus writes:

'A yellow shower of leaves is now continually falling from all the trees in the country. A few moments only seem to have passed since they were buds; and in a few moments, more they will have disappeared! It is one advantage of a rural situation, which it affords many hints of the rapidity with which life flies, which do not occur in towns and cities. It is impossible for a man, conversant with such scenes as surround me, not to advert daily to the shortness of his existence here, admonished of it as he must be by ten thousand objects. There was a time when I could contemplate my present state, and consider myself as a thing of the day, with pleasure; when I numbered the seasons, as they passed in swift rotation, as a schoolboy numbers the days that interpose between the next vacation, when he shall see his parents, and enjoy his home again. To make so just an estimate of a life like this, is no longer in my power. The consideration of my short continuance here, which was once grateful to me, now fills me with regret. The only consolation left me on this subject is, that the voice of the Almighty can, in one moment, cure me of this mental infirmity. That He can, I know by experience; and there are reasons for which I ought to believe that he will. But from hope to despair is a transition that I have made so often, that I can only consider the hope which may come, and which I sometimes believe will, as a short prelude of joy, to a miserable conclusion of sorrow that shall never end. Thus are my brightest hopes clouded; and thus, to me, is hope itself become like a withered flower, that has lost both its hue and its fragrance. I ought not to have written in this dismal strain to you, nor did I intend it; you have more need to be cheered than saddened; but a dearth of other themes constrained me to choose myself for a subject, and of myself I can write no otherwise.' Some individuals not acquainted with the peculiarity of Cowper's case, have remarked, without due consideration, that he paid more attention to Homer than to the Bible. 'The truth was,' as has been recently well observed, 'that Homer was his occupation, and the Bible, to his diseased imagination, an interdicted book; at least, as to any ray of hope which it could afford to console his agitated spirits.' Religion, it may be truly said, was never out of his thoughts. If he introduced it less frequently into his letters than on former occasions, it was not because he was less alive to its importance; so far was this from being the case, that when he did speak of it, it was in terms of the highest admiration. His mental aberration, however, led him to imagine that to him it was a forbidden subject; that though it was the duty of others to make things divine the subjects of their frequent and most attentive consideration, it was equally his duty to refrain from intermeddling with them at all. Entertaining the same opinion of religion as ever, and having an equally fervent desire to participate of its enjoyments, he regretted this deeply; he regarded his case as most mysterious, but never once spoke of it in the language of impatience or complaint. His views of the divine government were such that though God had been pleased to deal with him in great severity, yet no expression ever escaped his lips that would lead anyone to suppose he imagined him unjust or even unkind.

Early in December 1790, Cowper had a short but severe attack of that nervous fever to which he was very subject, and which he dreaded above all other disorders, because it generally preceded a severe paroxysm of melancholy. Happily, on this occasion, it lasted only for a short time; and in a letter to Mrs. King, dated the last day of the year, he thus records his feelings on the occasion:

'I have lately been visited with an indisposition much more formidable than that which I mentioned to you in my last—a nervous fever, a disorder to which I am subject, and which I dread above all others, because it comes attended by a melancholy perfectly unsupportable. This is the first day of my complete recovery, the first in which I have perceived no symptoms of my terrible malady. I wish to be thankful to the Sovereign Dispenser both of health and of sickness, that, though I have felt cause enough to tremble, He gives me now encouragement to hope that I may dismiss my fears, and expect an escape from my depressive malady. The only drawback to the comfort I now feel is the intelligence contained in yours, that neither Mr. King nor yourself are well. I dread always, both for my own health and for that of my friends, the unhappy influences of a year worn out. But, my dear Madam, this is the last day of it, and I resolve to hope that the new year shall obliterate all the disagreeables of the old one. I can wish nothing more warmly, than that it may prove a propitious year for you.'

In the autumn of this year Cowper had sent his 'Homer' to the press; and through the whole of the ensuing winter he was closely employed in correcting the proof-sheets, and making such alterations as he still thought desirable. The time which this consumed, and the indefatigable industry with which he engaged in it, will be seen by the following extracts:

'My poetical operations, I mean of the occasional kind, have lately been pretty much at a stand. I believe, in my last, that 'Homer,' in the present stage of the process, occupied me more intensely than ever. He still continues to do so, and threatens, till he shall be completely finished, to make all other composition impracticable. I am sick and ashamed of myself that I forgot my promise, but it is actually true that I did forget it. You, however, I did not forget; nor did I forget to wonder and be alarmed at your silence, being myself unconscious of my arrears. All this, together with various other trespasses of mine, must be set down to the account of Homer; and, wherever he is, he is bound to make his apology to all my correspondents, but to you in particular. True it is that if Mrs. Unwin did not call me from that pursuit, I should forget, in the ardour with which I persevere in it, both to eat and to drink, if not to retire to rest! This zeal has increased in me regularly as I have proceeded, and in an exact ratio, as a mathematician would say, to the progress I have made towards the point at which I have been aiming. You will believe this, when I tell you that, not contented with my previous labours, I have actually revised the whole work, and have made a thousand alterations in it since it has been in the press. I have now, however, tolerably well satisfied myself at least, and trust that the printer and I shall trundle along merrily to the conclusion.'

In the commencement of 1791, Cowper's long-tried friend, Mr. Newton, lost his wife, also named Mary. She died in January, after many months of severe suffering, borne with exemplary fortitude and patience. She had always taken a lively interest in Cowper's welfare; and, when she resided at Olney, had frequently assisted Mrs. Unwin in the arduous duty of watching over the poet, during his painful mental depression. Her decease, therefore, was sure to affect him deeply; and the following extracts from his letters to Mr. Newton, on this trying occasion, will not fail to be interesting:

'Had you been a man of the world, I should have held myself bound, by the law of ceremonies, to have sent you long since my tribute of condolence. I have sincerely mourned with you; and though you have lost a wife, and I only a friend, yet do I understand too well the value of such a friend as Mrs. Newton, not to have sympathized with you very nearly. But you are not a man of the world; neither can you, who have the scripture, and the Giver of the scripture to console you, have any need of aid from others, or expect it from such spiritual imbecility as mine." It affords me sincere pleasure that you enjoy serenity of mind, after your great loss. It is well in all circumstances, even in the most afflictive, with those who have God for their comforter. You do me justice in giving entire credit to my expressions of friendship for you. No day passes in which I do not look back to the days that are fled, and consequently none in which I do not feel myself affectionately reminded of you, and of her whom you have lost for a season. I cannot even see Olney spire from any of the fields in the neighbourhood, much less can I enter the town, and still less the vicarage, without experiencing the force of those mementos, and recollecting a multitude of passages to which you and yours were parties. The past would appear a dream, were the remembrance of it less affecting. It was, in the most important respects, so unlike my present moment, that I am sometimes almost tempted to suppose it a dream! But the difference between dreams and realities long since elapsed, seems to consist chiefly in this: that a dream, however painful and pleasant at the time, and perhaps for a few ensuing hours, passes like an arrow through the air, leaving no trace of its flight behind it; but our actual experiences make a lasting impression. We review those which interested us much when they occurred, with hardly less interest than in the first instance; and whether few years or many have intervened, our sensibility makes them still present—such a mere nullity is time, to a creature to whom God gives a feeling heart and the faculty of recollection.'

In June 1791, having completed his long and arduous undertaking—the translation of 'Homer,' he thus writes to Mr. Newton on the occasion:

'Considering the multiplicity of your engagements, and the importance, no doubt, of most of them, I am bound to set the higher value on your letters; and, instead of grumbling that they come so seldom, to be thankful to you that they come at all. You are now going into the country, where, I presume, you will have less to do. I am rid of 'Homer.' Let contrive to exchange letters more frequently than for some time past. You do justice to me, and to Mrs. Unwin, when you assure yourself that to hear of your health will give us pleasure. I know not, in truth, whose health and well-being could give us more. The years that we have seen together will never be out of our remembrance; and, so long as we remember them, we must remember you with affection. In the pulpit, and out of the pulpit, you have laboured in every possible way to serve us; and we must have a short memory, indeed, for the kindness of a friend, could we by any means become forgetful of yours. It would grieve me more than it does, to hear you complain of the effects of time, were not I also myself the subject of them. While he is wearing out you and other dear friends of mine, he spares not me; for which I ought to account myself obliged to him, since I should otherwise be in danger of surviving all that I have ever loved—the most melancholy lot that can befall a mortal. God knows what will be my doom hereafter; but precious as life necessarily seems to a mind doubtful of its future happiness, I love not the world, I trust, so much, as to wish a place in it when all my beloved shall have left it. As to Homer, I am sensible that, except as an amusement, he was never worth my meddling with; but as an amusement, he was to me invaluable. As such, he served me more than five years; and in that respect I know not at present where I shall find his equal. You oblige me by saying that you will read him for my sake. I verily believe that any person of a spiritual turn may read him to some advantage.'

It appears that Cowper had no expectation of again seeing his *Homer* until it was actually before the public. Johnson, the publisher, however, unexpectedly to him, sent him an interleaved copy of the work, recommending him to revise it again, before the sheets were worked off. On this occasion, he thus writes to his friend, Mr. Newton:

'I did not foresee, when I challenged you to a brisker correspondence, that a new engagement of all my leisure time was at hand, a new, and yet an old one. An interleaved copy of my Homer arrived soon after from Johnson, in which he recommended it to me to make any alterations that might yet be expedient, with a view to another impression. The alterations that I make are indeed but few and they are also short; not more, perhaps, than half a line in two thousand. The lines are, I suppose, nearly forty thousand in all; and to revise them critically must consequently be a work of time and labour. I suspend it, however, for your sake, until the present sheet be filled, and that I may not seem to shrink from my own offer. Were I capable of envying a good man, I should envy Mr. Venn, and Mr. Berridge, and yourself, who have spent, and while they last will continue to spend, your lives in the service of the only Master worth serving; labouring always for the souls of men, and not to tickle their ears, as I do. God knows how much rather I would be the obscure tenant of a lath and plaster cottage, with a lively sense of my interest in a Redeemer, than the most admired object of public notice without it. Alas! what is a whole poem, even one of Homer's, compared with a single aspiration that finds its way immediately to God, though clothed in ordinary language, or perhaps not articulated at all. These are my sentiments as much as ever they were, though my days are all running to waste among Greeks and Trojans. The night cometh when no man can work; and if I am ordained to work to any better purpose, that desirable period cannot be far distant. My day is beginning to shut in, as every man's must, who is on the verge of sixty.'

CHAPTER XV. Publication of his Homer—To whom dedicated—Benefits he had derived from it—Feels the want of employment—Mrs. Unwin's first attack of paralysis—Manner in which it affected Cowper—Remarks on Milton's labours —Reply to Mr. Newton's letter on original composition—Continuance of his depression—First letter from Mr. Hayley—Unpleasant circumstance respecting it —Mr. Hayley's first visit to Weston—Kind manner in which he was received—Mrs. Unwin's second severe paralytic attack—Cowper's feelings on the occasion —Mr. Hayley's departure—Cowper's warm attachment to him—Reflections on the recent changes he had witnessed—Promises to visit Eartham—

Makes preparations for the journey—Peculiarity of his feelings on the occasion.

On 1 July 1791, Cowper's Homer appeared. After so many years' incessant toil, it was not to be expected that he would feel otherwise than anxious respecting the reception it met with from the public. He had laboured indefatigably to produce a faithful and free translation of the inimitable original, and he could not be indifferent to the result. To Mrs. King he thus writes on the occasion:

'My Homer is gone forth, and I can sincerely say—Joy go with it! What place it holds in the estimation of the generality I cannot tell, having heard no more about it since its publication, than if no such work existed. I must except, however, an anonymous eulogium from some man of letters, which I received about a week ago. It was kind in a perfect stranger, as he avows himself to be, to relieve me, in some degree at least, at so early a day, from much of the anxiety that I could not but feel on such an occasion: I should be glad to know who he is, only that I might thank him.'

Cowper, very properly, dedicated the Iliad to his noble relative Earl Cowper, and the Odyssey to the dowager Countess Spencer, whom, in one of his letters he thus describes:

'We had a visit on Monday from one of the first women in the world; I mean, in point of character and accomplishments,— the Dowager Lady Spencer! I may receive, perhaps, some honours hereafter, should my translation speed according to my wishes, and the pains I have taken with it; but shall never receive any that I esteem so highly; she is indeed worthy to whom I shall dedicate, and may but my Odyssey prove as worthy of her, I shall have nothing to fear from the critics.'

Whether it arose from the unreasonable expectations of the public, or from the utter impossibility of conveying all the graces and the beauties of these unrivalled poems in a translation, it is certain that the volumes, when they appeared, did not give that satisfaction, either to the author or to his readers, which had been anticipated. It would perhaps be difficult, if not impossible, to assign a better reason for the imperfection of Cowper's translation, if imperfection it deserves to be called, than that mentioned by his justly admired biographer, Mr. Hayley.

'Homer is so exquisitely beautiful in his own language, and he has been so long an idol in every literary mind, that any copy of him, which the best of modern poets can execute, must probably resemble in its effect, the portrait of a graceful woman, painted by an excellent artist for her lover ; the lover, indeed, will acknowledge great merit in the work, and think himself much indebted to the skill of such an artist; but he will never acknowledge, as in truth he never can feel, that the best of resemblances exhibits all the grace that he discerns in the beloved original. So fares it with the admirers of Homer; his very translators themselves feel so perfectly the power of this predominant affection, that they gradually grow discontented with their own labour, however approved in the moment of its supposed completion. This was so remarkably the case with Cowper. In process of time, we shall see him employed upon what may almost be called his second translation, so great were the alterations he made on a deliberate revisal of the work for a second edition. And in the preface to that edition, he has spoken of his own labour with the most frank and ingenuous veracity. Yet of the first edition it may, I think, be fairly said, that it accomplished more than any of his poetical predecessors had achieved before him. It made the nearest approach to that sweet majestic simplicity which forms one of the most attractive features in the great prince and father of poets.'

If Cowper had derived no other benefit from his translation than that of constant employment for so long a time, when he stood so much in need of it, it would have been to him invaluable, as the best and most effectual remedy for that inordinate sensibility to which he was subject. Besides this, however, it procured him other advantages of paramount importance; it improved the general state of his health; it introduced him to a circle of literary friends, whom he would otherwise never have known, and who, when they once knew him, could not fail to feel affectionately interested in his welfare; it brought him into closer contact with those with whom he had previously been acquainted, by inducing him to avail himself of their kind offers and assistance in the transcribing way, It is said that Broome assisted Pope very largely in his translation of Homer; but Cowper had no assistant in that way. All the Throckmorton family, Lady Hesketh, Mrs. Johnson, and many others, helped him as transcribers, and only as such. which, to a mind like his, could not fail to become a source of almost uninterrupted enjoyment; it established his reputation as a most accomplished scholar, and unquestionably ranked him among the highest class of poets.

A living writer has well remarked, that 'to Cowper's translation of Homer, we are beholden, not only for the pleasure which a perusal will be sure to afford to reasonable and patient readers but we may attribute to its happy possession of his mind all the beautiful and inimitable letters, which appear in his correspondence, during the progress of that work. The exercise of his morning studies made him relish with keener zest the relaxation of his social hours, or those welcome opportunities of epistolary converse with the absent, in which it is evident that much of the little happiness allowed to him lay. He is never more at home, consequently never more amiable, sprightly, and entertaining, and even poetical, than in his correspondence, when he pours out all the treasures of his mind and the affections of his heart, upon the paper which is to be the speaking representative of himself to those he loves. It has often been regretted that instead of this labour in vain, as the translation of Homer has sometimes seemed to many, he had not spent an equal portion of time and talent on original composition. The regret is at least as much bestowed in vain, as was that labour; for there is no well-founded reason to suppose, from the momentary jeopardy in which he lived, of being plunged into sudden, irretrievable despondence, that if he had been otherwise employed he could have maintained even that small share of health and cheerfulness which he enjoyed.'

It was not to be expected that a mind like Cowper's could remain for any lengthened period unemployed. Accustomed as he had long been to intense application, when he had completed his great work, he immediately felt the want of some other engagement. To a mind less active than his, replying to his correspondents, now become most numerous, would have been employment amply sufficient— especially as he was considerably in arrears with them, owing to his previous labours. This, however, was not enough for Cowper. He wanted something more worthy of his powers; something that required more vigour of thought, and demanded more severe application. Several of his friends again urged him to original composition, and they would have been successful, had he not, about this time, received a letter from his publisher, of whose judgment and integrity he had always entertained a high opinion, recommending him to prepare materials for a splendid edition of Milton. To this proposal Cowper immediately assented. He had always expressed himself delighted with Milton's poetry, and on one occasion, in a letter to his friend Mr. Unwin, had thus ventured to defend his character from the severe censures cast upon him by Johnson, in his 'Lives of the Poets:'

'I have been well entertained with Johnson's biography, for which I thank you. With one exception, and that an important one, I think he has acquitted himself with his usual good sense and sufficiency. His treatment of Milton is unmerciful to the last degree. He has belaboured that great poet's character with the most industrious cruelty. As a man, he has hardly left him the shadow of one good quality. Churlishness in his private life, and a rancorous hatred of everything royal in his public, are the two colours with which he has smeared all the canvas. If he had any virtues, they are not to be found in the Doctor's picture of him, and it is well for Milton that some sourness in his temper is the only vice with which his memory has been charged; it is evident enough, that if his biographer could have discovered more, he would not have spared him. As a poet, he has treated him with severity enough, plucked one or two of the most beautiful feathers out of his muse's wing, and trampled them under his great foot. He has passed sentence of condemnation upon Lycidas, and has taken occasion from that charming poem, to expose to ridicule (what is indeed ridiculous enough) the childish prattling of pastoral compositions, as if Lycidas was the prototype and pattern of them all. The liveliness of the description, the sweetness of the numbers, the classical spirit of antiquity that pervades it, go for nothing. I am convinced, by the way, that he has no ear for poetical numbers, or that it was stopped by prejudice against the harmony of Milton's. Was there ever anything so delightful as the music of the *Paradise Lost*? It is like that of a fine organ; has the fullest and the deepest tones of majesty, with all the softness and elegance of the Dorian flute.

Variety without end, and never equalled, unless perhaps by Virgil. Yet the Doctor has little or nothing to say upon this copious theme, but talks something about the unfitness of the English language for blank-verse, and how apt it is, in the mouth of some readers, to degenerate into declamation.'

Cowper had no sooner made up his mind on the subject of his new engagement, than he communicated it to his correspondents. To one he writes:

'I am deep in a new literary engagement, being retained by my bookseller as editor of an intended most magnificent edition of Milton's poetical works. This will occupy me as much as Homer did, for a year or two to come; and when I have finished it, I shall have run through all the degrees of my profession, as author, translator, and editor. I know not that a fourth could be found; but if a fourth can be found, I dare say I shall find it. I am now translating Milton's Latin poems. I give them, as opportunity offers, all the variety of measures that I can. Some I render in heroic rhymes, some in stanzas, some in seven, some in eight-syllable measure, and some in blank verse. They will altogether make an agreeable miscellany for the English reader. They are certainly good in themselves, and cannot fail to please, but by the fault of their translator.'

One of his most esteemed correspondents, the Rev. Walter Bagot, attempted to dissuade him from entering upon his new engagement, and urged him to publish in a third volume what original pieces he had already composed, added to a translation of Milton's Latin and Italian poems. Had this plan been suggested to him earlier, he would have pursued it, as he thus writes to his friend on the subject:

'As to Milton, the die is cast. I am engaged, have bargained with Johnson, and cannot recede. I should otherwise have been glad to do as you advise, to make the translation of his Latin and Italian poems part of another volume, for with such an addition, I have nearly as much verse in my budget as would be required for the purpose.'

From some expressions in a letter to Rev. Mr. Hurdis, the author of 'The Village Curate,' with whom Cowper had entered into a correspondence a few months previous to this, and to whom he had written several most interesting letters, it would appear as if he entered upon his new engagement rather precipitately, and without due consideration. 'I am munch obliged to you for wishing that I were employed on some original work, rather than in translation. To tell the truth, I am of your mind; and unless I could find another Homer, I shall promise (I believe) and vow, when I have done with Milton, never to translate again. But my veneration for our great countryman is equal to what I feel for the Grecian; and consequently I am happy, and feel myself honourably employed, whatever I do for Milton. I am now translating his *Epitaphium Damonis*; a pastoral, in my judgment, equal to any of Virgil's Bucolics, but of which Dr. Johnson (so it pleased him) speaks, as I remember, contemptuously. But he who never saw any beauty in a rural scene, was not likely to have much taste for a pastoral.'

Among other consequences resulting from his new undertaking, one of the most gratifying to himself was, its becoming the means of introducing him to an acquaintance with his esteemed friend and future biographer, Mr. Hayley. This important event in Cowper's life, for so it afterwards proved,—is related with so much beauty and simplicity by Mr. Hayley in his life of Cowper, and reflects a lustre so bright on both the biographer and the poet, that we cannot do better than give it in his own words. Mr. Hayley thus relates the circumstance—'As it is to Milton that I am in a great measure indebted for what I must ever regard as a signal blessing, the friendship of Cowper, the reader will pardon me for dwelling a little on the circumstances that produced it; circumstances which often lead me to repeat those sweet verses of my friend, on the casual origin of our valuable attachments.'

'Mysterious are His ways whose power
Brings forth that unexpected hour,
When minds that never met before
Shall meet, unite, and part no more.
It is the allotment of the skies,
The hand of the supremely wise,
That guides and governs our affections,
And plans and orders our connections.'

'These charming lines strike with peculiar force on my heart, when I recollect that it was an idle endeavour to make us enemies, which gave rise to our intimacy, and that I was providentially conducted to Weston at a season when my presence there afforded peculiar comfort to my affectionate friend, under the pressure of a very heavy domestic affliction which threatened to overwhelm his very tender spirits. The entreaty of many persons whom I wished to oblige, had engaged me to write a life of Milton, before I had the slightest suspicion that my work could interfere with the projects of any man; but I was soon surprised and concerned in hearing that I was represented in a newspaper as an antagonist of Cowper. I immediately wrote to him on the subject, and our correspondence soon endeared us to each other in no common degree. The series of his letters to me I value, not only as memorials of a most dear and honourable friendship, but as exquisite examples of epistolary excellence.'

The above interesting extract will have informed the reader that Mr. Hayley paid Cowper a visit at Weston; this visit, however, so gratifying to both parties, did not take place until the beginning of May 1792. In the December previous, Cowper met with a more severe domestic calamity than he had lately experienced. Mrs. Unwin, his affectionate companion, who had watched over him with so much tenderness and anxiety, for so many years, was suddenly attacked with strong symptoms of paralysis. In a letter to his friend, Mr. Rose, dated 21st December, 1791, Cowper thus relates this painful event:

'On Saturday last, while I was at my desk, near the window, and Mrs. Unwin at the fireside opposite to it, I heard her suddenly exclaim, 'Oh! Mr. Cowper, don't let me fall!' I turned, and saw her actually falling, and started to her side just in time to prevent her. She was seized with a violent giddiness, which lasted, though with some abatement, the whole day, and was attended with some other very alarming symptoms. At present, however, she is relieved from the vertigo, and seems in all respects better. She has been my faithful and affectionate nurse for many years, and consequently has a claim on all my attentions. She has them, and will have them, as long as she wants them, which will probably be, at the least, a considerable time to come. I feel the shock, as you may suppose, in every nerve. God grant that there may be no repetition of it. Another such a stroke upon her would, I think, overset me completely; but at present I hold up bravely.'

Notwithstanding the interruption of Cowper's studies, occasioned by Mrs. Unwin's indisposition, and by the extreme slowness of her recovery, he had now become so much accustomed to regular employment, and had derived from it so many advantages, that he could not possibly remain inactive. In the month of February, we find him thus employed. 'Milton, at present, engrosses me altogether. His Latin pieces I have translated, and have begun with the Italian. I shall proceed immediately to deliberate upon and settle the plan of my commentary, which I have hitherto had but little time to consider. I look forward to it for this reason with some anxiety. I trust that this anxiety will cease, when I have once satisfied myself about the best manner of conducting it.'

Cowper's knowledge of mankind, and of the natural workings of the human heart, might, from his secluded situation, have been supposed to be extremely superficial. It was, however, on the contrary, most deep, and extensive. To his friend Mr. Rose, who had met with some unkind and ungrateful treatment, he writes:

'You are learning what all learn, though few at so early an age, that man is an ungrateful mortal; and that benefits too often, instead of securing a due return, operate rather as provocations to ill treatment. This I take to be the *summum malum* of the human heart. Towards God, we are all guilty of it, more or less; but between man and man, we may thank God for it, that there are some exceptions. He leaves this principle to operate in some degree against himself in all, for our humiliation, I suppose; and because the pernicious effects of it in reality cannot injure him, he cannot suffer by them: but he knows, that unless he should restrain its influence on the dealings of mankind with each other, the bands of society would be dissolved, and all the charitable intercourse at an end amongst us. It was said of Archbishop Cranmer,' Do him an ill turn, and you make him your friend forever;' of others it may be said, 'Do them a good one and they will be forever your enemies' It is the grace of God only that makes the difference.'

We have already informed our readers, that Cowper's engagement, as the editor of Milton became the means of introducing him to Mr. Hayley. He received the first letter from that gentleman in March 1792. An incident occurred respecting this letter, which ought not to go unrecorded; as it might have proved fatal to that friendship, which became to both the poets a source of the purest enjoyment. Neither of these talented individuals had, at that time, any knowledge of each other. Mr.

Hayley had read Cowper's productions, with no ordinary emotions of delight, and had consequently conceived the highest respect for their unknown author; and nothing could have occasioned him greater surprise, as well as uneasiness, than to be represented as the opponent of one whom he so highly respected. No sooner was he apprised of it, than he wrote to Cowper. generously offering him the materials that he had collected, with as much assistance as it was in his power to afford, and being unacquainted with his address, directed his letter to the care of Johnson, his publisher. Either through the carelessness or inadvertence of Johnson, this letter remained in his hands for a considerable time, and was not delivered to Cowper till six weeks after it had been written. Immediately on receiving it, Cowper wrote to Mr. Hayley, explaining the cause of this apparently long delay, and from that time an interchange of many most interesting letters took place, which subsequently led to a friendship the most cordial and ardent, which it was only in the power of death to dissolve. In a letter to Lady Hesketh, Cowper thus adverts to this circumstance:

'Mr. Hayley's friendly and complimentary letter, from some unknown cause, at least to me, slept six weeks in Johnson's custody. It was necessary I should answer it without delay; accordingly I answered it the very evening on which I received it, giving him to understand, among other things, how much vexation the bookseller's folly had cost me, who had detained it so long, especially on account of the distress that I knew it must have occasioned to him also. From his reply, which the return of the post brought me, I learn that in the long interval of my non-correspondence he had suffered anxiety and mortification enough; so that I dare say he made twenty vows never to hazard again either letter or compliment to an unknown author. What, indeed, could he imagine less, than that I meant by such obstinate silence to tell him, that I valued neither him nor his praises, nor his proffered friendship; in short, that I considered him as a rival, and, therefore, like a true author, hated and despised him. He is now, however, convinced that I love him, as indeed, I do, and I account him the chief acquisition that my verse has ever procured me. Brute should I be if I did not, for he promises me assistance in his power.'

To Mr. Hayley, at the commencement of Cowper's correspondence with him, and after the above unpleasant occurrence had been satisfactorily accounted for, he thus expresses his anxiety that the friendship thus formed might be lasting;—' God grant that this friendship of ours may be a comfort to us all the rest of our days, in a world where true friendships are rarities, and especially, where suddenly formed, they are apt soon to terminate. But, as I said before, I feel a disposition of heart towards you which I never before felt for one whom I had never seen; and that shall prove itself, I trust, in the event, a propitious omen. It gives me the sincerest pleasure that I hope to see you at Weston; for as to any migrations of mine, they must, I fear, notwithstanding the joy I should feel in being a guest of yours, be still considered in the light of impossibilities. Come then, my friend, and be as welcome, as the country people say here, as the flowers in May. I am happy, I may say, in the expectation, but the fear, or rather the consciousness, that I shall not answer on a nearer view, makes it a trembling kind of happiness, and invests it with many doubts. Bring with you any books that you think may be useful to my commentatorship, for with you for an interpreter, I shall be afraid of none of them. And in truth, if you think you shall want them, you must bring books for your own use also, for they are an article with which I am heinously unprovided; being much in the condition of the man whose library Pope describes, as—

No mighty store!
His own works neatly bound, and little more.'

Mr. Hayley's projected visit, anticipated so fondly, both by himself and by Cowper, took place in May 1792. The meeting proved reciprocally delightful. Though Cowper was now in his sixty-first year, he felt none of the infirmities of advanced life, but was as active and vigorous, both in mind and body, as his best friends could wish to see him. Mrs. Unwin had nearly recovered from her late severe attack, and as her health was every day progressively improving, there seemed every probability of their enjoying a long continuance of domestic comfort. Mr. Hayley thus describes the manner in which he was received, and his sensations on the occasion:

'Their reception of me was kindness itself; I was enchanted to find that the manners and conversation of Cowper resembled his poetry, charming by unaffected elegance, and the graces of a benevolent spirit. I looked with affectionate veneration and pleasure on the lady, who, having devoted her life and fortune to the service of this tender and sublime genius, in watching over him with maternal vigilance, through so many years of the darkest calamity, appeared to be now enjoying a reward justly due to the noblest exertions of friendship, in contemplating the health, and the renown of the poet, whom she had the happiness to preserve. It seemed hardly possible to survey human nature in a more touching, and a more satisfactory point of view. Their tender attention to each other, their simple, devout gratitude for the mercies which they had experienced together, and their constant but unaffected propensity to impress on the mind and heart of a new friend, the deep sense which they incessantly felt, of their mutual obligations to each other, afforded me very singular gratification.'

This scene of exquisite enjoyment to all parties, as is frequently the case in a world like ours, was suddenly exchanged for one of the deepest melancholy and distress. Mr. Hayley has related the painful event with so much tenderness and simplicity that we cannot do better than present it to our readers in his own words.

'After passing our mornings in social study, we usually walked out together at noon; in returning from one of our rambles round the pleasant village of Weston, we were met by Mr. Greatheed, an accomplished minister of the gospel, who resides at Newport Pagnel, and whom Cowper described to me in terms of cordial esteem. He came forth to meet us, as we drew near the house, and it was soon visible, from his countenance and manner, that he had ill news to impart. After the tenderest preparation that humanity could devise, he informed Cowper that Mrs. Unwin was under the immediate pressure of a paralytic attack. My agitated friend rushed to the side of the sufferer. He returned to me in a state that alarmed me in the highest degree for his faculties: his first speech was wild in the extreme; my answer would appear little less so, but it was addressed to the predominant fancy of my unhappy friend, and with the blessing of heaven, it produced an instantaneous calm in his troubled mind. From that moment he rested on my friendship with such mild and cheerful confidence, that his affectionate spirit regarded me as sent providentially to support him in a season of the severest affliction.'

The best means to promote the recovery of Mrs. Unwin that could have been used under similar circumstances were resorted to. Happily, they proved, to a considerable degree, successful, and she gradually recovered both her strength and the use of her faculties. The effect of this attack, however, upon Cowper's tender mind, was, in the highest degree, painful. This will not, perhaps, be surprising, when it is recollected how sincerely he was attached to his afflicted inmate, and how deeply he interested himself in everything that related to her welfare. The following beautiful lines will convey to the reader some idea of the exalted opinion he had formed of her character:

'Mary! I want a lyre with other strings,
Such aid from heaven as some have feigned they drew,
An eloquence scarce given to mortals, new
And undebased by praise of meaner things I
That ere through age or woe I shed my wings,
I may record thy worth, with honour due,
In verse as musical as thou art true—
Verse that immortalizes whom it sings!

But thou hast little need: there is a book
By seraphs writ, with beams of heavenly light
On which the eyes of God not rarely look!
A chronicle of actions, just and bright!
There all thy deeds, my faithful Mary, shine,
And since thou own'st that praise, I spare thee mine.'

The following extracts from Cowper's correspondence, immediately after this painful event, describe satisfactorily the state of his mind:

'I wish with all my heart, my dearest cousin, that I had not ill news for the subject of this letter; my friend, my Mary, has again been attacked by the same disorder that threatened me last year with the loss of her, of which you were yourself a witness. The present attack has been much the severest. Her speech has been almost unintelligible from the moment that she was struck: it is with difficulty she can open her eyes; and she cannot keep them open, the muscles necessary for that purpose being contracted; and as to self-moving powers from place to place, and the right use of her hand and arm, she has entirely lost them. I hope, however, she is beginning to recover; but her amendment is indeed very slow, as must be expected at her time of life. I am as well myself, and indeed better, than you have ever known me in such trouble. It has happened well for me that, of all men living, the man best qualified to assist and comfort me, is here; though, till within these few days 1 never saw him, and a few weeks since had no expectation that I ever should. You have already guessed that I mean Hayley—Hayley, who loves me as if he had known me from my cradle. When he returns to town, as he must, alas! He will pay his respects to you. He has, I assure you, been all in all to us, on this very afflictive occasion. I absolutely know not how to live without him?'

Mr. Hayley left Weston early in June, at which time many pleasing symptoms of Mrs. Unwin's ultimate recovery began to appear. Cowper's letters to his friend after his departure, which were written almost daily, afford ample proofs of the warmth of his affection for him, and of the deep interest he took in promoting Mrs. Unwin's recovery. He thus commences his first letter to Mr. Hayley:

'All's Well! These words I place as conspicuously as possible, and prefix them to my letter, to save you the pain, my friend and brother, of a moment's anxious speculation. Poor Mary proceeds in her amendment, and improves, I think, even at a swifter rate than when you left her. The stronger she grows, the faster she gathers strength, which is perhaps the natural course of recovery. Yesterday was a noble day with her; speech almost perfect—eyes, open almost the whole day, without any effort to keep them so—and her step, wonderfully improved! Can I ever honour you enough for your zeal to serve me? Truly, I think not. I am, however, so sensible of the love I owe you on this account, that I every day regret the acuteness of your feelings for me, convinced that they expose you to much trouble, mortification, and disappointment. I have, in short, a poor opinion of my destiny, as I told you when you were here; and though I believe that if any man living can do me good you will, I cannot yet persuade myself that even you will be successful in attempting it.

I rose this morning, wrapt round with a cloud of melancholy, and with a heart full of fears, but if I see my Mary's amendment a little advanced, I shall be better.

Of what materials can you suppose me made, if, after all the rapid proofs you have given me of your friendship, I do not love you with all my heart, and regret your absence continually. But you must permit me to be melancholy now and then; or, if you will not, I must be so without your permission; for that sable thread is so interwoven with the very thread of my existence as to be inseparable from it, at least while I exist in the body. Be content, therefore; let me sigh and groan, but always be sure that I love you. You will be well assured that I should not have indulged myself in this rhapsody about myself and my melancholy, had my present state of mind been of that complexion, or had not our poor Mary seemed still to advance in her recovery. It is a great blessing that, feeble as she is, she has invincible courage, and a trust in God's goodness that nothing shakes. She is certainly, in some degree, better than she was yesterday; but how to measure the degree, I know not, except by saying, that it is just perceptible.'

In a letter dated 11th June, 1792, Cowper thus discloses his state of mind to Lady Hesketh. 'My dearest cousin, thou art ever in my thoughts, whether I am writing to thee or not, and my correspondence seems to grow upon me at such a rate, that I am not able to address thee so often as I would. In fact, I live only to write letters. Hayley is, as you see, added to the number of my correspondents, and to him I write almost as duly as I rise in the morning. Since I wrote last, Mrs. Unwin has been continually improving in strength, but at so gradual a rate, that I can only mark it by saying, that she moves every day with less support than the former. On the whole, I believe she goes on as well as can be expected, though not quite so well as to satisfy me.

'During the last two months, I seem to myself to have been in a dream. It has been a most eventful period, and fruitful to an uncommon degree, both in good and in evil. I have been very ill, and suffered excruciating pain. I recovered, and became quite well again. I received within my doors a man, but lately an entire stranger, and who now loves me as his brother, and forgets himself to serve me. Mrs. Unwin has been seized with an illness, which for many days threatened to deprive me of her, and to cast a gloom, an impenetrable one, on all my future prospects. She is now granted to me again. A few days since I should have thought the moon might have descended into my purse as likely as any emolument, and now it seems not impossible. All this has come to pass with such rapidity as events move with in romance indeed, but not often in real life. Events of all sorts creep or fly exactly as God pleases. '

While Mr. Hayley was at Weston, he had persuaded Cowper and Mrs. Unwin to promise him a visit at Eartham, sometime in the summer. Believing it would greatly improve Mrs. Unwin's health, and be an agreeable relaxation to Cowper, after the anxiety of mind he had felt respecting his beloved invalid, Mr.

Hayley wrote several pressing invitations to induce them to come as early as possible. The following extracts will shew the state of Cowper's mind respecting it. To Mr. Bull he writes, 'We are on the eve of a journey, and a long one. On this very day, we set out for Eartham, the seat of my brother bard, Mr. Hayley, on the other side of London, nobody knows where, a hundred and twenty miles off. Pray for us, my friend, that we may have a safe going and return. It is a tremendous exploit, and I feel a thousand anxieties when I think of it. But a promise made to him when he was here, that we would go if we could, and a sort of persuasion that we can if we will, oblige us to it. The journey and the change of air, together with the novelty to us of the scene to which we are going, may, I hope, be useful to us both; especially to Mrs. Unwin, who has most need of restoratives.'

To Mr. Newton he thus discloses his feelings on the subject. 'You may imagine that we, who have been resident in one spot for so many years, do not engage in such an enterprise without some anxiety. Persons accustomed to travel would make themselves merry with mine; it seems so disproportioned to the occasion. Once I have been on the point of determining not to go, and even since we fixed the day, my troubles have been almost insupportable. But it has been made a matter of much prayer, and at last it has pleased God to satisfy me, in some measure, that his will corresponds with our purpose, and that he will afford us his protection. You, I know, will not be unmindful of us during our absence from home; but will obtain for us, if your prayers can do it, all that we would ask for ourselves —the presence and favour of God, a salutary effect of our journey, and a safe return.'

Anxious to enjoy the pleasure of Cowper's company at Eartham, Mr. Hayley, in his letters to the poet, urged him by no means to defer his visit till late in the summer. From Cowper's replies we select the following interesting extracts. 'The weather is sadly against my Mary's recovery; it deprives her of many a good turn in the orchard, and fifty times have I wished this very day, that Dr. Darwin's scheme of giving rudders and sails to the icelands, that spoil all our summers, were actually put into practice. So should we have gentle airs instead of churlish blasts, and those everlasting sources of bad weather, being once navigated into the southern hemisphere, my Mary would recover as fast again. We are both of your mind respecting the journey to Eartham, and that July, if by that time she have strength for the journey, will be better than August. This, however, must be left to the Giver of all good. If our visit to you be according to his will, he will smooth our way before us, and appoint the time of it; and I thus speak, not because I wish to seem a saint in your eyes, but because my poor Mary actually is one, and would not set her foot over the threshold unless she had, or thought she had, God's free permission. With that she would go through floods and fire, though without it she would be afraid of everything—afraid even to visit you, dearly as she loves, and much as she longs to see you.'

In another letter to Mr. Hayley, he writes:

'The progress of the old nurse in Terence is very much like the progress of my poor patient in the road of recovery. I cannot indeed say that she moves but advances not, for advances are certainly made, but the progress of a week is hardly perceptible. I know not, therefore, at present, what to say about this long-postponed journey; the utmost that it is safe for me to say at this moment is this,—you know that you are dear to us both; true it is that you are so, and equally true, that the very instant we feel ourselves at liberty, we will fly to Eartham. You wish me to settle the time, and I wish with all my heart to do so; living in hopes, meanwhile, that I shall be able to do it soon. But some little time must necessarily intervene. Our Mary must be able to walk alone, to cut her own food, and to feed herself, and to wear her own shoes,—for the present she wears mine. All these things considered, my friend and brother, you will see the expediency of waiting a little before we set off to Eartham. We mean, indeed, before that day arrives, to make a trial of her strength; how far she may be able to bear the motion of a carriage, a motion that she has not felt these seven years. I grieve that we are thus circumstanced, and that we cannot gratify ourselves in a delightful and innocent project, without all these precautions; but when we have leaf-gold to handle, we must do it tenderly.'

The day was at length fixed for this long-intended journey; and the following letter to Mr. Hayley, written a day or two previously, describes Cowper's feelings respecting it:

'Through floods and flames to your retreat
I win my desp'rate way,
And when we meet, if e'er we meet,
Will echo your huzza!

'You will wonder at the word desperate in the second line, and in the third; but could you have any conception of the fears I have had to contend with, and of the dejection of spirits that I have suffered concerning this journey, you would wonder much that I still courageously persevere in my resolution to undertake it. Fortunately, for my intention, it happens that as the day approaches my terrors abate; for had they continued to be what they were a week ago, I must, after all, have disappointed you; and was actually once on the verge of doing it. I have told you something of my nocturnal experiences, and assure you now, that they were hardly ever more terrific than on this occasion. Prayer has, however, opened my passage at last, and obtained for me a degree of confidence, which I trust will prove a comfortable viaticum to me all the way. The terrors that I have spoken of would appear ridiculous to most, but to you they will not, for you are a reasonable creature, and know well that to whatever cause it be owing (whether to constitution or to God's express appointment) I am hunted by spiritual hounds in the night season. I cannot help it. You will pity me, and wish it were otherwise; and though you may think there is much of the imaginary in it, will not deem it, for that reason, an evil less to be lamented. So much for fears and distresses. Soon, I hope, they will all have a joyful termination, and I and my Mary be skipping with delight at Eartham.'

The protracted indisposition of Mrs. Unwin, and the preparation which Cowper thought it necessary to make for his journey, had entirely diverted his mind from his literary undertaking. To Mr. Hayley, on this point, he thus writes:

'I know not how you proceed in your *Life of Milton*, but I suppose not very rapidly, for while you were here, and since you left us, you have had no other theme but me. As for myself, except my letters and the nuptial song I sent you in my last, I have literally done nothing since I saw you. Nothing, I mean, in the writing way, though a great deal in another; that is to say, in attending my poor Mary, and endeavouring to nurse her up for the journey to Eartham. In this, I have hitherto succeeded tolerably well, and I had rather carry this point completely than be the most famous editor of Milton the world has ever seen, or shall see. As to this affair, I know not what will become of it. I wrote to Johnson a week since, to tell him that the interruption of Mrs. Unwin's illness still continuing, and being likely to continue, I knew not when I should be able to proceed. The translations, I said, were finished, except the revisal of a part. I hope, or rather wish, that at Eartham I may recover that habit of study which, inveterate as it once seemed, I now appear to have lost—lost to such a degree, that it is even painful for me to think of what it will cost me to acquire it again.'

About this time, at the request of a much esteemed relative, Cowper sat to Abbot the painter for his portrait; and the following playful manner in which he adverts to the circumstance, exhibits the peculiarity of his case, and shows that though he was almost invariably suffering under the influence of deep depression, he frequently wrote to his correspondents in a strain the most sprightly and cheerful:

'How do you imagine I have been occupied these last ten days? In sitting, not on cockatrice eggs, nor yet to gratify a mere idle humour, nor because I was too sick to move, but because my cousin Johnson has an aunt who has a longing desire for my picture, and because he would therefore bring a painter from London to draw it. For this purpose, I have been sitting, as I say, these ten days; and am heartily glad that my sitting-time is over. The likeness is so strong, that when my friends enter the room where the picture is, they are startled, astonished to see me where they know I am not.

Abbot is painting me so true,
That (trust me) you would stare,
And hardly know, at the first view.
If I were here or there.

Miserable man that you are, to be at Brighton, instead of being here, to contemplate this prodigy of art, which therefore you can never see, for it goes to London next Monday, to be suspended awhile at Abbot's, and then proceeds into Norfolk, where it will be suspended forever.'

CHAPTER XVI. Journey to Eartham—Incidents of it—Safe arrival—Description of the place—Employment there—Reply to a letter from Mr. Hurdis, on the death of his sister — State of Cowper's mind at Eartham—His great attention to Mrs. Unwin—Return to Weston — Interview with General Cowper — Safe arrival at their beloved retreat — Regrets the loss of his studious habit — Warmth of his affection for Mr. Hayley—Dread of January—Prepares for a second edition of Homer — Commences writing notes upon it — Labour it occasioned him—His close application—Continuance of his depression — Judicious consolatory advice he gives to his friends—Letter to Rev. J. Johnson on his taking orders—Reply to Mr. Hayley respecting a joint literary undertaking.

Cowper and Mrs. Unwin set out for Eartham, in the beginning of August 1792. It pleased God to conduct them thither in safety; and though considerably fatigued with their journey, they were much less so than they had anticipated. Cowper's letters to his friends after his arrival, describe his feelings on the occasion in a manner the most pleasing:
'Here we are, at Eartham, in the most elegant mansion that I ever inhabited, and surrounded by the most beautiful pleasure

grounds that I have ever seen; but which, dissipated as my powers of thought are at present, I will not undertake to describe. It shall suffice me to say that they occupy three sides of a hill, which in Buckinghamshire might well pass for a mountain, and from the summit of which is beheld a most magnificent landscape, bounded by the sea, and in one part by the Isle of Wight, which may also be seen plainly from the window of the library in which I am writing. It pleased God to carry us both through the journey with far less difficulty and inconvenience than I expected; I began it indeed with a thousand fears, and when we arrived the first evening at Barnet, found myself oppressed in spirit to a degree that could hardly be exceeded. I saw Mrs. Unwin weary, as well she might be, and heard such noises, both within the house and without, that I concluded she would get no rest. But I was mercifully disappointed. She rested, though not well, yet sufficiently. Here we found our friend Rose, who had walked from his house in Chancery Lane to meet us, and to greet us with his best wishes. At Kingston, where we dined the second day, I found my old and much valued friend, General Cowper, whom I had not seen for thirty years, and but for this journey should never have seen again: and when we arrived at Ripley, where we slept the second night, we were both in a better condition of body and of mind than on the day preceding. Here we found a quiet inn that housed, as it happened, that night, no company but ourselves, we slept well and rose perfectly refreshed, and except some terrors that I felt at passing over the Sussex Hills at moonlight, met with little to complain of, till we arrived about ten o'clock at Eartham. Here we are as happy as it is in the power of earthly good to make us. It is almost a paradise in which we dwell; and our reception has been the kindest that it was possible for friendship and hospitality to contrive.'

While at Eartham, Cowper and Mr. Hayley employed the morning hours that they could bestow upon books, in revising and correcting Cowper's translation of Milton's Latin and Italian Poems. In the afternoon, they occasionally amused themselves by forming together a rapid metrical version of Andreini's Adamo.

Cowper's tender solicitude for Mrs. Unwin, however, rendered it impossible for them to be very attentive to these studies. Of the anxiety of Cowper respecting Mrs. Unwin, Mr. Hayley thus writes:

'I have myself no language sufficiently strong or sufficiently tender, to express my just admiration of that angelic compassionate sensibility with which Cowper watched over his aged invalid. With the most singular and most exemplary tenderness of attention, he incessantly laboured to counteract every infirmity, bodily and mental, with which sickness and age had conspired to load the interesting guardian of his afflicted life.'

At Eartham, Cowper's portrait was taken by Romney, in crayons, in his best style, and, in the poet's own opinion, ' with the most exact resemblance possible.' This picture is now in his kinsman's possession, and is justly esteemed by him as invaluable.

Cowper had been at Eartham but a few days when he received a letter from his friend Mr. Hurdis, informing him of the loss he had sustained by the death of a beloved sister. His compassionate heart immediately prompted him to write the following reply:

'Your kind but very affecting letter found me not at Weston, to which place it was directed, but in a bower in my friend Hayley's garden, at Eartham, where I was sitting with Mrs. Unwin. We both knew, the moment we saw it, from whom it came; and observing a red seal, both comforted ourselves that all was well at Burwash; but we soon felt that we were called not to rejoice, but to mourn with you; we do indeed sincerely mourn with you; and, if it will afford you any consolation to know it, you may be assured that every eye here has testified what our hearts have suffered for you. Your loss is great, and your disposition, I perceive, such as exposes you to feel the whole weight of it. I will not add to your sorrow by a vain attempt to assuage it; your own good sense and the piety of your principles will suggest to you the most powerful motives of acquiescence in the will of God. You will be sure to recollect, that the stroke, severe as it is, is not the stroke of an enemy, but of a Friend and a Father; and will find, I trust, hereafter, that like a Father, he has done you good by it. Thousands have been able to say, and myself as loud as any of them, "It has been good for me that I have been afflicted;" but time is necessary to work us to this persuasion; and in due time it will no doubt be yours. May the Comforter of all the afflicted who seek him, be yours. God bless you.'

The following extracts from letters to Lady Hesketh, dated Eartham, describe his feelings while he remained there:

'I know not how it is, my dearest cousin, but in a new scene like this, surrounded by strange objects, I find my powers of thinking dissipated to a degree that makes it difficult for me even to write a letter, and even a letter to you; but such a letter as I can, I will, and I have the fairest chance of succeeding this morning; Hayley, Romney, and Hayley's son, being all gone to the sea for bathing. The sea, you must know, is nine miles off, so that, unless stupidity prevent, I shall have opportunity to write, not only to you, but to poor Hurdis also, who is broken-hearted for the loss of his favourite sister, lately dead. I am, without the least dissimulation, in good health; my spirits are about as good as you have ever seen them; and if increase of appetite, and a double portion of sleep, be advantageous, such are the benefits I have received from this migration. As to that gloominess of mind which I have felt these twenty years, it cleaves to me even here; and could I be translated to Paradise, unless I left my body behind me, would cleave to me even there also. It is my companion for life, and nothing will ever divorce us. Mrs. Unwin is evidently the better for her jaunt, though by no means so well as she was before her last attack, still wanting help when she would rise from her seat, and a support in walking; but she is able to take more exercise than when at home, and move with rather a less tottering step. God knows what he designs for me; but when I see those who are dearer to me than myself, distempered and enfeebled, and myself as strong as in the days of my youth, I tremble for the solitude in which a few years may place me.

'This is, as I have already told you, a delightful place; more beautiful scenery I have never beheld, nor expect to behold; but the charms of it, uncommon as they are, have not in the least alienated my affections from Weston. The genius of that place suits me better; it has an air of snug concealment, in which a disposition like mine feels peculiarly gratified; whereas here I see from every window woods like forests, and hills like mountains, a wilderness, in short, that rather increases my natural melancholy, and which, were it not for the agreeables I find within, would convince me that mere change of place can avail but little.'

On the 17th September, 1792, Cowper and Mrs. Unwin left Eartham for their beloved retreat at Weston. Their parting interview with their friends at Eartham, who had heaped upon them everything that the most affectionate kindness could invent, was deeply interesting to all parties, but particularly affecting to the sensitive mind of Cowper. According to a previous arrangement, the poet and Mrs. Unwin dined and spent the day with General Cowper, at Kingston, who had come there on purpose to have the pleasure of Cowper's company, probably for the last time. A recollection of this so powerfully affected the poet's mind, that the pleasure of the interview was hardly greater than the pain he felt at parting with his venerable and beloved kinsman. The peculiar and burdened state of Cowper's mind respecting this visit, he thus describes:

'The struggles that I had with my own spirit, labouring, as I did, under the most dreadful dejection, are never to be told. I would have given the world to have been excused. I went, however, and carried my point against myself, with a heart riven asunder. I have a reason for all this anxiety, which I cannot relate now; the visit, however, passed off well, and I returned with a lighter heart than I had known since my departure from Eartham, and we both enjoyed a good night's rest afterwards.' The good providence of God conducted these travellers in safety to their home, where they arrived on the evening of the second day after they set out from Eartham. The unusual excitement occasioned by so long a journey, and by such a profusion of interesting objects, would, in ordinary cases, and in minds of almost any form, which had been so long confined to one spot, be very likely to be succeeded by considerable depression. Such was, however, much more likely to be the case on a mind like Cowper's. Accordingly we find, that when he arrived at Weston, - be was, for a considerable time, subject to an unusual degree of depression. The following extracts from his letters to his friend Hayley describe the state of his mind, and show how much he was then under the influence of his distressing malady:

'Chaos himself, even the chaos of Milton, is not surrounded more with confusion, nor has a mind more completely in a hubbub, than I experience now. A bad night, succeeded by an east wind, and a sky all in sables, have such an effect on my spirits, that if I did not consult my own comfort more than yours, I should not write to-day, for I shall not entertain you much; yet your letter, though containing no very pleasant tidings, has afforded me some relief. It tells me, indeed, that you have been dispirited yourself; all this grieves me, but then there is warmth of heart and a kindness in it that do me good. I will endeavour not to repay you in notes of sorrow and despondence, though all my sprightly chords seem broken. In truth, one day excepted, I have not seen the day when I have been cheerful since I left you. My spirits, I think, are almost constantly lower than they were; the approach of winter is perhaps the cause, and if it be, I have nothing better to expect for a long time to come. I began a long letter to you yesterday, and proceeded through two sides of the sheet, but so much of my nervous fever found its way into it, that, on looking over it this morning, I determined not to send it. Your wishes to disperse my melancholy would, I am sure, prevail, did that event depend on the warmth and sincerity with which you frame them; but it has baffled both wishes and prayers, and those the most fervent that could be made, so many years, that the case seems hopeless.'

These frequent, and indeed almost continual attacks of depression, combined with the attention that Cowper paid to promote the comfort, and facilitate the recovery of Mrs. Unwin, prevented him entirely from persevering in his literary undertaking. In his letters, he makes this a subject of particular regret. The benefits he had derived from his regular habits of study during his translation of Homer, made him anxious to be again regularly employed. To his friend Mr. Rose, he thus describes the state of his mind in this respect:

'I wish that I were as industrious and as much occupied as you, though in a different way; but it is not so with me. Mrs. Unwin's great debility is of itself a hindrance, such as would effectually disable me. I may now and then find time to write a letter, but I shall write nothing more. I cannot sit with my pen in my hand and my books before me, while she is in effect in solitude, silent, and looking at the fire. To this hindrance, that other has been added, of which you are aware, a want of spirits, such as I have never known when I was not absolutely laid by, since I commenced an author. How long I shall be continued in these uncomfortable circumstances, is known only to Him, who, as He will, disposes of us all.

'I may yet be able, perhaps, to prepare the first book of Paradise Lost for the press before it will be wanted, and Johnson himself seems to think (here will be no haste for the second. But poetry is my favourite employment, and my poetical operations are in the meantime suspended; for while a work to which I have bound myself remains unaccomplished, I can do nothing else.'

To his friend Hayley, he thus writes:

'Yesterday was a day of assignation with myself, a day of which I had said, some days before it came, when that day comes, I will, if possible, begin my dissertations. Accordingly, when it came, I prepared to do so; filled a letter-case with fresh paper, furnished myself with a pretty good pen, and replenished my inkbottle; but partly from one cause, and partly from another, chiefly, however, from distress and dejection, after writing and obliterating about six lines, in the composition of which I spent near an hour, I was obliged to relinquish the attempt. An attempt so unsuccessful could have no other effect than to dishearten me, and it has had that effect to such a degree, that I know not when I shall find courage to make another. At present I shall certainly abstain from it, since I cannot well afford to expose myself to the danger of a fresh mortification.'

He thus again writes to Mr. Hayley, 25th Nov. 1792.

'How shall I thank you enough for the interest you take in my future Miltonic labours, and the assistance you promise me in the performance of them? I will, at some time or other, if I live, and live a poet, acknowledge your friendship in some of my best verses, the most suitable return one poet can make to another; in the meantime, I love you, and am sensible of all your kindness. You wish me warm in my work, and I ardently wish the same, but when I shall be so, God only knows. My melancholy, which seemed a little alleviated for a few days, has gathered about me again, with as black a cloud as ever; the consequence is absolute incapacity to begin. Yet I purpose, in a day or two, to make another attempt, to which, however, I shall address myself with fear and trembling, like a man who, having sprained his wrist, dreads to use it. I have not, indeed, like such a man, injured myself by any extraordinary exertion, but seem as much enfeebled as if I had. The consciousness that there is so much to do, and nothing done, is a burden I am not able to bear. Milton especially is my grievance, and I might almost as well be haunted by his ghost, as goaded with continual reproaches for neglecting him. I will therefore begin; I will do my best, and if, after all, that best prove good for nothing, I will even send the notes, worthless as they are, that I have already; a measure very disagreeable to myself, and to which nothing but necessity shall compel me.'

To his friend, Mr. Newton, who had ventured to express his apprehensions lest his Miltonic labours should become too severe, he thus writes, 9th Dec. 1792:

You need not be uneasy on the subject of Milton; I shall not find that labour too heavy for me, if I have health and leisure. The season of the year is unfavourable to me respecting the former, and Mrs. Unwin's present weakness allows me less of the latter than the occasion seems to call for. But the business is in no haste; the artists employed to furnish the embellishments are not likely to be very expeditious; and a small portion only of the work will be wanted from me at once, for the intention is to deal it out to the public piece-meal. I am, therefore, under no great anxiety on that account. It is not indeed an employment that I should have chosen for myself, because poetry pleases and amuses me more, and would cost me less labour properly so called. All this I felt before I engaged with Johnson, and did, in the first instance, actually decline the service, but he was urgent, and at last I suffered myself to be persuaded. The season of the year, as I have already said, is particularly adverse to me, yet not in itself, perhaps, more adverse than any other; but the approach of it always reminds me of the same season in the dreadful seventy-three, and the more dreadful eighty-six. I cannot help terrifying myself with doleful misgivings and apprehensions; nor is the enemy negligent to seize all the advantage that the occasion gives him. Thus, hearing much from him, and having little or no sensible support from God, I suffer inexpressible things till January is over. Even then, whether it is that increasing years have made me more liable to it, or that despair, the longer it lasts, grows naturally darker, I find myself more inclined to melancholy than I was a few years since. God only knows where this will end; but where it is likely to end, unless he interpose powerfully in my favour, all may know.

In the same plaintive, though in a less hopeless strain, he again writes:

'I have neither been well myself, nor is Mrs. Unwin, though better, so much improved in her health, as not still to require my continual assistance. My disorder has been the old one, to which I have been subject so many years, and especially about this season—a nervous fever; not, indeed, so oppressive as it has sometimes proved, but sufficiently alarming both to Mrs. Unwin and myself; and such as made it neither easy nor proper for me to use my pen while it continued. I am tolerably free from it, a blessing, which I attribute partly to the use of suitable medicine, but chiefly to a manifestation of God's presence vouchsafed to me He has not cast me off forever.

'Our late visit to Eartham was a pleasant one, as pleasant as Mrs. Unwin's weakness, and the state of my spirits, never very good, would allow. As to my health, I never expected that it would be much improved by the journey; nor have I found it so. But the season was, after the first fortnight, extremely unfavourable, stormy and wet, and the prospects, though grand and magnificent, yet rather of a melancholy cast, and consequently not very propitious to me. The cultivated appearance of Weston suits my frame of mind far better, than wild hills that aspire to be mountains, covered with vast unfrequented woods, and here and there affording a peep, between their summits, at the distant ocean. Hayley is one of the most agreeable of men, as well as one of the most cordial of friends; but the scenery would have its effect, and though delightful in the extreme to those who had spirits to bear it, was too gloomy for me. I have made the experiment, only to prove, what indeed I knew before, that creatures are physicians of little value, and that health and cure are from God only. Henceforth, therefore, I shall wait for those blessings from Him, and expect them at no other hand.'

On another occasion, to the same correspondent, he again writes:

'Oh for the day when your expectations of my final deliverance shall be verified! At present it seems very remote, so distant, indeed, that hardly the faintest streak of it is visible in my horizon. The glimpse with which I was favoured about a month ago, has never been repeated, but the depression of my spirits has. The future appears as gloomy as ever, and I seem to myself to be scrambling always in the dark, among rocks and precipices, without a guide, but with an enemy ever at my heels, prepared to push me headlong. Thus I have spent twenty years, but thus I shall not spend twenty years more: long before that period arrives, the grand question concerning my everlasting weal or woe will be decided.'

To a lady with whom he occasionally corresponded, he thus discloses his feelings:

'I would give you consolation, madam, were I not disqualified for that delightful service by a great dearth of it in my own experience. I too often seek, but cannot find it. I know, however, there are seasons when, look which way we will, we see the same dismal gloom enveloping all objects. This is itself an affliction; and the worse, because it makes us think ourselves more unhappy than we are. I was struck by an expression in your letter to Hayley, where you say that you 'will endeavour to take an interest in green leaves again.' This seems the sound of my own voice reflected to me from a distance; I have so often had the same thought and desire. A day scarcely passes, at this season of the year, when I do not contemplate the trees so soon to be stript, and say, 'perhaps I shall never see you clothed again.' Every year, as it passes, makes this expectation more reasonable; and the year with me cannot be very distant when the event will verify it. Well, may God grant us a good hope of arriving, in due time, where the leaves never fall, and all will be right!'

In a letter to Mr. Newton, written 12th June, 1793, Cowper thus expresses himself respecting the state of his mind, and that of Mrs. Unwin. 'You promise to be contented with a short line, and a short one you must have, hurried over in a little interval I have happened to find, between the conclusion of my morning task and breakfast. Study has this good effect, at least, it makes me an early riser, a wholesome practice, from which I have never swerved since March. The scanty opportunity I have, I shall employ in telling you what you principally wish to be told, the present state of Mrs. Unwin's health and mine. In her I cannot perceive any alteration for the better, and must be satisfied, I believe, as indeed I have great reason to be, if she does not alter for the worse. She uses the orchard-walk daily, but always supported between two, and is still unable to employ herself as formerly. But she is cheerful, seldom in much pain, and has always strong confidence in the mercy and faithfulness of God. As to myself, I have invariably the same song to sing—well in body, but sick in spirit; sick, nigh unto death.

I could easily set my complaint to Milton's tune, and accompany him through the whole passage, on the subject of a blindness more deplorable than his; but time fails me. Prayer, I know, is made for me; and sometimes with great enlargement of heart by those who offer it: and in this circumstance consists the only evidence I can find that God is still favourably mindful of me, and has not cast me off forever.'

Notwithstanding his gloomy forebodings, Cowper escaped any very severe attack of depression, in the dreaded month of the ensuing January, and as the spring advanced he became as busily engaged as he had ever been, partly in his Miltonic labours, but chiefly in preparing materials for a second edition of Homer. He had long been carefully revising the work, and had judiciously availed himself of the remarks of his friends, as well as of the criticisms of the reviewers. As soon, therefore, as it was determined to republish it, he made the best use of these materials, and in a few weeks prepared the work a second time for the press, in its new and much improved form. It was thought advisable, in a second edition, to publish notes, for the assistance of unlearned readers; and the labour and research required to furnish these, occasioned Cowper much severe application, as the following extracts will shew:

19th March, 1793. I am so busy every morning before breakfast, strutting and stalking on Homeric stilts, that you must account it an instance of marvellous grace and favour that I write even to you. Sometimes I am, seriously, almost crazed with the multiplicity of matters before me, and the little or no time that I have for them; and sometimes I repose myself after the fatigue of that distraction, on the pillow of despair; a pillow which has often served me in time of need, and is become, by frequent use, if not very comfortable, at least convenient. So reposed, I laugh at the world and say— Yes, you may gape, and expect both Homer and Milton from me, but I'll be hanged if ever you get them. In

Homer, however, you must know I am advanced as far as the fifteenth book of the Iliad, leaving nothing behind that can reasonably offend the most fastidious; and I design him for a new dress as soon as possible, for a reason which any poet may guess if he will but thrust his hand into his pocket.'

Excusing himself for not having written to his correspondents, who all prized a letter from him as a treasure, he again remarks:

My time, the little that I have, is now so entirely engrossed by Homer, that I have, at this time, a bundle of unanswered letters by me, and letters likely to be so. Thou knowest, I dare say, what it is to have a head weary with thinking; mine is so fatigued that I am utterly incapable of sitting down to my desk again for any purpose whatever.'

It cannot be ascertained, precisely, what compensation Comper received for his productions; from his own statements, however, there is reason to believe that Johnson, his publisher, remunerated him liberally for his labour. Whenever the poet had occasion to advert to the subject in his correspondence, it was never in the language of complaint, but often of satisfaction, and sometimes of commendation.

To Mr. Rose he writes:

'I must send you a line of congratulation on the event of your transaction with Johnson, since you, I know, partake with me on the pleasure I receive from it. Few of my concerns have been so happily concluded. I am satisfied with my bookseller, as I have substantial cause to be, and account myself in good hands; a circumstance as pleasant to me as any other part of my business, for I love dearly to be able to confide with all my heart in those with whom I am connected, of what kind soever the connection may be.'

On the same subject, he writes to his kinsman, humourously adverting to the little property that had been bequeathed him by his ancestors. 'The long muster-roll of my great and small ancestors I signed, and dated, and sent up to Mr. Blue-mantle on Monday, according to your desire. Such a pompous affair, drawn out for my sake, reminds me of the old fable of the mountain in parturition, and a mouse the produce. Rest undisturbed, say I, thou lordly, ducal, and royal dust! Had they left me something handsome, I should have respected them more. But perhaps they did not know that such a one as I should have the honour to be numbered among their descendants. Well! I have a little bookseller that makes me some amends for their deficiency. He has made me a present; an act of liberality which I take every opportunity to blazon, as it well deserves.' The present here referred to was a hundred pounds, which Johnson (to his honour be it recorded,) presented to the poet above the sum stipulated in their agreement.

During this year, several of Cowper's correspondents were visited either with domestic affliction, or with painful bereavements. On such occasions, all the sensibility and sympathy of his peculiarly tender mind never failed to be called into lively exercise. The deep depression of his own mind did not deter him from attempting, at least, to alleviate the distress of others. To Mr. Hayley, who had recently lost a friend, he thus writes:

'I truly sympathize with you under your weight of sorrow, for the loss of our good Samaritan. But be not broken-hearted, my friend; remember, the loss of those we love is the condition on which we live ourselves; and that he who chooses his friends wisely from among the excellent of the earth, has a sure ground to hope concerning them when they die, that a merciful God will make them far happier than they could be here, and that we shall join them soon again: this is solid comfort, could we but avail ourselves of it, but I confess the difficulty of doing so always. Sorrow is like the deaf adder, that hears not the voice of the charmer, charm he never so wisely; and I feel so myself for the death of Austen, that my own chief consolation is that I had never seen him. Live yourself, I beseech you, for I have seen so much of you that I can by no means spare you, and I will live as long as it shall please God to permit. I know you set some value upon me, therefore, let that promise comfort you, and give us not reason to say, like David's servants, "We know that it would have pleased thee more if all we had died, than this one, for whom thou art inconsolable." "You have still Romney and Carwardine, and Guy, and me, and my poor Mary, and 1 know not how many beside; as many I suppose as ever had an opportunity of spending a day with you. He who has the most friends, must necessarily lose the most; and he whose friends are numerous as yours, may the better spare a part of them. It is a changing transient scene: yet a little while, and this poor dream of life will be over with all of us. The living, and they who live unhappy, they are indeed the subjects of sorrow.'

To his esteemed friend, Rev. Mr. Hurdis, who, as above related, had lost one beloved sister, and was in great danger of losing another, he thus writes, June 1793:

'I seize a passing moment, merely to say that I feel for your distresses, and sincerely pity you, and I shall be happy to learn from your next that your sister's amendment has superseded the necessity you feared of a journey to London. Your candid account that your afflictions have broken your spirits and temper, I can perfectly understand, having laboured much in that fire myself, and perhaps more than any man. It is in such a school that we must learn, if we ever truly learn it, the natural depravity of the human heart, and of our own in particular, together with the consequence that necessarily follows, namely, our indispensable need of the atonement, and our inexpressible obligations to Him who made it. This reflection cannot escape a thinking mind, looking back on those ebullitions of fretfulness and impatience to which it has yielded in a season of great affliction.'

To the Rev. Walter Bagot, who had recently lost a dear friend, he writes:

'While your sorrow for our common loss was fresh in your mind, I would not write, lest a letter on so distressing a subject should be too painful both to you and me; and now that I seem to have reached a proper time for doing it, the multiplicity of my literary business will hardly afford me leisure. Both you and I have this comfort when deprived of those we love—at our time of life we have every reason to believe that the separation cannot be long. Our sun is setting too; and when the hour of rest arrives, we shall rejoin your brother, and many whom we have tenderly loved, our forerunners in a better country.'

Early in the spring of this year, 1793, Cowper's esteemed relative, Mr. John Johnson, after much mature and solemn deliberation, had resolved to take holy orders. Cowper had always regarded him with the most paternal affection, and had wished that he should enter upon the important office of a Christian minister with a high sense of the greatness of the work, and with suitable qualifications for a proper discharge of its solemn duties. In accordance with these wishes, when Mr. Johnson, in a previous year, had relinquished his intentions of taking orders at that time, Cowper had thus addressed him:

'My dearest of all Johnnys, I am not sorry that your ordination is postponed. A year's learning and wisdom, added to your present stock, will not be more than enough to satisfy the demands of your function. Neither am I sorry that you find it difficult to fix your thoughts to the serious point at all times. It proves, at least, that you attempt, and wish to do it, and these are good symptoms. Woe to those who enter on the ministry of the gospel without having previously asked, at least from God, a mind and spirit suited to the occupation, and whose experience never differs from itself, because they are always alike vain, light, and inconsiderate. It is, therefore, matter of great joy to me to hear you complain of levity, as it indicates the existence of an anxiety of mind to be freed from it.'

The gratification it afforded Cowper to find that his beloved relative entered into the ministry with scriptural views and feelings, is thus expressed:

'What you say of your determined purpose, with God's help, to take up the cross, and despise the shame, gives us both great pleasure: in our pedigree is found one, at least, who did it before you. Do you the like, and you will meet him in heaven, as sure as the scripture is the word of God. The quarrel that the world has with evangelical men and doctrines, they would have with a host of angels in human form, for it is the quarrel of owls with sunshine; of ignorance with divine illumination. The Bishop of Norwich has won my heart by his kind and liberal behaviour to you, and if I knew him I would tell him so. I am glad that your auditors find your voice strong, and your utterance distinct; glad, too, that your doctrine has hitherto made you no enemies. "You have a gracious Master, who, it seems, will not suffer you to see war in the beginning. It will be a wonder, however, if you do not find out, sooner or later, that sore place in every heart which can ill endure the touch of apostolic doctrine. Somebody will smart in his conscience, and you will hear of it. I say not this to terrify you, but to prepare you for what is likely to happen, and which, troublesome as it may prove, is yet devoutly to be wished; for, in general, there is little good done by preachers till the world begins to abuse them. But understand me aright. I do not mean that you should give them unnecessary provocation, by scolding and railing at them, as some, more zealous than wise, are apt to do. That were to deserve their anger. No; there is no need of it. The self-abasing doctrines of the gospel will, of themselves, create you enemies; but remember this for your comfort—they will also, in due time, transform them into friends, and make them love you as if they were your own children. God give you many such; as, if you are faithful to his cause, I trust he will.'

Several of the poet's friends now became apprehensive that his severe application to Homer, added to the distress which they knew he would feel for the situation of Mrs. Unwin, would be seriously injurious to his health; to prevent which they gave him pressing invitations to favour them with a visit, as he had done Mr. Hayley. Lady Hesketh used all her efforts to succeed, as did also both Mr. Rose and Mr. Greatheed, but in vain. Had his literary engagements permitted him to comply with their kind requests, the health of his beloved inmate was such as to become an insuperable obstacle. His attachment to Mr. Greatheed, however, strongly inclined him to accept his invitation, as he thus writes:— 'Your kind offer to us of sharing with you the house which you at present inhabit, added to the short but lively description of the scenery that surrounds it, wants nothing to win our acceptance, should it please God to give Mrs. Unwin a little more strength, and should I ever be master of my time, so as to be able to gratify myself with what would please me most. But many have claims upon us, and some who cannot absolutely be said to have any, would yet complain, and think themselves slighted, should we prefer rocks and caves to them. In short, we are called so many ways, that these numerous demands are likely to operate as remora, and to keep us fixed at home. My dear mother's kindred, in Norfolk, are dying to see me; and my cousin Johnny holds me under a promise to make my first trip thither. The same promise I have hastily made to visit Sir John and Lady Throckmorton, at Bucklands. Hayley, in his last letter, gives me reason to expect the pleasure of seeing him, and his dear boy Tom, in the autumn. He will use all his eloquence to draw us to Eartham. How to reconcile such clashing promises, and give satisfaction to all, would puzzle me had I nothing else to do; and therefore the result will probably be, that we shall find ourselves obliged to go no-where, because we cannot go every-where.'

> Much to my own, though little to thy good,
> With thee (not subject to the jealous mood !)
> A partnership of literary ware!
> But I am bankrupt now, and doomed henceforth
> To drudge in descant dry, or other's lays—
> Bards, I acknowledge, of unequall'd worth!
> But what is commentator's happiest praise?
> That he has furnished lights for other eyes,—
> Which they who need them use, and then despise.'

About this time Mr. Hayley appears to have applied to Cowper for his assistance in a joint literary undertaking, of some magnitude, with himself and two other distinguished literary characters. Anxious, however, as Cowper was on all occasions to oblige his friend, he could not give his consent to this measure. His reply, given partly in poetry and partly in prose, with that happy playfulness peculiar to himself, while it shows the peculiar state of his mind, exhibits, at the same time, so much of that amiable modesty by which he was always distinguished, that it cannot be read without interest.

'Dear architect of fine chateaux in air,
Worthier to stand for ever if they could,
Than any built of stone, or yet of. wood.
For back of royal elephant to bear!
Oh, for permission from the skies to share,

'What remains for me to say on this subject, my dear brother, I will say in prose. There are other impediments to the plan you propose, which I could not comprise within the bounds of a sonnet. My poor Mary's infirm condition makes it impossible for me, at present, to engage in work such as you propose. My thoughts are not sufficiently free; nor have I, nor can I by any means find, opportunity; added to which comes a difficulty which, though you are not at all aware of it, presents itself to me under a most forbidding appearance. Can you guess it? No, not you: neither, perhaps, will you be able to imagine that such a difficulty can possibly exist. If your hair begins to bristle, stroke it down again; for there is no need why it should erect itself. It concerns me, not you. I know myself too well not to know that I am nobody in verse, unless in a corner and alone, and unconnected in my operations. This is not owing to want of love to you, my brother, or the most consummate confidence in you—I have both in a degree that has not been exceeded in the experience of any friend you have, or ever had. But I am so made up—I will not enter into a philosophical analysis of my strange constitution, in order to detect the true cause of the evil,—but, on a general view of the matter, I suspect that it proceeds from that shyness which has been my effectual and almost total hindrance on many other important occasions, and which I should feel, I well know, on this, to a degree that would perfectly cripple me. No! I shall neither do, nor attempt, anything of consequence more, unless my poor Mary get better: nor even then, unless it should please God to give me another nature. I could not thus act in concert with any man, not even with my own father or brother, were they now alive! Small game must serve me at present, and till I have done with Homer and Milton. The utmost that I aspire to, and Heaven knows with how feeble a hope, is to write, at some future and better opportunity, when my hands are free, The Four Ages. Thus I have opened my heart unto thee.'

On another occasion, he thus plaintively writes:

'I find that much study fatigues me, which is a proof that I am somewhat stricken in years. Certain it is that, ten or sixteen years ago, I could have done as much, and did actually do much more, without suffering the least fatigue, than I can possibly accomplish now. How insensibly old age steals on us, and how often it is actually arrived before we suspect it! Accident alone; some occurrence that suggests a comparison of our former with our present selves, affords the discovery. Well, it is always good to be undeceived, especially in a matter of such importance.'

To a person less intimately acquainted with Cowper than Mr. Hayley was, the above reply would have been amply sufficient to have prevented him from making any further application of a similar nature. He, however, was not to be thus easily diverted from his purpose. Of the talents of Cowper he had justly formed the highest opinion, and had wisely concluded, that if they could only be again brought fairly and fully into exercise, in the composition of original poetry, the result would be every thing that could be wished. Immediately, therefore, on receiving the above letter, he proffered Cowper his own assistance, and the assistance of two other esteemed friends, in composing the projected poem, 'The Four Ages,' and proposed that it should be their joint production. His principal object was, unquestionably, to induce Cowper to employ his unrivalled talents. The pleasure he anticipated in having such a coadjutor, gratifying as it must have been to his feelings, was only a secondary consideration.

Averse as Cowper was to the former proposal, he immediately consented to this, and the following extract will show what were his feelings on the occasion:

'I am in haste to tell you how much I am delighted with your projected quadruple alliance, and to assure you that, if it please God to afford me health, spirits, ability, and leisure, I will not fail to devote them all to the production of my quota in 'The Four Ages.' You are very kind to humour me as you do, and had need be a little touched yourself with all my oddities, that you may know how to administer to mine. All whom I love do so, and I believe it to be impossible to love heartily those who do not. People must not do me good in their way, but in my own, and then they do me good indeed. My pride, my ambition, and my friendship for you, and the interest I take in my own dear self, will all be consulted and gratified, by an arm-in-arm appearance with you in public; and I shall work with more zeal and assiduity at Homer; and when Homer is finished, at Milton, with the prospect of such a coalition before me. I am at this moment, with all the imprudence natural to poets, expending nobody knows what, in embellishing my premises, or rather the premises of my neighbour Courtenay, which is more poetical still. Your project, therefore, is most opportune, as any project must needs be, which has so direct a tendency to put money into the pocket of one so likely to want it.'

Ah, brother poet! send me of your shade.
And bid the zephyrs hasten to my aid;
Or, like a worm unearthed at noon, I go,
Dispatched by sunshine to the shades below.'

It is deeply to be regretted that the pleasing anticipations of both Mr. Hayley and Cowper, respecting this joint production, were never realized. Had this poem been written, it would in all probability, have been equal to any that had ever been published. Cowper was, however, at this time, rapidly sinking into that deep and settled melancholy which it now becomes our painful duty to describe, and in which he continued during the remaining period of his life, notwithstanding the united and indefatigable exertions of his friends to afford him relief.

A short time before this attack we find him giving the following description of the state of his mind to Mr. Hayley.

I am cheerful upon paper sometimes, when I am absolutely the most dejected of all creatures. Desirous, however, to gain something myself by my own letters, unprofitable as they may and must be to my friends, I keep melancholy out of them as much as I can, that I may, if possible, by assuming a less gloomy air, deceive myself, and by feigning with a continuance, improve the fiction into reality.'

In October, Mr. Rose, accompanied by Lawrence the painter, paid Cowper a visit; and the poet was again prevailed upon, though not without reluctance, to sit for his portrait. Adverting to the circumstance, he remarks, sportively:

'Yet once more my patience is to be exercised, and once more I am made to wish that my face had been moveable, to put on and take off at pleasure, so as to be portable in a band-box, and sent off to the artist.'

The peculiarity of his case, and the depression under which he laboured, even at the time he wrote the above playful remarks, will be seen by the close of the same letter:

'I began this letter yesterday, but could not finish it till now. I have risen this morning covered with the ooze and mud of melancholy. For this reason, I am not sorry to find myself at the bottom of my paper: for had I more room, perhaps I might make an heart ache at Eartham, which I wish to be always cheerful.'

CHAPTER XVII. Mr. Hayley's second visit to Weston—Finds Cowper busily engaged—Great apprehensions respecting him— Mrs. Unwin's increasing infirmities—Cowper's feelings on account of them—Vigour of his own mind at this period—Severe attack of depression—Deplorable condition to which he was nmu reduced—Management of his affairs kindly undertaken by Lady Hesketh— Mr. Hayley's anxieties respecting him—Is invited by Mr. Greatheed to pay Cowper another visit—Complies with the invitation—Arrival at Weston—How he is received by Cowper—Inefficiency of the means employed to remove the depression—Handsome pension allowed by his Majesty—His removal from Weston to Norfolk, under the care of the Rev. J. Johnson— Death of Mrs. Unwin—How it affected Cowper.

In the beginning of November 1793, Mr. Hayley made his second visit to Weston. He found Cowper in the enjoyment of apparent health; and though incessantly employed, either on Homer or Milton, pleasing himself with the society of his young kinsman from Norfolk, and his friend Mr. Rose, who had arrived from the seat of Lord Spencer in Northampton Shire, with an invitation from his lordship to Cowper and his guests, to pay him a visit. All Cowper's friends strongly recommended him to avail himself of this mark of respect from an accomplished nobleman whom he cordially esteemed. Their entreaties, however, were entirely in vain; his constitutional shyness again prevailed, and he commissioned his friends, Rose and Hayley, to make an apology to his lordship for declining so honourable an invitation. The manner in which Cowper employed his time during the continuance of his friend Mr. Hayley at Weston, is pleasantly described in the following extract from a letter to Mrs. Courtenay, 4th Nov. 1793:

I am a most busy man, busy to a degree that sometimes half distracts me: but if complete distraction be occasioned by having the thoughts too much and too long attached to any single point, I am in no danger of it, with such perpetual whirl are mine whisked about from one subject to another. When two poets meet, there are fine doings, I can assure you. My *Homer* finds work for Hayley, and his *Life of Milton* work for me; so that we are neither of us one moment idle. Poor Mrs. Unwin in the meantime sits quiet in her corner, laughing at us both, and not seldom interrupting us with some question or remark, for which she is occasionally rewarded by me with a 'hush!' Bless yourself, my dear Catherina, that you are not connected with a poet, especially that you have not two to deal with!'

Mr. Hayley remained at Weston more than a fortnight, affording Cowper just time to revise his friend's manuscript Life of Milton; of which, in a gratulatory letter to his friend Hurdis, who was then a successful candidate for the professorship at Oxford, he remarks:

'When your short note arrived, which gave me the agreeable news of your victory, our friend of Eartham was with me, and shared largely in the joy that I felt on the occasion. He left me a few days since. During his continuance here, we employed all our leisure hours in the revisal of his Life of Milton. It is now finished, and a very finished work it is, and one that will do great honour, I am persuaded, to his biographer, and the excellent man of injured memory who is the subject of it.'

During Mr. Hayley's visit, he saw, with great concern, that the infirmities of Mrs. Unwin were rapidly sinking her into a state of the most pitiable imbecility. Unable any longer to watch over the tender health of him whom she had guarded for so many years, and unwilling to relinquish her authority, her conduct at this period presented that painful spectacle, which we are occasionally called to witness, of declining nature seeking to retain that power which it knows not how to use, nor how to resign. The effect of these increasing infirmities on her whom Cowper justly regarded as the guardian of his life, added to apprehensions which he now began to feel, that his increasing expenses, occasioned by Mrs. Unwin's protracted illness, would involve him in difficulties, filled him with the greatest uneasiness; and the depressing influence it had upon his mind, became painfully evident to all his friends. So visibly was such the case, that Mr. Hayley felt fully persuaded that, unless some speedy and important change took place in Cowper's circumstances, his tender mind would inevitably sink under the multiplicity of its cares. To effect this desirable object, as far as was in his power, he embraced the earliest opportunity, after leaving Weston, of having an interview with Lord Spencer, and of stating to him undisguisedly the condition of the afflicted poet. His lordship entered feelingly into the case, and shortly afterwards mentioned it to his Majesty. It was owing to this that his majesty, sometime afterwards, granted to Cowper such a pension as was sufficient to secure to him a comfortable competence for the remainder of his life. It is however deeply to be regretted that this seasonable and well-merited bounty was not received till the poet's mind was enveloped in that midnight gloom from which it never afterwards wholly emerged.

It is not improbable that this catastrophe was in some degree hastened by the incessant attention which Cowper now paid to the revisal of his Homer, and the deep sympathy he felt for his afflicted inmate. For though he felt it a great relief that his publisher kindly left him at liberty to postpone his Miltonic labours, yet was he compelled, in order to prepare the notes and illustrations of Homer, and to get the work again through the press, to rise very early, and to labor hard for many hours; only quitting this labour for his attention to Mrs. Unwin; which, though it might be more grateful to his feelings, had, perhaps, a much more depressing influence upon his mind.

The increasing infirmities of Mrs. Unwin did not, in the slightest degree, diminish Cowper's regard for her; on the contrary, they seemed rather to augment it, as the following beautiful poem, written about this time, will show:

TO MARY.

Written in the autumn of 1793. Published by Hayley, 1803. There is a MS. copy in the Cowper Museum at Olney, from which the tenth verse was first printed by T. Wright in 1900.

THE twentieth year is well-nigh past
Since first our sky was overcast;
Ah, would that this might be the last!
My Mary!
Thy spirits have a fainter flow,
I see thee daily weaker grow—
'Twas my distress that brought thee low,
My Mary!

Thy needles, once a shining store,

For my sake restless heretofore,
 Now rust disus'd, and shine no more,
My Mary!

For though thou gladly wouldst fulfil
 The same kind office for me still,
 Thy sight now seconds not thy will,
My Mary!

But well thou play'd'st the housewife's part,
 And all thy threads with magic art
 Have wound themselves about this heart,
My Mary!

Thy indistinct expressions seem
 Like language utter'd in a dream;
 Yet me they charm, whate'er the theme,
My Mary!

Thy silver locks, once auburn bright,
 Are still more lovely in my sight
 Than golden beams of orient light,
My Mary!

For could I view nor them nor thee,
 What sight worth seeing could I see?
 The sun would rise in vain for me,
My Mary!

Partakers of thy sad decline,
 Thy hands their little force resign;
 Yet, gently prest, press gently mine,
My Mary!

And then I feel that still I hold
 A richer store ten thousandfold

Than misers fancy in their gold,
My Mary!

Such feebleness of limbs thou prov'st,
That now at every step thou mov'st
Upheld by two; yet still thou lov'st,
My Mary!

And still to love, though prest with ill,
In wintry age to feel no chill,
With me is to be lovely still,
My Mary!

But ah! by constant heed I know,
How oft the sadness that I show
Transforms thy smiles to looks of woe,
My Mary!
And should my future lot be cast
With much resemblance of the past,
Thy worn-out heart will break at last—
My Mary!

Some individuals, for want of duly considering all the circumstances of Cowper's case, have remarked that his language, on many occasions, to his inestimable Mary, partook more of the fondness of the husband than was seemly or decorous. 'The fact is,' as an able critic well observes, 'that his feelings naturally partook of the peculiarity of his situation, which had rendered him an object of maternal solicitude to his elder companion, rather than, what he otherwise would have been, her equal partner and protector. But it was well known to his friends, that their engagements to each other would have been consummated by legal ties and the closest union, but for the distemper which more than once prevented its taking place, after the day had been as repeatedly fixed. And the age of both parties, it was probably thought, rendered the step inexpedient at a later period. That Cowper, the most affectionate and most grateful of beings, should love, and that most tenderly, the faithful friend to whom he was so deeply indebted, whose companionship had been attendant on his happiest days, and was the only solace of long years of darkness;—that this love should be more than is implied by mere friendship; all this is so natural and so intelligible, that one cannot but reprobate the ingenuity that could extract matter of scandal from such materials. The manner in which Cowper, in all his letters, associates Mrs. Unwin with himself (in one instance playfully subscribing their joint names Guillaume—Marie) plainly indicates that the common nature of their interests, and the sacred character of their intimacy, were sufficiently understood by their friends, as well as that there was nothing equivocal about the circumstances of their domestic interaction. If anyone, after acquainting himself with the case, can harbour a doubt on the point, we leave him to the misgivings and degrading conceptions of a polluted imagination.'

It has been rashly asserted, that it would have been better had Cowper's companion been younger and less serious; and Mrs. Unwin has been unfeelingly reproached with a deficiency of cheerfulness that rendered her unfit to be the poet's associate; to which the critic above cited judiciously replies:

'It is scarcely worthwhile to advert to useless surmises and unprofitable peradventures; but we will give our opinion, that the appointment of Providence was in this instance, as in every other, wiser than the wisdom of the world. Excitement of a gentle description was undoubtedly beneficial to Cowper's mind: the stimulus supplied by the presence of Lady Hesketh, and other gay accomplished friends, had for a time the happiest effect; but, like all other stimulants, its efficacy was soon spent. Familiarity with an object, while it may strengthen its power over our affections, of necessity renders it less capable of ministering that excitation which things of a novel or occasional kind produce. The sprightliest companion would have failed, after a time, to cheer by her gaiety; and something more than sprightliness was requisite, to qualify for the arduous task which devolved upon

Cowper's companion, in the awful season of his deepest dejection, when, but for Mrs. Unwin's strength of mind and unwearied fidelity, he must have been consigned to the hired nurse and the medical practitioner. With her, it ought not to be forgotten, he shared some of his happiest hours; and to her he was indebted for all the alleviation of which his gloomiest seasons were susceptible. If she could not excite, she could soothe him; and what the heart requires for its happiness, is an object on which the affections can repose The fact is, that Mrs. Unwin was an eminently pious woman, and this was, with some of Cowper's friends, her real offence. Those who chose to ascribe his melancholy to his religion, naturally regarded Mr. Newton and Mrs. Unwin as persons who had contributed to his distemper. We have seen how judiciously the former acquitted himself as a correspondent; and we have reason to believe that in the latter, Cowper had a not less judicious companion. It was she who urged him, in the first instance, to employ his mind in poetical composition. Though religion was, for the most part, an interdicted, because an unapproachable theme, yet he could never have been happy, united to one who was not in his estimation religious; and there were bright moments in which he could have relished no other association. (*Eclectic Review*, March 1824)

Cowper retained his admirable powers in their full vigour, during the whole of 1793, and until the middle of January of the following year. His letters, written subsequently to Mr. Hayley's visit, though but few, afford unquestionable proofs that his talents had not suffered the slightest diminution. The following extract, in reply to some remarks on a disputed passage in his Homer, will show that his faculties were then unimpaired. To Mr. Hayley, 5th January 1794, he writes:

'If my old friend would look into my preface, he would find a principle laid down there which perhaps it would not be easy to invalidate, and which, properly attended to, would equally secure a translation from stiffness and from wildness. The principle I mean is this—' Close, but not so close as to be servile! free, but not so free as to be licentious! A superstitious fidelity loses the spirit, and a loose deviation the sense of the translated author—a happy moderation in either case is the only possible way of preserving both.'

'Imlac, in Rasselas, The *History of Rasselas, Prince of Abissinia,* often abbreviated to *Rasselas,* is an apologue about happiness by Samuel Johnson. says—I forget to whom, 'You have convinced me that it is impossible to be a poet.' In like manner, I might say to his Lordship, You have convinced me that it is impossible to be a translator; to be one on his terms at least, is, I am sure, impossible. On his terms, I would defy Homer himself, were he alive, to translate the Paradise Lost into Greek. Yet Milton had Homer much in his eye when he composed that poem;—whereas Homer never thought of me or my translation. There are minutiae in every language, which, translated into another, would spoil the version. Such extreme fidelity is, in fact, unfaithful. Such close resemblance takes away all likeness. The original is elegant, easy, and natural; the copy is clumsy, constrained, unnatural. To what is this owing? To the adoption of terms not congenial to your purpose, and of a context, such as no man writing an original would make use of. Homer is everything that a poet should be. A translation of him, so made, will be everything a translation of Homer should not be, because it will be written in no language under heaven. It will be English and it will be Greek, and therefore it will be neither. He is the man, whoever he may be (I do not pretend to be that man myself)—he is the man best qualified as a translator of Homer, who has drenched, and steeped, and soaked himself in the effusions of his genius, till he has imbibed their colour to the bone, and who, when he is thus dyed through and through, distinguishing what is essentially Greek from what may be habited in English, rejects the former and is faithful to the latter, as far as the purposes of fine poetry will permit, and no further; this, I think, may be easily proved. Homer is everywhere remarkable for ease, dignity, energy of expression, grandeur of conception, and a majestic flow of numbers. If we copy him so closely as to make everyone of these excellent properties of his absolutely unattainable, which will certainly be the effect of too close a copy, instead of translating, we murder him. Therefore, after all his Lordship has said, I still hold freedom to be an indispensable requisite. Freedom, I mean, with respect to the expression; freedom so limited as never to leave behind the matter, but at the same time indulged with a sufficient scope to secure the spirit, and as much as possible of the manner: I say as much as possible, because an English manner must differ from a Greek one, in order to be graceful, and for this there is no remedy. Can an ungraceful awkward translator of Homer be a good one? No; but a graceful, easy, natural, faithful version of him, will not that be a good one? Yes: allow me but this, and I insist upon it, that such a one may be produced on my principles, and can be produced on no other. Reading his Lordship's sentiments over again, I am inclined to think that in all I have said, I have only given him back the same in other terms. He disallows both the absolutely free and the absolutely close; so do I, and if I understand myself, have said so in my preface. He wishes to recommend a medium, though he will not call it so; so do I; only we express it differently. What is it then that we dispute about? I confess my head is not good enough to-day to discover.'

This was almost the last letter Cowper wrote to Mr. Hayley, and, with a very few exceptions, the last that he ever wrote at all. Standing, as he now did, on the borders of that deep pit of despair into which he was almost immediately plunged, he thus writes to his friend Rose:

'I have just ability enough to transcribe, which is all that I have to do at present; God knows that I write, at this moment, under the pressure of sadness not to be described.' Shortly after he had forwarded this, he experienced a more severe attack of depression than he had ever before felt; which paralyzed all his powers, and which continued almost wholly unmitigated through the remaining period of his life. The situation to which he was now reduced, was deeply affecting; imagination can scarcely picture to itself a scene of wretchedness more truly deplorable. Mrs. Unwin's infirmities had reduced her to a state of second childhood; a deep-seated melancholy, which nothing could remove, preyed upon Cowper's mind, and caused him to shun the sight of all except the individual who was utterly incapable of rendering him any assistance; his domestic expenses were daily increasing, and as his capabilities of providing for that increase were now entirely suspended, there was every probability of his being involved in pecuniary embarrassment. The providence of God, however, which had watched over and preserved him during the whole of his life, and had appeared on his behalf in several instances of peculiar distress, in a manner truly striking and affecting, did not abandon him in his present painful emergency. Lady Hesketh, his amiable cousin and favourite correspondent, now generously undertook the arduous task of watching over the melancholy poet and his feeble associate. The painful duties of this important office, which everyone who is at all acquainted with the great anxiety of mind required in all cases of mental aberration, will admit to be in no ordinary degree arduous, she discharged with the utmost Christian tenderness and affection. Nor did she discover any disposition to relinquish her charge, though it made considerable inroads upon her health, owing to the confinement and exertion it required, until an opportunity offered of placing these interesting invalids under the care of those who she knew would feel the greatest pleasure in laying themselves out for their comfort.

Hearing nothing from Cowper for several days beyond the time when he was accustomed to write, Mr. Hayley began to fear that his apprehensions respecting his friend's health were realized. He did not, however, receive the painful intelligence of his relapse until sometime afterwards, when he was informed of it by a letter from Lady Hesketh, detailing the particulars of his distressing case. About this time, the Rev. Mr. Greatheed paid him a visit. Such, however, was the distressing state to which Cowper was now reduced, that he refused to see anyone but his own domestics, on whatever friendly terms he might have been with them formerly. The hopes that his friends had cherished of his recovery, in some degree at least, as the summer advanced, were now entirely cut off; and they were all fully persuaded that unless some improvement took place in the state of his mind, the worst consequences were to be apprehended. The best advice had been taken without the slightest benefit, and the case began to appear altogether hopeless. It occurred to Lady Hesketh, that probably the presence of Mr. Hayley might cheer the poet's mind, and rouse him from his present state of almost absolute despair. She suggested this to Mr. Greatheed, but said she could not venture to mention the subject in her letters to Mr. Hayley, as it appeared unreasonable to request a person to come so great a distance, with so little real chance of success. Mr. Greatheed immediately wrote the following letter to Mr. Hayley on the subject, which describes the melancholy condition to which Cowper was then reduced, and the great anxiety of mind manifested by his friends on his behalf:

'Dear Sir, Lady Hesketh's correspondence has acquainted you with the melancholy relapse of our dear friend at Weston; but I am uncertain whether you know that within the last fortnight he has refused food of every kind, except now and then a very small piece of toasted bread, dipped generally in water, sometimes mixed with a little wine. This, her Ladyship informs me, was the case until last Saturday, since when he has eaten a little at each family meal. He persists in refusing to take such medicines as are indispensable to his state of body. In such circumstances, his long continuance in life cannot be expected. How devoutly to be wished is the alleviation of his sufferings and distress! You, dear Sir, who know so well the worth of our beloved and admired friend, will sympathize with us in this affliction, and deprecate his loss, doubtless, in no ordinary degree. You have already most effectually expressed and proved the warmth of your friendship. I cannot think that anything but your society would have been sufficient, during the infirmity under which his mind has long been oppressed, to support him against the shock of Mrs. Unwin's paralytic attack. I am certain that nothing else could have prevailed upon him to undertake the journey to Eartham. You have succeeded where his other friends knew they could not, and where they apprehended that no one could. How natural, therefore, is it for them to look to you, as most likely to be instrumental, under the blessing of God, to bring him relief in the present distressing and alarming crisis. It is, indeed, not a little unreasonable to ask any person to take such a journey, to witness so melancholy a scene, with an uncertainty of the desired success, increased as the present difficulty is, by Mr. Cowper's aversion to all company. On these accounts, Lady Hesketh does not ask it of you, rejoiced as she would be at your arrival. Am not I, dear Sir, a very presumptuous person, who, in the face of all opposition, dare do this? lam emboldened by these two powerful supporters—conscience and experience. Were I at Eartham, I would certainly undertake the journey I have presumed to recommend, for the bare possibility of restoring Mr. Cowper to himself, to his friends, and to the public' Mr. Hayley was too affectionately attached to Cowper, to hesitate for a moment what steps he should take on the receipt of this letter. The remotest probability of his being useful to his afflicted friend was amply sufficient to have induced him to undertake a much longer journey than this, to whatever dangers and inconveniences it might have exposed him. He accordingly made immediate arrangements for a visit to Weston, where he arrived a few days afterwards, with his son, a youth of great promise, to whom Cowper was affectionately attached. Little or no benefit, however, resulted from this visit. The suffering invalid was too deeply overwhelmed by his malady to show even the slightest symptoms of satisfaction at the appearance of one whom he had ever been accustomed to welcome with such affectionate delight. His acute anguish had nearly extinguished all the finest faculties of his mind, and annihilated, at least for a time, all the best affections of his heart. He seemed to shrink from every human creature, and if he allowed any one, except his own domestics, to approach him, it was with so much obvious reluctance and aversion that no benefit could be expected to arise from the interview. The only exception was in the case of Mr. Hayley's son, in whose company he would occasionally for a short time seem pleased; which Mr. Hayley attributed 'partly to the peculiar charm which is generally found in the manners of tender ingenuous children; and partly to that uncommon sweetness of character which had inspired Cowper with a degree of parental partiality towards this highly promising youth.' The united efforts, however, of both father and son, could not produce the slightest alleviation of Cowper's sufferings.

Shortly after Mr. Hayley's arrival at Weston, Lady Hesketh embraced the opportunity of leaving her interesting invalids for a few days in his charge, that she might, by a personal interview, consult the eminent Dr. Willis—who had prescribed so successfully in the case of his Majesty George III.—on the subject of Cowper's malady. Lord Thurlow had written to the doctor in Cowper's behalf, and at his and Lady Hesketh's request, he was induced to visit the interesting sufferer at Weston. Here again, however, the expectations of his friends were greatly disappointed; as the doctor's skill on this occasion proved wholly unsuccessful.

Mr. Hayley remained at Weston for some weeks, exerting all the means that ingenuity could invent, or that affection could dictate, to afford some relief to his suffering friend; he had, however, the mortification to perceive that his well-directed efforts were useless. The circumstances, in which Cowper was now placed, were exceedingly unfavourable to mental relief. Associated with one whose daily increasing infirmities were rapidly reducing her to a state of the most affecting imbecility; the constant sight of which was, of itself, almost sufficient to have produced melancholy in a tender mind like Cowper's, it was hardly probable that, under such circumstances, he should recover from his deeply-rooted malady. And yet to have separated him from the being with whom he had been so long associated, would have been an act of cruelty which he would not, in all probability, have survived. All that could be done was to mitigate, as much as possible, the sufferings of each individual, and to persevere in the use of such means as would be most likely, under such circumstances, to promote the poet's recovery, leaving the event at His disposal, who, in a manner altogether unexpected, had formerly appeared for him on several distressing occasions.

One morning in April, 1794, while Mr. Hayley was at Weston, musing, as he and Lady Hesketh were sometimes accustomed to do, over the melancholy scene of Cowper's sufferings, with aching and almost broken hearts, at the utter inefficacy of every measure that had been taken to afford him relief, they were suddenly almost overjoyed at the receipt of a letter from Lord Spencer, announcing it to be his majesty's gracious intention to allow Cowper the grant of such a pension for life, as would secure to him an honourable competence.1 The only subject of regret, connected with this pleasing circumstance, was, that he whom it was chiefly intended to benefit, and who, if he had been free from his distressing malady, would have been gratified in the highest degree at this instance of royal generosity, was in a condition that rendered it impossible for him to receive even the faintest glimmering of joy on the occasion. It was, however, fondly hoped by his friends, that he would ultimately recover, and that the day would at length arrive, when he would be able gratefully to acknowledge this princely beneficence. Well was it, indeed, for his friends, that they supported their minds by indulging these hopes of amendment. Had they known that he was doomed to pass six years in the same depressed and melancholy condition, with scarcely a single alleviation, and was, at the expiration of that lengthened period, to leave the world without emerging from this midnight gloom, they would themselves have almost become the subjects of despair. Such, however, was the case; and it is doubtful, though Cowper subsequently recovered in some slight degree from his depression, whether he was ever in a condition fully to appreciate the value of his majesty's grant.

Mr. Hayley's departure from Weston, which was now become to him as much a scene of suffering as it had formerly been of enjoyment, he thus affectingly records:

'After devoting a few weeks at Weston, I was under the painful necessity of forcing myself away from my unhappy friend, who, though he appeared to take no pleasure in my society, expressed extreme reluctance to let me depart. I hardly ever endured an hour more dreadfully distressing than the hour in which I left him. Yet the anguish of it would have been greatly increased, had I been conscious that he was destined to years of this dark depression, and that I should see him no more.

FOOTNOTE: In Mr. Greatheed's sketch of the poet's life, the amount of this grant is stated to have been nominally, 300. £ per annum, but reduced to little more than 200.£ by customary fees of office.

I still indulged the hope, from the native vigour of his frame, that as he had formerly struggled through longer fits of the depressive malady, his darkened mind would yet emerge from this calamitous eclipse, and shine forth again with new lustre. These hopes were considerably increased at a subsequent period: but alas! They were delusive! for though he recovered sufficient command of his faculties to write a few occasional poems, and to retouch his ' Homer,' yet the prospect of his perfect recovery was never realized; and I had beheld the poet of unrivalled genius, the sympathetic friend, and the delightful companion, for the last time!'

Cowper remained in the same most distressing state from the time of Mr. Hayley's departure, which was in the spring of 1794, until the summer of 1795. During the whole of this time he was most affectionately watched over by his amiable cousin; she procured for him the best medical advice, and employed every means that promised the slightest chance of proving beneficial. All these, however, were ineffectual to lighten that ponderous burden which incessantly pressed upon and weighed down his spirits. He had now been eighteen months in this deplorable state, and, instead of becoming better, if any alteration had taken place, it was evidently for the worse. Lady Hesketh's health was beginning to fail, owing to the intense anxiety of mind she had experienced for so long a period; and it became at length desirable to adopt some other means for his recovery. At this seasonable juncture, the Rev. J. Johnson providentially arrived, and willingly shared with Lady Hesketh the task of superintending the interesting sufferer. It occurred to Mr. Johnson one day, while reflecting on the inefficacy of the air at Weston, in the poet's case, that perhaps a summer's residence by the seaside might prove of great advantage. On mentioning the subject to Lady Hesketh, she concurred in the opinion, and all the poet's friends strongly recommended the measure. Mr. Johnson kindly undertook the charge of both these interesting individuals, and their removal from Weston took place under his immediate guidance on the 28th July, 1795.

Happily for Cowper and his beloved companion, as well as for their friends, they all regarded this departure from Weston as merely temporary, and indeed, this was all that was originally intended. Had the poet been aware that he was taking his final leave of his endeared residence, his regret, in passing for the last time over its threshold, would have been inexpressible. Had it been known too, that he was bidding farewell for the last time, to his deservedly beloved cousin, Lady Hesketh, the anguish of both would probably have been insupportable; and had his kinsman been aware of the task he was then undertaking, it would probably have unfitted him entirely for the proper discharge of its duties. How strikingly is the wisdom and the benevolence of God often displayed in that concealment which he throws around the operations of his providence!

To guard as much as possible against the effect of noise on the shattered nerves of Cowper, his kinsman took care to have a relay of horses ready on the skirts of the towns of Bedford and Cambridge, by which means he passed through those places without stopping. Their first resting place was at the quiet village of St. Neots; here they stopped for the night. During the evening, Cowper and his kinsman walked several times up and down the churchyard; and the peaceful scenery of the spot had so happy an effect upon his spirits, that he conversed with much composure on the subject of Thomson's Seasons, and the circumstances under which they were probably written.

'This gleam of cheerfulness,' remarks Mr. Johnson, 'with which it pleased God to visit the afflicted poet at the commencement of his journey, though nothing that may be at all compared with it was ever again exhibited in his conversation, was yet a subject of grateful remembrance to him; for though it vanished from the breast of Cowper like the dew of the morning, it preserved the sunshine of hope in his kinsman's mind as to the final recovery of his revered relative, and that cheering hope never forsook him till the object of his incessant care was sinking into the valley of the shadow of death.'

They rested the second day at Boston Mills, a quiet and convenient spot, and arrived in the evening of the Thursday at North Tuddenham, in Norfolk. Here they were accommodated with a commodious parsonage-house, by the kindness of the Rev. Leonard Shelford, with whom Mr. Johnson had previously arranged for their reception, fearing lest the activity and bustle that occasionally prevailed in the vicinity of his own house, situated in the market-place at East Dereham, should harass and perplex the tender mind of Cowper.

During the poet's continuance at Tuddenham, it being a season of the year very favourable for walking, he was prevailed upon by his kinsman to make frequent excursions near this retired spot. On one occasion, he reached the house of his cousin, Mrs. Bodham, at Mottishall, where was suspended, in one of the rooms, his own portrait by Abbot. The sight of it awakened in his mind the recollection of the comparative tranquillity he enjoyed when he sat to that artist, and wrung from him a passionately expressed wish, that similar comfort and peace might yet return.

They continued in their new residence only a very short time. In the following August Mr. Johnson conducted them to Mundesley, a village on the Norfolk coast, hoping that a situation by the sea-side might prove amusing to Cowper, and become ultimately the means of reviving his spirits. Here they remained till the following October, without appearing to derive any benefit whatever. While in this situation Cowper, who had long discontinued all correspondence with his friends, ventured to write the following letter to the Rev. Mr, Buchanan, which, while it shews the melancholy depression under which he still laboured, proves that he was not without some occasional intermissions of pleasure:

'I will forget for a moment that, to whomsoever I may address myself, a letter from me can no otherwise be welcome than as a curiosity. To you, sir, I address this, urged to it by extreme penury of employment, and the desire I feel to learn something of what is doing, and has been done, at Weston (my beloved Weston) since I left it.

'The coldness of these blasts, even in the hottest days, has been such that, added to the irritation of the salt spray with which they are always charged, they have occasioned me an inflammation in the eyelids, which threatened, a few days since, to confine me entirely; but by absenting myself as much as possible from the beach, and guarding my face with an umbrella, that inconvenience is in some degree abated. My chamber commands a very near view of the ocean, and the ships, at high water, approach the coast so closely, that a man, furnished with better eyes than mine, might, I doubt not, discern the sailors from the window. No situation, at least when the weather is clear, can be more pleasant; which you will easily credit, when I add, that it imparts something a little resembling pleasure, even to me. Gratify me with news of Weston! If Mr. Gregor, and your neighbours the Courtenays, are there, mention me to them in such terms as you see good. Tell me if my poor birds are living. I never see the herbs I used to give them, without a recollection of them, and sometimes am ready to gather them, forgetting that I am not at home.'

The utmost efforts that ingenuity, exerted by the purest sympathy, could make, were employed by these accomplished and excellent clergymen, to induce Cowper to keep up this correspondence, in hopes that it would prove, at least, some little alleviation to his melancholy. Unhappily, however, his distemper rendered them all abortive. Change of scene was resorted to as the next expedient, and he visited, successively, under the direction and care of his kinsman, Hasboro, Catfield, Holt, Fakenham, Reephoon, Aylsham, and North Walsham, performing the excursion on one occasion by sea. All, however, proved to be of little use; neither the effect of air and exercise, nor the change of scene, had any tendency to remove his depression.

In the beginning of October, 1795, Mr. Johnson took the two interesting invalids to his own residence at Dereham, where they remained about a month, when they removed to Dunham Lodge, which was then unoccupied, and was pleasantly situated in a park, a few miles from Swaffham, and which, from that time, became their settled residence. Here they were constantly attended by two of the most interesting females that could possibly have been selected, Miss Johnson and Miss Perowne. The latter took so lively an interest in Cowper's welfare, and exerted so much ingenuity in attempting to produce some alleviation of his sufferings, that he ever afterwards honoured her with his peculiar regard, and preferred her attendance to that of every other individual by whom he was surrounded; and she continued her kind attention to him to the close of his life.

'The providence of God (as Mr. Hayley justly remarks) was strikingly displayed towards Cowper, in supplying him with attendants, during the whole of his life, peculiarly suited to the exigencies of mental dejection.'

In April, 1796, Mrs. Unwin's daughter, accompanied by her husband, Mr. Powley, paid her aged parent a visit, and was not a little gratified, deeply as they commiserated the poet's depression, to find that neither his own acute sufferings, nor the long and debilitating affliction of Mrs. Unwin, had diminished, in the slightest degree, the fond attachment he felt for his infirm companion. The visit of these exemplary individuals was productive of much advantage, as it led to the practice of reading a portion of the Bible, daily, to Cowper and Mrs. Unwin, which had not been done in his presence for a length of time, from an apprehension that he was unwilling to hear it. Mrs. Powley accustomed herself to read a chapter to her parent every morning, whether the poet were absent or not; no reluctance, however, was evinced by him to hear what was read, and on the departure of Mrs. Powley, the poet's kinsman, pleased with the discovery that his afflicted relative would listen to the voice of inspiration, persevered in the practice, taking care always to read to Mrs. Unwin when Cowper was present. Encouraged, too, by the result of the above experiment, he ventured, as he himself states, 'in the course of a few days, to call the members of the family to prayers in the same room where Cowper was, instead of assembling in another apartment, as they had hitherto done, under the influence of misconception, as it proved, with regard to his ability to attend the service. On the first occurrence of this new arrangement, of which no intimation had been previously given him, he was preparing to leave the room, but was prevailed on to resume his seat, by a word of soothing and whispered entreaty.'

Cowper's melancholy depression remained unalleviated. In June 1796, however, an incident occurred, which for a time, though it removed not his dejection, revived the spirits of his friends, and cheered them with the hope of his ultimate recovery. Mr. Johnson invariably procured copies of all such new publications as were likely to interest the mind of Cowper; and as Cowper had discontinued the use of his pen, and manifested considerable disinclination to read himself, his kinsman kindly undertook to read these publications to his relative whenever suitable opportunities offered. About this time, Mr. Wakefield published his edition of Pope's *Homer*. It occurred to Mr. Johnson, who always readily embraced the slightest incident that seemed likely to diminish the anguish of his afflicted relative, that this work might probably excite the poet's attention sufficiently to rouse him, in some degree, from his dejection. He immediately, therefore, procured a copy, and ingeniously placed it in a conspicuous part of a large unfrequented room, through which he knew Cowper would have to pass, in his way from Mrs.

Unwin's apartments, and in which he was aware it was Cowper's practice, daily, to take some turns, observing, previously, to his afflicted relative, that the work contained some occasional comparison of Pope with Cowper. The plan succeeded far beyond Mr. Johnson's expectation; to his agreeable surprise, he discovered, the next day, that Cowper had not only found the passages to which he had adverted, but had corrected his translation at the suggestion of some of them. Perceiving that the poet's attention was arrested, it was vigilantly cherished by the utmost efforts of Mr. Johnson; and from that time Cowper regularly engaged in a revisal of his own version, and for some weeks produced almost sixty new lines a day. He continued this occupation so steadily, and with so much deliberation, that all his friends began to rejoice at the prospect of his almost immediate recovery. Their hopes, however, were of short duration. In a few weeks, he again relapsed into the same state of hopeless depression.

In the ensuing autumn, Mr. Johnson again made trial of a change of air, and of scene, and removed the family to the delightful village of Mundesley. But no apparent benefit resulted from this change, though the air and the walks of that favourite village, both inland and marine, were fully tried: and towards the close of Oct. 1796, it was thought desirable to remove the family to Mr. Johnson's house at Dereham, and to remain there during the winter, as the Lodge was at too great a distance from Mr. Johnson's churches. The poet's friends were much pleased to find their apprehension, that a residence in town would injure the poet, groundless, and that the bustle of the place was by no means distressing to his tender spirit.

In the following December, it became evident that Mrs. Unwin's life was rapidly drawing to a close; she had been gradually sinking for a considerable time; and on the seventeenth day of this month, in the 72nd year of her age, she peacefully, and without a groan or a sigh, resigned her happy spirit into the hands of her Redeemer. Her life had been distinguished by the most fervent and unaffected piety, which she had displayed in circumstances the most trying and afflicting; and her end was peace. The day before she expired, Cowper, as he had long been accustomed to do at regular periods, spent a short time with his afflicted and long-tried friend and although to his inmates he appeared so absorbed in his own mental anguish, as to take little if any notice of her condition, it was evident afterwards that he clearly perceived how fast she was sinking. He saw her, for the last time, about an hour before she expired; and, notwithstanding the intensity of his own distress, he was much affected, though he clearly perceived that she enjoyed the utmost tranquillity. He saw the corpse once after her decease; and after looking at it attentively for a short time, he suddenly withdrew, under the influence of the strongest emotions. She was buried in the north aisle of East Dereham church, on the night of the 23rd December, 1796, by torch-light, lest her removal during the day should have been too severe a shock for the poet's feelings. The funeral was attended by her son-in-law and daughter, Mr. and Mrs. Powley, besides Mr. Johnson and several members of his family, and a marble tablet was raised to her memory, with the following inscription:

IN MEMORY OF

MARY,
WIDOW OF THE REV. MORLEY UNWIN, AND
MOTHER OF THE REV. WILLIAM CAWTHORN UNWIN,
BORN AT ELY, 1724,
BURIED IN THIS CHURCH, 1796.

Trusting in God with all her heart and mind,
This woman proved magnanimously kind;
Endured affliction's desolating hail,
And watched a poet through misfortune's vale.
Her spotless dust, angelic guards defend!
It is the dust of Unwin, Cowper's friend!
That single title in itself is fame,

For all who read his verse revere her name.'

Had Cowper been in the enjoyment of health, and had his mind been entirely free from his gloomy forebodings, at the time of Mrs. Unwin's decease, so tender were his feelings that it would undoubtedly have proved to him one of the severest shocks he had ever experienced. Such, however, was the absorbing influence of his melancholy depression, that he never afterwards referred to the event, even in the most distant way, nor did he even make the slightest inquiries respecting her funeral. A more striking proof of the intense anguish of his own sufferings cannot possibly be given. Dreadful, indeed, must have been those feelings that could have produced in his tender mind an insensibility so great, to the loss of such a friend! An insensibility, let it be remembered, over which he had no control, but which was occasioned entirely by the benumbing influence of his dreadful malady.

CHAPTER XVIII. Cowper undertakes the revisal of his Homer—Depth of his depression—Means pursued by his kinsman to remove it—Lady Spencer's visit to the poet—His removal to Mundesley—His letter to Lady Hesketh— Returns to Dereham—Manner in which he was occasionally employed—His last original poem—His declining strength—New models a passage in his Homer —Rapid increase of his weakness—Last illness and death—Description of his person, his disposition, his piety—His attachment to the Established Church— His religious sentiments—Depth of his piety—His aversion to flattery and ostentation—The warmth of his friendship—His industry and perseverance — Manly independence—Happy manner in which he could console the afflicted—Occasional intervals of enjoyment—Rhyming letter, *etc.*

In the summer of 1797, Cowper's health appeared in some measure to improve, and in the following September, at the earnest entreaty of his kinsman, he resumed the revisal of his Homer. Notwithstanding the severity of his mental anguish, he persevered in it, with some occasional interruption, until May 8,

1799, on which day he completed the work. It was evidently owing to the influence exerted by Mr. Johnson on the mind of Cowper, that he was induced to end this great work. And it would have been exceedingly difficult, if not utterly impossible, to have found an individual who could, with so much tenderness, have exerted an influence so beneficial over the distressed mind of the poet. He was indefatigable in his efforts to divert his mind from the melancholy depression, which spread its pernicious influence over his soul. During the whole of the summer of 1798, he endeavoured, by frequent change of scene, sometimes residing for a week or two at Mundesley, and then returning to Dereham, to restore the mind of his revered relative to its proper tone. Though he had not the satisfaction to see his efforts crowned with complete success, yet he was pleased to perceive them prove in some degree, at least, beneficial to the interesting sufferer. In his concise sketch of Cowper's life, prefixed to the poet's works, he 'records it as a subject of much gratitude, that a merciful Providence should again have appointed his afflicted relative the employment alluded to, as, more than anything else, it diverted his mind from a contemplation of its miseries, and seemed to extend his breathing, which was at other times short, to a depth of respiration more compatible with ease.

The happy means employed by Mr. Johnson to induce Cowper to complete the revisal of his Homer, and its successful result, ought not to go unrecorded. He thus relates it in the excellent sketch above referred to:

'His kinsman resolved, if it were possible, to re-instate him in the revisal of his Homer. One morning, therefore, after breakfast, in the month of September, 1797, he placed the commentaries on the table one by one, namely, Villoison, Barnes, and Clarke, opening them all, together with the poet's translation, at the place where he had left off a twelvemonth before; but talking with him as he paced the room, upon a very different subject, namely, the impossibility of the things befalling him, which his imagination had presented; when, as his companion had wished, Cowper said to him, 'And are you sure that I shall be here till the book you are reading is finished.' 'Quite sure,' replied his kinsman, ' and that you will also be here to complete the revisal of your Homer, (pointing to the books,) if you will resume it to-day.' As he repeated these words, he left the room, rejoicing in the well-known token of their having sunk deep into the poet's mind, namely his seating himself on the sofa, taking up one of the books, and saying, in a low and plaintive voice, 'I may as well do this, for I can do nothing else.'

In July, 1798, the Dowager Lady Spencer paid the afflicted poet a visit. Had he been in the enjoyment of health, he would undoubtedly have received her with the greatest respect and affection, and the conversation between them would have been equally pleasing to both parties; but such was his melancholy depression, that he seemed to derive no pleasure from the visit, and could not be prevailed upon to converse with his distinguished visitor with any apparent pleasure.

While residing at Mundesley, in October 1798, Cowper felt himself so far relieved from his depressive malady as to undertake, without solicitation; to write to Lady Hesketh. The following extract from this letter, will show the severity of his mental anguish, even at that period:

You describe delightful scenes, but you describe them to one who, if even he saw them, could receive no delight from them; who has a faint recollection, and so faint as to be like an almost forgotten dream, that once he was susceptible of pleasure from such causes. The country that you have had in prospect has been always famed for its beauties; but the wretch who can derive no gratification from a view of nature, even under the disadvantage of her most ordinary dress, will have no eyes to admire her in any. In one day,—in one minute, I should rather have said,—she became an universal blank to me, and though from a different cause, yet with an effect as difficult to remove as blindness itself.'

Mr. Johnson again removed from Mundesley to Dereham, towards the end of October, and pursuing their journey, on this occasion, with himself, Miss Perowne, and Cowper, in the post-chaise, they were overturned. Cowper discovered no particular alarm on the occasion, and through the blessing of Providence, they all escaped unhurt.

As soon as Cowper had finished the revisal of his Homer, Mr. Johnson laid before him the papers containing the commencement of his projected poem, *The Four Ages*. He, however, declined undertaking it, as a work far too important for him to attempt in his present situation. Several other literary projects, of easier accomplishment, were then suggested to him by his kinsman, who was aware of the great benefit he had derived from employment, and was seriously apprehensive that the want of it would add to his depression ; but all were objected to by the poet, who at length replied, that he had just thought of six Latin verses, and if he could do anything it must be in pursuing something of that description. He, however, gratified his friends, by occasionally employing the powers of his astonishing mind, which remained in full vigour, in the composition of some short original poems. In this way he produced the poem entitled *Montes Glaciales*, founded upon an incident, which he had beard read from the Norwich paper, several months previous; to which, at the time, owing to his depression, he appeared to pay no attention. This poem he afterwards, at the request of Miss Perowne, translated into Latin. Translation was his principal amusement; sometimes from Latin and Greek into English, and occasionally from English into Latin. In this way, he translated several of *Gay's Fables*, and communicated to them, in their new dress, all that ease and vivacity which they have in the original. Thus employed, he continued, with some intermissions, almost to the close of his life.

The last original poem he composed was entitled The Cast-Away, and was founded upon an incident related in *Anson's Voyage*, of a mariner who was washed overboard in the Atlantic, and lost; which he remembered to have read in that work many years before, and which he appears to have regarded as bearing a close resemblance to his own case.

THE CASTAWAY

Obscurest night involv'd the sky,
    Th' Atlantic billows roar'd,
When such a destin'd wretch as I,
    Wash'd headlong from on board,
Of friends, of hope, of all bereft,
His floating home forever left.

No braver chief could Albion boast
    Than he with whom he went,
Nor ever ship left Albion's coast,
    With warmer wishes sent.
He lov'd them both, but both in vain,
Nor him beheld, nor her again.

Not long beneath the whelming brine,
    Expert to swim, he lay;
Nor soon he felt his strength decline,
    Or courage die away;
But wag'd with death a lasting strife,
Supported by despair of life.

He shouted: nor his friends had fail'd
    To check the vessel's course,
But so the furious blast prevail'd,
    That, pitiless perforce,

They left their outcast mate behind,
And scudded still before the wind.

Some succour yet they could afford;
    And, such as storms allow,
The cask, the coop, the floated cord,
    Delay'd not to bestow.
But he (they knew) nor ship, nor shore,

Whate'er they gave, should visit more.

Nor, cruel as it seem'd, could he
    Their haste himself condemn,
Aware that flight, in such a sea,
    Alone could rescue them;
Yet bitter felt it still to die
Deserted, and his friends so nigh.

He long survives, who lives an hour
    In ocean, self-upheld;
And so long he, with unspent pow'r,
    His destiny repell'd;
And ever, as the minutes flew,
Entreated help, or cried—Adieu!

At length, his transient respite past,
    His comrades, who before
Had heard his voice in ev'ry blast,
    Could catch the sound no more.
For then, by toil subdued, he drank
The stifling wave, and then he sank.

No poet wept him: but the page
    Of narrative sincere;
That tells his name, his worth, his age,
    Is wet with Anson's tear.
And tears by bards or heroes shed
Alike immortalize the dead.

I therefore purpose not, or dream,
    Descanting on his fate,
To give the melancholy theme
    A more enduring date:
But misery still delights to trace
Its semblance in another's case.

No voice divine the storm allay'd,
　　No light propitious shone;
When, snatch'd from all effectual aid,
　　We perish'd, each alone:
But I beneath a rougher sea,
And whelm'd in deeper gulfs than he.

　　Anxious as all his friends now were, that he should he constantly employed, as affording the best remedy for his depression, they were frequently pained to see him reduced to a state of hopeless inactivity, owing to the severity of his mental anguish. At these seasons what suited him best was, Mr. Johnson's reading to him, which he was accustomed to do, almost invariably for a length of time every day. And so industriously had he persevered in this method of relieving the poet's mind, that after having exhausted numerous works of fiction, which had the power of attracting his attention, he began to read to the afflicted poet his own published writings. Cowper evinced no disapprobation of this, until they arrived at the history of *John Gilpin*, when he entreated his relative to desist.

　　It became evident towards the close of 1799 that his bodily strength was rapidly declining, though his mental powers, notwithstanding the unmitigated severity of his depression, remained unimpaired. In January 1800, Mr. Johnson observed in him many symptoms, which he thought very unfavourable. This induced him to call in additional medical advice. His complaint was pronounced to be, not as has been generally stated, dropsical, but a breaking up of the constitution. Remedies, however, were tried, and he was recommended to take as much gentle exercise as he could bear. To this recommendation, he discovered no particular aversion, and Mr. Johnson induced him to venture out in a post chaise, as often as circumstances would permit. But it was with considerable difficulty he could be prevailed upon to use such medicines as it was thought necessary to employ.

About this time his friend Mr. Hayley wrote to him, expressing a wish that he would new model a passage in his translation of the Iliad, in which mention is made of the very ancient sculpture in which Daedalus had represented the Cretan dance for Ariadne. 'On the 31st January,' says Mr. Hayley, 'I received from him his improved version of the lines in question, written in a firm and delicate hand. The sight of such writing from my long-silent friend inspired me with a lively, but too sanguine hope, that I might see him once more restored. Alas! the verses which I surveyed as a delightful omen of future letters from a correspondent so inexpressibly dear to me, proved the last effort of his pen.'

Cowper's weakness now very rapidly increased, and by the end of February it had become so great as to render him incapable of enduring the fatigue of his usual ride, which was hence discontinued. In a few days, he ceased to come down stairs, though he was still able, after breakfasting in bed, to adjourn to another room, and to remain there until the evening. By the end of the ensuing March, he was compelled to forego even this trifling exercise. He was now entirely confined to his bedroom; but was still able to sit up to every meal, except breakfast.

His friend Mr. Rose, about this time, paid him a visit; but his complicated maladies had produced so melancholy a change upon his mind, that he expressed no pleasure at the arrival of one whom he had previously been accustomed to greet with the most cordial reception. Mr. Rose remained with him till the first week in April, witnessing with much sorrow the sufferings of the afflicted poet, and kindly sympathizing with his distressed relations and friends. Little as Cowper had appeared to enjoy his company, he evinced symptoms of considerable regret at his departure.

Both Lady Hesketh and Mr. Hayley would have followed the humane example of Mr. Rose, in visiting the dying poet, had they not been prevented by circumstances over which they had no control. The health of the former had suffered considerably by her long confinement with Cowper, at the commencement of his last attack, and the latter was detained by the impending death of a darling child.

Mr. Johnson informs us, in his sketch of the poet's life, that, 'on the 19th of April the weakness of this truly pitiable sufferer had so much increased that his kinsman apprehended his death to be near. Adverting, therefore, to the affliction, as well of body as of mind, which his beloved inmate was then enduring, he ventured to speak of his approaching dissolution as the signal of his deliverance from both these miseries. After a pause of a few moments, which was less interrupted by the objections of his desponding relative than he had dared to hope, he proceeded to an observation more consolatory still—namely, that in the world to which he was hastening, a merciful Redeemer, who had prepared unspeakable happiness for all his children, and therefore for him . To the first part of this sentence he had listened with composure, but the concluding words were no sooner uttered than he passionately broke into entreaties that his companion would desist from any further observations of a similar kind; clearly proving that though he was on the eve of being invested with angelic light, the darkness of delusion still veiled his spirit.'

On the following day, which was Sunday, he revived a little. Mr. Johnson, on repairing to his room, after he had discharged his clerical duties, found him in bed and asleep. He did not, however, leave the room, but remained watching him, expecting he might, on awaking, require his assistance. Whilst engaged in this melancholy office, and endeavouring to reconcile his mind to the loss of so dear a friend, by considering the gain which that friend would experience, his reflections were suddenly interrupted by the singularly varied tone in which Cowper then began to breathe. Imagining it to be the sound of his immediate summons, after listening to it for several minutes, he arose from the foot of the bed on which he was sitting, to take a nearer, and, as he supposed, a last view of his departing relative, commending his soul to that gracious Saviour, whom, in the fulness of mental health, he had delighted to honour. As he put aside the curtains, Cowper opened his eyes, but closed them again without speaking, and breathed as usual. On Monday, he was much worse; though, towards the close of the day, he revived sufficiently to take a little refreshment. The two following days he evidently continued to sink rapidly. He revived a little on Thursday, but, in the course of the night appeared exceedingly exhausted; some refreshment was presented to him by Miss Perowne, but, owing to a persuasion that nothing could afford him relief, though without any apparent impression that the hand of death was already upon him, he mildly rejected the cordial with these words, the last he was heard to utter, 'What can it signify?'

Early on Friday morning, the 25th, a decided alteration for the worse was perceived to have taken place. A deadly change appeared in his countenance. In this insensible state he remained until a few minutes before five in the afternoon, when he gently, and without the slightest apparent pain, ceased to breathe, and his happy spirit escaped from that body, in which, amidst the thickest gloom of darkness, it had so long been imprisoned, and took its flight to the regions of perfect purity and bliss. In a manner so mild and gentle did death make its approach, that though his kinsman, his medical attendant, and three others were standing at the foot of the bed, with their eyes fixed upon his dying countenance, the precise moment of his departure was unobserved by any.

'From this mournful period,' writes Mr. Johnson, 'till the features of his deceased friend were closed from his view, the expression which the kinsman of Cowper observed in them, and which he was affectionately delighted to suppose an index of the last thoughts and enjoyments of his soul in its gradual escape from the depths of despondence, was that of calmness and composure, mingled as it were with holy surprise.'

He was buried in that part of Dereham Church called St. Edmund's Chapel, on Saturday, May 2, 1800; and his funeral was attended by several of his relatives. In a literary point of view, his long and painful affliction had ever been regarded as a national calamity; a deep and almost universal sympathy was felt in his behalf; and by all men of learning and of piety, his death was looked upon as an event of no common importance.

"'Tis o'er—the last sad scene is clos'd—thy heart
Shall bleed no longer;—thy severest Task
At length perform'd, with pious obsequies,
Slow to the silent grave, the funeral train
Thy cold remains convey; richly bedew'd
With pity's tenderest tear.'

As Cowper died without a will, his amiable and beloved relation, Lady Hesketh, kindly undertook to become his administratrix. She raised a tablet to his memory with the following inscription:—

IN MEMORY OF
WILLIAM COWPER, Esq.
BORN IN HERTFORDSHIRE, 1731.
BURIED IN THIS CHURCH,

Ye who with warmth the public triumph feel
Of talents dignified by sacred zeal,
Here, to devotion's bard, devoutly just,
Pay your fond tribute, due to Cowper's dust!
England, exulting in his spotless fame,
Ranks with her dearest sons his favourite name;
Sense, fancy, wit, suffice not all to raise
So clear a title to affection's praise:
His highest honours to the heart belong—
His virtues formed the magic of his song.

'Three years ago,' writes the reviewer in the British Critic, of July, 1833, 'we availed ourselves of the opportunity afforded by a residence in the neighbourhood of Dereham, a small town, remarkable for nothing save the memory of him who has made it almost sacred ground, to make a long-purposed visit to the grave of Cowper. We were not aware, when we arrived, that Sarah Harrison, the faithful servant who attended Cowper and Mrs. Unwin during their last years was then living in the place; but we eagerly sought her out, when we had acquired the pleasing intelligence. The cottage in which this faithful domestic resided, is situate at the end of the principal street, and presented something of a poetical appearance, in the beautiful flowers with which it was ornamented. We shall not soon forget the hours we passed, in listening to every trait of the departed poet. The tears came into our eyes when we thought of his daily visits to the bedside of poor Mrs. Unwin, where he sat folded up in the curtains, the most pitiable of sufferers.'

It is scarcely necessary to add anything on the subject of Cowper's character, after the ample delineation, which has already been given of it in this memoir. We shall subjoin the following brief remarks, which could not so conveniently be introduced into any other part of the narrative.

Cowper was of the middle stature; he had an open and expressive countenance, indicating much thoughtfulness, and almost excessive sensibility. His eyes were more remarkable for the expression of tenderness than of penetration. The general character of his countenance partook of that sedate cheerfulness which so strikingly characterizes all his original productions, and which never failed to impart a peculiar charm to his conversation. His limbs were more remarkable for strength than for delicacy of form. He possessed a warm temperament; and he says of himself, in a letter to his cousin, Mrs. Bodham, dated February 27, 1790, that he was naturally 'somewhat irritable;' but if he was, his religious principle had so subdued that tendency, that his kinsman, who was intimately acquainted with him the last ten years of his life, never saw his temper ruffled in a single instance.

His manners were generally somewhat shy and reserved, particularly to strangers; when, however, he was in perfect health, and in such society as was quite congenial to his taste, they were perfectly free and unembarrassed; his conversation was unrestrained and cheerful, and his whole deportment was the most polite and graceful, especially to females, towards whom he conducted himself on all occasions with the strictest delicacy and propriety.

Much as Cowper was admired by those who knew him only as a writer, or as an occasional correspondent, he was infinitely more esteemed by his more intimate friends; indeed, the more intimately he was known, the more he was beloved and revered.

Nor was this affectionate attachment so much the result of his brilliant talents, as it was of the real goodness of his disposition, and constant gentleness of his demeanour.

Cowper was emphatically, in the strictest and most scriptural sense of the term, a good man. His goodness, however, was not the result of mere effort, unconnected with Christian principles, nor did it arise from the absence of those evil dispositions of which all have reason, more or less, to complain; on the contrary, all his writings prove that he felt and deplored the existence of evil affections, and was only enabled to repress them by a cordial reception of the gospel of Christ, and the diligent use of the strength supplied from above to every real believer. Nor was the goodness of Cowper a mere negative goodness, leading him only to avoid doing evil; it is evident, from many passages both in his poetic and prose productions, that he ever looked upon his talents, not as his own, but as belonging to him from whom he had received them. Under the influence of this impression, all his best and most important original productions were unquestionably written. Desirous of communicating to his fellow men the same invaluable benefits which he had himself received, and incapable of attempting it in any other way than that of becoming an author, he took up his pen and produced those unrivalled poems, which, while they delight the mere literary reader by their elegance, beauty, and sublimity, are no less interesting to the Christian for the accurate and striking delineations of real religion with which they abound.

And surely, long as Charity and Truth,
Have place in human bosoms; long as charms
Of Conversation, or Retirement please;
Long as Expostulation's warning voice
Raises her shrillest cry in British ears;
Or Hope exalts and animates the soul,
His verse shall flourish; and sensations most
Of love and rev'rence shall embalm his page.'
—Shewell's tribute,

Cowper was warmly attached to the religion of the Established Church, in which he had been trained up, and which, like his friend Mr. Newton, he calmly and deliberately preferred to any other. But his attachment was not that of the narrow-minded bigot, which blinds the mind to the excellences of every other religious community; on the contrary, it was the attachment of the firm and steady friend of religious liberty, in the most genuine sense of the term. Of a sectarian spirit he was ever the open and avowed opponent. He sincerely and very highly respected the conscientious of all parties. In one of his letters to Mr. Newton, adverting to a passage in his writings that was likely to expose him to the charge of illiberality, he thus writes: — 'When I wrote the passage in question I was not at all aware of any impropriety in it. I am, however, glad you have condemned it; and though I do not feel as if I could presently supply its place, shall be willing to attempt the task, whatever labour it may cost me; and rejoice that it will not be in the power of the critics, whatever else they may charge me with, to accuse me of bigotry, or a design to make a certain denomination odious at the hazard of the public peace. I had rather my book should be burnt, than a single line guilty of such a tendency should escape me.'

Poets have almost invariably been charged with adulation, whenever they have ventured to eulogise an individual of exalted rank, however much he may have been distinguished by his virtues and his talents. In many cases, they have undoubtedly merited this censure; but there are some honourable exceptions, and amongst this class, Cowper is pre-eminently distinguished. Of this weak and often criminal tendency, he had the utmost abhorrence; and in some instances, it maybe doubted whether he did not carry his aversion to flattery almost to an opposite extreme; withholding praise where he knew it was due. The following lines occur almost at the commencement of his *Table Talk*. After painting the portrait of that most estimable monarch, George the Third, in language as just as it is beautiful, he, abruptly exclaims:—

Guard what you say; the patriotic tribe
Will sneer, and charge you with a bribe;—a bribe!
The worth of his three kingdoms I defy
To lure me to the baseness of a lie:
And of all lies, (be that one poet's boast,)
The lie that natters, I abhor the most.'

In the character of Cowper there was not the slightest particle of ostentation; on no occasion did he assume any airs of consequence; he never aimed or wished to be thought what he was not. Everything in the shape of affectation was the object of his disgust. He loved simplicity without rudeness, and detested that squeamish mimicry of fine feeling which frequently, either under the assumed garb of superior sanctity, or of ardent friendship, conceals the most pitiable imbecility and ignorance.

Cowper's religious sentiments were undoubtedly those generally termed Calvinistic, not including, however, under that term, any of those perversions of great scriptural truths which are frequently, but falsely, charged upon Calvinism. On no occasion did we find him speaking of the character of God in such language as would lead any, who were sincerely desirous of approaching Him in the way of His own appointment, to doubt of a gracious reception at his hands. His own case, indeed, must be excepted, as his melancholy depression ever led him to regard himself as a solitary instance of the severity of God, and of his reversal of his otherwise immutable decree. His views of the atonement, and of the infinite extent of its efficacy, were such as led him, whenever he had occasion to advert to it, to represent it truly, as a solid ground of hope to every sinner, whatever might have been his former character. He felt an entire conviction that he whose infinite compassion had prompted him to make provision for the restoration of fallen man to his favour, intended it to be universally beneficial; and that the perverseness and obstinacy of men were the only reasons why it was not so. That he should have regarded his own case as an exception, and should, consequently, have passed the greater part of his life in the bitterness of despair, is a discrepancy which we are persuaded will, in the present life, forever remain unaccounted for. To assert, as some have done, on no other foundation than that of mere opinion, that had he not been religious he would never have been melancholy, is utterly at variance with all the leading facts of his history. To every well-regulated mind it will be abundantly evident, that whatever reasons may be assigned for the affecting peculiarity of his case, the deep concern he felt for religion could never have been the cause. On the contrary, it will appear clearly to have been much more likely to become the best remedy, as in fact, the events of his life prove it to have been, though, owing to some unaccountable organic conformation, much less completely so than might have been hoped.

Perhaps no individual ever felt more fully the authority of religion in his heart, or obeyed it more completely in his life, than Cowper. The apprehension for his ultimate safety, by which he was so continually harassed, injurious as was its influence on his mind, never relaxed, in any degree, that severe watchfulness which religion had taught him to exercise over his thoughts and conduct. On the contrary, they seem rather to have operated as a continual check upon those corrupt inclinations that are common to our fallen nature; and to which even Cowper was not a stranger. It would be absurd to say he had no imperfections; he felt them; he often mourned over them; and the vivid perception he had of them, associated, as it invariably was, with a strong constitutional tendency to melancholy, often filled him with the greatest anxiety and dread. His conceptions of the purity of that sublime morality inculcated in the gospel, and of the paramount importance of a holy life in its professors, were such as led him to regard the least deviation from the strictest line of Christian duty, in his own case at least, as an entire disqualification for the reception of spiritual comfort. No individual's conscience was ever more tremblingly alive to the importance of habitual watchfulness and uniform consistency of conduct. He could make ample allowances for the imperfections of others, but nothing could tempt him to make any for his own.

No person was ever more alive to the pleasures of real friendship, or had ever formed more correct conceptions of its obligations and advantages. His inimitable stanzas on this most interesting subject, which are perhaps superior to anything that has ever been written upon it, prove incontestably that he understood what were its indispensable prerequisites, and his whole conduct through life shews that he felt the full force of that sentiment which he so admirably described. It is difficult to make extracts from a poem every line of which is almost alike excellent: but we cannot deny ourselves the pleasure of quoting the following admirable lines:

Who hopes a friend, should have a heart
Himself, well-furnished for the part,
And ready on occasion,
To show the virtue that he seeks;
For 'tis an union that bespeaks
A just reciprocation.

A man renowned for repartee
Will seldom scruple to make free
With friendship's finest feeling;
Will thrust a dagger at your breast,
And tell you 'twas a special jest,

By way of balm for healing.

Beware of tattlers! keep your ear
Close stopt against the tales they bear.
Fruits of their own invention!
The separation of chief friends
Is what their business most intends—
Their sport is your dissension.

Religion should extinguish strife
And make a calm of human life:
But even those who differ
Only on topics left at large,
How fiercely will they meet, and charge,
No combatants are stiffer.

Then judge, before you choose your man,
As circumspectly as you can;
And having made election,
See that no disrespect of yours,
Such as a friend but ill endures,
Enfeeble his affection.

As similarity of mind,
Or something not to be defined.
First rivets our attention;
So manners decent and polite,
The same we practised at first sight,
Must save it from declension.

The man who hails you Tom or Jack,
And proves, by thumps upon your back,
His sense of your great merit;
Is such a friend, that one had need
Be very much his friend indeed,
To pardon or to bear it.

Some friends make this their prudent plan,
Say little, and hear all you can;
Safe policy, but hateful!
So barren sands imbibe the shower.
But render neither fruit nor flower;
Unpleasant and ungrateful.

They whisper trivial things, and small;
But to communicate at all
Things serious, deem improper.
Their feculence ^{impurity} and froth they show,
But keep their best contents below;
Just like a simmering copper.

Pursue the theme, and you will find
A disciplined and furnished mind
To be at least expedient;
And, after summing all the rest,
Religion ruling in the breast,
A principal ingredient.

True friendship has, in short, a grace,
More than terrestrial in its face,
That proves it heav'n-descended:
Man's love of woman's not so pure,
Nor when sincerest, so secure,
To last till life is ended.

    The exquisite sensibility of Cowper, and the real goodness of his disposition, with his entire abhorrence of cruelty, whether practised by man towards his own species, or towards any part of the Creator's works, are evinced by the following striking lines:"

I would not enter on my list of friends,
Though graced with polished manners and fine sense,

Yet wanting sensibility, the man
Who needlessly sets foot upon a worm.
An inadvertent step may crush the snail
That crawls at evening in the public path;
But he that has humanity, forewarned,
Will tread aside, and let the reptile live.
Ye, therefore, who love mercy, teach your sons
To love it too. The spring time of our years
Is soon dishonoured and defiled in most
By budding ills, that ask a prudent hand
To check them. But, alas! none sooner shoots,
If unrestrained, into luxuriant growth
Than cruelty, most devilish of them all!
Mercy, to him that shows it, is the rule
And righteous limitation of its art,
By which Heaven moves in pardoning' guilty man;
And he that shews none, being ripe in years,
And conscious of the outrage he commits,
Shall seek it, and not find it, in his turn.

Liberty has always been a soul-inspiring theme with poets. On no subject has the muse sung in sweeter strains, or towered to heights that are more sublime. Cowper has given ample proofs that his muse felt all the fire of this ennobling theme. In his Table Talk, some beautiful lines will be found on this interesting subject, so dear to the heart of every Englishman; but in his most masterly production, the Task, he thus sings—

'Tis liberty alone that gives the flower
Of fleeting life its lustre and perfume,
And we are weeds without it. All constraint
Except what wisdom lays on evil men,
Is evil; hurts the faculties, impedes
Their progress in the road of science; blinds
The eyesight of discovery; and begets
In those that suffer it a sordid mind,—

Bestial—a meagre intellect, unfit
To be the tenant of man's noble form.
Thee, therefore, still, blameworthy as thou art,
Thee I account still happy, and the chief
Among the nations, seeing thou art free,'
My native nook of earth! Thy clime is rude,
Replete with vapours, and disposes much
All hearts to sadness, and none more than mine;
Yet, being free, I love thee for the sake
Of that one feature, can be well content,
Disgraced as thou hast been, poor as thou art,
To seek no sublunary rest beside.
But once enslaved, farewell. I could endure
Chains nowhere patiently; and chains at home,
Where I am free by birthright, not at all!'

The liberty thus sung by Cowper was not, however, that lawless restraint which, under the sacred name of liberty, would burst asunder all those bands which hold society together, and introduce confusion infinitely more to be dreaded than the most absolute despotism. It was not the wild unrestrained liberty of the ferocious mob; it was the liberty that is compatible with wholesome restraint, and with the due administration of law. It was the liberty not of disorder but of discipline, as will be seen by the following beautiful lines:

'Let Discipline employ her wholesome arts;
Let magistrates alert perform their parts,
Not skulk, or put on a prudential mask,
As if their duty was a desperate task.
Let active laws apply the needful curb,
To guard the peace that riot would disturb;
And liberty, preserved from wild excess,
Shall raise no feuds for armies to suppress.
When Tumult lately burst his prison door,
And set plebeian thousands in a roar,

When he usurped Authority's just place,
And dared to look his master in the face;
When the rude rabble's watchword was—'Destroy!'
And blazing London seemed a second Troy I
Liberty blushed, and hung her drooping head—
Beheld their progress with the deepest dread;
Blushed that effects like these she could produce,
Worse than the deeds of galley-slaves let loose;
She loses in such storms her very name,
And fierce Licentiousness should bear the blame!'

Powerful as were the charms of subjects like these to Cowper, there were others of a different character which he held more dear, and ever regarded as more important. Like his great predecessor, Milton, he had made the sacred scriptures his constant study; not so much because he admired the sublime imagery of the holy penmen, (alive as he was to their beauties in this respect) as because he felt the power of the truth upon his heart; which, notwithstanding the severe pressure of his malady, would sometimes yield him an interval of pleasure. It was undoubtedly on one of these happy occasions that he penned the following lines, so strikingly descriptive of the refined pleasure with which the Christian can view the works of nature.

He looks abroad into the varied field
Of nature; and though poor, perhaps, compared
With those whose mansions glitter in his sight,
Calls the delightful scenery all his own:
His are the mountains, and the valleys his,
And the resplendent rivers: his to enjoy
With a propriety that none can feel,
But who, with filial confidence inspired,
Can lift to heaven an unpresumptuous eye,
And smiling say—My Father made them all!
Are they not his by a peculiar right?
And by an emphasis of interest his,

Whose eye they fill with tears of holy joy;
Whose heart with praise, and whose exalted mind
With worthy thoughts of that unwearied love
That planned, and built, and still upholds a world
So clothed with beauty for rebellious man?
Yes! Ye may fill your garners, ye that reap
The loaded soil; and ye' may waste much good
In senseless riot; but ye will not find
In feast, or in the chase, in song or dance,
A liberty like his, who, unimpeached
Of usurpation, and to no man's wrong,
Appropriates nature as his Father's work,
And has a richer use of yours than you.'

Although Cowper, towards the close of his life, before he received his Majesty's pension, owing to the heavy expenses occasioned by his own and Mrs. Unwin's illness, was scarcely able to keep his expenditure within the limits of his income, yet he was never once heard to complain, nor even to indulge the slightest disposition to be otherwise than contented in the station in which Providence had placed him. Writing to his intimate friend, Mr. Hill, on one occasion, whom he appears to have made his treasurer, he remarks, (Your tidings respecting the slender pittance yet to come, are, as you observe, of a melancholy cast. Not being gifted, however, by nature with the means of acquiring much, it is well that she has given me a disposition to be contented with little. I have now been so many years habituated to small matters, that I should probably find myself incommoded by greater, and, may I but be enabled to shift, as I have been hitherto, unsatisfied wishes will not trouble me much.'

On another occasion, to the same individual he writes,' I suppose that you are sometimes troubled on my account, but you need not. I have no doubt that it will be seen, when my days are closed, that I served a Master who would not suffer me to want anything that was good for me. He said to Jacob, "I will surely do thee good;" and this he said not for his sake only, but for ours also, if we trust in him. This thought relieves me from the greatest part of the distress I should else suffer in my present circumstances, and enables me to sit down peacefully upon the wreck of my fortune.' The same sentiment is still more forcibly expressed in the following lines:

Fair is the lot that's cast for me;
I have an Advocate with Thee:
They whom the world caresses most
Have no such privilege to boast.
Poor though I am, despised, forgot,
Yet God, my God, forgets me not;
And he is safe, and must succeed,
For whom the Lord vouchsafes to plead.'

Cowper was through life, the warm, though not the blind admirer of the British constitution; and though he made no pretensions to the character of a politician, yet he took the liveliest interest in all that related to the honour and prosperity of his country. In one of his letters to Mr. Newton, he thus writes:
'I learned, when I was a boy, being the son of a man that loved his country, to glow with that patriotic enthusiasm which is apt to break forth into poetry, or at least to prompt a person, if he has any inclination that way, to poetical endeavours. After I was grown up, and while I lived in the Temple, I produced several halfpenny ballads, two or three of which had the honour of being popular. But, unhappily, the ardour I felt upon the occasion, disdaining to be confined within the bounds of fact, pushed me upon uniting the prophetical with the poetical character, and defeated its own purpose. I am glad it did. The less there is of this sort in my productions the better. The stage of national affairs is such a fluctuating scene, that an event which seems probable to-day becomes impossible to-morrow; and unless a man were indeed a prophet, he cannot, but with the greatest hazard of losing his labour, bestow his rhymes upon future contingencies,

which, perhaps, are never to take place but in his own wishes, and in the reveries of his own fancy.

The time which Cowper bestowed upon his translation of Homer, and the indefatigable diligence with which he laboured in this great work, notwithstanding his melancholy depression, until he had completed it, prove that he was not easily to be diverted from what he had once undertaken; and that few men were equal, and perhaps none superior to him in those essential qualities of a truly great mind,—industry and perseverance.

It might be imagined that Cowper's very retired manner of life had deprived him of that manly independence of mind, which is a prime constituent in the character of every great man; but several incidents are related of him, which go to prove that such was very far from being the case. His conduct to Mr. Unwin and Mr. Newton, who both in their turns, at different times, thought themselves entitled to complain of some neglect, proves that he allowed not the claims of friendship to intrench upon his right to judge at all times for himself. Alluding to Mr. Newton's displeasure, he remarks to another friend:

'If he says more on the subject, I shall speak freely, and perhaps please him less than I have already done.' Almost in the same breath, however, evincing his deep knowledge of human nature, he adds:

'But we shall jumble together again, as people who have an affection for each other at the bottom, never fail to do.'

On one occasion, some friend having remarked to Cowper that he knew a person who wished to see a sample of his verse, before subscribing for his edition of Homer, he replied, that 'when he dealt in wine, or cloth, or cheese, he would give samples, but of verse never.' The same independence he evinced on another occasion, writing to the friend whom he had employed to negotiate for the publication of his second volume of poetry, he remarks, 'If Johnson should stroke his chin, look up to the ceiling, and cry Humph! Anticipate him, I beseech you, at once, by saying that you know I should be very sorry he should undertake for me to his own disadvantage, or that my volume should be in any degree pressed upon him.'

The depressive malady under which Cowper laboured through the greater part of his life, might naturally be supposed to have disqualified him entirely for the kind office of comforting those who were in distress. In truth, however, no one had better learned the divine skill of strengthening the weak mind, of encouraging the timid and trembling believer, of lifting up the hands that were hanging down, wiping the tear of sorrow from the mournful eye, and directing the Christian to look alone to heaven for support in all his difficulties. His poems abound with passages the most tender and consolatory; enforcing, with an eloquence persuasive and almost irresistible, humble submission to the Divine will, in circumstances the most discouraging. The following lines, forming part of a poetic epistle to a lady in France, show how admirably he could pour the healing oil of comfort into the wounded spirits of others, though he was unable to assuage the grief of his own.

The path of sorrow, and that path alone.
Leads to the land where sorrow is unknown;
No traveller ever reached that blessed abode
Who found not thorns and briars on the road.
The world may dance along the flowery plain,
Cheer'd as they go by many a sprightly strain,
Where nature has her mossy velvet spread,'
With unshod feet they yet securely tread,
Admonish'd, scorn the caution and the friend
Bent all on pleasure, heedless of its end.
But He, who knew what human hearts would prove,
How slow to learn the dictates of his love;
That hard by nature, and of stubborn will,
A life of ease would make them harder still;
In pity to a chosen few, designed
To escape the common ruin of their kind.
Called for a cloud to darken all their fears,

And said—Go spend them in the vale of tears
O balmy gales of soul-reviving air,
O salutary streams that murmur there,
These flowing from the fount of grace above!
Those breathed from lips of everlasting love!
The flinty soil indeed their feet annoys,
Chill blasts of trouble nip their springing joys,
An envious world will interpose its frown,
To mar delights superior to its own,
And many a pang, experienced still within,
Reminds them of their hated inmate, sin!
But ills of every shape and every name,
Transformed to blessings, miss their cruel aim,
And every moment's calm that soothes the breast,
Is given in earnest to eternal rest.
Ah! be not sad! although thy lot be cast
Far from the flock, and in a boundless waste;
No shepherd's tents within thy view appear,
But the Chief Shepherd even there is near.
Thy tender sorrows and thy plaintive strain
Flow in a foreign land, but not in vain;
Thy tears all issue from a source divine,
And every drop bespeaks a Saviour thine.'

Notwithstanding the almost unmitigated severity of Cowper's sufferings, there were seasons in which he enjoyed some internal tranquillity, and was enabled to exercise a trembling, if not an unshaken confidence in the Almighty. It was undoubtedly on one of these occasions that he penned the following lines—

'I see, or think I see, a glimmering from afar—
A beam of day that shines for me, to save me from despair.

Forerunner of the sun, it marks the pilgrim's way:
I'll gaze upon it while I run, and watch the rising day.'

On one of these occasions, when a gleam of light shot across his path, dissipating for a short interval his fears, he composed the following lines, left unfinished in his pocket-book, and received from one of his personal attendants by the late Rev. John Sutcliffe, of Olney. At what period of his life they were written, we cannot tell. It might probably have been at some moment of sunshine, towards the close of his sufferings.

To Jesus, the crown of my hope,
My soul is in haste to be gone,
Oh, bear me, ye cherubim, up,
And waft me away to his throne.
My Saviour! whom absent 1 love,
Whom not having seen, I adore,
Whose name is exalted above
All glory, dominion, and power:
Dissolve thou the bond that detains
My soul from her portion in thee,
And strike off these adamant chains,
And make me eternally free. When that happy era begins,
When arrayed in thy beauty I shine,
Nor pierce any more by my sins
The bosom on which I recline;—

Had it not been for Cowper's depressive malady, he certainly would have been, on all occasions, the most lively and agreeable companion. Even as it was, it must not be imagined that in his conversation he was never sprightly and cheerful. Frequently, when his own heart was weighed down with grief, arising from the severity and peculiarity of his malady, such an air of innocent pleasantry and humour, delicate and perfectly natural, ran through his conversation and correspondence, as could not fail to delight all who happened to be in his company, or who were occasionally favoured with the productions of his pen. It would be easy to produce proofs of this, both from his poetry and prose. His rhyming letter to Mr. Newton, in which there is such a happy mixture of the grave and the gay, as scarcely any other writer could produce, evinces the occasional sprightliness of his mind:

'My very dear friend, I am going to send, what, when you have read, you may shake your head, and say, I suppose there's nobody knows whether what I have got, be verse or not; by the tune and the time, it ought to be rhyme, but if it be, did you ever see, of late or yore, such a ditty before I I have writ Charity, not for popularity, but as well as I could, in hopes to do good; and if the reviewer should say, to be sure, the gentleman's muse wears Methodist shoes, you may know by her pace, and talk about grace that she and her bard have little regard, for the taste and fashions, and ruling passions, and hoydening play of the modern day; and though she assume a borrowed plume, and now and then wear a tittering air, 'tis only her plan to catch if she can, the giddy and gay, as they go that way, by a production on a new construction; she has baited her trap, in hopes to snap, all that may come, with a sugar plum. His opinion in this will not be amiss; 'tis what I intend, my principal end, and if I succeed, and folks should read, till some are brought to a serious thought, I shall think I am paid, for all I have said, and all I have done, though I have run, many a time, after a rhyme, as far as from hence, to the end of my sense, and by hook or by crook, write another book, if I live and am here another year.

'I have heard before, of a room with a floor, laid upon springs, and such like things, with so much art, in every part, that when you went in, you were forced to begin a minuet pace, with an air and a grace, swimming about, now in and now out, with a deal of state, in a figure of eight, without pipe or string, or any such thing; and now I have writ, in a rhyming fit, what will make you dance, and as you advance, will keep you still, though against your will, dancing away, alert and gay, till you come to an end, of what I have penned, which that you may do ere madam and you are quite worn out with jiggling about, I take my leave, and here you receive, a bow profound, down to the ground, from your humble me, W. C.

The following *jeu d'esprit*, lighthearted display of wit and cleverness, especially in a work of literature. written by the poet, as descriptive of one of his rural excursions, through the whole of which runs a strain of pleasantry, innocent, and perfectly natural, shews that his life was not one unbroken series of despair, but that he enjoyed, occasionally, at least, some lucid intervals, when, to gratify his friends, he would trifle in rhyme, with an affectionate and endearing gaiety. As it has never been published in any of his works, the reader will not regret its having a place here.

I sing of a journey to Clifton, a village near Olney
We would have performed if we could:
Without cart or barrow to lift on
Poor Mary or me through the mud.
Sle, sla, slud,
Stuck in the mud.
Oh, it is pretty to wade through a flood.

So away we went slipping and sliding.
Hop, hop,—a-la mode de deux frogs;
'Tis near as good walking as riding,
When ladies are dressed in their clogs.
Wheels, no doubt,
Go briskly about,
But they clatter, and rattle, and make such a rout.

DIALOGUE.

SHE:
'Well—now I protest it is charming;
How finely the weather improves;
That cloud, though, is rather alarming,
How slowly and stately it moves!'

HE:

'Pshaw I never mind, 'Tis not in the wind,
We are travelling south, and shall leave it behind.'
SHE:
I am glad we are come for an airing,
For folks may be pounded and penn'd.
Until they grow rusty, not caring
To stir half a mile to an end.'

HE:
'The longer we stay,
The longer we may;
It's a folly to think about weather or way.'

SHE:
'But now I begin to be frighted,
If I fall, what a way I should roll'
I am glad that the bridge was indicted;
Stay! Stop! I am sunk in a hole.'

HE:
Nay, never care,
'Tis a common affair,
You'll not be the last that will set a foot there.'

SHE:
'Let me breathe now a little and ponder,
On what it were better to do; hat terrible lane I see yonder,
I think we shall never get through.'

HE:
'So think I,—
But by the bye,
We never shall know, if we never should try.'

SHE:

But should we get there, how shall we get home? What a terrible deal of bad road we have pass'd,
Slipping and sliding; and if we should come
To a difficult stile, I am ruined at last.
Oh, this lane!
Now it is plain,
That struggling and striving is labour in vain.'

HE.

Stick fast there, while I go and look.'

SHE.

'Don't go away, for fear I should fall!'

HE:
I have examined it every nook,
And what you have here is a sample of all:
Come, wheel around,
The dirt we have found,
Would buy an estate at a farthing a pound.'
'Now sister Ann,' ^{Lady Austen} the guitar you must take,
Set it and sing it, and make it a song;
I have varied the verse for variety's sake,
And cut it off short because it was long.
"Tis hobbling and lame,
Which critics won't blame,
For the sense and the sound, they say should be the same.

CHAPTER XIX. Cowper's scholastic attainments—Character as a writer —Originality of his productions—Comparison between him and other poets—The severity of his sarcasm— Review of his original poems—Table Talk—Expostulation—Hope—Charity— Conversation—Retirement—The Task—His minor poems—His prose productions—Remarks on his letters—List of his works—Extract from an anonymous critic—Lines descriptive of his poetic character—On seeing his picture—On visiting his garden and summer-house.

Cowper's attainments as a scholar were highly respectable; he was master of four languages besides his own: Greek, Latin, Italian, and French; and though his reading was by no means so extensive as that of some, it was turned to better account, as he was a most thoughtful and attentive reader, and it was undoubtedly amply sufficient for every purpose, with a genius so brilliant, and a mind so original as his.

As a writer, Cowper's powers of description, both in poetry and prose, were of the highest order; equalled by few, and excelled by none. His richly cultivated mind, united to an imagination as brilliant as it was chaste, enabled him to paint the visible beauties of the material, as well as the ideal charms of the moral world, with an ease and felicity equally delightful. No one could describe the feelings of the heart with more vivid force, or knew better how to levy contributions on the rich and varied scenes of nature. He possessed all the requisite qualifications for a poet of the highest class—a familiar acquaintance with the ancient classics; a comprehensive mind, well stored with accurate information on almost every subject; a fertile genius; a rich fancy; an excursive, but chaste imagination; to all which were added, an extensive knowledge of the varied feelings of the human heart, and a most deeply-seated sense of the solemn claims of religion. The productions of Cowper were eminently and entirely his own; he neither borrowed from nor imitated anyone. He copied from none, either as to his subjects, or the manner of treating them. All was the creation of his own inventive genius. Adverting to this circumstance in one of his letters, he thus writes:

'I reckon it among my principal advantages as a composer of verses, that I have not read an English poet these thirteen years, and but one these twenty years. Imitation even of the best models is my aversion; it is a servile and mechanical trick, which has enabled many to usurp the name of author, who could not have written at all if they had not written upon the pattern of some original. But when the ear and the taste have been much accustomed to the style and manners of others, it is almost impossible to avoid it, and we imitate, in spite of ourselves, Justin the same proportion as we admire.' Cowper's mode of expressing his thoughts was entirely original. His blank verse is not the blank verse of Milton, or of any other poet. His numbers, his pauses, his diction, are all his own,— without transcription, and without imitation. If he thinks in a peculiar train, it is always as a man of genius, and, what is better still, as a man of ardent and unaffected piety. His predecessors had circumscribed themselves, both in the choice and management of their subjects, by the observance of a limited number of models, who were thought to have exhausted all the legitimate resources of the art. 'But Cowper,' says a great modern critic,' at once ventured to cross this enchanted circle, and thus regained the natural liberty of invention, and walked abroad in the open field of observation as freely as those by whom it was originally trodden. He passed from the imitation of poets to the imitation of nature, and ventured boldly upon the representation of objects which none before him had imagined could be employed in poetic imagery. In the ordinary occupations, occurrences, and duties of domestic life, he found a multitude of subjects for ridicule and reflection, for pathetic and picturesque description, for moral declamation and devotional rapture, which would have been looked upon with disdain or despair by all his predecessors. He took as wide a range in language too, as in matter; and shaking off the tawdry incumbrance of that poetical diction which had nearly reduced poetry to a skilful collection of a set of appropriated phrases, he made no scruple to set down in verse every expression that would have been admitted in prose; and to take advantage of all the varieties and changes of which our language is susceptible.'

It has been justly remarked, 'that between the poetry of Cowper and that of Dryden and Pope, and some of their successors, there is an immense difference. It would be easy to show how little he owed to his immediate forerunners, and how much his immediate followers have been indebted to him. All the cant phrases, all the technicalities of the former school, he utterly threw away; and by his rejection of them they became obsolete. He boldly adopted cadences of verse unattempted before, which though frequently uncouth, and sometimes scarcely reducible to rhyme, were not seldom ingeniously significant and signally energetic. He feared not to employ colloquial, philosophical, and judicial idioms, and forms of argument and illustration, which enlarged the vocabulary of poetical terms, less by recurring to obsolete ones, than by hazardous and generally happy innovations of his own invention, which have since become dignified by usage; but which Pope and his imitators durst not have touched. The eminent adventurous revivers of English poetry, about thirty years ago, Southey, Wordsworth, and Coleridge, in their blank-verse, trode directly in the steps of Cowper; and, in their early productions at least, were each in a measure what he had made them. Cowper may be legitimately styled the father of this triumvirate, who are, in truth, the living fathers of an innumerable company of modern poets, whom no ingenuity can well classify and arrange.'

The poetry of Cowper is in the highest degree deserving the honourable appellation of Christian poetry. He consecrated his muse to the service of that pure and self-denying religion taught by Christ and his apostles. In this respect his poems differed from the productions of any writers that had then appeared, with the exception of Milton and Young. Both these individuals, though they wrote on religious subjects, yet in all probability wrote less under the influence of purely pious feelings, than for the purpose of procuring fame; with Cowper, however, the desire of doing good predominated over every other feeling: and the hope of emolument, nay, even the love of fame itself, was looked upon as subordinate to this great object, the last to which poets generally pay any consideration. To Young, Cowper was evidently superior in everything that constitutes real poetic excellence; and equal to Milton in the ease and elegance of his compositions, and in the vivacity and beauty of his imagery, though seldom, and perhaps never, rising to that majestic sublimity to which the author of Paradise Lost sometimes soared; and in which he stands unrivalled among modern, if not among ancient poets. Milton's matchless poem is a most sublime description of the great facts of the Christian system; every line of it fills the reader with surprise. Hurried on through a profusion of imagery the most splendid and grand, and never inelegant, tawdry, or ungraceful, the mind becomes astonished, and is much more powerfully affected than the heart. But we look in vain for those touching appeals to the affections with which Cowper's poetry abounds, and which come home to the hearts and affections of all.

> 'Poet and saint, to him is justly given,
> The two most sacred names of earth and heaven.'

In the productions of Milton and Young, there is not much of practical, and still less of experimental piety. They confined themselves chiefly to the leading facts of religion. Cowper, on the contrary, whose views of the Christian system were equally, if not more comprehensive, describes, with unequalled simplicity and beauty, those less splendid but not less useful parts of religion, which his predecessors had left almost untouched; hence the superiority of his muse to theirs in these respects. No uninspired orator ever so happily and so strikingly described the operations of Divine grace upon the human soul. The gospel had come home to him, not in word only, but in demonstration of the Spirit, and in power. He not only possessed a comprehensive knowledge of gospel truth, which enabled him, whenever he had occasion, to describe and illustrate, with all the force and beauty of poetic enchantment, that solid foundation on which the Christian builds his hopes, but he had himself felt the powerful efficacy of these truths on the heart, when truly and cordially received. This accounts for the unrivalled felicity with which he describes the happy influence of Christianity in all cases where it is rightly embraced, unless, as in his own case, its influence be prevented by some unaccountable bodily distemper. Treating the great peculiarities of the Christian system—the depravity of man—the necessity of regeneration—the efficacy of the atonement—access to God, through the Divine Spirit—justification by faith, with others of a like kind, not merely as subjects of inquiry, but as things which had been to him matters of actual experience, it is no wonder that his muse sometimes carried him to a depth of Christian feeling, unsung, and not attempted before. As he himself, in his poem on Charity, beautifully sings—

When one that holds communion with the skies
Has fill'd his urn where these pure waters rise,
And once more mingles with us meaner things;
'Tis e'en as if an angel shook his wings;
Immortal fragrance fills the circuit wide,
That tells us whence his treasures are supplied.'

'Cowper,' as Mr. Hayley justly observes, 'accomplished, as a poet, the sublimest object of poetic ambition,—he dissipated the general prejudice which held it hardly possible for a modern author to succeed in sacred poetry. He has proved that verse and devotion are natural allies. He has shewn that true poetical genius cannot be more honourably or more delightfully employed than in diffusing through the heart and mind of man a filial affection for his Maker, with a firm and cheerful trust in his word. He has sung in a strain, in some degree at least equal to the great subject, the blessed advent of the Messiah; and perhaps it will not be expecting too much, to hope that his poetry may have no inconsiderable influence in preparing the world for the cordial reception of all the rich blessings, which this event was intended to introduce.'

Up to the period when Cowper's productions were given to the world, it was foolishly imagined impossible successfully to employ the graces and beauties of poetry on the side of virtue. A great modern critic had inconsiderately declared that 'contemplative piety cannot be poetical.' Had he asserted only, that it had very rarely been so, the assertion would not have been untrue. It would, indeed, have coincided with the views entertained by Cowper himself; for, of his predecessors' productions, with few exceptions, no one could have formed a more correct opinion, as will appear by the following lines:

'Pity religion has so seldom found
A skillful guide into poetic ground!
The flowers would spring where'er she deigned to stray,
And every muse attend her in her way.
Virtue indeed meets many a rhyming friend,
And many a compliment politely penned;
But unattired in that becoming vest
Religion weaves for her, and half undressed,
Stands in the desert, shivering and forlorn,
A wintry figure, like a withered thorn.'

This censure, severely as it may fall on most of Cowper's predecessors, was not unjust. His muse, however, was the first to show, successfully, that poetry may be made the handmaid of practical and experimental, as well as of contemplative religion. When he gave to the world the productions of his unrivalled pen, they saw, indeed:

'...A bard all fire,
Touched with a coal from heaven, assume the lyre.
And tell the world, still kindling as he sung,
With more than mortal music on his tongue.
That he who died below, and reigns above,
Inspires the song, and that his name was love.'

It must be acknowledged that Cowper sometimes dipped his pen in gall. Some expressions the most bitterly sarcastic are to be found in his poems. Of his first volume it was said, by one of his friends, 'There are many passages delicate, many sublime, many beautiful, many tender, many sweet, and many acrimonious.'

Cowper's satire, however, though keen and powerful as a whip of scorpions, was employed only to expose and punish the openly profligate, and the hypocritical professors of religion. Everything in the shape of deception he held in perfect detestation. The castigation of vice, of ignorance, or of dissimulation, was his object, when he became a satirist. If he held up philosophy to ridicule, it was that glare of false philosophy, which, instead of being beneficial to men, only led them from the plain and beaten track of truth, into paths of error and misery. He never wantonly, for the sake only of his own gratification, inflicted his satiric lash on a single individual. He became a satirist, not to give vent to a waspish, revengeful, and malicious disposition, (to feelings of this kind he was an entire stranger) but for the same purpose as the holy prophets of old were satirists, to expose, in mercy to mankind, the hideous deformity of those vices, which have ever been the fruitful parents of misery to mankind. As one has admirably remarked, 'His satire was the offspring of benevolence. Like the Pelian spear, [A huge weapon made from an ash tree. Grown on Mount Pelion. Only Achilles was capable of using this spear, which was said to have healing properties.] it furnished the only cure for the wound it had inflicted. Where he must blame, he pities; where he condemns, it is with regret. His censures display no triumphant superiority, but rather express a turn of feeling such as we might suppose angels to indulge in at the prospect of human frailty.'

To take a comprehensive review of the poet's original productions, in the order in which they appeared, would require a much greater space than it would be prudent to devote to it here. Table Talk is a dialogue, carried on with uncommon spirit and vivacity, in which a variety of most interesting topics are happily introduced, and descanted on with great force and beauty. At the close, he exposes with great force, the ignoble ends to which the muse has too often been made subservient; preferring, as every well-regulated and pious mind must do, the humblest efforts of the pious muse, to its loftiest flights in the cause of vice.

A. 'Hail, Sternhold, then; and Hopkins, hail!
B. Amen.
If flattery, folly, lust, employ the pen;
If acrimony, slander, and abuse,
Give it a charge to blacken and traduce;
Though Butler's wit, Pope's numbers, Prior's ease,
With all that fancy can invent to please,
Adorn the polish'd periods as they fall,
One madrigal of theirs is worth them all.

A. 'Twould thin the ranks of the poetic tribe,
To dash the pen through all that you proscribe.
B. No matter—we could shift when they were not;
   And should, no doubt, if they were all forgot.

The Progress of Error is much more serious than its predecessor is; and though it contains passages of unrivalled excellence, it exhibits occasional marks of weakness, and is less beautiful than any other in the volume. It was the first production of the poet's pen after his severe attack of depression, though it was not deemed advisable to make it the first poem in the volume. The poet invokes his muse to sing—

'By what unseen and unsuspected arts,
The serpent Error twines round human hearts;
Tell where she lurks, beneath what flow'ry shades,
That not a glimpse of genuine light pervades,
The poisonous, black, insinuating worm,
Successfully conceals her loathsome form.'

The following beautiful description of the gospel has ever been admired, but never equalled:—

O how unlike the complex works of man,
Heaven's easy, artless, unencumber'd plan;
No meretricious graces to beguile,

No clust'ring ornaments to clog the pile;
From ostentation as from weakness free
It stands, like the cerulean arch we see,
Majestic in its own simplicity,
Inscribed above the portal from afar,
Conspicuous as the brightness of a star,
Legible only by the light they give,
Stand the soul-quickening words— *Believe and Live.*

The following inimitable delineation of the believer's confidence, could only be written by one who had enjoyed it himself:—

'All joy to the believer! He can speak—
Trembling, yet happy; confident, yet meek.
Since the dear hour that brought me to thy foot,
And cut up all my follies by the root,
I never trusted in an arm but thine,
Nor hoped but in thy righteousness divine:
My prayers and alms, imperfect and defiled,
Were but the feeble efforts of a child;
However perform'd, it was their brighter part
That they proceeded from a grateful heart j
Cleans'd in thine own all-purifying blood.
Forgive their evil, and accept their good;
I cast them at thy feet—my only plea
Is what it was—dependence upon thee;—
While struggling in the vale of tears below,
That never fail'd, nor shall it fail me now.'

Expostulation, founded on a sermon by Mr. Newton, is an impassioned appeal to men, in almost all conditions, on behalf of religion; it abounds with imagery the most grand, impressive and awful, exhibiting proofs of the poet's deep acquaintance with the inspired prophetic records. After tracing, in the history of the Jews, the sins and punishment of that people, the poet enumerates the sins of Britain, takes an interesting review of our civil and religious liberty, and then urges upon us, with all the vehemence and authority of a prophet, the superior obligations under which we are laid by our preeminent advantages; closing the poem with the following plaintive but exquisite lines:—

>'My soul shall sigh in secret, and lament
>A nation scourg'd, yet tardy to repent:
>I know the warning song is sung in vain,
>That few will hear, and fewer heed the strain;
>But if a sweeter voice, and one design'd
>A blessing to my country and mankind,
>Reclaim the wand'ring thousands, and bring home
>A flock so scatter'd, and so wont to roam,
>Then place it once again between my knees;
>The sound of truth will then be sure to please;
>And truth alone, where'er my life be cast
>In scenes of plenty or in pining waste,
>Shall be my chosen theme, my glory to the last.

Hope is less impassioned than its predecessor, but not less striking. It is written throughout with great elegance, beauty, and force, and the sentiments it breathes are purely evangelical. It commences with an estimate of human life, formed by two individuals; one in the decrepitude of age, the other in the bloom of youth. Both are skillfully drawn; each look at the same things through a distorted medium, and as the poet sings—

>'Thus things terrestrial wear a different hue,
>As youth or age persuades, and neither true.'

The character of the loiterer is finely drawn, and the irksomeness of a life spent without a plan, is happily exposed. Hope is, then, made to appear as the only remedy for the ills of life. It is not, however, that vain and illusive expectation with which men too generally rest content, which is shown to be thus beneficial, but the hope of the gospel; built on the immovable foundation of faith in the Redeemer's merits, preceded, invariably, by the converting grace of the Divine Spirit, and followed by a holy and consistent life. Thus,—

>'From fading good derives, with chercic art,
>That lasting happiness, a thankful heart:
>Hope, with uplifted foot, set free from earth,
>Pants for the place of her ethereal birth;
>On steady wings sails through th' immense abyss,
>Plucks amaranthine joys from bow'rs of bliss.
>And crowns the soul while yet a mourner here,
>With wreaths like those triumphant spirits wear.
>Hope, as an anchor, firm and sure, holds fast
>The Christian vessel, and defies the blast.
>Hope! Nothing else can nourish and secure
>His newborn virtues, and preserve her pure.'

This poem is a masterly defence of the gospel. The arguments, which assert the immoral tendency of its peculiar doctrines are fairly met and refuted. Not only is it shown to be friendly to virtue, but essential to its actual existence. Among the great variety of characters introduced, not one is feebly drawn. The poem never becomes insipid, flat, or dull. Without ever losing sight of his principal object, to elucidate gospel hope, the poet introduces his reader to various scenes and characters, fixes his attention, and not unfrequently, there is reason to believe, carries conviction to his mind.

Charity is a poem of less vigour; but equally instructive, admonitory, and delightful. After some admirable lessons, illustrative of the utility of our social affections, the poet describes, in glowing terms, the advantages of commerce, not overlooking the evils with which it has been connected, owing to the avarice of mankind; one of the greatest of which he describes as the odious traffic in slaves.

In *Conversation*, the poet appears in the character of a teacher of manners, as well as of morals; and delineates with exquisite and unerring skill, many of the follies and frailties of life. The loquacious—the incommunicative—the noisy and tumultuous—the disputatious—the scrupulous and irresolute — the furious and intractable—the ludicrous—the censorious—the peevish—the bashful—with others of similar kind, may here find their character drawn by the pen of a master, in the liveliest colours, and with striking accuracy.

Retirement was ever a favorite theme with the poet; and his muse here seemed to revel in a strain the most tender, and yet sometimes the most sublime. The description he gives of the ineffable delight enjoyed by the Christian, while surveying the works of creation, has never been surpassed. Towards its close he sublimely sings—

> These are thy glorious works, thou source of good!
> How dimly seen, how faintly understood!
> Thine, and upheld by thy paternal care,
> This universal frame, thus wondrous fair;

The poet happily ridicules the fallacy of supposing it impossible to be pious while following the active pursuits of life, and in the same happy strain, he exposes the absurdity of seeking retirement as an excuse for indolence.

> 'An idler is a watch that wants both hands,
> As useless when it goes, as when it stands.
> Absence of occupation is not rest;
> A mind quite vacant is a mind distressed.'

This poem contains the most striking picture of melancholy that was ever drawn: and it is impossible to read it without remarking how aptly it depicts the poet's own distressing condition, when suffering under his severe paroxysms of depression.

The Task however, is by far the poet's greatest production, and had he written nothing else, would have immortalized his name, and given him a place among the highest class of poets. Here his muse kindled into its happiest inspirations, and burst forth into its sublimest strains. Commencing with objects the most familiar, and in a manner inimitably playful, the poet touches on a vast variety of subjects, many of them unsung and unattempted before, scattering wherever he goes

'From grave to gay, from lively to severe,'

an exuberance of beauty and elegance, which enchains the reader, carrying him through the muse's adventurous track, without the least restraint, and without a moment's uneasiness. The transitions are the happiest imaginable; after delineating one object with matchless felicity and force, presenting it in shapes almost endlessly diversified; ere he is aware of it, another and another start up before the reader, with magical effect, but without the slightest confusion, or the least violation of perspicuity. This admirable poem may be repeatedly read with increasing delight. It yields an almost inexhaustible, source of pleasure and instruction. The reader rises from its perusal, not only filled with astonishment at the mighty powers of its author, but what is of equal, and perhaps of greater importance, with feelings of the most unfeigned esteem for the poet, and with sentiments of benevolence towards all mankind.

The poem opens with a most amusing but rapid historical survey of seats, bringing it down to the elegant sofa, which, however, he soon quits, taking an excursive bound into the rural scenery around his favourite Weston; describing his rambles in the park, and through the village, delineating the reflections they suggested, in a manner so perfectly natural as at once justifies the poet's own remark, 'My descriptions are all from nature, not one of them second-hand; and my delineations of the heart are from my own experience, not one of them borrowed from books, or in the least degree conjectural.'

To make descriptive poetry interesting, the principal objects of the scene described must be selected and presented to the imagination in terms, and by the use of figures, the most lively and agreeable. When this is happily done, the reader accompanies the poet in all his peregrinations, to participate in all his pleasures and regrets, and in fact becomes as it were his bosom companion. This was never more happily effected than by Cowper, in several passages in this poem. One almost seems to be rambling with the poet through Weston park, listening to the delightful sounds of the rural spot, enjoying the cool shade of the colonnade, or sauntering through the avenue into the gothic temple in the wilderness, or admiring the stately elms, or the rustic bridge, or enjoying the sweet solitude of the shrubbery. Every step we take with him convinces us that we are in the company of one who not only viewed nature with a painter's eye, and felt her influence with a poet's heart, but who looked up through nature to nature's God, with the devout feelings of a Christian philosopher, admiring much the displays of his glory in creation, but far more the manifestations of his love in the gospel.

In the second book, entitled the *Time-piece*, the poet makes an admirable use of his deep acquaintance with the writings of the ancient prophets, which, so far from injuring his style, as some have most erroneously stated, imparted to it that dignity and force which it would not otherwise have possessed. Had this book no other claim upon our notice, it would be rendered invaluable by its opening remarks on the odious system of slavery. Adverting to the signs of the times, which were then sufficiently portentous, he satirizes the follies, and denounces the vices of the age, warning the guilty of their approaching doom; and with eloquence the most persuasive, urging the necessity of a speedy and effectual reformation. His picture of the Christian minister is exquisitely drawn, and must ever be admired:

> Would I describe a preacher such as Paul
> Were he on earth, would hear, approve, and own;
> Paul should himself direct me: I would trace
> His master-strokes, and draw from his design.

In the third book, *The Garden,* the poet enters upon a widely different subject, expatiating in a most delightful manner on the pleasures to be derived from the seclusion of a retired life. Even here, however, be pours forth occasionally a strain of satirical invective on vice. Indeed, throughout the whole of this charming and most instructive poem we find him exposing the vices, lashing the follies, and fixing the stamp of vanity upon the pursuits of men; not as many of his contemporaries had done, for the mere purpose of degrading human nature, by making it the subject of satirical raillery and invective, but for a purpose far more important. A modern critic has well observed, 'that eternity forms the back-ground of every moral picture wherein Cowper describes human life; and the general occupations of mankind appear to him not only idle, but criminal, when they occupy exclusively, or consume profusely, that time on which everlasting happiness may depend.'

The fourth book takes the reader from the rural scenery of summer and autumn, to the snug and comfortable fire-side of a winter's evening; introducing him into the company of one, who, while he ridicules the vain and delusive amusements of mankind, feels for those who pursue them the tenderest pity. The following book changes the subject from a winter's evening to the rural occupations of a frosty morning, whence the poet leads us to the discussion of the horrors of war, and the blessings of civil and religious liberty. After depicting these with his usual felicity and force, he adverts to the liberty of the gospel, that liberty wherewith Christ makes the believer free.

The scene of the last book is laid in the same season of the year, being entitled *Winter's Walk at Noon.* It embraces a great variety of subjects, and is throughout most instructive, admonitory, and beautiful.

Triclinium is the least attractive poem from Cowper's pen, but not the least useful. Like most of his productions, it was written not to please himself, nor to gratify his friend Unwin, to whom it was inscribed, but to answer some important end, as we learn from his own description. 'The purpose of this poem is to censure the want of discipline, and the scandalous inattention to morals, that prevail in schools, especially in the largest, and to recommend private tuition as preferable on all accounts; to call upon fathers to become tutors to their own sons— where that is practicable: where it is not, to take home to them a domestic tutor; and where neither can be done, to place them under the care of some judicious individual whose attention is limited to a few. Having had a public education himself, and being consequently aware of its advantages and disadvantages, it will not be denied that Cowper was able to pronounce an opinion on the subject; and whatever allowances may be made for his constitutional temperament, some attention ought nevertheless to be paid to the arguments he adduces in favour of his sentiments on this important subject.

The poet's minor productions, which have been found sufficiently numerous to make a volume of themselves, exclusive of his translations of Madame Guyon, and of the Olney Hymns, are all eminently happy in both sentiment and expression. Even those which are on trifling incidents, where he allowed his muse to gambol and revel with gaiety the most amusing and humorous, convey sentiments not infrequently of great importance, and exhibit the character of the poet in the most amiable light. In not a few of these smaller poems, however, we find Cowper making that his theme which was ever his favourite subject, breathing forth in strains of the softest and sweetest melody, sentiments the most pious and devout.

As a translator, Cowper was eminently distinguished for his fidelity. It was with him an affair of conscience, as he himself remarked, to make the author speak his own and not the translator's sentiments. If his *Homer* be less interesting to general readers, than the favourite work of his predecessor, it is not because it is less to be admired as a translation, which, in the opinion of all competent judges, is far from being the case, but because Pope made it his sole object to produce a fascinating and pleasing poem, from the materials of Homer's mine; while

Cowper's object was to produce an English poem as much like the original as the genius of the language would admit. That he has succeeded admirably in all those parts of the poem which are capable of poetical management in our language, none will deny; and it may be doubted whether in those familiar details where he appears to have failed, it will ever be in the power of an English poet to succeed, so as to give this poem all the ease and dignity which it has in the original.

Cowper wrote but little prose with a view to publication; the little, however, that he did write proves, that had he made it his study, he would have been as much distinguished for the felicity and purity of his style in this department of literature as in the other. The three papers appended to his life by Mr. Hayley, written at the age of twenty-five, and inserted in the Connoisseur, on Babbling, on Improprieties common in Parochial Congregations, and on Conversation, are distinguished by great simplicity and purity of style. The same may be said of the translation of Van Leer's letters: and the preface to his Homer equals anything of the kind that was ever written.

The letters of Cowper are unquestionably among the best productions of this interesting class that are to be found in the English language. Easy and natural, and everywhere simple and elegant, without the slightest affectation of formality, or the most distant approach to that studied and artificial style which invariably destroys the beauty of such productions, they never fail to interest and delight the reader; and will ever be regarded as perfect models of epistolary correspondence. Their peculiar charm is, perhaps, to be attributed chiefly, if not entirely, to that affectionate glow of sincere friendship, by which they are so preeminently distinguished. Fascinating as they are to every reader of taste, from the chaste and unornamented style in which they are composed, from their easy and natural transitions, and from their concise, yet sufficiently copious descriptions, it is to that ardent and genuine affection which runs through the whole of them, causing the reader to peruse them with almost as much interest as if they were addressed to him personally, that they are principally indebted for their universal popularity.

To the above remarks on Cowper's letters, we have great pleasure in adding the following testimony of a late distinguished scholar and writer, the Rev. Robert Hall, of Bristol, whose eloquence was unrivalled, and whose powers, being all consecrated to the cause of religion, rendered him an ornament to the age in which he lived. In a letter to Mr. Johnson, he thus writes. 'It is quite unnecessary to say that I perused the letters with great admiration and delight. I have always considered the letters of Mr. Cowper as the finest specimens of the epistolary style in our language. To an air of inimitable ease and carelessness, they unite a high degree of correctness, such as could result only from the clearest intellect, combined with the most finished taste. I have scarcely found a single word which is capable of being exchanged for a better. Literary errors I can discern none. The selection of the words, and the structure of the periods, are inimitable; they present as striking a contrast as can well be conceived, to the turgid verbosity which passes at present for fine writing, and which bears a great resemblance to the degeneracy which marks the style of *Ammianus Marcellinus*, [a fourth century soldier and historian.] as compared to that of Cicero or Livy. A perpetual effort and struggle is made to supply the place of vigour; garish and dazzling colours are substituted for chaste ornament; and the hideous distortions of weakness for native strength. In my humble opinion, the study of Cowper's prose may, on this account, be as useful in forming the taste of young people as his poetry.'

The facility with which Cowper wrote these letters, would lead us to imagine that he was an entire stranger to those nervous sensations not unfrequently experienced by the most intelligent individuals, when called to address strangers, especially if they are much above their own rank in life. The following playful remarks, however, will show that he felt them on some occasions very acutely. 'I am glad that I happened to cast my eye upon your appeal, respecting your letter to his lordship. A modest man, however able, has always some reasons to distrust himself upon extraordinary occasions. Nothing is so apt to betray us into absurdity, as too great a dread of it; and the application of more strength than enough is sometimes as fatal as too little; but you have escaped very well. For my own part, when I write to a stranger, I feel myself deprived of half my intellects. I suspect that I shall write nonsense, and I do so. I tremble at the thought of an inaccuracy, and become absolutely ungrammatical. I feel myself sweat. I have recourse to the knife and the pounce. I correct half a dozen blunders, which in a common case I should not have committed, and have no sooner despatched what I have written, than I recollect how much better I could have made it; how easily and genteelly I could have relaxed the stiffness of the phrase, and have cured the insufferable awkwardness of the whole, had they struck me a little earlier. Thus we stand in awe of we know not what, and miscarry through mere desire to excel.'

The notice we have already taken of Cowper's productions, renders it unnecessary that we should view them any further in detail. We cannot, however, suppress the following admirable observations of an anonymous critic, subjoined to Mr. Hayley's *Life* of the poet:

'The noblest benefits and delights of poetry can be but rarely produced, because all the requisites for producing them so seldom meet. A vivid mind and happy imitative power may enable a poet to form glowing pictures of virtue, and almost produce in himself a short-lived enthusiasm of goodness. But although even these transient and factitious movements of mind may serve to produce grand and delightful effusions of poetry, yet when the best of these are compared with the poetic productions of a genuine lover of virtue, a discerning judgment will scarcely fail to mark the difference. A simplicity of conception and expression: a conscious and therefore unaffected dignity; an instinctive adherence to sober reason, even amid the highest flights; an uniform justness and consistency of thought; a glowing, yet temperate ardour of feeling; a peculiar felicity, both in the choice and combination of terms, by which even the plainest words acquire the truest character of eloquence, and which is rarely to be found except where a subject is not only intimately known, but cordially loved; these, I conceive, are the features peculiar to the real votary of virtue, and which must of course give to his strains a perfection of effect never to be attained by the poet of inferior moral endowments. I believe it will be granted that all these qualities were never more perfectly combined than in the poetry of Milton. And I think, too, there will be little doubt that the next to him, in every one of these instances, beyond all comparison, is Cowper. The genius of the latter certainly did not lead him to emulate the songs of the Seraphim. But though he pursues a lower walk of poetry than his great master, he appears no less the enraptured votary of pure unmixed goodness. Nay, perhaps he may in this one respect possess some peculiar excellences, which may make him seem more the bard of Christianity. That divine religion infinitely exalts, but it also deeply humbles the mind it inspires. It gives majesty to the thoughts, but it impresses meekness on the manners, and diffuses tenderness through the feelings. It combines sensibility and fortitude, the lowliness of the child, and the magnanimity of the hero.

'The grandest features of the Christian character were never more gloriously exemplified than in that spirit which animates the whole of Milton's poetry. His own Michael does not impress us with the idea of a purer or more awful virtue than that which we feel in every portion of his majestic verse; and he no less happily indicates the source from which his excellence was derived, by the bright beams, which he ever and anon reflects upon us from the sacred scriptures. But the milder graces of the gospel are certainly less apparent. What we behold is so awful, it might almost have inspired a wish, that a spirit equally pure and heavenly might be raised to illustrate, with like felicity, the more attractive and gentler influences of our divine religion. In Cowper, above any poet that ever lived, would such a wish seem to be fulfilled. In his charming effusions we have the same spotless purity, the same elevated devotion, the same vital exercise of every noble and exalted quality of the mind, the same devotedness to the sacred scriptures and to the peculiar doctrines of the gospel. The difference is, that instead of an almost reprehensive dignity, we have the sweetest familiarity; instead of the majestic grandeur of the Old Testament, we have the winning graces of the New; instead of those thunders by which angels were discomfited, we have, as it were, the still small voice of Him who was meek and lowly of heart. May we not then venture to assert, that from that spirit of devoted piety which has rendered both these great men liable to the charge of religious enthusiasm, but which, in truth, raised the minds of both to a kind of happy residence

'In regions mild, of calm and serene air,
Above the smoke and stir of this dim spot,
Which men call earth—'

A peculiar character has been derived to the poetry of them both, which distinguishes their compositions from those of almost all the world besides. I have already enumerated some of the superior advantages of a truly virtuous poet, and presumed to state that these are realized in an unexampled degree in Milton and Cowper. That they both owed this eminence to their vivid sense of religion, will, I conceive, need no demonstration, except what will arise to every reader of taste and feeling on examining their works. It will here, I think, be seen at once, that that sublimity of conception, that delicacy of virtuous feeling, that majestic independence of mind, that quick relish for all the beauties of nature, at once so pure and so exquisite, which we find ever occurring in them both, could not have existed in the same unrivalled degree, if their devotion had been less intense, and of course their minds more dissipated amongst low and distracting objects.

To the above remarks on the poet's character, we subjoin with much pleasure the two following exquisite pictures of him, one drawn undesignedly by himself, and the other by the Rev. Dr. Randolph of Bath, on seeing his portrait by Lawrence.

Nature, exerting an unwearied power,
Forms, opens, and gives scent to every flower;
But seldom (as if fearful of expense)
Vouchsafes to man a poet's just pretence—
Fervency, freedom, fluency of thought,
Harmony, strength, words exquisitely sought;
Fancy, that from the bow that forms the sky,
Brings colours, dipt in heaven, that never die;
A soul exalted above earth; a mind
Skilled in the characters that form mankind;
And as the sun, in rising beauty drest,
Looks to the westward from the dappled east,
And marks, whatever clouds may interpose
Ere yet his race begins, its glorious close;
An eye like his, to catch the distant goal;
Or ere the wheels of verse begin to roll,
Like his to shed illuminating rays
On every scene and subject it surveys:
Thus graced, the man asserts a poet's name,
And the world cheerfully admits the claim.'

COWPER.
Sweet Bard! whose mind, thus pictured in thy face,
O'er every feature spreads a nobler grace;
Whose keen but soften'd eye appears to dart
A look of pity through the human heart;
To search the secrets of man's inward frame;
To weep with sorrow o'er his guilt and shame;
Sweet Bard! with whom, in sympathy of choice,
I've oft-times left the world, at Nature's voice,

To join the song that all the creatures raise
To carol forth their great Creator's praise;
Or, rapt in visions of immortal day,
Have gazed on Truth in Zion's heavenly way—
Sweet Bard! may this, thine image all I know,
Or ever may, of Cowper's form below,
Teach one who views it with a Christian's love
To seek and find thee in the realms above.'
—Rev. Dr. Randolph.

The following exquisite lines were written by the late amiable and talented Jane Taylor, on visiting the poet's garden and summerhouse at Olney, which, in one of his letters, he playfully designated his 'Verse Manufactory.'

'Are these the trees? Is this the place?
  These roses—did they bloom for him?
Trod he these walks with thoughtful pace?
  Passed he amidst these borders trim ?

Is this the bower?—a humble shed,
  Methinks it seems for such a guest!
Why rise not columns, dome bespread,
  With Art's elaborate fingers drest?
Art waits on wealth, there let her roam,

Her fabrics rear, her temples gild;
  But Genius, when she seeks a home,
Must send for Nature's self to build.
  This quiet garden's humble bound,

This humble roof, this rustic fane,
  With playful tendrils twining round,
And woodbines peeping at the pane;
  That tranquil tender sky of blue,

Where clouds of golden radiance skim,
  Those ranging trees of varied hue,—
These were the sights that solaced him.
  We stept within:—at once on each

A feeling steals, so undefined;
  In vain we seek to give it speech—
'Tis silent homage paid to Mind.
  They tell us here he thought and wrote,
On this low seat, reclining thus;

Ye garden breezes, as ye float,
  Why bear ye no such thoughts to us?
Perhaps the balmy air was fraught
  With breath of heaven;—or did he toil

In precious mines of sparkling thought,
  Concealed beneath the curious soil?
Did zephyrs bear, on golden wings,
  Rich treasures from the honeyed dew?

Or are there here celestial springs
  Of living waters whence he drew?
And here he suffered!—this recess,
  Where even nature fail'd to cheer,

Has witness'd oft his deep distress,
  And precious drops have fallen here!
Here are no richly sculptured urns,
  The consecrated dust to cover;

But nature smiles and weeps by turns,
  In memory of her fondest lover.'

CHAPTER XX.

Reflections to which the poet's life give rise—Remarks on introducing religious truths, occasionally, to the insane—Mistakes made respecting real religion—Importance of leaving all events to the sovereign disposal of Providence—Ways of God often inscrutable, but never wrong—Impossibility of being able to fathom them— Great need of caution in our remarks upon his dispensations—Remarks on afflictions—Liability of our mental powers to derangement—Their continuance a call for gratitude—Cowper's example not injured by his affliction—Best remedy for spiritual despondency— Reflections on the closing scene of the poet's life—Tributary lines—Elegy on his death.

 The history of Cowper's life, and the incidents of his peculiar case, give rise to so many useful reflections, and involve consequences so important to the best interests of mankind, that we cannot imagine an apology for the following remarks to be in the least degree requisite. It has already been proved in this memoir, that Cowper's religion, so far from inducing or aggravating his despondency, became its best, and indeed its only alleviation. And were it not for the unwarrantable assertions not long since made by an anonymous essayist, who has unblushingly affirmed, in despite of facts the most indisputable, that Cowper's mind was surrounded with super stition, that his nervous disease was deepened into a religious horror by his opinions, that the flood of light which burst upon his mind at his conversion, and which brought with it peace and joy, was nothing but the false fire of insanity; and that the transport he experienced after his conversion, was the mere natural consequence of highly-wrought feeling, to which the gloom he subsequently experienced was to be ascribed,—were it not, we repeat, for assertions thus glaringly false, we should not have deemed any further remarks needful.
 On no other principle than that of the blindness of heart, which is natural to fallen man, but which is rendered more inveterate by the fostering influence of prejudice and error, can we account for the intense aversion to every thing like evangelical

religion and real spirituality of mind, which individuals who can make or give credit to such assertions as the above, must feel. How clearly is it thus shown that the human heart, in its unregenerate state, will resist the clearest proofs, and distort the plainest facts, if it can thereby lower the claims of the character of vital religion. Looking at Cowper's case dispassionately, with a mind unfettered by prejudice, it will be seen, that before he had any correct views of religion, and indeed previously to his feeling anything more than a few transient convictions on this subject, he had laboured under deep mental aberration. The dread of appearing before the House of Lords, and the consequences which he saw would certainly result from his not retaining the situation that was offered him, were the first predisposing causes of his malady; the views of the gospel he subsequently embraced could have no share in its origin ;—his acquaintance with them at that time, to say the best of it, being extremely vague and superficial.

Dr. Johnson, who possessed the best means of obtaining information on the subject, speaking of the origin of Cowper's malady, and shewing that his religion could not be the cause, remarks, that 'to the poet's aberration of mind was indisputably owing all the gloominess of his character, a point,' he adds, 'which I am the more anxious to establish, as it has been unjustly charged on his religious opinions. But no; the unhappiness of this amiable man is to be referred to the cause already stated; and that again, to an excess of hypochondriacal affection, induced, in the first instance, as I have repeatedly heard a friend of his and mine observe, by his having, in very early life, checked an erysipelatous complaint of the face; which rendered him ever after liable to depression of spirits. Under the influence of one of these attacks, attended with evident mental obliquity, he was impressed with an idea, originating in a supposed voice from heaven, that the Author of his life had recalled the boon. This was rapidly followed by another, to this effect: that as he had failed to restore it in the intervening moment, the punishment of his disobedience would be everlasting destruction.'

'Now I would ask' continues Dr. J. 'those who have charged the unhappiness of this pitiable sufferer on his religious opinions,—to the operation of what theological tenets they can warrantably ascribe the supposition, not only of so preposterous a demand, but of a denunciation, under such circumstances more preposterous still, as referred to the supreme Being? It will be readily conceded, I trust, that, as no known system of divinity can justly be charged with such absurd principles, so that which Cowper adopted (whatever it might be), and through the influence of which on his divine poem, 'The Task,' he obtained the high eulogium of being—

'With more than painter's fancy blest, with lays
Holy as saints to heav'n aspiring raise'

unquestionably cannot. And if this be granted, his unhappiness must undoubtedly be referred solely to his aberration of mind.'

It is evident that in Cowper, almost from his infancy, there was a strong constitutional tendency to nervous sensibility, which was doubtless the result chiefly, if not entirely, of physical organization. In what degree his mental hallucination depended upon, or was produced by this, it would be difficult, if not impossible, to determine, and is a subject on which different individuals may form different, and even opposite views; and a question, as a recent critic remarks, which is 'better left to the discussion of physiologists and medical philosophers. That his intellectual condition depended, in some measure, on the action of the nervous system, must be evident to everyone who remembers that his paroxysms of severe distraction were invariably attended with, and sometimes preceded by, a specific nervous disorder. Hence, in all probability, there was in him, at least on these occasions, an almost absolute subjection of his mind to external influences, whether of depression or excitement. His feelings, he himself declared, were all of the intense kind, and he never derived a little pleasure from anything in the course of his life.'

It is well known that intense personal anxiety or mental perturbation of any kind will frequently induce that ruinous habit of despondency, which often becomes the prelude to partial — and sometimes to complete insanity. Permitting the imagination to dwell entirely on the terrific and gloomy pictures of its own creation, suggested by pre-existing depression, has a most injurious effect, and, in not a few instances, produces a reaction on the diseased state of intelligence out of which it grew, thus operating alternately as cause and effect. At such a crisis, when the mind is enfeebled and enervated by its own reflections, and when the sufferer may be said to stand on the very brink of insanity, if any object of intense interest, but the consolatory truths of religion, be presented to his mind, it is more than probable that the hallucination will become complete. Even these truths themselves, though they contain the only balm that can heal the soul, will not always in the first instance, as was the case with the poet, alleviate the sufferer's anguish. Nor can we venture to assert that they would, in every case, be subsequently followed by the same result as in his; freeing him from his desponding fears, and filling his mind with delightful serenity and peace, not for a short season only, but for the lengthened period of nine years. We are, however, well assured, that in most, if not in all cases, this expedient might be resorted to with perfect safety; and in many cases, we are disposed to think, with the probability of benefit, if not with entire success. On this subject, we fully concur in the following judicious remarks of a modern reviewer:—

'We are far from being disposed to deny, that the truths of religion may administer consolation even to persons labouring under mental disorder. In defiance of the sneers of the infidel, we will venture to suggest, whether even in the sunless, comfortless recesses of the asylums which conceal the outcasts of reason, there may not be subjects to whom the divine proclamation of mercy would, in intervals of intelligence, be most appropriate? Does it follow that because the reason is dethroned, and the mind is darkened, there are not gleams of intelligence, during which objects of hope and future realities might flash comfort into the

soul? Are there no pauses in which the faculties might rally for a while and collect materials for a prayer? Though the human temple is thus devastated, may not even its ruins be at times visited by the Spirit of its Divine Architect —its lawful inhabitant? We do not fear to be misunderstood: we trust we shall not be willfully misrepresented. It requires the most correct judgment, and the nicest discrimination, to handle the mind, either under the apprehensions of death, or under the influence of physical ailment; and too much caution cannot well be exercised in pronouncing upon the results of the most promising impressions. All that we would insist upon is, that the subjects of mental distemper are not, at all seasons, uniformly out of the reach of moral instruction and religious consolation ; and that, therefore, among the requisites for a competent superintendence of such patients, we should consider religious character as not less indispensable than medical skill. It was a providential circumstance for Cowper, that every requisite qualification met in Dr. Cotton, in whom he found at once a physician and a friend.
Eclectic Review, Second Series, Vol. VI, 327.

Some individuals, whom we feel constrained very highly to respect, in their anxiety to maintain what they call the honour of religion, will perhaps fear, that thus to bring it into contact with minds of this class, and with persons in these circumstances, would injure its reputation in the estimation of the worldly minded, fortifying them in their prejudices against the gospel, and increasing their lamentable antipathy to all its spiritual requirements. In reply to this, the critic above quoted, very properly remarks:

'Religion can have nothing to fear from the most degrading associations with which it may be connected. The evidence on which Christianity rests is unimpaired, its authority remains undiminished, its essential character and its heavenly tendency continue the same, through whatsoever medium they are contemplated, or whatsoever be the pretence on which the obedience of the heart is withheld. Call it Methodism, fanaticism, madness—religion under no change, in consequence of the terms by which it is designated. [*Eclectic Review*, second series, vol. 6, page 32] It may be found in active combination with a morbid intellect, or a perverted imagination. To confound the wise, it may be permitted that religion should be sometimes associated with human weakness and human folly. It is a salutary trial, a moral exercise of the faculties as influenced by the dispositions of the heart, to witness the genuine element of piety mingling with deformity and wretchedness so uninteresting, and even so loathsome, that religion constitutes their sole redeeming attraction. Nay, sometimes it shall be difficult to discover the identity of religion in cases where, though disguised and hidden beneath the infirmities of our poor shattered nature, it really exists. It is the triumph of religion that "it saves to the uttermost," objects on which perhaps divine compassion alone bestows the attention of pity, or which are even capable of being saved. So unreasonable as well as pernicious are the prejudices entertained against spiritual religion, in consequence of the tasteless or forbidden forms of individual character in which it may be enveloped, or of the uncertainty which may sometimes attach to the boundary of religious principle and human infirmity.' We have seen, that in Cowper's case the exciting (we do not say the physical) cause of his depression, in the first instance was his excessive dread of appearing at the bar of the House of Peers. So completely was he, at that juncture, unmanned and overpowered, that had any subject of deep and intense interest been presented to his mind, it would doubtless have super induced the calamity, which did actually befall him. It was the same in this case with religion, in itself considered, as with any other important subject; but it may be doubted whether, had the subject been of a different kind, he would so speedily have obtained relief. The pitiful attempt to account for Cowper's malady by ascribing it to his religion, or, as some would call it, his enthusiasm, can be made only by those who are entirely ignorant of its nature, and who are themselves, on this account, the subjects of commiseration.

Let it only be considered that, instead of a religion of gloom, and perturbation, and weakness, we discover in Cowper's case, a religion, which enlivens while it calms and strengthens the mind. In the place of dark despondency and peevish irritation, his religion filled it with serenity, peace, and heavenly consolation. It was a religion which, placing in its true light the comparative importance of temporal and eternal things, rectifies the corrupt bias that too generally leads us to prefer the former to the latter. Who would not be content to be in that frame of mind in which Cowper must have lived, when he penned those admirable letters—so full of Christian experience, during the interval between his conversion and his subsequent severe mental attack, a period of nearly nine years.

There can be little doubt that the individuals who, in spite of all that has been or can be urged, continue to ascribe Cowper's melancholy to his religion.

The truth is that the obstinacy of these individuals on this subject arises from the vague and erroneous notions they entertain of religion, making it consist not in that entire renovation of the heart, by the power of divine grace—that very moral change which everyone must undergo, before we can become truly pious, and which God alone can produce.

The following admirable remarks of a distinguished female writer, well deserve consideration:

'That superficial thing, which by mere people of the world is dignified by the appellation of religion, though it brings just that degree of credit which makes part of the system of worldly Christians, neither brings comfort for this world nor security for the next. Outward observances, indispensable as they are, are not religion. They are the accessary, but not the principle; they are important aids and adjuncts, but not the thing itself; they are its aliment, but not its life: the fuel, but not the flame; the scaffolding, but not the edifice. Religion can no more subsist merely by them, than it can subsist without them. They are divinely appointed, and must be conscientiously observed; but observed as a means to promote an end, and not as an end in themselves.'

Here it is that those individuals, who attribute Cowper's depression to his religion, stumble. Attempting to construct a religion, not on the apostacy and consequent ruined state of man, on which alone it can rest with safety, but on man's supposed moral ability, unaided by the Holy Spirit, to obey all the divine commands; and dreading nothing so much as what they call religious enthusiasm, but which would, in most cases, be much more properly designated Christian energy, it is not surprising that they should speak in disparaging terms of the poet's warm and animated piety, as it displayed itself in his conduct and letters, during the first few years of his religious experience; stigmatizing it sarcastically, as consisting in ecstasies,' 'spiritual revelry,' 'exhausting experiences.'

Let it, however, be remembered, that this excitement, as they are pleased to term it, continued for the long space of nine years; the ninth part of which would have been more than sufficient to have prostrated, if not destroyed, the firmest constitution, had it been, as those individuals would fain persuade us, nothing but mere excitement. It was the same excitement essentially, though doubtless less ardent, as that which pervaded the bosom of the divine Redeemer himself, and of all his disciples. Nor can it be doubted, that had these individuals lived in the apostolic age, they would have branded the lively and active zeal of Paul with some such epithets as they have applied to that of the poet's.

It is the furthest from our wish to misrepresent those individuals, who have spoken reproachfully of Cowper's religion. Were it a subject of trifling importance, we should have allowed it to pass unnoticed. We look upon it, however, as an affair not to be trifled with, involving the consideration of points in the Christian system of the highest moment, and indeed essentially fundamental. Not that it is of any material consequence, what opinions we may form of Cowper's religion, or of any other person's religion, in itself considered. If, however, our opinion goes to invalidate any one fundamental truth of the gospel, it becomes then a matter of infinite importance, in the proper adjustment of which too much pains cannot be taken.

One great object of the enemy of mankind, is to surround them as much as possible with an atmosphere of delusion and deceit, thereby either obscuring the rays of divine truth, and rendering them less likely to penetrate their minds; or giving them such distorted views of it, as answers the same ruinous purpose. Misleading them thus, by false lights, he renders them insensible to their impending danger, until ruin overwhelms them, and their everlasting hopes are dashed in pieces. Hence arises the importance of at least making an earnest Christian effort to save them from being turned aside by a deceived heart. Indeed, if our Lord more than hinted, on several occasions, the probability of many being lost, who call themselves Christians, and who boasted of their supposed conformity to his will, how cautious ought we to be, lest the light that is in us should be darkness.

Very few delusions have been practised upon mankind by the arch-deceiver more successfully, than that of blinding their minds to those cardinal truths in the Christian system—human depravity, the spirituality of religion, and the necessity of divine influence, in order to its attainment. Unhappily, he has been most successful among that class who are deservedly esteemed as the most amiable, and these are almost the only persons who are likely to attribute Cowper's malady to his religion. Substituting their own natural dispositions or acquirements for true piety, and resolving all religion into external virtues, they ridicule the subject of renewing grace, despise the doctrine of Christian sanctification, and thus show themselves to be lamentably ignorant of the true nature of Christian holiness. Do not the words of our Saviour come to such individuals as a solemn warning;—" Except your righteousness exceed the righteousness of the Scribes and Pharisees, ye shall in no wise enter into the kingdom of heaven."

Of those who make the most determined stand against the influence of divine grace, a greater proportion will often be found among the apparently amiable and virtuous, than among the turbulent and vicious. And it must not be concealed, though it is matter of deep regret, that there often exists in this class of men of moral character, so predominant a tendency proudly to wrap up their minds in the impenetrable veil of their own supposed goodness, that according to all probability, their dislodgement from the strong holds of human sufficiency, in which they have entrenched themselves, is a far more difficult work than the conviction of individuals notoriously vicious. The great danger there is that these sober, temperate, and respectable individuals, who are thus opposed to the gospel, and who regard Cowper's malady as the effect of his religion, should persist in their error, to their final and inevitable ruin, will, it is hoped, be admitted as a sufficient apology for the lengthened observations we have made on this subject.

After all, in remarking upon the cause of Cowper's malady, it is perhaps much better, instead of indulging in any vain conjectures, as to its more immediate physical or moral causes, to regard it as one of those dispensations of Providence, which the Almighty permits occasionally to occur, to teach us a lesson we are all so unwilling to learn—that He is the sovereign disposer of all events, and that he has consequently a right to do as seemeth him good, both in the armies of heaven and among the inhabitants of earth, without asking the consent of his creatures, or making them acquainted with the reasons for his conduct. In such circumstances, our duty unquestionably is—and it is equally our privilege properly to discharge it,—to believe with unshaken confidence, that God will never exercise his dominion wantonly or capriciously, or to the infliction of one unnecessary pang on any of his creatures; but that though "his judgments are a great deep, and his ways past finding out," it is not because they are in themselves confused and intricate, but "because his thoughts are not as our thoughts, nor his ways as our ways. For as far as the heavens are above the earth, so far are his ways above our ways, and his thoughts above our thoughts."

Taking this view of the poet's history, we need not, as some individuals, from amiable but much mistaken motives, have done, blink any facts of the case, under the apprehension that their disclosure would be injurious to the interests of piety. A zeal for the reputation of religion must not be exerted in such a way as to impeach the wisdom of God; which can hardly fail to be the case when it induces us to conceal what he has done, or what he has permitted to occur, lest by making it known, the cause of religion should be injured. As well might we conceal any part of his word because it happened not to accord with our views of what may be deemed injurious or beneficial, which, indeed, some have even had the hardihood and impiety to attempt.

No one, having the common feelings of humanity, can be otherwise than deeply affected by the recital of Cowper's sufferings. To see an amiable and eminently pious individual labouring under a hopeless depression, and dragging through a miserable existence, for more than half the period of his days, must excite the commiseration of the most unfeeling; and even where the sufferer happened not to be distinguished for his talents, the application itself would be more than enough to call forth the warmest sympathy—how much more was this likely to be the case when it was allied to genius and talents like Cowper's! Under such circumstances our hearts, if unchanged and unsubdued by divine grace, are greatly in danger of charging God foolishly; vainly attempting to scan the wonderful works of him who is perfect in wisdom; rashly arraigning Lis dispensations at our bar, and perversely speaking of them in terms that would at least imply defect; as if infinite benevolence could wantonly or unnecessarily inflict pain; or infinite wisdom, by random and wild conjectures, could possibly be mistaken. How much better would it become us to be found in the posture of child-like humility, acknowledging with holy serenity and calmness of mind, the equity of all the divine administrations; acquiescing implicitly in all his decisions, and assuring ourselves, as we have abundant reason to do, that no circumstance connected with the afflictions of any individual, as to its severity or the length of its continuance, can escape his notice, or occur without his permission. He is a God of judgment, and though he submits not the volume of his mysterious purposes to our gaze, but seals it up in the secrecy of his all-comprehending mind, yet he directs all the movements of his providence with unerring certainty and precision, regulating those events, which to us seem the most contradictory, on principles of the strictest equity; so as to make the entire whole, glorious, and perfect; the least alteration of which, could it possibly be made, would mar and deface its beauty.

The truth is, as the writer last quoted has well remarked, that 'some little tincture of latent infidelity mixes itself in almost all our reasonings on these topics. We do not constantly take into the account a future state. We want God to clear himself as he goes; we cannot give him such long credit as the period of human life. He must every moment be vindicating his character against every skeptical cavil; he must unravel his plan to every shallow critic; he must anticipate the knowledge of his design before its operations are completed. If we may adopt a phrase in use among the vulgar, we will trust him no further than we can see him. Though he has said, "judge nothing before the time," we judge instantly, of course rashly, and in general falsely.'

We act not thus inconsiderately, in giving our opinions of the works of men. We judge it imbecile and foolish to make any decisive remarks, of either censure or praise, respecting an unfinished undertaking. In our courts of judicature, sentence is not pronounced in the midst of a trial, nor until all the evidence is collected, circumstantially detailed, and finally summed up. Shall we not treat the schemes of infinite wisdom with as much respect as we do the actions of men? Is it only the operations of infinite mercy that we cannot trust? or is it the Judge of all the earth only, on whose decisions we cannot depend 1

The impropriety, and indeed we may justly say, impiety of these hasty decisions, will be apparent, when it is remembered that many events and circumstances do not, and indeed cannot, appear to our present feeble senses in their true light.

Surrounded with the mists of darkness, of prejudice, and of impurity, our knowledge at the best must be extremely limited, obtained only by much labour and research, and retained frequently with the greatest difficulty. We are apt to form a high opinion of our attainments and penetration; fancying that we can discover with certainty, the way in which things ought to be managed; forgetting that our powers of combination and of computation are so imperfect, that we soon become baffled, perplexed, and confused in our calculations. Owing to the obstacles we have to surmount, and the misconceptions to which we are liable, the prejudices to which we are exposed, the intricacies of error we have to disentangle, and the brevity of human life, our acquisition of knowledge is necessarily slow, and confined within very circumscribed limits. Those whose powers are the most capacious, whose extensive attainments and wonderful grasp of thought fill us with astonishment, arrived not at their knowledge at one stride, but by tedious and difficult and persevering efforts; and are, after all, the most ready to acknowledge the feebleness of their powers, and the imperfection of their views.

Our information, be it ever so extensive must necessarily be confined to events that are past or present; of the future we know nothing: the occurrences of the next hour are impenetrable to our perceptions; indeed we cannot fully or perfectly comprehend anything that we see around us, or feel within us. Even those subjects with which we are the most familiar, and with which we can hardly persuade ourselves we are not perfectly acquainted, when they come to be more deeply looked into, present difficulties which no human sagacity can solve. Ought it then to surprise us, that an impenetrable gloom should conceal the clemency and wisdom of the divine procedure, as regards some circumstances connected with our earthly destiny? The chain of divine providence may appear, to the dim eye of unawakened men, broken, or at least inextricably entangled; while the great agent who constructed it knows that it is perfectly coherent, and that the whole is irresistibly conducive to the end designed.

Everything is fully known to the divine mind at one intuitive glance; the terms past, present, and future, cannot be applied to the prescience of God. One day is with the Lord as a thousand years, and a thousand years as one day. Vast as is the extent of his dominion, and innumerable as are the different orders of creatures that are under his control, all their separate interests are by him carefully observed, and all their individual wants constantly supplied; as much so, indeed, as if they were, separately considered, the only individuals in existence. It is no greater exertion of mind to Omniscience to superintend each subdivision of existence than to overlook the whole: nor can any confusion arise from such an observance to perplex an infinite intelligence. That Almighty Being who spake the universe into existence by his word, and whose presence fills universal nature, cannot be supposed to find it difficult to watch over the interests of every separate individual. If a sparrow falls not to the ground without his notice, and if he numbers the very hairs of our head, can we imagine that any event will be permitted to befall us, with which he is not perfectly acquainted?

Whether there be cases, as has been supposed by some of our best writers on providence, in which God inflicts personal suffering, solely for the benefit of a nation or a community, irrespective of any separate disciplinary ends, it is impossible for creatures like ourselves, who at the best can only discern objects like these through a thick and hazy atmosphere, to determine. In every separate case, there may be, and we indeed have no doubt there are reasons, which respect the sufferer himself, which may be either retrospective, or prospective, preservative or preventative; upon which, however, it would be rash presumption in us to pronounce any decision. It should satisfy us, that " he chastens us, not for his pleasure, but for our profit, that we may be partakers of his holiness;" and having his promise to encourage us, we ought to believe in every case, whatever appearances there may be to the contrary, "that all things shall work together for good to them that love God, to them who are the called according to his purpose."

The administration of human affairs is occasionally so happily managed as to make a single measure productive of private as well as of public good; and why may we not suppose that the infinitely wise God invariably conducts his affairs to accomplish this double object. Because we have it not in our power in many instances, Ado a public good without inflicting an unmerited private injury, shall we conclude that he cannot do it, who can make even the wrath of man to praise him, while the remainder of that wrath he restrains?

The truth is that in all our speculations on providential events we cannot be too cautious. It is easy enough to launch out into the abyss, but how soon shall we find ourselves beyond our depth. Had we that perfect knowledge of contingent events, which God alone can possess,—could we discern the nice movements of every separate wheel in the vast machine of providence,—and were we able to disentangle this intricate subject, so as to pursue its endless windings and turnings, we should everywhere behold displays of consummate wisdom, exerted invariably in the production of happiness, in the best possible way, and at the least possible expense of individual or general suffering. It is not, however, necessary or even desirable that we should see this; the secret purposes of the Almighty are far better concealed in the fathomless abyss of his own councils. "Secret things belong unto the Lord: but the things that are revealed, to us and to our children forever."

The erroneous opinions we form of sensible objects, in consequence of their powerful association with the operation of our own minds, deteriorated by the principles of corruption inherent in our fallen nature, need to be removed by the quickening energy of Divine grace, before we can bow with calm and holy serenity to the sovereign disposals of Providence. Then, and not till then, shall we cheerfully acquiesce in its decisions; and, instead of vainly attempting to pry into its concealed and mysterious operations, by assigning this or that second cause or causes, for every afflictive visitation, we shall rest perfectly satisfied that every event, with all the attending circumstances, are under the direction of that God who hath done, and who will do, all things well. Looking at Cowper's extraordinary sufferings, and forgetting that the present life is not one of reward but of trial, and that severe, protracted, personal affliction, so far from being, in cases generally, a proof of the divine displeasure, is almost invariably to be regarded as a token of his favour—" for whom the Lord loveth he chasteneth,"—superficial observers may be tempted erroneously to conclude it was for the punishment of some enormous sin, which either he or his ancestors had committed. In confutation of this groundless surmise, for which the facts of the case prove satisfactorily there is not the slightest foundation, it will be sufficient to remark, that this is a most fallacious method of reasoning on all such occasions; as our Lord himself remarked, in reference to those who had perished by the fall of the tower of Siloam:

"Suppose ye," said he to those who regarded this as a judgment of God upon the individuals who thus suffered a premature death, "that they were sinners above all men, because they suffered such things 1 I tell you, nay: but except ye repent, ye shall all likewise perish."

This was the error into which Job's friends fell, and which led them so severely to aggravate the severity of the patriarch's sufferings; an error which the pride of the human heart prompts it to commit, vainly imagining it can scan the purposes of the Almighty, and that he cannot have reasons for his conduct towards any of his creatures which can elude its penetration. That it was groundless in the patriarch's case, we have the clearest proofs; nor are the proofs that it was so in the poet's, less satisfactory. How much better would it become us, instead of arrogantly exerting our ingenuity in the discovery of imaginary causes for the divine conduct, to submit humbly to his will, devoutly inquiring, what lessons of useful instruction we may learn from every separate event. Cultivating such a disposition, we should not fail to derive much advantage even from the sorrowful details of Cowper's history.

What an affecting proof have we, in the poet's case that it is not in the power of the greatest natural or acquired talents, even when associated with genuine and unaffected piety, to render its possessor permanently happy, if it pleases God to derange, in ever so slight a degree, our mental powers.

> Man is a harp whose chords elude the sight,
> Each yielding harmony disposed aright;
> The screws revers'd
> (a task which, if he please,
> God in a moment executes with ease),
> Ten thousand strings at once go loose,
> Lost, till he tune them, all their power and use.'

The uninterrupted enjoyment of our mental powers, in full vigour and activity, is a blessing for which we can never be sufficiently grateful. Is it not, however, to be feared, that by many it is very much overlooked, if not entirely forgotten? Never, perhaps, was a Christian more happily situated than was Cowper during his residence at Huntingdon, and at Olney, previous to his second severe mental attack. Associated with individuals perfectly to his taste, who, like himself, lived under the smiles of the divine favour, and commencing a literary undertaking with his friend, Mr. Newton, which must have afforded him the highest gratification, his situation was truly delightful; when suddenly his sky became darkened, and an awful cloud of despair, thicker than midnight, gathered around him, from which he never afterwards wholly emerged. Individuals distinguished for their genius and acquirements, will do well to take a lesson from this affecting case. Their sky may now be serene and their prospects bright, there may not be even the slightest appearance of a change, and yet, in a short time, a cloud, dense and horrid, may come over them, and shroud them in the deepest gloom. How truly may it be said, "Verily, every man at his best estate is altogether vanity."

When we consider the extreme delicacy of the mechanism essential to the vigorous exertion of mental power—the injury which we have reason to believe it sustained by man's original defection—the debilitating and enfeebling power which we are sure the indulgence of vicious passions must have upon it— and the facility with which the great Creator can derange its operations, partially or entirely, by the suspension or extinction of functions too minute for human observation, our surprise is, not that it should ever be impaired, but that it should not be so much more frequently. It is not improbable but its occasional suspension, and even sometimes its total extinction, may be permitted to take place, to make us sensible on whom we are dependent for its continuance. The individual who has yielded his mind to the benumbing influence of sin, whose long indulgence in vicious practices has besotted his understanding, hardened his heart, and rendered him utterly insensible of Divine mercies, may pass by this favour, as he will do every other, unheeded, regarding it as too common for notice. The Christian, on the contrary, remembering to whom he is indebted for a blessing which he so highly values, while he simply depends upon, and devoutly supplicates, God for its continuance, will most gratefully express his obligations to heaven for its enjoyment.

The same grateful emotions, mingled with the kindest sympathy for the deep depression of the poet, should be felt by the Christian whose experience is happily of a brighter cast. Living in the enjoyment of the divine favour, and, by the aid of the Divine Spirit, being enabled to stretch forth the hand of faith, and though perhaps with some trembling, yet with sufficient confidence, to lay hold on that promise which he finds as an anchor to his soul, sure and steadfast, instead of regarding it as the effect of his own care or efforts, he should gratefully exclaim, "Who maketh me to differ, and what have I that I have not received?" Such favoured individuals will do well constantly to remember how entirely they are dependent on Divine aid, for the continuance of their faith and hope, and how impossible it is to insure its permanent enjoyment in any other way than by the diligent and proper use of those means which God has instituted for the maintenance of our piety and the stability of our hope; means in which, owing to the poet's melancholy aberration, he never dared to engage, saying, when invited so to do, 'Had I the universe, I would give it to go with you; but I dare not do it against the will of God.' How thankful ought we to be, that we are not the subjects of such a delusion!

It must not be imagined that the force or beauty of Cowper's example is in any degree diminished by the hallucination under which he laboured; since, in fact, the influence of religion upon his mind was never suspended, even when, under the influence of his hopeless depression, he forbore to pray. The piety that shines through all his despondency, and his entire submission to the divine will, even though, as he erroneously supposed, its fiat was his own destruction, prove that through the whole of his bewilderment his heart was singularly right with God. It was doubtless owing to his malady, that he confined his attention so entirely to his own feelings, instead of looking to the finished work of the Redeemer, and to the infinite sufficiency of his atonement. Many Christians, however, it is to be feared, who are not suffering under mental depression, bring upon themselves much disquietude, by making their own feelings the measures of their joys and sorrows. Their mind thus becomes the prey of its own objects, and they might just as well expect to grow in strength by watching their appetite, as to grow in grace merely by watching their own internal feelings. The object placed before us in the gospel, as the foundation upon which our faith is to rest, and on which we are to lean, for repose and safety, in every spiritual conflict, is the great sacrifice of the Redeemer, whom it exhibits to our view as the mighty God, the everlasting Father, and the Prince of Peace, setting him forth as the propitiation for our sins, declaring it to be "a faithful saying, and worthy of all acceptation, that he came into the world to save sinners;" assuring us that he is "able to save unto the uttermost all that come unto God by him;" reminding us of the Saviour's invitation,

"Come unto me, All ye that are weary and heavy laden, and I will give you rest." If, instead of looking to this foundation, and fixing our eye upon these promises, in an hour of conflict and of trial, we look into ourselves for comfort, we shall assuredly meet with disappointment. All solid comfort can flow only to ruined and depraved man from the Cross, and can only be received by faith. The highest attainments we can make in the Christian life, will never warrant us to expect it from ourselves. Imperfection and guilt, more or less, attaches to the best of our performances, and if we have no better source to repair to for comfort, when the shafts of the enemy fly thick around us, disappointment must be our lot.

The best, and we may say the only, remedies for spiritual despondency, are a believing and comprehensive view of the character and perfections of Christ, with earnest, fervent, and persevering prayer that the Divine Spirit would apply these great principles with power to our hearts. Of this we may be assured, that had it not been for Cowper's malady, these remedies would have been, in his case, completely successful, and his faith would have shone with unusual lustre. His despondency was, in no degree, the result of religious declension, but arose solely from a mental aberration. He never lost his relish for religion, though he looked upon it as a forbidden subject; his attachment to the gospel remained undiminished, and his love to the Redeemer unabated; and though his malady would not permit him to use them, he retained, to the close of life, an unalterable regard for all the ordinances and means of religion.

The closing scene of a life like Cowper's, was one of peculiar solemnity. 'Had his piety been of a less decided character,' as a pious critic has well remarked, 'there might have been room for regret, that ere he died he gave not some pleasing sign of having escaped from his delusion; but it should seem that his physical powers were too exhausted to admit of that transient illumination of the faculties, which, in cases of derangement, is generally the presage of death. It is, however, a consideration of small moment on which side the river the vision of the 'open gate of heaven' burst upon the soul. That dark passage once effected by the poet, every doubt was over. And if the state of separate consciousness admits of the perception of the objects of sense, it must have been with a peculiar emotion of exultation that his spirit surveyed the breathless form in which it had been entombed, and adopted the triumphant challenge of the last enemy, *"O Death! Where is thy sting?"* Might we but imagine its detention for a while near the scene of its former sufferings, it would be to represent to ourselves the solemn joy with which it would contemplate the deposit of that poor corruptible frame in the dust, as seed cast into the furrow, anticipating, as the last act of faith, that moment when the universal chorus shall arise, "O Grave, where is thy victory?"

Freed from that tabernacle of clay in which it had been so long imprisoned, how triumphant must have been the flight of his happy spirit to the regions of unending felicity and peace. In what sublime strains must his muse, now that its energies were entirely unimpeded, have sung the high praises of heaven! How joyfully must he have gazed upon the glorified Redeemer, while he exultingly joined that assembled multitude who had washed their robes, and made them white in the blood of the Lamb; whose number was "ten thousand times ten thousand, and thousands of thousands," and who, with a loud voice, were saying, "Worthy is the Lamb that was slain, to receive power, and riches, and wisdom, and strength, and honour, and glory and blessing, for ever and ever."

With much pleasure, we add the following interesting lines, the production of an amiable individual, J. T. Shewell, Esq., one of the poet's warmest admirers:

TRIBUTE TO COWPER'S MEMORY

"Twas thine to make the purposes of song
Nobly subservient to truth's awful cause;
Its sacred dictates thy acknowledge guide;
Thy highest treasure, thy supreme delight,

At once thy consolation and thy theme.
Not like the fool, improvident and vain,
Who laid his weak foundation on the sands
Of human wisdom; that, when winds and waves
Of trial and affliction shook the house,
It sank beneath the overwhelming flood:
But rather like the wise, who having built,
With prudent caution, and a single eye
To that which shall withstand the wreck of time,
His mansion on the everlasting rock;
Unmov'd beheld it firm abide the assault
Of weary elements, and stand secure.
Thy life's a wholesome lesson, good for all
Who woo instruction in the walks of time,
To ponder well, and haply thus extract
A balsam from thy tears; though nature shrinks
Reluctant to receive the unwelcome cup.
Afflictions are the ministers of love,
By heav'n appointed—happy if they serve
To bring us nearer home! to wean our hearts
From toys and trifles; and to fix them there,
Where only lasting happiness is found!
Mortality's frail garments cast aside;
Corruptible put off for incorrupt;
And with the Lamb's unspotted robes array'd,
Made meet to mingle with th' angelic train
Of that celestial city; all whose walls
Are sure salvation, and whose gates are praise .
Thou'rt safely landed on th' immortal coast,
Where in full triumph the Messiah reigns.
There,—midst the splendours of eternal day,
Applauding angels hail thee welcome guest;
There, ever sheltered from the darksome clouds,
That hover'd o'er thy doubting path whilst here,
And often seem'd to thy distemper'd eye,
Awfully low'ring, as with tempests fraught;

Thy fears now all are hush'd, and every pang
Of time and sense, in sure possession lost.
Beauty for ashes; oh! the blest exchange!
And oil of joy to mourning now succeeds.
Wak'd-by His voice who tun'd thy trembling strings,
With genuine fervour of seraphic fire,
New songs of gladness from thy lyre ascend,
Sweeter than all the poet sang before;
Whilst thou, rejoicing, join'st the general praise
Of thy Redeemer, wise in all his ways;
And own'st, with gratitude, his sov'reign skill,
Who sometimes "wounds to heal, but "ne'er to kill."

Printed in Great Britain
by Amazon